PROGRESS IN BEHAVIOR MODIFICATION

Volume 4

DISCARD

CONTRIBUTORS TO THIS VOLUME

Alan S. Bellack

Douglas A. Bernstein

Edward B. Blanchard

Leonard H. Epstein

Anthony M. Graziano

Nathan Hare

Alan E. Kazdin

Donald J. Levis

Michael T. Nietzel

Clifford R. O'Donnell

PROGRESS IN BEHAVIOR MODIFICATION

EDITED BY

Michel Hersen

Department of Psychiatry
Western Psychiatric Institute and Clinic
University of Pittsburgh School of Medicine
Pittsburgh, Pennsylvania

Richard M. Eisler

Department of Psychiatry and Human Behavior
University of Mississippi Medical Center
Jackson, Mississippi

Peter M. Miller

Weight Control Center
Hilton Head Hospital
Hilton Head Island, South Carolina

Volume 4

1977

ACADEMIC PRESS   NEW YORK   SAN FRANCISCO   LONDON

A Subsidiary of Harcourt Brace Jovanovich, Publishers

ACADEMIC PRESS, INC.
111 Fifth Avenue, New York, New York 10003

United Kingdom Edition published by
ACADEMIC PRESS, INC. (LONDON) LTD.
24/28 Oval Road, London NW1

LIBRARY OF CONGRESS CATALOG CARD NUMBER: 74–5697

ISBN 0–12–535604–8

PRINTED IN THE UNITED STATES OF AMERICA

CONTENTS

A Review of the Theoretical Rationale and Empirical Support for the Extinction Approach of Implosive (Flooding) Therapy
Donald J. Levis and Nathan Hare

LIST OF CONTRIBUTORS

Numbers in parentheses indicate the pages on which the authors' contributions begin.

ALAN S. BELLACK (1), Department of Psychology, University of Pittsburgh, Pittsburgh, Pennsylvania

DOUGLAS A. BERNSTEIN (119), Department of Psychology, University of Illinois, Urbana-Champaign, Illinois

EDWARD B. BLANCHARD (163), Department of Psychiatry, University of Tennessee Center for the Health Sciences and Tennessee Psychiatric Hospital and Institute, Memphis, Tennessee

LEONARD H. EPSTEIN (163), Psychology Department, Auburn University, Auburn, Alabama

ANTHONY M. GRAZIANO (251), Psychology Department, State University of New York at Buffalo, Buffalo, New York

NATHAN HARE (299), Department of Psychology, State University of New York at Binghamton, Binghamton, New York

ALAN E. KAZDIN (39), Department of Psychology, The Pennsylvania State University, University Park, Pennsylvania

DONALD J. LEVIS (299), Department of Psychology, State University of New York at Binghamton, Binghamton, New York

MICHAEL T. NIETZEL (119), Department of Psychology, University of Kentucky, Lexington, Kentucky

CLIFFORD R. O'DONNELL (69), Department of Psychology and Social Welfare Development and Research Center, University of Hawaii, Honolulu, Hawaii

PREFACE

Progress in Behavior Modification is a multidisciplinary serial publication encompassing the contributions of psychology, psychiatry, social work, speech therapy, education, and rehabilitation. In an era of intense specialization, it is designed to bring to the attention of all workers in behavior modification, in a yearly review format, the most timely issues and developments in the field. Inasmuch as several journals are presently devoted entirely to publishing articles on behavior modification, and in consideration of the fact that numerous other journals are now allowing an increased allotment of pages to articles dealing with behavioral techniques, even the most diligent reader will find it difficult to keep abreast of all new developments in the field. In light of the publication explosion in behavior modification, there is a real need for a review publication that undertakes to present yearly in-depth evaluations that include a scholarly examination of theoretical underpinnings, a careful survey of research findings, and a comparative analysis of existing techniques and methodologies. In this serial publication we propose to meet this need.

Theoretical discussion, research methodology, assessment techniques, treatment modalities, control of psychophysiological processes, and ethical issues in behavioral control will be considered. Discussions will center on a wide spectrum of child and adult disorders. The range of topics will include, but will not be limited to, studies of fear behavior, measurement and modification of addictive behaviors, modification of classroom behaviors, remedial methods for the retarded and physically handicapped, descriptions of animal analogs, the effects of social influences on behavior, the use of drugs in behavioral approaches, and the contribution of behavior therapy to the treatment of physical illness.

Progress in Behavior Modification will present a diversity of views within the field. We will, on occasion, solicit discussions from theoreticians, researchers, or practitioners not directly associated with behavior modification. Cross-fertilization of ideas, *when maintained at the empirical level,* can be most rewarding and often leads to refinements in theory, research, and practice. In short, we propose not only to review critically developments in behavior modification at a particular point in time, but also to identify new directions and point toward future trends at all levels of inquiry.

Michel Hersen
Richard M. Eisler
Peter M. Miller

CONTENTS OF PREVIOUS VOLUMES

PROGRESS IN BEHAVIOR MODIFICATION

Volume 4

BEHAVIORAL TREATMENT FOR OBESITY: APPRAISAL AND RECOMMENDATIONS[1]

ALAN S. BELLACK

Department of Psychology
University of Pittsburgh
Pittsburgh, Pennsylvania

I. INTRODUCTION

The treatment of obesity or overweight has become a highly conspicuous topic in the behavior modification literature. The amount of material has been sufficient that reviews have recently appeared in several behavioral journals (Abramson, 1973; Bellack, 1975; Hall & Hall, 1974) as well as in nonbehavioral literature (Jordan & Levitz, 1975; Stunkard, 1972). At least two books dealing with behavioral approaches to obesity are in preparation (Foreyt, 1976; Williams, Martin, & Foreyt, 1976) and several recent survey books on behavior modification have included chapters on obesity

[1] Preparation of this manuscript was supported in part by Grant MH 26176-01 from the National Institute of Mental Health.

1

(Leitenberg, 1976; Yates, 1975). This rapid and marked rise to prominence has been similar to that seen in behavioral applications to other disorders. Early reviews of nonbehavioral treatments for obesity indicated that traditional methods had had almost no impact on what was (and still is) a national health problem (Stunkard & McLaren-Hume, 1959). Large numbers of untreatable individuals were thus available for clinical research that offered the possibility of success. Behavioral explanations for obesity were apparent: eating (overeating) was highly reinforcing. Given an available population, an objective dependent variable (weight), and a learning-based causal explanation, the disorder was ripe for behavioral intervention. In keeping with the spirit of the 1960s, early approaches often involved aversive conditioning (e.g., Kennedy & Foreyt, 1968; Meyer & Crisp, 1964; Stollak, 1967). This strategy soon gave way, however, and, paralleling the general development of behavioral techniques, cognitive approaches (e.g., Cautela, 1972) and self-control (e.g., Bellack, 1976; Mahoney, 1974; Wollersheim, 1970) became the treatments of choice (Abramson, 1973; Bellack, 1975). By 1972, the famous Stunkard and McLaren-Hume (1959) statement about the intractability of obesity had been modified to the following: ". . . both greater weight loss during treatment and superior maintenance of weight loss after treatment indicate that behavior modification is more effective than previous methods of treatment for obesity" (Stunkard, 1972, p. 398). Additional testimony to the efficacy of behavioral treatments appeared in the Discussion sections of most experimental articles and in several of the previously cited reviews (e.g., Abramson, 1973; Bellack, 1975; Hall & Hall, 1974).

In a continuing parallel with the general development of behavior modification, the initial enthusiasm has dampened somewhat, and positive claims for obesity treatments have recently been challenged. Some of the foremost contributors to the behavioral approach have begun to question basic premises (e.g., Hall, Hall, Hanson, & Borden, 1974; Mahoney, 1975a). A more critical view is offered by Yates (1975), who has entitled his chapter on obesity: "When Behavior Therapy Fails: II. Obesity." He states, ". . . it is clear that is it (sic) not really surprising that behavior therapists have had little success with the problem of obesity as yet on a long term basis and that there will have to be some radical rethinking of the approaches thus far adopted" (p. 148).

Questions are thus raised regarding which (if any) of these conclusions are valid and what the effectiveness of behavioral approaches is at this time. This article is devoted to a consideration of these questions. The text is divided into two major sections. The first focuses on a critical review of the experimental literature, with an emphasis on methodology and outcome. The second section deals with broader issues in treatment and treatment research which cut across specific studies and techniques. Throughout, the focus is on outpatient applications with adults. The degree of therapeutic control over food availability and major reinforcers with children and inpatients alters the nature of treatment and the issues involved with those populations (see Harmatz & Lapuc, 1968; Moore & Crum, 1969).

II. EFFECTIVENESS OF BEHAVIORAL TECHNIQUES

In the discussion thus far, the label "behavioral approaches" has been used as if there were only one specific behavioral technique that has been applied. In fact, numerous procedures (e.g., aversive conditioning, covert conditioning, self-monitoring, self-reinforcement) have been used alone and in combination, with varying degrees of control and success. However, almost all approaches have been based on a common, two-part conception of obesity. First, obesity is presumed to result from an energy imbalance: consumption of more energy than is expended. Second, this energy imbalance occurs as a function of overeating, which persists because eating has immediate positive consequences, whereas the negative consequences (e.g., obesity, heart disease) are delayed. (The presumed reasons why only some people become obese pertain to the idiosyncratic nature of individual learning histories.) Therefore, all behavioral interventions have attempted to alter the energy balance by achieving a reduction in the quantity of either all food or certain high calorie foods eaten. This goal has been approached in one of two ways: (1) modification of the consequences of eating (e.g., by applying immediate aversive consequences for excessive eating), or (2) modification of the antecedents of eating (e.g., alteration of the environment such that high caloric food is unavailable). The latter approach has typically been referred to as *stimulus control*, which term will be applied for the remainder of this paper. These two strategies have been applied both as independent treatment techniques and in varying combinations with one another. Investigations emphasizing consequence control will be reviewed first, followed by review of investigations using either antecedent control alone or combinations of both approaches.

Modification of the Consequences of Eating

As stated above, initial applications of behavioral principles to the treatment of obesity emphasized the use of aversive stimulation, in an effort to alter the immediate reinforcement valence of eating. In one of the earliest reports, Meyer and Crisp (1964) displayed highly desirable foods to two clinical patients and administered electric shocks contingent upon physical approach to the food items. Both reports were uncontrolled case studies; Meyer and Crisp reported positive results for one patient and negative results for the other. In another uncontrolled case study, Kennedy and Foreyt (1968) reported the successful application of an avoidance conditioning paradigm in which noxious odors were paired with the aroma of preferred food items. In a subsequent investigation, Foreyt and Kennedy (1971) employed noxious odors in an aversive conditioning paradigm. Weight loss for the experimental group was 13 lbs. in 9 weeks of treatment and losses were partially maintained through a 48-week follow-up period. This study contained several design flaws which limit the conclusions that can be drawn. The experimental subjects were substantially younger than control subjects and they attended regular group meetings, while control subjects had no on-going contact with therapists. Experimental subjects were also required to self-monitor (SM) their eating. The reactive effects of SM on eating behavior have been clearly demonstrated (e.g., Romanczyk, 1974; Stuart, 1971). Therefore, the specific contribution of aversive conditioning to the weight loss cannot be determined in this study.

Tyler and Straughan (1970) recruited subjects from a weight loss club and instructed them to hold their breath while visualizing themselves eating fattening foods. This was the sole intervention employed and it did not result in significant weight loss. Stollak (1967) employed electric shock as an aversive stimulus. Subjects in an aversive conditioning group were required to monitor their food intake and attend biweekly meetings with the therapist. Monitoring records were discussed and electric shock was administered when consumption of high-calorie foods was mentioned. A group matched to the aversive conditioning group with the exception of the aversive contingency lost more weight than the conditioning group, which did not differ from an untreated control group. The shock in this procedure was not administered contingent upon eating or thoughts of eating but on reports of eating; it might well be that treatment was aversively conditioned, rather than inappropriate eating.

Mann (1972) employed a single subject reversal design with multiple replications to examine a contingency contracting procedure. Subjects initially deposited a number of valuables with him and signed contracts authorizing him to establish weight loss contingencies for return of the items. Depending on the particular contingency in force, failure to meet weight loss goals during the treatment period could result in permanent forfeiture of items. The contracts varied throughout the program, and included options for relatively immediate reinforcement (three times per week) and two forms of delayed reinforcement (every two weeks and for the entire treatment period). The treatment was highly effective, and reversal of phases indicated that aversive contingencies (item loss) for failure to meet criteria were more effective than participation alone or positive reinforcement (item return) for meeting criteria. Despite the positive results, this procedure has questionable generality. First, it is unlikely that many clients would afford their therapist such extensive control by depositing highly valued items. Second, the application of powerful aversive contingencies resulted in undesirable patterns of weight loss. Subjects often took diuretics and laxatives in order to meet criteria. This practice is both unhealthy and not conducive to long-term behavior change and maintenance of loss once contingencies are terminated. Third, while Mann did not include a follow-up phase, he did subsequently discover that effects were not well maintained (Mann, personal communication).

Morganstern (1974) successfully applied aversive conditioning with a single subject in a multiple baseline design. Monitoring of eating behavior prior to initiation of treatment indicated that a major factor in the client's weight problem was excessive consumption of several high calorie food items (candy, cookies, doughnuts); treatment was thus designed to reduce eating of those particular foods. Cigarette smoking was identified as a highly aversive stimulus for the subject. Conditioning trials involved the client puffing on a cigarette while she chewed one of the target foods. Treatment was applied sequentially to each food and the client reported significant reduction of her consumption. Weight loss occurred gradually throughout treatment concurrent with conditioning and continued through a 6-month follow-up period.

An alternative to the use of externally administered aversive consequation is the use of cognitive stimuli, as in covert sensitization (Cautela, 1972). This procedure avoids potential negative concomitants of other forms of aversive conditioning (e.g., Mann, 1972).

Furthermore, the covert stimuli are portable, allowing the client to apply them in vivo, when actually involved in the target behavior. Cautela (1972) reported successful application of covert sensitization in uncontrolled case studies. In contrast, Morganstern (1974) turned to cigarette smoke as an aversive stimulus when his client failed to respond to a covert procedure. Sachs and Ingram (1972) examined the effects of covert sensitization on eating behavior in an analogue study. They compared a standard sensitization procedure with a backward conditioning variation (nausea images were terminated prior to imagination of target foods rather than being presented simultaneously). The two procedures were equally effective in reducing consumption rates of two target foods. However, this study has several critical methodological faults. Consumption rates were based on self-monitoring records which were not subjected to independent reliability checks. Self-monitoring has reactive effects on behavior and has questionable reliability (Kazdin, 1974). It is thus uncertain whether reported changes were accurate and whether (any) changes were due to the conditioning procedures or to SM and/or experimental demand and expectancy factors.

Manno and Marston (1972) conducted a treatment study in which they compared covert sensitization, covert positive reinforcement, and an attention placebo condition. Although both treatment groups lost significantly more weight than the control group, weight losses were considerably less than the 1 lb. per week presumed to be a minimum for a clinically meaningful intervention (Bellack, 1975; Hall & Hall, 1974).[2] Foreyt and Hagen (1973) found no difference in weight loss between a covert sensitization and a placebo group, and Janda and Rimm (1972) found nonsignificant differences between a sensitization group, an attention-placebo group, and a no-contact control group. Janda and Rimm conducted posttreatment interviews with their subjects and discovered that three of the six treated subjects did not find the imagery to be aversive. Those three subjects lost a mean of only 2.3 lbs., while the other three subjects (who found the imagery aversive) lost a mean of 21 lbs. This difference is intriguing but must be viewed cautiously as it is based

[2] Rate of weight loss has become a frequent criterion for evaluating the clinical effectiveness of weight-control programs, although it is rarely subjected to statistical analysis. Most programs advise subjects to lose weight at a moderate rate: 1 to 2 lbs. per week. Therefore, a minimum rate of loss of 1 lb. per week would indicate that goals were at least minimally met. The applicability of this criterion for long-term programs (e.g., 6 months) and for the grossly obese (e.g., 100 lbs. overweight) is uncertain, but it appears to be a viable standard for most short-term programs with moderately overweight individuals.

on post hoc self-reports. A modified version of sensitization was examined in a recent study by Elliott and Denney (1975). They compared a sensitization group, a sensitization group receiving false physiological feedback (suggesting their arousal to the imagery), and an attention-control group. All groups also were instructed to self-monitor eating in vivo. There were no differences between the groups after 4 weeks of biweekly treatment; all lost 3.5 to 5 lbs. While these losses meet the 1 lb. per week criterion, it is quite possible that they resulted from the short-term reactive effects of SM (Bellack, Glanz, & Simon, 1976; Stuart, 1971) (see discussion of SM, Section III, C).

An alternative strategy for the application of aversive stimulation is the "induced anxiety" procedure described by Bornstein and Sipprelle (1973a, 1973b). This technique involves the induction and termination of anxiety (independent of eating or food stimuli) such that subjects learn to first tolerate and then control a degree of physiological discomfort. As described by Bornstein and Sipprelle, this procedure resembles anxiety management training (Suinn & Richardson, 1971). While the rationale for this approach is unclear and the procedures imprecisely specified, Bornstein and Sipprelle (1973b) first reported its successful application in an uncontrolled case study. In a controlled group study, an induced anxiety group lost significantly more weight than a group receiving training in deep muscle relaxation, and two control groups. Furthermore, the weight losses were maintained through a 6-month follow-up period. This approach warrants further investigation, whereby the parameters of the technique and characteristics of subjects, experimenters, and treatment sessions are more clearly elucidated and controlled.

On the whole, the results of investigations and clinical applications of aversive conditioning procedures are not positive. The reports by Mann (1972) and Morganstern (1974) indicate that aversive contingencies can be effective, but in the Mann (1972) study the concomitants of the weight changes made the procedure somewhat undesirable. There are several general issues which must be considered in evaluating the potential utility of these approaches. The *first* issue pertains to the nature of the aversive stimuli used. The aversiveness of stimuli cannot be presumed on the basis of face validity, but must be empirically determined for each individual (Berecz, 1973). The potential difficulty in the nonempirical identification of aversiveness is clearly demonstrated by the Janda and Rimm (1972) study in which one-half of the subjects retrospectively reported their imagery to be nonaversive. It seems likely that this difficulty was duplicated in other studies involving covert sensitization. In addition to level of aversiveness, the specific nature of the stimulus is also an issue. There are some data to suggest that aversive stimuli function best when they affect the same sense modality as the target substance. Elkins (1974) and Seligman (1970) have reported that powerful and persistent flavor aversions can be best produced in response to such gustatory stimuli as nausea and malodorous and unpleasant tasting substances. In this regard, some of the most positive reports for aversive conditioning involved such stimuli (e.g., Foreyt & Kennedy, 1971; Morganstern, 1974).

A *second* issue concerns the determination of the target for aversive conditioning. Weight loss (Mann, 1972) and specific fattening target foods (Morganstern, 1974) have been the most common targets. However, the form of consumption (see Mills, Sobell, & Schaeffer (1971) on aversive conditioning with alcoholics), the circumstances of eating (e.g., when, where), and daily caloric totals (Schwartz & Bellack, 1976) are alternative targets. Unlike the client described by Morganstern (1974), overweight for most people is not a function of overconsumption of a few specific foods (e.g., Nisbett, 1972; Schachter, 1971), and it is unlikely that reducing consumption of only a few food items would be sufficient to generate significant weight loss. Applying contingencies solely to weight loss is also problematic (e.g., Mahoney, 1974) as the primary difficulty is eating behavior (and energy expenditure); weight loss is an indirect and often much delayed consequence of eating behaviors. In general, aversive conditioning should be most effective when powerful, relevant stimuli are applied contingent upon focal behaviors or stimuli. Other general guidelines about the effective application of aversive stimuli (e.g., massed vs. spaced practice, relative merits of avoidance and punishment paradigms, and schedules) also should be given greater attention. The investigations discussed so far have not, in general, applied conditioning procedures of maximal form for sufficiently extended or intense periods to allow for clear-cut conclusions to be drawn.

The *third* issue pertains to the role of aversive conditioning in the overall treatment program. A behavioral maxim relative to punishment is that it teaches the subject what not to do, but not what he should do. The client in a weight reduction program should be taught the appropriate adaptive behaviors necessary to achieve a healthy rate of weight loss while having balanced nutritional intake and to maintain the loss after termination of contingencies. Application of aversive conditioning alone is, therefore, contraindicated under most circumstances. While research is necessary to isolate the effects of such conditioning and identify its critical parameters, investigators should explore the use of aversive conditioning in multifactor programs. For example, aversive conditioning might be applied initially to reduce consumption of specific problem foods followed by a broad-based self-control and exercise program in which new eating habits and an appropriate energy balance are established.

III. MODIFICATION OF ANTECEDENT CONTROL AND COMBINED PROGRAMS

As already described, the initial learning-based conception of obesity emphasized the consequation of eating. More recently, the predominant view has placed greater emphasis on the antecedent stimuli that elicit eating. This shift in focus has been in response to Schachter's (1971) "stimulus bound" hypothesis of obesity. Schachter has hypothesized that the obese not only eat proportionately *more* that the nonobese, but that they eat *differently*. More specifically, they eat in response to external stimuli such as the sight and smell of food, time of day, where they are, what they are doing, and with whom they are at the time. They also have a maladaptive eating style. They eat too rapidly, too much, take large bites, etc. In contrast, the nonobese eat in moderation, primarily in response to internal, hunger-produced proprioceptive stimuli. Ferster, Nurnberger, and Levitt (1962) had earlier come to a similar conclusion about the obese individual's eating behavior, although they did not hypothesize a fundamental deficit or stimulus boundedness in the obese. The implications of the Schachter model are clear. If the obese individual eats in response to antecedents as opposed to (or in addition to) consequences, an effective weight reduction program would have to modify the antecedents to which the individual was exposed *or* modify his eating habits such that he begins eating in response to physiological needs. Treatment focusing solely on consequence modification should have, at best, temporary effects, as it would not deal with a fundamental source of the eating problem.

This model of obesity has led to the development of a number of parallel treatment programs (e.g., Bellack, Rozensky, & Schwartz, 1974a; Ferster *et al.,* 1962; Jeffrey, Christensen, & Pappas, 1972; Stuart, 1971; Wollersheim, 1970). By far the most systematized and influential version of this approach is the Stuart and Davis (1972) program; it has been published commercially and is available as either a therapist manual or patient handbook. All of the programs share three common elements: (1) reduction of calorie intake (usually by about 1000 calories per day from baseline consumption); (2) increase in energy expenditure through exercise (Stuart and Davis, for example, suggest aerobics); (3) modification of the form of eating behavior (e.g., speed) and the circumstances under which it occurs. The latter component is unique to the "stimulus control" approach. First, clients are instructed to engage in a variety of behaviors which are designed to restructure the environment such that they are exposed to fewer eating stimuli. Simultaneously, they are also expected to engage in a variety of behaviors which serve to reduce the impact of stimuli which cannot be avoided. In consequence, it is expected that the individual will cease to be controlled by external stimuli and will begin to eat primarily in response to proprioceptive hunger stimuli.

A list of the most commonly employed procedures is shown in Table I. The items are designed for self-application in the natural environment, have different degrees of generality, and are differentially difficult to apply. Subjects are typically presented with a list of these recommendations and attend group meetings at which the procedures and their applications are discussed. Most of the studies to be discussed below have employed idiosyncratic versions of this basic treatment strategy. Characteristically, a subset of the stimulus control procedures has been applied and the three program elements (calorie reduction, exercise, stimulus control) have been given differential emphasis. In addition, they are also frequently supplemented by any of a variety of other techniques which are designed to facilitate (consequate) their application (e.g., self-monitoring, social or financial contingencies, self-reinforcement). The literature review presented below will focus first on those studies which were designed (to a great extent) to investigate the overall effectiveness of the general treatment approach. Studies which involved comparisons or evaluations of program parameters will then be separately reviewed.

A. Evaluations of the Stimulus Control (SC) Package

Research reporting negative results does not often find its way into the literature. Nevertheless, there have been a few published studies in which SC programs have not been effective. Penick, Filion, Fox, and Stunkard (1971) compared an SC program with a traditional psychotherapy condition. Although more SC than psychother-

TABLE I

Procedures to Reduce Stimulus Control of Eating[a]

Modification of Meal Quantity

1. Eat slowly: gradually increase minimal time allowed for each meal.
2. Take small bites.
3. Put eating utensil (or food item) down while chewing.
4. Take one helping at a time.
5. Leave table for a brief period between helpings.
6. Eat one food item at a time (e.g., finish meat before taking vegetable).
7. Serve food from kitchen rather than placing platter on table.
8. Use small cups and plates.
9. Leave some food on plate at end of meal.

Modification of Meal Frequency

1. Do nothing else while eating.
2. Eat in only one place, sitting down (preferably not in the kitchen and not where you engage in other activities).
3. Eat only at specified times.
4. Set the table with a complete place setting whenever eating.
5. Wait a fixed period after urge to eat before actually eating.
6. Engage in an activity incompatible with eating when urge to eat appears.
7. Plan a highly liked activity for periods when the urge to eat can be anticipated (e.g., read evening newspaper before bedtime).

Modification of Types of Food Eaten

1. Do not buy prepared foods or snack foods.
2. Prepare lunch after eating breakfast and dinner after lunch (to avoid nibbling).
3. Do grocery shopping soon after eating.
4. Shop from a list.
5. Eat a low-calorie meal before leaving for a party.
6. Do not eat while drinking coffee or alcohol.

---

[a]Reprinted from Bellack, A. S. Behavior therapy for weight reduction. *Addictive Behaviors*, 1975, 1, 73–82.

apy subjects lost substantial amounts of weight, both procedures were only moderately successful and the overall differences in weight loss were not significant. Harris and Bruner (1971) reported on the results of two separate studies. An SC procedure was found to be less effective than a condition in which financial contingencies for weight loss were the sole treatment. In the second study, an SC group did not differ from a control group. Both studies were marked by excessively high (up to 40%) dropout rates. In a study lacking statistical evaluation of data, Hall (1972) also reported an SC condition to be ineffective. While the results of these studies are difficult to interpret, therapist factors were not controlled and, therefore, cannot be discounted. Penick *et al.* (1971) used different therapists for the different treatment groups, and in the Hall (1972) and Harris and Bruner (1971) studies all groups were seen by the same (one) therapist. Specific details of application were also unclear.

Most published reports have found more positive results. Stuart (1967, 1971) successfully applied the procedures in several uncontrolled case studies. Harris (1969) described a study in which subjects in two similar SC groups lost more weight than subjects in a no-contact control group. However, this study did not control for social reinforcement and modeling effects; SC subjects attended weekly group meetings led by a therapist who also lost weight, while control subjects had no on-going treatment contact. One of the most carefully controlled and well-documented investigations of SC programs was conducted by Wollersheim (1970). She compared an SC condition with three control conditions: a social pressure group, a verbal psychotherapy group, and a waiting list control group. Subjects in the SC condition attended weekly group meetings in which procedures were presented and discussed and social reinforcement was provided for weight loss. While all three treatment groups lost weight, the SC group lost significantly more than the other groups. SC subjects lost more than 1 lb. per week and maintained the weight losses through an 8-week follow-up period. As is typical of many of the other studies to be described below, the SC condition in this study included two possibly potent treatment elements in addition to SC per se: social reinforcement and self-monitoring. The effects of the three-element SC package cannot be isolated from the effects of those other techniques on the basis of this study.

Jordan and Levitz (1973) reported positive results for an SC program (including SM) in an uncontrolled study. Subsequently, Levitz and Stunkard (1974) conducted a large-scale controlled evaluation of SC procedures in the context of a commercial self-help group (TOPS). The SC procedure was significantly more effective than control conditions. While weight losses for SC groups were relatively small, any success with such a refractory group (older subjects who had already been dieting unsuccessfully for an extended period) is notable. The Stuart and Davis (1972) program was examined in a study by Abrahms and Allen (1974). Two SC groups (SC supplemented by either social or financial contingencies for weight change) were compared with each other and with groups receiving either social reinforcement for weight loss only or no treatment. The two SC conditions were equally effective and both were significantly more effective than both control conditions. Weight losses for SC groups were maintained through an 8-week follow-up, although subjects in the social-reinforcement-only group lost sufficient additional weight during this period that group differences were no longer significant.

Effective application of SC techniques was also reported in two studies by Balch and Ross (1974, 1975). In the first investigation, subjects completing an SC program lost significantly more weight than subjects who failed to attend meetings regularly and a waiting list group. The second study did not involve a comparison of treatment groups. Hagen (1974) examined the format in which SC programs are administered. A bibliotherapy application, in which the program was administered by mail, was compared to two conditions which included weekly group meetings and a waiting list control. The bibliotherapy group lost as much weight as the two weekly meeting groups, and all three lost significantly more than the control group. Weight losses were maintained through a 4-week follow-up. Bellack, Schwartz, and Rozensky (1974b) and Hanson, Borden, Hall, and Hall (1976) also found that SC programs could be successfully administered with minimal therapist–client contact. In the Bellack et al. study, SC groups having mail contact and brief weekly meetings with the therapist lost similar amounts of weight and both lost significantly more than a group which received the same information as the two contact groups but which had no on-going therapist contact. These results suggest that while weekly face-to-face meetings are not necessary, some regular therapist contact is required if the SC procedures are to be applied effectively. Subjects in the Bellack et al. study were instructed to monitor all of their food intake, again beclouding the effectiveness of SC procedures per se. Hanson et al. (1976) compared five groups: (1) waiting list, (2) attention placebo, (3) self-management (SC), (4) self-management presented in a programmed text and with high therapist–group contact, and (5) self-management in a programmed text with low therapist–group contact. Subjects in each of the three SC groups lost a significant amount of weight. Those three groups did not differ from one another and all three differed from the two control groups. While the results were maintained through a 10-week follow-up, only subjects receiving SC by mail continued to lose weight after the formal treatment period was concluded.

On balance, the results from this set of studies provide positive support for the utility of SC procedures. While few of the studies contained adequate experimental controls to make conclusions clear-cut, the consistency of positive findings makes a fairly persuasive argument. However, almost all of the studies supplemented the SC procedures with additional therapeutic elements; the specific and relative contributions of calorie reduction, exercise, and stimulus control procedures cannot be determined. While the inclusion of additional program elements precludes clear component differentiation, this procedure is clinically justifiable. The SC package as described above consists of therapeutic instructions for self-modification. It does not seem likely that individuals suffering from a chronic dysfunction, such as obesity, in which reinforcement patterns and the behavioral repertoire facilitate current eating practices, would be able to lose weight simply on the basis of having received some new information. Rather, self- or externally imposed contingencies for application of new behaviors are undoubtedly necessary if behavior is to change. The results for the no-contact group reported by Bellack *et al.* (1974b) are representative of this issue. The SC procedures might well be effective as the core of a more complex program, but it is unlikely that they are effective by themselves.

B. Financial Contingencies (FC)

A consequation procedure that has been widely employed is the application of financial contingencies for weight and/or behavior change. Characteristically, subjects are required to deposit a sum of money with the experimenter before treatment begins. This money is then returned at weekly meetings contingent upon the subject meeting a preset criterion (e.g., loss of 2 lbs.). If the criterion is not met, the money is forfeited, and either divided among subjects meeting the criterion or donated to some agency or group that is considered to be aversive to the individual. The contingencies can be applied by the therapist or by the client himself.

One of the earliest examples of this approach was reported by Harris and Bruner (1971). Subjects in an FC condition were reinforced for weight loss at a rate of 50¢ or $1.00 per pound as the sole form of treatment. In one study FC subjects lost more weight than subjects in a control condition, but regained the weight by the end of a 10-month follow-up. In a second study, FC subjects did not differ from a control group. In a subsequent study Harris and Hallbauer (1973) found no difference between two FC groups and a control group at the end of treatment, but both treatment groups had lost significantly more than the control group by the end of a 7-month follow-up. Contingencies were self-determined by the subjects and averaged 76¢ per pound. Weight losses were not substantial during either the treatment or follow-up phases.

In an unusual variant of the FC approach, Hall (1972) reinforced weight loss with her own funds rather than securing deposits from the subjects. She reported that FC subjects lost more weight than subjects under an SC condition. However, Hall served as therapist for all subjects in a reversal design. Abrahms and Allen (1974) compared the effects of FC and social reinforcement combined with social reinforcement alone for application of the Stuart and Davis (1972) program. Both treatment groups showed better results than a no-treatment group, and the weight losses were maintained through an 8-week follow-up. Social reinforcement might have been powerful enough that any possible impact of the FC procedure was masked. Hall, Hall, DeBoer, and O'Kulitch (1976) compared groups receiving SC alone, SC plus FC, FC alone, and two control conditions. Subjects in the FC troups could earn between $1.00 and $2.25 per week, depending on how much weight they lost. The three treatment groups had all lost significantly more weight than the control groups by the end of treatment, but only the combined group maintained the losses through a 6-month follow-up period. This finding suggests that the FC procedure facilitated the development of new eating habits (via SC), which thus resulted in long-term maintenance. Jeffrey and Christensen (1975) also found that a combined SC and FC group maintained losses during an extended follow-up period, although the effects of the FC procedure were not isolated by the methodology.

Another investigation of therapist-managed financial contingencies was reported by Rozensky and Bellack (1976). They compared an FC procedure with a self-control condition and a minimal contact control. All subjects initially made equal financial deposits, which were refunded to FC subjects on a contingent basis and to other subjects noncontingently at the conclusion of the program. All groups also received instructions in SC techniques. Subjects in the self-control group were required to monitor their anticipated food consumption immediately prior to eating, mailing their monitoring records to the therapist daily. Subjects in the self-control and FC groups reported for weekly weight checks at which time FC subjects were reinforced for weight loss at a rate of $2.00 per pound. Both treatment conditions were more effective than the control condition, with losses being maintained through a 7-week follow-up period. However, the FC condition was not effective for all subjects. Subjects were initially categorized as either high or low self-controllers on the basis of an analogue self-reinforcement task (Bellack & Tillman, 1974). Low self-controllers lost similar amounts of weight in the two treatment conditions. In contrast, high self-controllers lost 10.70 lbs. in the self-control condition and 2.60 lbs. (less than minimal contact subjects) in the FC condition. These results strongly suggest that there is an interaction between treatment form and subject style which must be taken into account. In particular, caution is advised in the application of programs which place a premium on external management.

An alternative to therapist-managed contingencies is to instruct the subject to manage and administer consequation by himself. As it has typically been applied, this procedure requires subjects to make a financial deposit with the therapist, but in contrast to externally managed programs, subjects physically administer contingencies themselves, in private. This approach has several potential advantages over external management, including greater subject involvement, ease of administration, and avoidance of negative reactions toward the therapist (e.g., when response cost is invoked). In addition, if this procedure were effective, the major advantage would be that subjects would be taught a self-management skill which they could apply independent of any active therapeutic involvement (e.g., Thoresen & Mahoney, 1974). The first investigations of self-managed FC were conducted by Mahoney, Moura, and Wade (1973), who compared four conditions: self-administered reward for weight loss, self-punishment for weight gain, self-monitoring (of weight and eating urges), and a waiting list group. The self-reward group lost significantly more weight than the waiting list group and maintained losses through a follow-up period. The other three groups did not differ from one another. All groups received SC instructions, again indicating that some supplemental reinforcement is necessary for their application. While this study suggests that self-reward can be effective, the procedure did not apply adequate controls over the administration of self-punishment. Also, there is some suggestion that self-punishment subjects did not comply with instructions as well as self-reinforcement subjects. The comparison of reward and punishment procedures is thus limited. In a subsequent study, Mahoney (1974) compared self-reward for weight loss, self-reward for habit change (based on SC procedures), self-monitoring of eating habits, and a waiting list group. Self-reward for habit change was significantly more effective than each of the other conditions; these subjects continued to lose weight during the 9-week follow-up period. Self-reward for weight loss was only moderately effective, although it was significantly better than the no-treatment condition. There was no difference between the self-monitoring and no-treatment groups.

Further support for the utility of self-managed FC is provided by Jeffrey (1974a). He compared an externally managed FC procedure with two variations of self-managed FC. Contingencies were applied to *both* weight loss and habit change, and all subjects received SC instructions. One self-managed group was placed on a response cost program in which unearned money was to be forfeited, while the second group was told that unearned money would be returned at the end of the program. All three groups lost statistically significant amounts of weight. They did not differ from one another during treatment but only the self-managed groups maintained weight losses during a 6-week follow-up. While weight losses were statistically significant, the externally managed group lost at the relatively low rate of only .7 lb. per week. The results for the self-managed groups are clear, but those for the external group are somewhat confounded by expectancy attributions. Subjects in this condition were explicitly told that success depended on therapist control, while self-management subjects were told that they were responsible for their own success. Given that weight loss necessarily involves self-management in outpatient treatment, the external control expectancy might have had countertherapeutic effects. If therapist management is to be applied, it should (probably) be offered as a supplement to self-management, not as a complete alternative.

The utility of supplemental financial contingencies is still uncertain. The results for externally managed programs are mixed; the only study involving differential, clinically significant effects for a therapist-managed FC procedure was conducted by Hall *et al.* (1976). In general, this technique has been no more effective than other procedures (e.g., social reinforcement, pre-eating, self-monitoring) which are simpler to administer and involve more naturalistic consequation (see Baer & Wolf, 1970). It also has potentially negative effects (e.g., Jeffrey, 1974; Rozensky & Bellack, 1976). However, further research is needed before this approach is rejected. The results of the Hall *et al.* (1976) study suggest that effects of the contingencies might not be evident until after a follow-up period. Most of the issues discussed above in the context of aversive conditioning are applicable here as well. FC programs have employed relatively mild contingencies. Reinforcements (and response cost penalties) have generally ranged from \$1.00 to \$2.00 per pound. As weight changes typically range from 1 to 2 lbs. per week, the total reward or penalty for a week's dieting effort is quite modest. In addition, they are applied on a delayed basis to an indirect product of the actual target behaviors (e.g., eating habits). Mahoney (1974), for example, found consequation of eating habits to be more effective than consequation of weight change. Not only is this a more appropriate target, but it requires the subject to self-monitor his on-going behavior. Such monitoring can have secondary reinforcing or discriminative stimulus properties, which would serve to mitigate the delay until the FC is applied.

The results for the three self-management studies are more positive; all three achieved clinically meaningful rates of loss that were stable through follow-up periods. One question raised by these studies pertains to the relative degree of self-management involved in the procedures employed. Subjects were required to deposit a sum of money with the experimenters as a condition of participation. The experimenter specified the nature (e.g., criteria and amounts) of the contingencies and required attendance at meetings and exposure to the contingency (e.g., subjects were weighed and ushered behind a screen where the money was kept). Despite attempts to suggest that experimenters were unaware of the application of rewards and punishments, they were aware; thus, it is not unlikely that subjects knew (or presumed) they were being checked. All of these elements combine to impose a considerable degree of external control over subject behavior. While the procedures appear to be effective, it would be desirable to compare them to a total self-management condition in which: (1) no deposit was retained, and (2) subjects established and administered their own contingencies at home. Schwartz and Bellack (1976) applied such a procedure and found extremely low rates of compliance; in the absence of external management, subjects did not contingently administer FC. (Eighteen of 47 subjects in two self-reinforcement conditions reported never using procedures; 18 others rated their compliance as 5 or less on a 10-point scale. Yet subjects in both groups lost significant amounts of weight.)

C. Self-Monitoring and Self-Reinforcement

Self-monitoring (SM) has become almost an integral part of the behavioral weight control package. One of the premises of the stimulus control model of obesity is that obese individuals are not aware of their eating behavior (e.g., how much, when, and where they eat). One goal of treatment, therefore, is to increase their awareness so that they can exercise appropriate control over their behavior. Self-monitoring appears to be a perfect vehicle for increasing such awareness. Further, SM has been shown to be reactive (see Kazdin, 1974), offering the possibility that eating could be controlled as well as observed by the use of SM. While several studies have employed SM solely as a data gathering procedure, primary interest lies in its utility as a therapeutic agent.

Mahoney *et al.* (1973) required subjects to keep daily records of their weight, diet-related thoughts, and instances of indulgence and restraint in eating. Subjects in the Mahoney (1974) study kept a daily log of eating habits (unspecified). These procedures did not have therapeutic effectiveness in either study. Stollak (1967) instructed subjects to keep a daily diary of food consumption (where, when, what was eaten). An SM group that met regularly with therapists to review the diary lost a significant amount of weight (more than 1 lb. per week). This condition was more effective than an SM–no-contact condition, and two SM conditions in which aversive stimuli were applied during treatment sessions. While initial weight losses were satisfactory, they were not maintained during the follow-up period.

Romanczyk, Tracey, Wilson, and Thorpe (1973) and Romanczyk (1974) compared two forms of SM (monitoring of calorie intake and monitoring of daily weight), with stimulus control packages supplemented by a set of consequation procedures (e.g., covert sensitization, financial contingencies). In both studies, SM groups received no supplemental weight control treatment (e.g., no contact, no stimulus control material), yet the SM calories group lost as much weight as the more intensive treatment groups. On the other hand, the groups that monitored weight did not differ from a no-treatment control group. The results for the SM calorie groups are especially surprising given that subjects received no supplemental information or training. However, these findings might be a function of the short treatment duration that was employed (4 weeks). While SM is known to be reactive (Kazdin, 1974), Stuart (1971) and Mahoney (1974) have reported that the effects of SM in weight control programs are only temporary. In the Mahoney (1974) study, for example, differences between SM and FC groups did not become apparent until the midpoint of treatment. Clinical observation, in general, suggests that many subjects lose some weight in the first few weeks of almost any program, but fail to maintain losses or quickly regain the lost weight.

These findings suggest that the results of the Romanczyk studies might have been different if treatment had been extended further.

The results reported above suggest that the focus of SM (e.g., weight, calories) can affect the therapeutic utility of self-observation. Another potential variable is the time at which the records are made. Monitoring at the time the target behavior occurs should be more accurate and provide more relevant feedback than delayed record keeping. In that regard, monitoring of (intended) eating immediately prior to consumption should have even more impact as it guarantees attention to relevant variables (in this case hunger, caloric values, etc.) at a point when behavior can still be modified. Such prebehavior monitoring would interrupt the stimulus-eating sequence and increase the likelihood of an appropriate response. This contention was examined in a series of studies by Bellack and his colleagues. Bellack *et al.* (1974a) compared pre-eating SM with post-eating SM, a stimulus control therapy group, and a no-contract control. The pre-eating SM condition was the most effective, and subjects in this group continued to lose weight through a 6-week follow-up period. The post-eating SM group did not differ from the no-contact control group and lost significantly less weight than the nonmonitoring group, which received an identical intervention with the exception of SM instructions. Such monitoring appears to have decreased the effectiveness of an otherwise potent intervention. The three treatment groups in this study attended weekly group meetings at which time monitoring records (for SM groups) and stimulus control techniques were discussed. Bellack *et al.* (1974b) evaluated pre-eating SM in the context of two low-therapist-contact conditions: (1) mail contact, in which subjects mailed SM records to the therapist daily, and received feedback in the mail weekly, and (2) mail contact plus feedback at weekly weight checks. The two procedures were equally (albeit moderately) effective, and subjects in those groups lost significantly more weight than those in a no-contact control group. In a third study, Rozensky and Bellack (1976) found pre-eating SM to be as effective as an FC program, and significantly better than a minimal-contact control condition. Weight losses exceeded 1 lb. per week and persisted through a 7-week follow-up.

Most of the programs employing stimulus control techniques have, directly or indirectly, emphasized the importance of self-management in the implementation of the procedures. Current conceptions of self-management (e.g., Kanfer, 1975; Thoresen & Mahoney, 1974) hold it to be a three-stage process: self-monitoring, self-evaluation, and self-reinforcement (SR). Any reactive effects of

SM would presumably be a function of covert self-evaluative and self-reinforcing operations that followed. However, if subjects are not explicitly directed to self-evaluate and administer SR, it cannot be presumed that consequation would be applied consistently. Explicit instructions for SR should, therefore, increase the likelihood of behavior change. Bellack (1976) compared the effectiveness of pre-eating monitoring with monitoring supplemented by SR. All subjects were required to monitor all eating plans, and one-half were instructed to self-reinforce by assigning a letter grade (in writing) to each diary entry. Grades were presumed to be secondary reinforcers for most subjects. Level of therapist contact was also varied such that one-half of each group mailed diary records to the therapist daily and received weekly feedback and one-half of each group had no on-going therapist contact. The SR procedure was significantly more effective than SM alone across both levels of contact. Weight losses for SR groups were well above 1 lb. per week and continued during the 6-week follow-up period; both SR groups had lost more than 5% of body weight by the end of the follow-up. As in the study reported by Bellack *et al.* (1974b), the SM mail-contact group lost a statistically significant but small amount of weight. While this procedure has been consistently effective, it should be supplemented by contingent reinforcement (e.g., social or explicit SR) if clinically meaningful results are to be achieved.

An alternative form of SR was described by Bellack *et al.* (1976). They instructed subjects to SM and evaluate the adequacy of each diary entry based on caloric value and eating style. Depending on the experimental condition, they were then required to either self-reward (for a good entry) or self-punish (for an undesirable entry). In the self-reward condition, a positive evaluation was followed by writing the word THIN in the diary and generating positive covert imagery (e.g., imagining oneself wearing a smaller dress or slack size). Under the self-punishment condition, a negative evaluation was to be followed by writing the word FAT next to the diary entry and generating aversive imagery (e.g., viewing one's body fat). Both self-reward and self-punishment were significantly more effective than a control condition and resulted in weight losses of more than 1 lb. per week. The results of these studies suggest that SR can be a highly useful technique in the treatment of obesity. It is portable, and thus can be applied immediately whenever the target behavior occurs. It can be applied to any form of target (e.g., calorie values, eating style, time, weight), and, given the variability of form of SR (e.g., imagery, activities, money), should be broadly applicable. Finally, it is a technique which requires minimum therapist intervention initially and, theoretically (e.g., Thoresen & Mahoney, 1974), can be self-initiated and applied after formal treatment ends. As discussed previously in the context of self-administered FC, this latter presumption requires further investigation. Schwartz and Bellack (1976) evaluated the effectiveness of Premack and financial reinforcement contingencies in the context of low therapist control. Subjects were responsible for administering their own contingency program based either on self- or therapist-determined criteria. They attended biweekly meetings at which their progress (and problems) were reviewed. While subjects in both conditions lost weight, they failed to apply the designated SR procedures. Furthermore, weight loss was not highly correlated with the degree of application. In contrast to the SR procedures employed by Bellack (1976) and Bellack *et al.* (1976), the Premack and FC procedures were tedious and complicated to administer and their application could not be easily monitored by therapists. In that regard, subjects in the Schwartz and Bellack (1976) study were also required to monitor eating behavior and calories and convert their performance to a numerical point total for administering SR. Subjects did comply with those instructions, with degree of compliance significantly correlated with weight loss.

D. Covert Conditioning Procedures

Clinical observation of individuals in weight reduction programs suggests that as time passes the saliency of initial reasons for losing weight becomes obscure or loses relevance. Both the aversive aspects of overweight and potential reinforcement stemming from lowered weight appear to succumb to the immediate aversiveness of dieting. As a function of this phenomenon, several researchers have hypothesized that increasing the saliency of those cues would facilitate weight loss. Tyler and Straughan (1970) and Horan and Johnson (1971) evaluated the effectiveness of coverant conditioning (Homme, 1965) to increase the occurrence of appropriate, diet-relevant cognitions. In both studies, subjects were instructed to emit negative coverants (e.g., "I am fat," "I am ugly") followed by positive coverants (e.g., "Thin people are attractive") at various times throughout the day. Tyler and Straughan instructed their subjects to emit coverants prior to engaging in Premack reinforcement (e.g., reading the newspaper, watching television); the coverant conditioning procedure was not supplemented by other weight control procedures, and it did not result in significant weight loss. Horan and Johnson compared four groups: (1) waiting list, (2) weight control information, (3) information plus coverants, and (4) information plus coverants reinforced by Premack reinforcers. The last-mentioned condition was the most effective, resulting in moderate weight losses (.7 lb per week) despite the fact that subjects emitted progressively fewer coverants each day throughout the treatment period. A higher rate of reinforced coverant emission might have resulted in greater weight losses.

Horan, Baker, Hoffman, and Shute (1975) evaluated the use of coverants in a three-way factorial design; they varied valence of coverants (positive vs. negative), the Premack reinforcer (eating vs. non-eating behaviors), and contact level (group meetings vs. minimum contact). The use of positive coverants was significantly more effective than negative coverants, whether emitted before eating or before other behaviors and with group meetings or minimal contact (although more subjects having group meetings lost large amounts of weight). Weight losses for positive coverant groups were more than 1 lb. per week. Horan et al. did not conduct a follow-up, as they presumed that a high rate of coverant emission would not be maintained over time. Given the positive and consistent results of this study (every positive coverant subject lost weight), this contention should be empirically examined, along with the utility of this procedure in sequence with other techniques.

Several investigations have been conducted in which covert sensitization has been paired with other weight control techniques (Harris, 1969; Romanczyk, 1974; Romanczyk et al. 1973). In each case the procedures were ineffective. However, as with the studies in which covert sensitization was applied in isolation, subjects received few conditioning trials, and aversiveness of imagery was not assessed. Further research is warranted in which optimal applications of covert sensitization are evaluated.

E. Compound Studies with Long-Term Follow-ups

Most of the studies reviewed thus far have either involved preliminary evaluations of new techniques or were designed to provide critical comparisons of technique variants. As a result, treatment durations and follow-up periods have been brief. Once the short-term efficacy of the behavioral approach was determined, a considerable amount of interest shifted to the long-term clinical efficacy of the techniques. Several reports have recently appeared in which compound programs involving SM, SR, stimulus control, and other procedures have been employed, with follow-ups of 6 months and longer.[3]

Hall (1973) conducted a 2-year follow-up on subjects from the Hall (1972) study; while there was not much stability of weights, the original treatment procedure had not been effective. In a series of uncontrolled case studies, Jeffrey, Christensen, and Katz (1976) attempted to fade therapist contact after long-term treatment. Two of four subjects regained lost weight after a 6-month follow-up period. Hall et al. (1974) compared two self-management programs with two control conditions. Both treatment conditions were significantly more effective than the controls at the end of the 10-week treatment period. Differences were reduced after a 3-month follow-up and were nonsignificant by the time of a 6-month follow-up. In response to these disappointing results, Hall, Hall, Borden, and Hanson (1975) examined techniques for increasing stability of changes. Three groups of subjects were given a 12-week course in behavioral weight management procedures. For the following 12 weeks, one group was required to attend biweekly meetings, a second group maintained biweekly contact by mail (they mailed monitoring diaries to the therapist), and the third group had no further contact. All groups had lost significant amounts of weight by the end of treatment, but only the mail-contact group successfully maintained weight losses. One-half of the continued-contact group continued to meet with their original therapist; they maintained losses while subjects who saw a new therapist regained weight. No data were presented on the degree to which SM instructions were followed by either of the contact groups or the mail group. The specific contributions of the two booster procedures and the differential results for the contact groups are thus difficult to evaluate. Furthermore, neither raw weights, percentage losses, or rates of loss were reported, precluding comparison with other studies. These results suggest that given appropriate support for an extended period, weight losses can be maintained. However, the nature of "appropriate support" is unclear.

Simon and Bellack (1976) conducted a similar investigation that employed parallel treatment groups. The initial treatment period

---

[3] A few reports have appeared in which telephone follow-ups were conducted. My own experience indicates that most participants (or volunteers) in weight control programs are not aware of their actual weight, especially if knowledge of their weight is aversive (as when they have not lost or have regained). Without demonstration that telephone follow-ups provide reliable and valid data, it would be safe to assume that such data are not accurate.

lasted 8 weeks rather than 12 and consisted of biweekly meetings rather than weekly meetings. Therapist contact was faded (for continuous contact subjects) from biweekly to every 3 weeks to 1 month by the end of the 6-month period. All groups lost more than 1 lb. per week during the initial period. Furthermore, the no-contact and mail group maintained losses during the subsequent 6-month period, and the continued-contact group continued to lose weight. Mail-contact subjects maintained weight losses despite the fact that they returned relatively few diary records (they did receive mailings from the therapist each week). Schwartz and Bellack (1976) were able to secure 6-month follow-up data from one-third of their subjects. Of the 24 individuals reweighed, nine continued to lose weight after treatment ended and seven regained some weight but maintained overall losses. Only three subjects who had lost weight during treatment weighed as much or more as they did prior to treatment.

This series of studies suggests that behavioral programs can have stable effects. The specific factors which result in stability are still unclear. These studies all varied, in undefined ways, in the manner in which programs were administered, the nature of therapist–client interactions, expectancy factors, and subject populations. This type of variability vastly complicates the integration of results. The Hall group, for example, emphasized group and therapist social pressure, while Simon and Bellack emphasized didactic material during meetings. Subjects in the Hall studies initially met for up to 12 sessions, while subjects in the Simon and Bellack study met for only five sessions. Thus, while the Simon and Bellack approach might have facilitated maintenance by placing greater initial emphasis on self-management, Hall's subjects received more training and might be expected to have mastered techniques more effectively. However, her sample was older and heavier and that might have been a factor. Furthermore, the studies had differential dropout rates; presuming that dropouts are often failures (see below), this further complicates interpretations of findings. The by now familiar refrain must be repeated: more research is needed to resolve these issues.

IV. DISCUSSION

Having surveyed the literature, we can now return to Yates' (1975) conclusion: Is the treatment of obesity an instance of failure for behavior modification? I think not. Applications of compound programs involving stimulus control and supplemental reinforcement have consistently resulted in clinically significant weight losses. These losses have generally been maintained over brief follow-up intervals, and there is some suggestion that given appropriate planning (e.g., fading contact, conducting booster sessions) the effects of treatment can be stable for more extended posttreatment periods. The results for programs emphasizing external consequation rather than self-management have generally been disappointing. However, this approach to treatment has not been sufficiently examined under optimal conditions. While Yates' position is too extreme in the negative direction, initial claims for the effectiveness of the behavioral approach are far too positive given the data currently available. Unanswered questions about the application of behavioral techniques far exceed the answered questions. The remainder of this article will be devoted to a discussion of some of the major issues still to be resolved.

A. Generality of Results

A number of factors make it difficult to integrate the results of different studies and draw conclusions about the generality of the findings.

1. MEASUREMENT

One of the factors that drew researchers to the study of obesity was the (presumed) objective nature of the treatment target: body weight. Indeed, the selection of a dependent variable and a strategy for data analysis have been a source of considerable controversy (Bellack & Rozensky, 1975). Body weight is not a pure measure of body fat, which is presumed to be a more critical factor in cosmetic and health reasons for weight loss (Mayer, 1968). Furthermore, weight loss is partially a function of initial weight (Mayer, 1968). Given these two factors, weight loss as the primary dependent measure was used less frequently. Other alternative measures were promulgated, including: percentage body weight lost (Bellack & Rozensky, 1975), percentage overweight lost (Mahoney, 1974), Weight Reduction Index (Jeffrey, 1974b), skinfold thickness (Franzini & Grimes, 1975), and residual change scores (Wollersheim, 1970). Data analysis procedures have included: analysis of variance (or Kruskal Wallace H) on raw weight loss, each of the derived scores, and arcsin conversions of derived scores; analysis of covariance (using initial weight as covariate); and repeated-measures analysis of variance in which pretreatment, posttreatment, and follow-up represent measurement points.

This plethora of variables and analysis strategies precludes meaningful comparisons between and among studies. A systematic review of measurement and data analysis procedures is beyond the scope of this paper. However, several recommendations are offered for future research: (1) pretreatment weights and weight losses should *always* be presented for *each* experimental *group;* (2) rate of weight loss should be presented; (3) if a derived score is to be used, data analyses should also be conducted on another variable; (4) repeated-measures analysis of variance should *not* be employed without direct report of weight lost and rate of loss (statistically significant differences from pre- to posttreatment can be based on actual losses of 1 or 2 lbs.).

2. TREATMENT DROPOUTS

Stunkard (1959) reported that traditional treatment methods had dropout rates of 20%–80%. While behavioral treatments have generally been better able to keep subjects in treatment, dropout rates of up to 40% are not uncommon and, in general, the problem of subject attrition has not been resolved. The dropout question has implications for both clinical evaluation of treatment utility and for data analysis in research (e.g., which subjects to include in analyses). The empirical issue is resolved if the subject is a true dropout and fails to report for the final weight check. However, many subjects for whom data are collected remain functional dropouts; that is, they attend meetings infrequently and/or do not comply with instructions. They often lose minimal amounts of weight or even gain weight. Not surprisingly, Balch and Ross (1974) found that subjects attending more than 75% of group meetings lost significantly more weight than subjects attending fewer than 75% of the meetings (the 75% attendance rate has been a general criterion for defining dropout status). Should such individuals be included in data analyses? It is unreasonable to assume that any treatment would be effective for everyone. Many individuals volunteering for weight reduction programs are not prepared to change their behavior and/or have insufficient incentive to lose weight. Therefore, such individuals should not be included in determining the success of a given treatment strategy. Conversely, a clinician or researcher who arbitrarily and retrospectively excludes "unmotivated" subjects from his reports will experience 100% "success." There is a critical need for research which attacks the problem of pretreatment assessment of subject—treatment compatibility so that incompatible clients can be counseled out of treatment, and faulty client—treatment matches can be avoided. In the meantime, researchers are advised to conduct data analyses *independently* on all subjects for whom data are available *and* on high attenders (or compliers) only. Paired with a report of percentage of noncompliers, this approach would provide a more complete picture of the effectiveness of a procedure. Calculations should be based on weight *loss* rather than weight *change,* so that a weight gain would appear as zero loss; this guideline is tantamount to assuming that anyone who gains weight while in a weight-control program is not an appropriate candidate.

3. DEMOGRAPHIC VARIABLES

A majority of studies have involved relatively young (mean ages of 21 to 30) and mildly overweight (mean weights from 150 to 175) subjects (e.g., college populations). There is some suggestion that heavier and older subjects have more difficulty losing weight (see Hall & Hall, 1974), leaving the generality of findings based on lighter, younger subjects in question. However, a number of studies have reported positive results with older noncollege populations (e.g., Balch & Ross, 1974; Hall *et al.,* 1975; Rozensky & Bellack, 1976; Simon & Bellack, 1976). In the single study designed to compare the two populations, Hall *et al.,* (1974) found a behavioral program to be equally effective for both groups. While caution is still advised in generalizing across populations, the assumption that current findings are applicable only to college populations is not supported. The one group of subjects with whom behavioral techniques have not been systematically applied is the grossly obese: individuals with weight loss goals of over 100 lbs. Given such factors as the period of time required to lose that much weight, and restrictions in mobility and life style, a different approach might be necessary with this group. Applicability of the behavioral package for this population should be empirically determined.

B. Individual Differences

The results (and conclusions) reported above represent the out-come of research-based applications of behavioral programs. Techniques have been administered on a group basis, in a "shotgun fashion" for brief periods. Subjects have been assigned to treatments at random and there has been a minimum of individual assessment and tailoring of treatments. It is somewhat surprising that techniques have been effective at all under such conditions. As with all behavioral interventions, treatment should be preceded by a functional analysis of the individual client's behavior (Ferster *et al.*, 1962). The items in Table I will not all be applicable for every client, and only those that are appropriate should be administered. It is unlikely that clients will apply all elements of a multicomponent intervention, and without guidance, they are as likely to select ineffective as effective elements. In addition, there is consistent evidence that the addition of inappropriate program elements can mitigate the value of an otherwise effective program (Bellack *et al.*, 1974a; Franzini & Grimes, 1975; Rozensky & Bellack, 1976). The importance of selecting appropriate reinforcers has been alluded to in previous sections. The form of reinforcement must be considered as well as the magnitude or valence. Morganstern (1974), for example, applied cigarette smoke as the aversive stimulus based on the idiosyncratic needs of his client after covert stimuli proved to be ineffective.

Intensive pretreatment assessment is also necessary prior to the use of self-management procedures (Bellack & Schwartz, 1976). Individuals will vary in their ability to effectively self-monitor, self-evaluate, and self-reinforce, as well as in their preference for self- or external management. Pretraining in self-management skills or a primary emphasis on external management is sometimes necessary. For example, Rozensky and Bellack (1976) classified subjects as high or low self-reinforcers based on their utilization of self-reinforcement on a verbal recognition memory task (see Bellack & Tillman, 1974). High self-reinforcers lost more weight than lows in a self-management program, and they lost less than a non-treatment group in an external control program. In a subsequent study, Bellack *et al.* (1976) found that high self-reinforcers lost significantly more weight than low self-reinforcers in a self-management program. They also maintained their losses better once therapist contact was terminated. Given that all weight reduction relies to some extent on self-management, pretreatment assessment of individual differences in self-control skills should receive much greater emphasis (Bellack & Schwartz, 1976).

The entire issue of treatment–subject matching demands greater attention (Mahoney & Mahoney, 1976). No treatments are universally applicable, yet guidelines for identifying appropriate treatments are lacking. Attempts to predict outcome based on demographic characteristics, motivation, and numerous personality scales have been unsuccessful. Aside from self-reinforcement (as described above), only locus of control has been found to relate to treatment outcome; Balch & Ross (1975) found low but significant correlations between locus of control and weight loss. However, overall scores on self-report scales and inventories are no more likely to be useful predictors in this context than they are in others (Bellack & Hersen, 1977). Success is more likely to be achieved by identifying and matching the functional demands of the program (e.g., "must monitor and evaluate calorie intake") with the skills of the client (e.g., "is a good self-observer but does not know caloric values of foods"). Unless and until effective pretreatment tests are developed for assessing relevant client characteristics, on-going evaluation through the use of single-subject research methodology (Hersen & Barlow, 1976) provides the only approach for systematically pairing client and treatment. It should be added that this emphasis on individual assessment does not preclude group application, simply that the economy of group application should not substitute for individualized assessment and treatment planning.

C. Strategies for Applying Techniques

Related to the issue of what technique is to be employed with a given client is the order in which techniques should be applied. Two factors suggest that simultaneous presentation of a multicomponent treatment package is not advisable. First, clients are not able to apply multiple techniques effectively at one time; practice, shaping, and reinforcement for specific performance are generally necessary. Second, clinical application ordinarily involves extended treatment (6 months rather than 6 weeks is common), during which time treatment needs change (e.g., reinforcers satiate, value of weight loss changes, environmental support and pressure vary) and new components must be added. Therefore, sequential application of procedures is desirable. For example, many clients lose weight in the first few weeks of treatment even without effective programs (e.g., Bellack *et al.*, 1976; Mahoney, 1974). Consequation procedures might then be reserved until that initial surge begins to subside. Aversive conditioning could be applied to specific problem foods or situations that present roadblocks. Coverant conditioning could be instituted if and when the value of weight loss becomes less apparent. Self-monitoring is often tedious and somewhat aversive; actual record keeping could be simplified or eliminated as covert SM becomes automatic. In general, behavioral intervention should not be conceptualized as a unitary package that is applied in a pro forma manner at the beginning of the treatment period; it must be viewed as a reactive intervention involving multiple components.

Another factor in applying behavioral programs is the nature and schedule of therapist contact. Many of the programs described above were administered in 6–12 weekly group therapy meetings. Therapists provided didactic information about weight loss and social reinforcement for compliance and weight change. Several investigations demonstrated that such a high level of therapist involvement was unnecessary (Bellack, 1976; Bellack et al., 1974b; Hagen, 1974; Hanson et al., 1976). However, while weekly meetings and intensive social consequation are not necessary, the therapist does play an apparently critical role. With the exception of one group in the Bellack (1976) study, no contact groups (given equivalent information) have not lost as much weight as groups receiving even minimal (e.g., mail) contact. The results for follow-up periods indicate that subjects rarely lose (much) additional weight after contact is terminated. Hall et al. (1975) found that an extended treatment group transferred to a new therapist was much less successful at maintaining weight losses than a similar group that continued contact with their original therapist. Finally, clinical data indicate that subjects in low-contact programs almost invariably report a desire for more contact, even when they are successful in losing weight. These results are difficult to interpret. While the therapist appears to be necessary, his function is uncertain. The effectiveness of mail contact procedures, in which both information-giving and social reinforcement are minimal, suggest that contact serves a different function. Bellack et al. (1974b) suggested that the therapist serves as a discriminative stimulus for dieting behavior. This hypothesis, analogous to the rationale for the use of coverant conditioning (e.g., Horan et al., 1975; Tyler & Straughan, 1970), assumes that when the individual diets, noncompliance with diet rules is aversive, but that the same behavior is not aversive if the individual does not perceive himself to be on a diet. Therefore, "forgetting" that one is dieting is a frequent response as it is negatively reinforcing. Therapist contact even at a low level precludes this response by serving as a repeated S^D for dieting. As with many of the other hypotheses offered in this paper, this too requires empirical investigation [it does not, for example, account for the Hall et al. (1975) data] .

There are times when the therapist is much more actively engaged as a social reinforcer for behavior and weight change. When such reinforcement is a primary factor in maintaining appropriate behavior, termination of contact becomes a problematic issue. Unless new behaviors have become habitual, reinforcement control must be shifted to the client himself or his natural environment (e.g., spouse, parents). Several recent investigations have dealt with this problem by fading therapist contact (Hall *et al.*, 1975; Jeffrey *et al.*, 1976; Simon & Bellack, 1976). This approach appears to be a highly promising alternative to sudden, extreme transitions from high levels of contact to no contact and should be explored further.

D. Eating Behavior

One of the primary goals of behavioral programs is modification of the eating patterns of clients. This is assumed to be necessary in order for them to lose weight during treatment, and to maintain losses after treatment. However, despite the importance given to this goal, research efforts have given it scant attention, focusing almost entirely on weight loss. Subjects have been provided with information about behavior change, but with few exceptions (e.g., Bellack *et al.*, 1976; Jeffrey, 1974a; Mahoney, 1974), reinforcement and monitoring procedures have focused on weight change (or calorie consumption). Weight has invariably been the sole dependent variable and behavior is presumed to have changed if weight is lost. As pointed out by Mahoney (1975a) and demonstrated clearly in the Mann (1972) study, loss of weight is not sufficient evidence to support that conclusion. While weight loss does imply an alteration in the energy balance, there are no data to indicate that losses have commonly resulted from increased exercise or improved eating style rather than from unsystematic reduction in caloric intake.

Efforts to assess changes in eating style have been limited to posttreatment questionnaires in which subjects are asked to estimate the degree to which they complied with treatment instructions. [Mahoney (1974) reviewed SM diaries, but he did not include the actual degree of reported behavior change.] Responses to such surveys are likely to be invalid and to overestimate compliance (e.g., Bellack & Hersen, 1977). While some posttreatment surveys have suggested that eating behavior was modified (e.g., Hagen, 1974; Wollersheim, 1970), others have suggested minimal compliance with program guidelines about eating style (e.g., Bellack *et al.*, 1974a; Schwartz & Bellack, 1976). Resolution of this question requires on-going monitoring of eating behavior (self- or other-monitoring) with reliability checks.

Along with a more effective evaluation of changes in eating behavior, further research is needed to determine the desirability and necessity of such changes. While the importance of permanent modification of eating behavior is emphasized by therapists and given lip service by clients, it is doubtful that most overweight individuals are actually willing to sacrifice on a permanent basis such potent reinforcement. For the majority of moderately overweight individuals, lowered weight is not sufficiently reinforcing to maintain a controlled eating style. This might be one reason why subjects do not continue to lose weight after treatment ends, even though (presumed) goals have not been met. Perhaps short-term intervention with moderate losses is an appropriate endeavor, rather than, as Yates (1975) concludes, an instance of failure. Support for this contention is provided by Nisbett (1972) and the "set point" or "ponderostat" theory of obesity. Nisbett hypothesizes that, as a function of genetics and early learning history, there is a physiological set point for amount of body fat. Homeostatic mechanisms function to maintain this quota of fat, and the set point is unmodifiable. The obese individual not only has a high set point, but as a function of social pressure, consistently diets, and is thus below optimal levels (despite the socially defined excess). Therefore, he is always hungry and is doomed to be hungrier the more weight (fat) he loses. This theory suggests not only that eating style is at most only part of the problem in obesity, but that if maintenance of lowered body weight is desirable, it requires a different and more intensive intervention than we have applied. The successful weight loser might have to learn to tolerate perpetual discomfort [it is possible that the induced anxiety procedure employed by Bornstein and Sipprelle (1973a, 1973b) was effective for that very reason].

In a seminal article appropriately entitled "Fat Fiction," Mahoney (1975a) has pointed out several of the as yet unvalidated beliefs which have guided behavioral weight control research. Along with some of the issues discussed above, he suggests that widespread acceptance of Schachter's "stimulus bound" model of obesity is premature, as are the related beliefs about the existence of fundamental differences in eating style between the obese and the nonobese. This reservation has been amplified elsewhere. Milich (1975) suggests that if it is valid at all, the theory is applicable only for some individuals with early-onset obesity. Several recent naturalistic studies of eating behavior of obese and nonobese individuals have not yet verified the existence of such assumed differences in eating style (Gaul, Craighead, & Mahoney, 1975; Mahoney, 1975b). An extensive review of this issue is beyond the scope of this paper; nevertheless, it does seem clear that several of our basic premises have been accepted in excess of what supportive data would justify. Furthermore, whether or not this or alternative hypotheses ultimately receive empirical support, it is unlikely that all obese individuals are obese as a function of a single, common, causal factor. As specified at the beginning of this section, it behooves the clinician to perform a functional analysis of the client's behavior, based on an objective assessment. Subjective determination of the source of dysfunction and treatment based on gross nosological classification (e.g., obesity) are contraindicated by the behavioral literature, in general, as well as by the literature on obesity.

Along with individualized interventions, we must also consider the application of far more comprehensive programs. Eating for many individuals is a primary source of reinforcement, entertainment, anxiety reduction, and a vehicle for interpersonal activity. Modification of eating behavior might require recruitment of environmental (e.g., spouse) support, training in alternative anxiety reduction techniques (e.g., systematic desensitization, assertion training), and the development of alternative sources of reinforcement. The commonplace occurrence of obesity in seemingly subclinical populations should not delude us into believing it is easier to modify than more "clinical"-appearing problems such as alcohol abuse. We can apply minimal interventions and achieve modest goals (e.g., moderate weight losses with minimal permanent behavior change). This accomplishment is greater than other treatment approaches can offer and is not to be disparaged. However, if the goal involves a major alteration of life style, a more comprehensive intervention will be required.

REFERENCES

Abrahms, J., & Allen, G. Comparative effectiveness of situational programming, financial pay-offs and group pressure in weight reduction. *Behavior Therapy*, 1974, 5, 391–400.

Abramson, E. E. A review of behavioral approaches to weight control. *Behaviour Research and Therapy*, 1973, 11, 547–556.

Baer, D. M., & Wolf, M. M. The entry into natural communities of reinforcement. In R. Ulrich, T. Stachnik, & J. Mabry (Eds.), *Control of human behavior*. Vol. 2. Glenview, Ill.: Scott, Foresman, 1970.

Balch, P., & Ross, A. W. A behaviorally oriented didactic-group treatment of obesity: An exploratory study. *Journal of Behavior Therapy and Experimental Psychiatry*, 1974, 5, 239–243.

Balch, P., & Ross, A. W. Predicting success in weight reduction as a function of locus of control: A unidimensional approach. *Journal of Consulting and Clinical Psychology*, 1975, 43, 119.

Bellack, A. S. Behavior therapy for weight reduction: An evaluative review. *Addictive Behaviors*, 1975, 1, 73–82.

Bellack, A. S. A comparison of self-monitoring and self-reinforcement in weight reduction. *Behavior Therapy*, 1976, 7, 68–75.

Bellack, A. S., Glanz, L., & Simon, R. Covert imagery and individual differences in self-reinforcement style in the treatment of obesity. *Journal of Consulting and Clinical Psychology*, 1976, in press.

Bellack, A. S., & Hersen, M. The use of self-report inventories in behavioral assessment. In J. D. Cone & R. P. Hawkins (Eds.), *Behavioral assessment: New directions in clinical psychology*. New York: Brunner/Mazel, 1977, in press.

Bellack, A. S., & Rozensky, R. H. The selection of dependent variables for weight reduction studies. *Journal of Behavior Therapy and Experimental Psychiatry*, 1975, 6, 83–84.

Bellack, A. S., Rozensky, R. H., & Schwartz, J. A comparison of two forms of self-monitoring in a behavioral weight reduction program. *Behavior Therapy*, 1974, 5, 523–530. (a)

Bellack, A. S., & Schwartz, J. Assessment for self-control programs. In M. Hersen & A. S. Bellack (Eds.), *Behavioral assessment: A practical handbook*. New York: Pergamon, 1976. Pp. 111–142.

Bellack, A. S., Schwartz, J., & Rozensky, R. The contribution of external control to self-control in a weight reduction program. *Journal of Behavior Therapy and Experimental Psychiatry*, 1974, 5, 245–250. (b)

Bellack, A. S., & Tillman, W. The effects of task and experimenter feedback on the self-reinforcement behavior of internals and externals. *Journal of Consulting and Clinical Psychology*, 1974, 42, 330–336.

Berecz, J. Aversion by fiat: The problem of "face validity" in behavior therapy. *Behavior Therapy*, 1973, 4, 110–116.

Bornstein, P. H., & Sipprelle, C. N. Group treatment of obesity by induced anxiety. *Behaviour Research and Therapy*, 1973, 11, 339–341. (a)

Bornstein, P. H., & Sipprelle, C. N. Induced anxiety in the treatment of obesity: A preliminary case report. *Behavior Therapy*, 1973, 4, 141–143. (b)

Cautela, J. R. The treatment of over-eating by covert conditioning. *Psychotherapy: Theory, Research and Practice*, 1972, 9, 211–216.

Elkins, R. L. Conditioned flavor aversions to familiar tap water in rats: An adjustment with implications for aversion therapy treatment of alcoholism and obesity. *Journal of Abnormal Psychology*, 1974, 83, 411–417.

Elliott, C. H., & Denney, D. R. Weight control through covert sensitization and false feedback. *Journal of Consulting and Clinical Psychology*, 1975, 43, 842–850.

Ferster, C. B., Nurnberger, J. I., & Levitt, E. B. The control of eating. *Journal of Mathetics*, 1962, 1, 87–109.

Foreyt, J. P. (Ed.) *Behavioral treatment of obesity*. Elmsford, N.Y.: Pergamon, 1976.

Foreyt, J. P., & Hagen, R. Covert sensitization: Conditioning or suggestion? *Journal of Abnormal Psychology*, 1973, 82, 17–23.

Foreyt, J. P., & Kennedy, W. A. Treatment of overweight by aversion therapy. *Behaviour Research and Therapy*, 1971, 9, 29–34.

Franzini, L. R., & Grimes, W. B. Contracting, Stuart's three-dimensional treatment, and a new criterion of change in behavior therapy of the obese. Paper read at the Association for Advancement of Behavior Therapy, San Francisco, December 1975.

Gaul, D. J., Craighead, W. E., & Mahoney, M. J. Relationship between eating rates and obesity. *Journal of Consulting and Clinical Psychology*, 1975, 43, 123–126.

Hagen, R. L. Group therapy vs bibliotherapy in weight reduction. *Behavior Therapy*, 1974, 5, 222–234.

Hall, S. M. Self-control and therapist control in the behavioral treatment of overweight women. *Behaviour Research and Therapy*, 1972, 10, 59–68.

Hall, S. M. Behavioral treatment of obesity: A two year follow-up. *Behaviour Research and Therapy*, 1973, 11, 647–648.

Hall, S. M., & Hall, R. G. Outcome and methodological considerations in the behavioral treatment of obesity. *Behavior Therapy*, 1974, 5, 352–364.

Hall, S. M., Hall, R. G., Borden, B. L., & Hanson, R. W. Follow-up strategies in the behavioral treatment of overweight. *Behaviour Reserach and Therapy*, 1975, 12, 167–172.

Hall, S. M., Hall, R. G., DeBoer, G., & O'Kulitch, P. Self-management, external management and self and external management combined compared with psychotherapy in the control of obesity. Submitted for publication, 1976.

Hall, S. M., Hall, R. G., Hanson, R. W., & Borden, B. L. Permanence of two self-managed treatments of overweight in university and community populations. *Journal of Consulting and Clinical Psychology*, 1974, 42, 781–786.

Hanson, R. W., Borden, B. L., Hall, S. M., & Hall, R. G. Use of programmed instruction in teaching self-management skills to overweight adults. *Behavior Therapy*, 1976, 7, 366–373.

Harmatz, M. G., & Lapuc, P. Behavior modification of overeating in a psychiatric population. *Journal of Consulting and Clinical Psychology*, 1968, 32, 583–587.

Harris, M. B. Self-directed program for weight control: A pilot study. *Journal of Abnormal Psychology*, 1969, 74, 2, 263–270.

Harris, M. B., & Bruner, C. G. A comparison of a self-control and a contract procedure for weight control. *Behaviour Research and Therapy*, 1971, 9, 347–354.

Harris, M. B., & Hallbauer, E. S. Self-directed weight control through eating and exercise. *Behaviour Research and Therapy*, 1973, 11, 523–529.

Hersen, M., & Barlow, D. H. *Single case experimental designs: Strategies for studying behavior change.* New York: Pergamon, 1976.

Homme, L. E. Control of coverants: The operants of the mind. *Psychological Record*, 1965, 15, 501–511.

Horan, J. J., Baker, S. B., Hoffman, A. M., & Shute, R. E. Weight loss through variations in the coverant control paradigm. *Journal of Consulting and Clinical Psychology*, 1975, 43, 68–72.

Horan, J. J., & Johnson, R. G. Coverant conditioning through a self-management application of the Premack Principle: Its effects on weight reduction. *Journal of Behavior Therapy and Experimental Psychiatry*, 1971, 2, 243–249.

Janda, L. H., & Rimm, D. C. Covert sensitization in the treatment of obesity. *Journal of Abnormal Psychology*, 1972, 80, 37–42.

Jeffrey, D. B. A comparison of the effects of external control and self-control on the modification and maintenance of weight. *Journal of Abnormal Psychology*, 1974, 83, 404–410. (a)

Jeffrey, D. B. Some methodological issues in research on obesity. *Psychological Reports*, 1974, 35, 623–626. (b)

Jeffrey, D. B., & Christensen, E. R. Behavior therapy vs "will power" in the management of obesity. *Journal of Psychology*, 1975, 90, 303–311.

Jeffrey, D. B., Christensen, E. R., & Katz, R. C. Behavior therapy weight reduction programs: Some preliminary findings on the need for follow-ups. *Psychotherapy: Theory, Research and Practice*, 1976, in press.

Jeffrey, D. B., Christensen, E. R., & Pappas, J. P. Developing a behavioral program and therapist manual for the treatment of obesity. Paper read at the American College Health Association, Atlanta, April, 1972.

Jordan, H. A., & Levitz, L. S. Behavior modification in a self-help group. *Journal of the American Dietetic Association*, 1973, **62**, 27–29.

Jordan, H. A., & Levitz, L. S. A behavioral approach to the problem of obessity. *Obesity/ Bariatric Medicine*, 1975, **4**, 58–69.

Kanfer, F. H. Self-management methods. In F. H. Kanfer & A. P. Goldstein (Eds.), *Helping people change*. New York: Pergamon, 1975. Pp. 309–355.

Kazdin, A. E. Self-monitoring and behavior change. In M. J. Mahoney & C. E. Thoresen (Eds.), *Self-control: Power to the person*. Monterey, Calif.: Brooks/Cole, 1974. Pp. 218–246.

Kennedy, W. A., & Foreyt, J. Control of eating behavior in an obese patient by avoidance conditioning. *Psychological Reports*, 1968, **22**, 571–576.

Leitenberg, H. (Ed.) *Handbook of behavior modification and behavior therapy*. Englewood Cliffs, N.J.: Prentice-Hall, 1976.

Levitz, L. S., & Stunkard, A. J. Therapeutic coalition for obesity: Behavior modification and patient self-help. *American Journal of Psychiatry*, 1974, **131**, 423–427.

Mahoney, M. Self-reward and self-monitoring techniques for weight control. *Behavior Therapy*, 1974, **5**, 48–57.

Mahoney, M. J. Fat fiction. *Behavior Therapy*, 1975, **6**, 416–418. (a)

Mahoney, M. J. The obese eating style: Bites, beliefs, and behavior. *Addictive Behaviors*, 1975, **1**, 47–54. (b)

Mahoney, M. J., & Mahoney, K. Treatment of obesity: A clinical exploration. In B. J. Williams, S. Martin, & J. P. Foreyt (Eds.), *Obesity: Behavioral approaches to dietary management*. New York: Brunner/Mazel, 1976, in press.

Mahoney, M., Moura, N., & Wade, T. The relative efficacy of self-reward, self-punishment and self-monitoring techniques. *Journal of Consulting and Clinical Psychology*, 1973, **40**, 404–407.

Mann, R. A. The behavior-therapeutic use of contingency contracting to control an adult behavior problem: Weight control. *Journal of Applied Behavior Analysis*, 1972, **5**, 99–109.

Manno, B., & Marston, A. R. Weight reduction as a function of negative covert reinforcement (sensitization) *vs* positive covert reinforcement. *Behaviour Research and Therapy*, 1972, **10**, 201–208.

Mayer, J. *Overweight: Causes, cost and control*. Englewood Cliffs, N.J.: Prentice-Hall, 1968.

Meyer, V., & Crisp, A. Aversion therapy in two cases of obesity. *Behaviour Research and Therapy*, 1964, **2**, 143–147.

Milich, R. S. A critical analysis of Schacter's externality theory of obesity. *Journal of Abnormal Psychology*, 1975, **84**, 586–588.

Mills, K. C., Sobell, M. B., & Schaeffer, H. Training social drinking as an alternative to abstinence for alcoholics. *Behavior Therapy*, 1971, **2**, 18–27.

Moore, C. H., & Crum, B. C. Weight reduction in a chronic schizophrenic by means of operant conditioning procedures: A case study. *Behaviour Research and Therapy*, 1969, **7**, 129–131.

Morganstern, K. P. Cigarette smoke as a noxious stimulus in self-managed aversion therapy for compulsive eating: Technique and case illustration. *Behavior Therapy*, 1974, **5**, 255–260.

Nisbett, R. E. Hunger, obesity, and the ventromedial hypothalamus. *Psychological Review*, 1972, **79**, 433–453.

Penick, S. B., Filion, R., Fox, S., & Stunkard, A. J. Behavior modification in the treatment of obesity. *Psychosomatic Medicine*, 1971, 33, 49–55.

Romanczyk, R. G., Self-monitoring in the treatment of obesity: Parameters of reactivity. *Behavior Therapy*, 1974, 5, 531–540.

Romanczyk, R. G., Tracey, D., Wilson, G. T., & Thorpe, G. Behavioral techniques in the treatment of obesity: A comparative analysis. *Behaviour Research and Therapy*, 1973, 11, 629–640.

Rozensky, R. H., & Bellack, A. S. Individual differences in self-reinforcement style and performance in self- and therapist-controlled weight reduction programs. *Behaviour Research and Therapy*, 1976, 14, 357–364.

Sachs, L., & Ingram, G. Covert sensitization as a treatment for weight control. *Psychological Reports*, 1972, 30, 971–974.

Schachter, S. Some extraordinary facts about obese humans and rats. *American Psychologist*, 1971, 26, 129–144.

Schwartz, J., & Bellack, A. S. Self-reinforcement and contracting in a behavioral weight reduction program. Submitted for publication, 1976.

Seligman, M. E. On the generality of the laws of learning. *Psychological Review*, 1970, 77, 406–418.

Simon, R., & Bellack, A. S. Individual differences in self-control behavior and long term stability in behavioral weight reduction programs. Submitted for publication, 1976.

Stollak, G. E. Weight loss obtained under different experimental procedures. *Psychotherapy: Theory, Research and Practice*, 1967, 4, 61–64.

Stuart, R. B. Behavioral control of overeating. *Behaviour Research and Therapy*, 1967, 5, 357–365.

Stuart, R. B. A three-dimensional program for the treatment of obesity. *Behaviour Research and Therapy*, 1971, 9, 177–186.

Stuart, R. B., & Davis, B. *Slim chance in a fat world.* Champaign, Ill.: Research Press, 1972.

Stunkard, A. Obesity and the denial of hunger. *Psychosomatic Medicine*, 1959, 21, 281–289.

Stunkard, A. New therapies for the eating disorders. *Archives of General Psychiatry*, 1972, 26, 391–398.

Stunkard, A. J., & McLaren-Hume, M. The results of treatment for obesity. *Archives of Internal Medicine*, 1959, 103, 79–85.

Suinn, R., & Richardson, F. Anxiety management training: A nonspecific behavior therapy program for anxiety control. *Behavior Therapy*, 1971, 2, 498–510.

Thoresen, C. E., & Mahoney, M. J. *Behavioral self-control.* New York: Holt, 1974.

Tyler, V., & Straughan, J. H. Coverant control and breath holding as techniques for the treatment of obesity. *Psychological Record*, 1970, 20, 473–478.

Williams, B. J., Martin, S., & Foreyt, J. P. (Eds.), *Obesity: Behavioral approaches to dietary management.* New York: Brunner/Mazel, 1976, in press.

Wollersheim, J. P. Effectiveness of group therapy based upon learning principles in the treatment of overweight women. *Journal of Abnormal Psychology*, 1970, 76, 462–474.

Yates, A. J. *Theory and practice in behavior therapy.* New York: Wiley, 1975.

EXTENSIONS OF REINFORCEMENT TECHNIQUES TO SOCIALLY AND ENVIRONMENTALLY RELEVANT BEHAVIORS

ALAN E. KAZDIN

Department of Psychology
The Pennsylvania State University
University Park, Pennsylvania

I. INTRODUCTION

Reinforcement techniques have been applied to a large number of treatment populations, target behaviors, and settings. Literature reviews have summarized and evaluated programs for psychiatric patients, the mentally retarded, individuals in classroom settings, delinquents, prisoners, drug addicts, alcoholics, and others (e.g., Braukmann & Fixsen, 1975; Davidson & Seidman, 1974; Gripp & Magaro, 1974; Kazdin, 1975c, 1977b; Kazdin & Craighead, 1973; Kennedy, 1976; Milan & McKee, 1974; Miller & Eisler, 1976; O'Leary & Drabman, 1971). Most reinforcement programs have been conducted in treatment, rehabilitation, and educational settings. Recently, however, reinforcement techniques have been extended to ameliorate social and ecological problems in the natural environment such as pollution, fuel consumption, racial integration, and others.

Extending operant conditioning principles to society is not new. Indeed, Skinner (1948) has advocated extrapolation of reinforcement techniques to design society. The focus of contemporary extensions of reinforcement to society are directed at select problems rather than to the design of society.[1] Increasingly, a wide range of community-relevant problems have been reported (Kazdin, 1975b). These extensions consist of implementing programs in community settings where social problems arise and, thus, constitute applications that attempt to change the natural environment.

The present article reviews the extensions of reinforcement techniques to socially and environmentally relevant problems. Applications of reinforcement are reviewed in the areas of pollution control and energy conservation, job performance and unemployment, community self-government, racial integration, and others. Potential obstacles and problems associated with the large-scale extension of reinforcement techniques to society are also discussed.

II. POLLUTION CONTROL
AND ENERGY CONSERVATION

Considerable attention has been focused on environmental conditions that affect the quality of human life. Various factors have made this attention salient including advances in technology, increases in the population, and a continued drain on natural resources. The concerns pertaining to human life have been reflected in such areas as pollution control and the utilization of limited environmental

---

[1] In fact, communes and experimental living projects have developed on a small scale to construct small communities based upon some of the recommendations in Skinner's *Walden Two*. Two notable practices are the Twin Oaks Community in Virginia (Kinkade, 1972) and the Experimental Living Project for college students in Kansas (Miller, 1976).

resources. Recently, operant techniques have begun to be applied to aspects of these environmental concerns. Four areas that have received attention are littering, recycling of waste material, conserving energy, and using mass transit.

A. Littering

Littering in public places is a matter of great concern not only for the unsightly pollution it creates but also for the monetary expense to remove litter. In the United States, litter control costs millions of dollars just to clean major highways (Keep America Beautiful, 1968). Although public appeals, general instructions to dispose of litter, and national campaigns are commonly employed, research suggests that these often do not alter littering (Baltes, 1973; Burgess, Clark, & Hendee, 1971; Ingram & Geller, 1975; Kohlenberg & Phillips, 1973).

Some studies have shown that prompts in the form of written messages or instructions can decrease littering (Geller, 1973, 1975). For example, Geller (1973) prompted the use of trash cans with written messages in separate studies in six different settings including a college classroom, the lobby of a university building, a college snack bar, a grocery store, and two movie theaters. The paradigm used to study littering in the university settings was to provide cups of lemonade free or for a small price. The messages written on the cups were related to littering. Generally, antilittering prompts were more effective than no prompts. Also, prompts which specified the location of trash containers where the cups could be disposed of decreased littering beyond the general prompt. Other studies in natural settings have shown that antilitter messages decrease littering and that messages which specify the methods of disposal are particularly effective (Geller, Witmer, & Orebaugh, 1976).

Incentives have been used frequently in diverse settings to control littering. For example, Clark, Burgess, and Hendee (1972) controlled litter in a national campground (over 100 acres). Litter (bags, beverage cans, bottles) was planted in the campground to provide a consistent level for the weekends of baseline and the program. During the program, seven families were asked whether the children would help with the litter accumulation. The children were told they could earn various items (e.g., shoulder patch, comic book, ranger badge, gum, and so on) for picking up litter and were given a large plastic bag. They were not told how much had to be collected to earn the reward. The amount of litter was markedly reduced during the incentive program. The children collected between 150 and 200 pounds of litter. The rewards given to them cost approximately $3.00. To accomplish the "clean-up" using camp personnel would have cost approximately $50 to $60.

Chapman and Risley (1974) decreased litter in an urban housing project area with over 390 low income families living in a 15 square block area. Litter was collected in such areas as residential yards, public yard areas, streets, and sidewalks. Three different experimental conditions were evaluated over the 5-month period of investigation, including making a verbal appeal (asking children to help clean up the litter and giving them a bag for litter deposit), providing a small monetary incentive for collecting a certain amount of litter (10¢ for filling up a litter bag), and providing the incentive for making yards clean rather than for merely turning in a volume of trash. The incentive procedures decreased the amount of litter. Payment for clean yards rather than for volume of collected litter tended to result in less litter in the yards of the housing project. The results clearly demonstrate the utility of reinforcement in a community setting in maintaining low levels of litter.

Other investigations have shown the effects of incentive systems in reducing littering in movie theaters (Burgess *et al.*, 1971), forest grounds (Powers, Osborne, & Anderson, 1973), schools (Baltes, 1973), football stadiums (Baltes & Hayward, 1974), and zoos (Kohlenberg & Phillips, 1973). In most of the littering studies, individuals receive incentives for collecting trash. A potential problem is that reinforcement is dependent upon the amount of trash collected rather than the amount of litter picked up. Possibly, individuals artificially produce trash (e.g., by tearing paper, or dumping the contents of trash cans into litter bags) rather than picking up litter. Another problem is that incentives for filling litter bags may lead individuals to pick up only the bulkier trash and bypass smaller pieces.

Hayes, Johnson, and Cone (1975) devised a procedure to ensure that the trash collected was littered trash and that all sizes of litter would be picked up. These investigators planted some litter onto the grounds of a youth correctional facility where the project was conducted. The litter that they planted was marked in ways only identifiable to the investigators (e.g., specific brands of matchbooks or candy wrappers creased in a special way; cigarette butts or paper items torn or marked with a dot of ink). The youths received an incentive (small monetary reward or a special privilege in the setting) for filling bags of litter. The incentive was delivered only if a marked item was included in the bag of collected litter. Thus, for an individual to ensure that the reinforcer was delivered, all trash had to be picked up in a given area. The program effectively increased picking up litter. The marked-item technique appears to provide a way of ensuring that the litter collected is from the area where litter is a problem.

In most of the above programs, someone is required to carefully monitor behavior and to administer the reinforcing consequences. The supervision required to administer the program raises the question of feasibility of conducting antilitter programs on a large scale. Powers et al. (1973) devised a program that suggests a way to resolve the problem of surveillance and supervision. These investigators placed litter cans and bags on the grounds of a camp site with no one to monitor behavior and administer consequences. Individuals in the setting who participated were able to label their bags filled with litter with their name, address, and similar information. Also, individuals indicated the reward they wanted for collecting litter which included either 25¢ or a chance to win $20 in a lottery. No one was present to administer the consequences because individuals received a letter with their money. Thus, it appears feasible to devise a system that does not require someone to administer immediate consequences.

B. Recycling "Waste" Material

A major concern related to littering is the accumulation of waste products in the environment. The accumulation of waste is not only unsightly but also poses problems of disposal and storage. Some waste material might be recycled. If waste products (e.g., cans, paper, returnable bottles) were recycled, they would become a resource rather than an accumulated waste. The use of biodegradable products such as certain detergents and food containers represent innovations to ameliorate the problem of accumulated waste. Reinforcement techniques have altered consumer purchase of materials that can be recycled, such as returnable rather than nonreturnable containers (Geller, Farris, & Post, 1973; Geller, Wylie, & Farris, 1971) and have increased collection of waste paper for recycling (Geller, Chaffee, & Ingram, 1975; Ingram & Geller, 1975).

Geller et al. (1973) increased the percentage of grocery store customers who bought returnable containers (defined as individuals who purchased at least 50% of their soft drinks in returnable bottles). During one intervention condition, customers were given a handbill urging them to purchase returnable bottles to save money (because there was a refund) and taxes (because less money would be spent collecting littered bottles) and to fight pollution (because nonreturnable bottles are permanent pollutants). On some occasions, the handbill stated that the purchase of the customer would be recorded on a chart and reported in a local newspaper and to the American Psychological Association. The "pollution chart," placed at the front of the store, indicated whether the customer had bought 50% of his drinks in returnable bottles. Providing the handbill increased purchase of returnable bottles. Variations of the basic procedure were not differentially effective.

Geller *et al.* (1975) increased the recycling of paper on a university campus. Several dormitories had collected waste paper from the students to be sold at a paper mill at $15 per ton and eventually recycled. Over a 6-week period, each of six dormitories received three different phases in a Latin Square design. During baseline, students were merely thanked for bringing in waste paper. One intervention consisted of a contest between a men's and women's dormitory. "Recycling contest" rules specified that the dorm with more paper would receive a $15 bonus. Another intervention consisted of a raffle in which each student who brought paper to the collection room received a ticket. Tickets drawn weekly earned prizes, including monetary certificates redeemable at clothing or grocery stores or for a piece of furniture, sleeping bag, and other items ranging in value from $4 to $30. Contest and raffle contingencies increased the amount of paper collected. The raffle contingency was superior to the contest contingency in the total amount of paper received and in the number of individuals who brought paper. Subsequent research has confirmed the efficacy of a raffle contingency in controlling paper collection in a university setting (Ingram, Chaffee, Rorrer, & Wellington, 1975; Ingram & Geller, 1975; Witmer & Geller, 1976). Overall, the research suggests that contests, raffles, and lotteries might be utilized on a larger scale to increase the amount of paper and, indeed, other materials that are recycled.

Extrinsic incentives are not always necessary to increase recycling. Reid, Luyben, Rawers, and Bailey (1976) merely informed residents of three apartment complexes of the location of recycling containers to be used to collect newspapers. Near the containers, which were placed in the laundry rooms of the apartment complexes, were instructions explaining the use of containers. Also, residents were briefly interviewed and prompted about the use of the containers prior to beginning the program. Increases in the amount of newspapers collected were marked relative to baseline levels over a several-week treatment period. These results suggest that behavior which may require relatively little effort or cost to the subjects can be altered by prompts and by providing a convenient means of performing the response. Additional research has replicated the effects of providing prompts and convenient collection containers in recycling newspaper in mobile home parks (Luyben & Bailey, 1975). However, providing incentives for depositing newspapers leads to greater collection of materials than does providing prompts alone.

C. Conserving Energy

Concern has increased over the use of fuel and energy including electricity, natural gas, and oil, all limited resources. Reinforcement techniques have been applied in several studies to control energy consumption in the home. In a project with one family, Wodarski (1975) reduced electrical energy consumption by providing points to the husband and wife for decreasing the number of minutes that specific major appliances were used (e.g., stereo, television, oven, heater). Energy saving behaviors such as turning off the dishwasher before the "dry" cycle began, using the charcoal grill instead of the oven, opening the oven door after use to circulate the heat in the room, and others also were reinforced with points. The points could be exchanged for food, money in the bank, entertainment, camping and hiking opportunities, and other events. In an ABAB design, contingent points were shown to reduce the number of minutes that electrical appliances were used. However, a one-week follow-up after the program was withdrawn indicated that energy consumption returned to baseline levels.

Similarly, Palmer, Lloyd, and Lloyd (1976) reduced the consumption of electricity of four families using variations of feedback or prompting techniques. Feedback consisted of providing daily information to each family of their meter readings indicating electricity consumption and a comparison of current electricity consumption with baseline levels. A second variation of feedback translated daily electricity consumption into monetary cost and provided the projected monthly bill based on that rate of consumption. Prompting consisted of telling individuals each day to conserve energy or providing a personal letter from the government encouraging conservation. The feedback and prompting conditions were equally effective in reducing consumption of electrical energy relative to baseline. A one-year follow-up indicated that electrical consumption tended to return to baseline levels for two of the three families still available.

Kohlenberg, Phillips, and Proctor (1976) reduced electricity consumption during peak periods of energy use with three families. Instructions to the families about the problems on consumption during peak periods and a request to avoid "peaking" did not reduce consumption during these periods. Feedback, consisting of a light placed in the house which came on during excessive energy consumption, moderately reduced consumption during peak periods. Relatively large reductions in consumption during peak periods were made when monetary incentives for a reduction in consumption was added to the feedback.

Similarly, Hayes and Cone (1976b) decreased use of electricity in four units of a housing complex for married university students. Feedback was effective but not as effective as monetary incentives for reduction of energy consumption. The average reduction for the incentive condition was 29% of baseline rate. Interestingly, in both the Kohlenberg *et al.* (1976) and Hayes and Cone (1976b) studies, merely providing information about the consumption of electricity and the energy utilized by various appliances and suggestions for decreasing consumption tended to be ineffective in altering behavior.

Winett and Nietzel (1975) compared the effects of information on how to reduce energy consumption with information, feedback, and monetary incentives for reduction in a study including 31 homes. Households in the feedback-incentive condition received information about weekly energy consumption and fixed payments depending upon the percentage reduction in energy (gas or electricity) relative to baseline. Also, special bonuses were given for the greatest reductions made in a weekly period. After a 4-week period, the feedback-incentive condition led to greater reduction in electricity and consumption than the information-only condition. Groups did not differ in gas consumption, which seemed to be closely related to weekly temperature. Group differences in electricity consumption were maintained at a 2-week follow-up but not at an 8-week follow-up assessment.

On a much larger scale, Seaver and Patterson (1976) studied 180 homes randomly selected from rural communities in a 4-month project designed to reduce fuel oil consumption. Homes were assigned randomly to one of three conditions: feedback, feedback plus commendation, and no treatment. In the feedback condition, households received slips at the time of fuel delivery about the amount of fuel consumed relative to the same period for the previous year and the dollars saved (or lost) in light of this reduced (or increased) consumption. In the feedback plus commendation condition, households received the above feedback information and, if there was a reduction of fuel consumption, a decal saying, "We are saving oil." The decal could not be exchanged for other events but served as a source of social recognition for fuel savings. In the no-treatment group, no intervention was implemented. Feedback-plus-commendation homes consumed significantly less fuel in the delivery period after the intervention than did the other two groups. The feedback and control groups were not different from each other.

D. Using Mass Transportation

A major source of energy consumption is the use of automobiles. Many people drive to work when mass transportation is available. Recently, the benefits of mass transportation have been stressed to reduce fuel consumption and pollutants in the air.

Token reinforcement has been extended on a large university campus to promote use of mass transit (Everett, Hayward, & Meyers, 1974). After baseline observations of the number of bus riders per day, a token system was implemented on one bus. A newspaper advertisement announced that the campus bus marked with a red star would provide tokens to each passenger. Tokens, consisting of wallet-sized cards that listed the back-up reinforcers, were presented with an exchange sheet that listed the cost of the back-up events. The tokens (each worth from 5 to 10¢) could be exchanged for a free bus ride, ice cream, beer, pizza, coffee, cigarettes, movies, flowers, records, or other items made available at local stores in the community. Ridership on the bus increased when the contingency was in effect and returned to baseline levels when the contingency was withdrawn. Ridership did not increase on a control bus that never received the token system.

This initial investigation is preliminary because the influence of the reinforcement system was particularly pronounced with those who walked rather than with those who used cars. Yet, the main goal of encouraging the use of mass transit is to increase ridership of those who ordinarily use cars. The results are extremely encouraging and suggest the utility of wider application.

E. Other Environmentally Relevant Responses

Other investigations have focused upon select environmentally relevant responses in university settings. For example, Hayes and Cone (1976a) altered the frequency with which students walked on the lawns rather than on the rock paths of a university campus. Different interventions were used to promote use of the paths, such as making it difficult to gain access to the lawn by obstructing with park benches the areas where students normally walked and by constructing a fence, and also by identifying the grassy area with a sign as a "mini park" and requesting people to avoid walking on the grass. Benches were the most effective means to reduce lawn walking. Interestingly, the signs which labeled the area as a park and requested people to avoid the grass also markedly reduced lawn walking.

With a different focus, Meyers, Artz, and Craighead (1976) decreased noise on four floors of university residence halls for female undergraduates. The frequency of discrete noises above a certain level (either 82 or 84 dB across different halls) served as the dependent measure. Although the procedures varied slightly across residences, generally treatment consisted of instructions to reduce noise, modeling, feedback, and reinforcement. Modeling consisted of having residents view students communicating quietly. Feedback included sounding a bell when noise exceeded the predetermined decibel level and providing charts informing residents of noise transgressions and points that were earned for low rates of trangressions. The points (exchangeable for money or credit toward a course grade) were delivered for decreasing the frequency of trangressions over time. The treatment package markedly decreased noise levels across residence halls although noise immediately returned to baseline or near-baseline rates when treatment was withdrawn.

III. JOB PERFORMANCE AND PROCUREMENT

A. On-the-Job Performance

Job performance is an area where operant techniques are already in wide use. Employees receive money for job performance and additional incentives such as promotions and recognition for superior performance and receive aversive consequences such as demotion or loss of job for poor performance. Systematic applications of operant techniques have enhanced job performance in industry.

Well-known applications of reinforcement in industry were conducted at Emery Air Freight Corporation (*Business Week,* 1971). In diverse areas of company operation, feedback, praise, and recognition were used to reinforce job performance. For example, in one application, the cost of delivering air freight was reduced by shipping several small packages in a single shipment rather than separately. Employees who worked on the loading dock received feedback using a checklist and praise for shipping in containers and thus saving costs. Use of the containers increased to 95% and remained at a high level for almost two years. Savings to the company as a result of the increased use of containers was estimated to be $650,000 per year.

Additional applications of operant principles have extended to selected areas of job performance. For example, token reinforcement was used to increase punctuality of workers in an industrial setting in Mexico (Hermann, deMontes, Dominguez, Montes, & Hopkins, 1973). Individuals who were frequently tardy for work (one or more minutes late) received a slip of paper daily for punctuality. The slips could be exchanged for maximum of $.80 at the end of each week. Tardiness decreased when tokens were provided for punctuality as demonstrated in an ABAB design. A control group of workers who did not receive tokens failed to decrease in tardiness.

Pedalino and Gamboa (1974) reduced absenteeism in a manufacturing–distribution center consisting of several plants. One plant was picked for behavioral intervention while four other plants served as controls (no treatment). The intervention consisted of a lottery in which an employee who came to work and was on time received an opportunity to choose a card from a deck of playing cards. At the end of each week, the individual would have five cards which were used as a poker hand. Several individuals who had the highest poker hands received $20 each week. The lottery reduced absenteeism, even when the lottery was eventually conducted every other week rather than every week. The effect of the lottery was convincingly demonstrated in an ABA design and in between-group comparisons with nontreated groups. However, a 22-week follow-up indicated that termination of the lottery was associated with a return of absenteeism to baseline rates.

Work performance has been the focus of various studies. For example, Pierce and Risley (1974) improved job performance of adolescent workers at a community recreation center. The workers enforced rules of the center, recorded the number of individuals engaging in activities, prepared the game rooms, and several other tasks. Merely providing explicit job descriptions and instructions to perform the tasks or providing wages independently of task completion led to relatively low work performance. In contrast, when pay was delivered for the number of tasks completed, performance increased markedly.

Another aspect of job performance that has been studied is the shortage of cash in the register of a small business (Marholin & Gray, 1976). In this study, the register receipts in a family-style restaurant were monitored. Cash shortages were defined as less cash in the register at the end of the day than the amount of cash received (as automatically recorded on an internal record of the register). After baseline, a response cost contingency was introduced in which any cash shortage equal to or greater than 1% of the day's total cash receipts was deducted from the cashiers' salaries for that day. The total cash shortage was simply divided by the number of people who worked at the register that day and the fine was paid. In an ABAB design, the response cost contingency markedly reduced cash shortfalls.

The investigations of reinforcement in industry suggest that inadequate job performance might easily be altered by providing contingent consequences. The alternative for inadequate performance usually is to terminate employment. Termination solves the problem of inadequate performance for the employer but not for the employee. Developing desirable performance increases the likelihood that the employee will retain his/her job and develop skills that otherwise might not be learned, thus decreasing employee turnover.

B. Obtaining Employment

Developing adequate work performance presupposes that the individual has a job or can obtain one once adequately trained. However, procuring a job is difficult in its own right. A major portion of jobs are obtained through informal contacts rather than from advertised positions (Jones & Azrin, 1973, Exp. 1). Employees often provide advance information about job openings to friends, acquaintances, and relatives before the information is generally available. Thus, a major task of job procurement is discovering existing job opportunities.

Jones and Azrin (1973, Exp. 2) evaluated the effect of token (monetary) reinforcement in obtaining information about jobs that actually resulted in employment. During baseline, an ad was placed in the newspaper under the auspices of the state employment agency, noting several occupational categories for which persons registered at the agency were qualified (e.g., stenographer, book-keeper, sales clerk, mechanic, janitor) and asked readers to call if they knew of positions. After one week, the advertisement was changed to indicate that anyone who reported a job opening that led to employment would receive $100. After one week, the original advertisement was reinstated. Over the 2 weeks of the baseline advertisement, only two calls were received and only one of these led to employment. During the one incentive week, 14 calls were received which resulted in eight instances of employment. Thus, the incentive program was markedly successful in procuring jobs.

Although the incentive condition may seem extravagant, the relative costs were less for the incentive than the no-incentive condition. In the incentive condition, the average cost per successful placement was $130 (which included the cost of the advertisement and the reward to persons who called in the jobs). In the no-incentive condition, the cost per successful placement was $470 (which included only the cost of the advertisement). These results strongly support the utility of monetary incentives for revealing job opportunities.

Azrin, Flores, and Kaplan (1975) expanded the job procurement program by developing a job-finding club. Unemployed persons who joined the club attended meetings in which methods of obtaining employment were reviewed, job leads were shared, and opportunities for job interview role playing were offered. Also, club members were paired so that each member would have a "buddy" to provide support and encouragement, were trained to systematically search for jobs from a variety of sources and to communicate with former employers, relatives, and friends about possible job opportunities, received instructions and training in dress and grooming and in developing a resumé, were encouraged to expand their job interests, and in general worked to enhance their desirability as an employee. In a careful experimental evaluation, job seekers who participated in the club found work within a shorter period and received higher wages than individuals who did not participate in the club. Indeed, after 3 months of participation in the club, 92% of the clients had obtained employment, compared to 60% of those who had not participated in the club.

Overall, the above studies suggest the utility of reinforcement techniques with the spectrum of employment-related issues. Obtaining job leads, procuring jobs, ensuring punctuality, attendance, and high levels of job performance have all been reliably altered with reinforcement techniques. Because employment systems are naturally enmeshed with monetary reinforcement, this area would seem to be an obvious candidate for further extensions of operant techniques.

IV. COMMUNITY SELF-GOVERNMENT

A major issue in government is to increase the involvement of people in decisions that affect their welfare. People can have some impact on decisions made about their own communities. Preliminary attempts have increased the involvement of lower socioeconomic individuals in community issues. For example, Miller and Miller (1970) increased the attendance of welfare recipients to a self-help group that met monthly to discuss such problems as receipt of welfare checks, medical allotments, and community problems such as urban renewal, school board policy, police problems, and city government. In an initial phase, the welfare counselor mailed notices to self-help group members indicating when the next meeting was scheduled. During the reinforcement phase, group members were informed that they could select various reinforcers if they attended the meeting. Reinforcers included Christmas toys for each child in a family and a wide range of rewards, including stoves, refrigerators, furniture, clothing, rugs, assistance in negotiating grievances, locating a suitable house, resolving court or police problems, finding jobs, and others. In an ABAB design, reinforcement for attendance increased the number of individuals who attended meetings. Moreover, while the contingency was in effect, new members were attracted to the self-help group.

Briscoe, Hoffman, and Bailey (1975) developed problem-solving skills in lower socioeconomic adolescents and adults who participated in a self-help project. The participants attended weekly board meetings designed to identify and solve community problems such as arranging to have repairs made to the community center, organizing social and educational events, discovering and distributing social welfare resources to the community, and providing medical care. Training developed problem-solving skills at the meetings which included identifying and isolating problems under discussion, stating and evaluating alternative solutions, selecting solutions, and making decisions. Verbal responses reflecting each of these problem-solving skills were developed in an individualized training program that utilized prompts, social reinforcement, modeling, and role playing. Training, evaluated in a multiple-baseline design, indicated that three different problem-solving skills (stating a problem, selecting solutions, and deciding on the action to be taken) were altered only when training was introduced. Up to 1-month follow-up, problem-solving behaviors were maintained even though training had ceased.

The above investigations suggest that reinforcement techniques can increase self-help skills in the community. Increased participation in activities and developing problem-solving skills provide entry responses to effective self-government. The effects of these and similar interventions on community change need to be explored further.

V. RACIAL INTEGRATION

Racial integration is a complex issue that has received little direct intervention by behavior modification techniques. The precise targets for increasing integration encompass diverse behaviors across a range of settings and target groups. Procedures to facilitate racial integration usually have been directed at changing attitudes, although changes in racial attitudes do not necessarily result in corresponding behavior change (Mann, 1959).

Some researchers have focused upon changing how individuals describe and evaluate others against whom they show racial bias. For example, Best, Smith, Graves, and Williams (1975, Exp. 1) used reinforcement techniques to alter the tendency of children to evaluate light-skinned (Euro-American) persons positively and dark-skinned (Afro-American) persons negatively. This racial bias has been demonstrated in a large number of studies with both Euro- and Afro-American children (cf. Williams & Morland, 1976, for review). Preschool children were trained with a teaching machine in which selection of light- or dark-skinned figures was differentially reinforced in the context of stories in which positive and negative descriptions were presented. Responses associated Afro-American characters with positive adjectives and Euro-American characters with negative adjectives were reinforced either with advance of the machine to the next story or by tokens (pennies exchangeable for candy). Racial bias was altered by the reinforcement procedures. The changes in bias were maintained up to 1 week and, to a lesser extent, up to 1 year after training. These results, and similar findings from other studies, show that operant techniques can alter children's tendencies to associate negative adjectives with Afro-American children (Edwards & Williams, 1970; McMurtry & Williams, 1972). Although these studies clearly demonstrate the change of attitudinal and laboratory-based responses involving racial bias, they do not indicate whether interracial social behaviors would vary. Additional research is necessary to show more clearly that behaviors in nonlaboratory settings can be altered.

An initial attempt to alter overt interracial social behavior was reported by Hauserman, Walen, and Behling (1973), who developed a program to socially integrate five black children in a predominantly white first-grade classroom. The students in class isolated themselves along racial lines for all activities of a social nature. To increase interracial interaction, all students in the class received tokens and praise for sitting with "new friends" during lunch. Sitting with new friends included interracial combinations of students although this was not specified to the students. Tokens were redeemable after lunch for a snack. Interracial interactions increased during the token and social reinforcement phase. Interestingly, interaction transferred to a free-play period immediately after lunch even though reinforcers were never provided for interracial socialization during this period. In the final phase of the ABA design, baseline conditions were reinstated and interracial interactions decreased. Although the effects were not maintained, this study suggests the amenability of interracial interaction to change as a function of consequences. Positive reinforcement of interracial interaction might provide another alternative to public appeals and forced integration.

VI. MILITARY TRAINING

An interesting application of operant principles has been in training individuals to function in the military. Of course, the military normally incoporates operant principles by providing promotion for desirable performance. However, structure of military training, particularly basic training, has been criticized because of its heavy reliance upon aversive control in the form of arbitrary punishments and unnecessary penalties (Datel & Legters, 1970). To ameliorate the aversive properties of military training, positive reinforcement has been emphasized.

In one program, a token economy was used during basic training (Datel & Legters, 1970). In the program, referred to as the merit system, merits were earned by the recruits for behaviors such as performance at daily inspections, training formations, proficiency in physical combat, written test performance covering areas of basic training, and work. The merits consisted of punches on a card that each recruit carried with him. The card specified the behaviors that needed to be performed, the back-up reinforcers, and the prices of these reinforcers. The back-up events consisted of privileges such as attending a movie or taking an overnight pass. At the end of 8 weeks and the completion of training, the total number of merits earned determined whether the individual was considered for promotion. Although several categories of behavior resulted in merits, usually provided by the drill sergeant, bonus merits could also be administered for exceptional performance of one's duties, as designated by the commanding officer.

Despite the desirability of emphasizing positive reinforcement, many of the behaviors that earned merits were not clearly specified, so that the discretion of the reinforcing agent could play a major role in one's earnings. For example, at the drill sergeant's daily evaluation, recruits received points based upon their attitudes, discipline, marching, attention in class, alertness, knowledge, interest, and deportment. Specific target responses may not have been clearly delineated and perhaps individuals received points for not engaging in aversive behaviors rather than in performing exceptionally well in these areas. In any case, the system represents a direct extension of the token economy to military training, although no evidence was provided regarding the program's success.

The military has used token reinforcement frequently in the rehabilitation of military personnel in a large number of psychiatric facilities (Chase, 1970). One of the more well-known programs treated soldiers who engaged in a variety of delinquent behaviors (Boren & Colman, 1970; Stayer & Jones, 1969). This program reported favorable follow-up data in returning problem soldiers to completion of their tour of duty.

VII. EVALUATION OF SOCIAL EXTENSIONS OF REINFORCEMENT TECHNIQUES

Extension of reinforcement techniques to social and environmental problems represents a promising area of research, in part because of the contemporary importance of the behaviors focused upon. In addition, characteristics of community, as opposed to treatment, settings offer advantages for implementing reinforcement programs. Initially, the natural environment already has a large-scale incentive system, namely, monetary reinforcement, which can be relied upon for behavior modification programs. Thus, a potent reinforcer is already available in the setting and need not be artificially introduced into the environment. Second, and related to the above, is that reinforcement is normally a part of social living so that the reinforcement system need not be withdrawn after behavior change has been achieved, as is usually the case with incentive systems conducted in treatment settings.

A third advantage of applying reinforcement techniques to social problems is that the interventions often can be evaluated in concrete terms. For many extensions to social behaviors, the main criterion is that a significant economic gain be realized. For example, reducing littering and energy consumption, recycling waste products, increasing use of mass transit, and increasing employment and job retention all have direct economic implications and can be evaluated by a cost–benefit analysis. There are other implications for evaluating social extensions of reinforcement techniques. For example, large-scale reductions of pollution are likely to have implications for physical health, particularly for diseases such as cancer (Cairns, 1975). Similarly, increasing employment may have implications for crime, psychiatric disorders, and alcohol consumption (cf. Jones & Azrin, 1973). Of course, these latter changes are likely to result only from the long-term effects of social interventions rather than from the more immediate economic gains.

Although preliminary research suggests that diverse socially relevant responses can be altered, it is important to consider the limitations of this research and the possible obstacles that may interfere with large-scale applications. The present discussion considers the limited applications of current research, the problems related to maintaining behaviors, and the unresponsiveness of some individuals to the contingencies. Finally, ethical implications of social extensions of reinforcement techniques are briefly discussed.

A. Limited Applications

The majority of investigations extending reinforcement techniques to social problems have had a relatively limited focus. Socially relevant behavior has been altered for only brief periods, in restricted locations, or for a relatively short time. For example, in some of the reports, energy conservation has been controlled in only one or a few families (e.g., Hayes & Cone, 1976b; Palmer *et al.*, 1976; Wodarski, 1975), job performance has been enhanced among a small number of workers (e.g., Hermann *et al.*, 1973; Pierce & Risley, 1974), use of mass transit has been increased on a single bus (Everett *et al.*, 1974), and interracial interaction has been increased for brief (30 minute) classroom periods (Hauserman *et al.*, 1973). Many of the interventions are not in effect for extended periods and may last only a few days (e.g., Clark *et al.*, 1972; Everett *et al.*, 1974; Hauserman *et al.*, 1973; Hayes & Cones, 1976b; Pierce & Risley, 1974), weeks (e.g., Geller *et al.*, 1973, 1975), or occasionally a few months (e.g., Palmer *et al.*, 1976; Seaver & Patterson, 1976).

There are exceptions to these studies that show relatively broad extensions of reinforcement techniques. For example, Pedalino and Gamboa (1974) increased attendance of industrial workers in an entire manufacturing plant. Seaver and Patterson (1976) focused on over 130 homes (after attrition) in their fuel conservation study. Chapman and Risley (1974) reduced littering in a high-density urban area of 15 square blocks. These latter studies suggest that social extensions of reinforcement can be implemented on a relatively broad scale.

A number of extensions of reinforcement practices to environmentally relevant behaviors have been implemented on university campuses (e.g., Everett *et al.*, 1974; Hayes & Cone, 1976a). For example, some studies have focused on students living in university housing facilities where the control over the population and reinforcing consequences as well as assessment of the target response may be somewhat easier than applications in other community settings (e.g., Hayes & Cone, 1976b; Meyers *et al.*, 1976). Possibly, the kind of control exerted over student behavior may not be readily available when programs are extended to the community at large. Fortunately, several studies have demonstrated the efficacy of diverse interventions in a wide range of community settings.

Current research has only begun to extend reinforcement to social problems. Thus, investigations have served primarily as demonstrational projects, suggesting that important behaviors in the natural environment are amenable to change through operant techniques. Additional demonstrations are needed to determine whether the techniques can be extended on a large scale for protracted periods. Indeed, programs may need to be implemented on a semipermanent basis to sustain gains made in overcoming unemployment, decreasing energy consumption, and other areas where the problems seem to be less than short term.

B. Maintenance of Behavior

Although reinforcement techniques in treatment settings have effectively altered a wide range of behaviors, the techniques required to maintain gains after the program has been terminated remain to be developed. Some techniques have been effective in maintaining behaviors but these have been inadequately tested (Kazdin, 1975a). If behaviors are difficult to maintain on a small scale in programs conducted in relatively well-controlled settings such as a psychiatric ward or classroom, they might be even less easily maintained in social extensions of reinforcement where there is less control over the environment. Research on social extensions of reinforcement has already shown that once the contingencies are withdrawn, behavior reverts to or approaches baseline rates (e.g., Best et al., 1975; Everett et al., 1974; Hayes & Cone, 1976b; Jones & Azrin, 1973, Exp. 2; Kohlenberg et al., 1976; Pedalino & Gamboa, 1974; Winett & Nietzel, 1975; Wodarski, 1975), although there are exceptions (e.g., Azrin et al., 1975). Thus, maintaining gains in community settings may be as problematic as it has been in more well-controlled situations.

Although response maintenance is an unresolved problem for reinforcement techniques in general, the problems eventually may prove to be less serious in social extensions of reinforcement than in the usual well-controlled situation. In most applications, behaviors are not maintained because the client leaves the treatment setting (e.g., psychiatric ward) and the program cannot be implemented or extended to the new setting (e.g., the community). Thus, behaviors developed in one setting change in response to the new contingencies. Reinforcement programs implemented in the community to solve social problems may not have to be withdrawn. For example, to control fuel consumption, monetary incentives may be offered to sustain conservation efforts. The incentive need not be withdrawn as in the usual program but can be permanently incorporated into the normal process of billing from the utilities company. Similarly, use of mass transit can be encouraged by automatically providing incentives (e.g., partial return of bus fares) for riding a bus. Essentially, the program to alter socially relevant behaviors can be built into the system and not be transitory. Similarly, transfer of training of behavior from one treatment setting to new settings is not likely to be a problem in the social extensions of reinforcement techniques as it is in institutional and treatment settings. In social extensions of reinforcement, the natural environment *is* the treatment setting and behavior is altered in the situation in which it is desired.

Although programs to alter socially relevant behaviors might be implemented on a long-term basis, no evidence is available to suggest that the techniques would be effective over an extended period. Indeed, the effect of social extensions of reinforcement may be due to the fact that they are novel and provide reinforcers that have not otherwise been available. In the long run, the efficacy of the reinforcer may decline along with the gains in the target behavior.

C. Unresponsiveness to the Contingencies

In many reinforcement programs, selected individuals fail to respond to the contingencies. This has been found with diverse populations, including psychiatric patients, the mentally retarded, children and adolescents in classroom settings, delinquents, and others (cf. Kazdin, 1973). The consistency of the finding suggests that extrapolations of reinforcement techniques on a larger social scale will encounter large numbers of individuals who do not respond to the contingencies. Indeed, in some studies reviewed on social extensions of reinforcement, individuals occasionally do not respond to the incentive system. For example, Seaver and Patterson (1976) found that 25% (*n*=14) of the households did not respond to the feedback and commendation procedure designed to reduce home fuel consumption. Possibly, the failure of a large number of individuals to respond could seriously limit the efficacy of any attempt at large-scale extensions of reinforcement techniques.

Actually, the failure of some individuals to respond may not be as crucial in the social extension of reinforcement as in treatment, rehabilitation, and educational applications. In these latter applications, the behavior of a particular patient or client is usually very important. If treatment does not affect the individual patient, it is simply unsuccessful. Yet, in the social extensions of reinforcement techniques, the performance of the individual is not necessarily as crucial. In dealing with a large number of individuals (e.g., a community), the behavior change of any given individual is not essential for the effectiveness of the intervention. The group of individuals to which the intervention is applied becomes the unit or "client," and the overall response of this unit determines the success of the intervention. It is not essential that each member of the unit change, only that an overall change is achieved. For example, it is not essential in increasing the use of mass transit that everyone or even most people ride buses rather than use their automobiles. Rather, it is important only that a sufficient number of people ride buses so that an economically significant reduction in fuel costs is achieved.

In most applications of reinforcement, the behavior change for an individual needs to be dramatic to effect therapeutic change (cf. Baer, Wolf, & Risley, 1968; Kazdin, 1977a). Small behavior changes usually do not achieve the original treatment goal. Interestingly, in social extensions, small changes in the behavior of individuals can have tremendous impact because the number of individuals is very large. For example, slightly reducing energy consumption of individual home owners, when multiplied by the large number of homes, constitutes a marked and economically significant effect.

The extensions of reinforcement techniques to social problems will not resolve the problem of individuals failing to respond to the contingencies. However, the lack of responsiveness of select individuals may not be as readily noticeable or detrimental to the overall goals of the program designed to alter a socially relevant behavior in the natural environment. Indeed, in many programs, the behavior of the individual may not even be monitored. For example, in decreasing littering in a natural setting (e.g., a park), the individuals who are in the setting constantly change over time. The goal of the intervention is to alter the frequency of littering independent of the particular individuals.

D. Ethical Implications

The use of reinforcement techniques in treatment and rehabilitation settings already has generated ethical disputes and litigation (e.g., Begelman, 1975; Davison & Stuart, 1975; Lucero, Vail, & Scherber, 1968). Ethical discussions revolve around such questions as what the treatment goals should be, the philosophical and moral underpinnings of such decisions, who shall be in the position to make decisions, and the abridgement of individual freedom (cf. Mahoney, Kazdin, & Lesswing, 1974). In many ways, the courts have operationalized some of these general concerns by specifying the behaviors that can and cannot be changed and the techniques that can be used to alter behavior (cf. Martin, 1975, for a review). For example, in the United States, patients may no longer be induced to engage in work to maintain the institution by earning privileges as has often been the case in many token economies (cf. Gripp & Magaro, 1974; Kazdin, 1977b).

Extensions of reinforcement to social problems may create even greater concern over the infringement of individual rights than contemporary treatment programs. Social extensions are directed at enhancing the general welfare of society and thus seek to control the behavior of large numbers of individuals. These extensions may be of concern because the large-scale application of reinforcement techniques may provide the individual citizen with little recourse but to respond to the contingencies. The infringement of rights may result from unchecked programs intended for the general good but differentially coercive to certain subgroups of individuals. The threat of injustice, normally present on a relatively small scale in treatment programs, could be multiplied by any large-scale extensions of reinforcement techniques to society.

Aside from the large-scale applications in terms of the number of individuals affected, social extensions may increasingly focus on behaviors that are more controversial than current areas of focus. For example, the general welfare of society may well be a function of the birth rate, eating habits, consumption of cigarettes, alcohol, and drugs, use of leisure time, exercise, and so on. Extensions of reinforcement into these areas would surely elicit protestations from many people. In general, the large-scale extension of reinforcement to social problems is likely to raise objections to the abridgement of individual freedoms. Indeed, theologians, psychologists, philosophers, and others have already discussed the implications of extending reinforcement techniques to social design (cf. Wheeler, 1973). The ethical implications will eventually need to be addressed to decide the limits of extending reinforcement practices both in terms of the behaviors and populations that are controlled.

VIII. CONCLUSION

Social extensions of reinforcement techniques have focused upon diverse behaviors related to littering, recycling waste material, energy consumption, use of mass transportation, job procurement and performance, community self-help skills, racial integration, and military training. Extension of behavior modification into these areas would seem to be extremely promising given the increased recognition of social and environmental problems. At this stage, extensions of behavior modification to social problems have been primarily of demonstrational value.

There are unresolved issues and problems associated with reinforcement techniques, such as maintaining behavior after a program is terminated and altering the behavior of individuals who initially fail to respond. These problems, evident in well-controlled treatment settings, also have appeared in some preliminary investigations of socially relevant behaviors in the community. It is unclear whether these and new problems will limit the efficacy of large-scale environmental interventions.

Interestingly, certain features of the natural environment lend themselves well to implementation of reinforcement programs. Initially, a potent reinforcement system (money) is already operative. In addition, once a program is implemented (e.g., to reduce energy consumption), it may be implemented on a relatively long-term or even permanent basis. The intervention can become a routine part of the social system and need not be withdrawn as is the case in most reinforcement programs. If the program can be implemented on a permanent basis, the problem of maintaining behavior should be resolved. Another advantage of social programs is that the problem of certain individuals failing to respond to the contingencies will not necessarily undermine the overall efficacy of the program. With social interventions, the change of any one individual is not essential as long as the overall goal for the group has been achieved.

It is too early to endorse reinforcement techniques as an unequivocal solution for any significant social problem addressed in the present article. The techniques to alter behavior on a large scale, directed toward the general good of society, remain to be researched. Current preliminary evidence suggests that behavior modification may play a role in altering social behaviors, although the long-term viability of this approach has not yet been demonstrated.

The widespread extension of reinforcement techniques to alter socially relevant behaviors depends upon more than simply developing an effective technology. The viability of a technology of social change will depend upon additional considerations pertaining to the social system itself. Two considerations include whether there will be incentives within the existing social system to support large-scale social change and whether the process of resolving some social problems will create new problems.

Initially, within the existing social system, it is unclear whether there would be support for large-scale performance of socially relevant behaviors. For example, business and government do not automatically gain from energy conservation and pollution control on the part of citizens. Indeed, if energy conservation were profitable economically, automobiles and homes could have been designed to conserve fuel long ago. The potential conflict of interest between factions of the social system could limit or delay the widespread implementation of programs to effect social change. The incentives to select business and government concerns could impede large-scale implementation of social programs even if these programs were known to be effective at this level.

An issue related to the large-scale implementation of social programs is that of the possible side effects of these programs. Altering an environmentally significant behavior on a large scale may have effects beyond those for which the program was designed. For example, reduced pollution and energy consumption could be achieved by promoting use of mass transit in place of automobiles. Yet, a large reduction in automobile use might alter economic and social patterns. The employment of many people would be threatened as the dependence upon automobiles and fuel decreased. The national and world economies could be influenced adversely.

Overall, the larger the scale upon which social programs are implemented, the more serious the threat of undesirable side effects of the programs. Given the social balance, eradication of a particular problem might introduce changes in other aspects of the system which might not be desirable (cf. Willems, 1974). The cost–benefit ratio of a given intervention may be difficult to evaluate because of the problems in balancing monetary and social costs throughout the system. In light of contemporary social problems, the demonstrated benefits of interventions, at least on a small scale, probably outweigh the potential deleterious effects, which remain to be investigated.

REFERENCES

Azrin, N. H., Flores, T., & Kaplan, S. J. Job-finding club: A group-assisted program for obtaining employment. *Behaviour Research and Therapy*, 1975, 13, 17–27.

Baer, D. M., Wolf, M. M., & Risley, T. R. Some current dimensions of applied behavior analysis. *Journal of Applied Behavior Analysis*, 1968, 1, 91–97.

Baltes, M. M. Operant principles applied to acquisition and generalization of nonlittering behavior in children. *Proceedings, 81st Annual Convention, American Psychological Association*, 1973, 8, 889–890.

Baltes, M. M., & Hayward, S. C. Behavioral control of littering in a football stadium. Paper read at the American Psychological Association, New Orleans, September 1974.

Begelman, D. A. Ethical and legal issues of behavior modification. In M. Hersen, R. M. Eisler, & P. M. Miller (Eds.), *Progress in behavior modification.* Vol. 1. New York: Academic Press, 1975. Pp. 159–189.

Best, D. L., Smith, S. C., Graves, D. J., & Williams, J. E. The modification of racial bias in preschool children. *Journal of Experimental Child Psychology,* 1975, **20**, 193–205.

Boren, J. J., & Colman, A. D. Some experiments on reinforcement principles within a psychiatric ward for delinquent soldiers. *Journal of Applied Behavior Analysis,* 1970, **3**, 29–37.

Braukmann, C. J., & Fixsen, D. L. Behavior modification with delinquents. In M. Hersen, R. M. Eisler, & P. M. Miller (eds.), *Progress in behavior modification.* Vol. 1. New York: Academic Press, 1975. Pp. 191–231.

Briscoe, R. V., Hoffman, D. B., & Bailey, J. S. Behavioral community psychology: Training a community board to problem solve. *Journal of Applied Behavior Analysis,* 1975, **8**, 157–168.

Burgess, R. L., Clark, R. N., & Hendee, J. C. An experimental analysis of anti-litter procedures. *Journal of Applied Behavior Analysis,* 1971, **4**, 71–75.

Business Week, New tool: "Reinforcement" for good work. December 18, 1971. Pp. 76–77.

Cairns, J. The cancer problem. *Scientific American,* 1975, **233**, 64–78.

Chapman, C., & Risley, T. R. Anti-litter procedures in an urban high-density area. *Journal of Applied Behavior Analysis,* 1974, **7**, 377–384.

Chase, J. D. *Token economy programs in the Veterans Administration.* Washington, D.C.: VA Department of Medicine and Surgery, 1970.

Clark, R. N., Burgess, R. L., & Hendee, J. C. The development of anti-litter behavior in a forest campground. *Journal of Applied Behavior Analysis,* 1972, **5**, 1–5.

Datel, W. E., & Legters, L. J. The psychology of the army recruit. Paper read at the American Medical Association, Chicago, June 1970.

Davidson, W. S., II, & Seidman, E. Studies of behavior modification and juvenile delinquency: A review, methodological critique, and social perspective. *Psychological Bulletin,* 1974, **81**, 998–1011.

Davison, G. C., & Stuart, R. B. Behavior therapy and civil liberties. *American Psychologist,* 1975, **7**, 755–763.

Edwards, C. D., & Williams, J. E. Generalization between evaluative words associated with racial figures in preschool children. *Journal of Experimental Research in Personality,* 1970, **4**, 144–155.

Everett, P. B., Hayward, S. C., & Meyers, A. W. The effects of a token reinforcement procedure on bus ridership. *Journal of Applied Behavior Analysis,* 1974, **7**, 1–9.

Geller, E. S. Prompting anti-litter behaviors. *Proceedings, 81st Annual Convention, American Psychological Association,* 1973, **8**, 901–902.

Geller, E. S. Increasing desired waste disposals with instructions. *Man-Environment Systems,* 1975, **5**, 125–128.

Geller, E. S., Chaffee, J. L., & Ingram, R. E. Promoting paper recycling on a university campus. *Journal of Environmental Systems,* 1975, **5**, 39–57.

Geller, E. S., Farris, J. C., & Post, D. S. Prompting a consumer behavior for pollution control. *Journal of Applied Behavior Analysis,* 1973, **6**, 367–376.

Geller, E. S., Witmer, J. F., & Orebaugh, A. L. Instructions as a determinant of paper-disposal behaviors. *Environment and Behavior,* 1976, in press.

Geller, E. S., Wylie, R. G., & Farris, J. C. An attempt at applying prompting and reinforcement toward pollution control. *Proceedings, 79th Annual Convention, American Psychological Association,* 1971, **6**, 701–702.

Gripp, R. F., & Magaro, P. A. The token economy program in the psychiatric hospital: A review and analysis. *Behaviour Research and Therapy*, 1974, 12, 205–228.

Hauserman, N., Walen, S. R., & Behling, M. Reinforced racial integration in the first grade: A study in generalization. *Journal of Applied Behavior Analysis*, 1973, 6, 193–200.

Hayes, S. C., & Cone, J. D. Decelerating environmentally destructive lawn-walking behavior. *Environment and Behavior*, 1976, in press. (a)

Hayes, S. C., & Cone, J. D. Reducing residential electrical energy use: Payments, information, and feedback. *Journal of Applied Behavior Analysis*, 1976, in press. (b)

Hayes, S. C., Johnson, V. S., & Cone, J. D. The marked item technique: A practical procedure for litter control. *Journal of Applied Behavior Analysis*, 1975, 8, 381–386.

Hermann, J. A., deMontes, A. I., Dominguez, B., Montes, F., & Hopkins, B. L. Effects of bonuses for punctuality on the tardiness of industrial workers. *Journal of Applied Behavior Analysis*, 1973, 6, 563–570.

Ingram, R. E., Chaffee, J. L., Rorrer, C. W., & Wellington, C. J. A community-integrated behavior modification approach to facilitate paper recycling. Paper read at the Southern Psychological Association, Atlanta, March 1975.

Ingram, R. E., & Geller, E. S. A community-integrated, behavior modification approach to facilitating paper recycling. *Catalog of Selected Documents in Psychology*, 1975, 5, 327.

Jones, R. J., & Azrin, N. H. An experimental application of a social reinforcement approach to the problem of job-finding. *Journal of Applied Behavior Analysis*, 1973, 6, 345–353.

Kazdin, A. E. The failure of some patients to respond to token programs. *Journal of Behavior Therapy and Experimental Psychiatry*, 1973, 4, 7–14.

Kazdin, A. E. *Behavior modification in applied settings*. Homewood, Ill.: Dorsey Press, 1975. (a)

Kazdin, A. E. Characteristics and trends in applied behavior analysis. *Journal of Applied Behavior Analysis*, 1975, 8, 332. (b)

Kazdin, A. E. Recent advances in token economy research. In M. Hersen, R. M. Eisler, & P. M. Miller (Eds.), *Progress in behavior modification*. Vol. 1. New York: Academic Press, 1975. Pp. 233–274. (c)

Kazdin, A. E. Methodology of applied behavior analysis. In T. A. Brigham & A. C. Catania (Eds.), *Applied behavior research: Analysis of social and educational processes*. New York: Irvington/Naiburg–Wiley, 1977. (a)

Kazdin, A. E. *The token economy: A review and evaluation*. New York: Plenum Press, 1977. (b)

Kazdin, A. E., & Craighead, W. E. Behavior modification in special education. In L. Mann & D. A. Sabatino (Eds.), *The first review of special education*. Vol. 2. Philadelphia: Buttonwood Farms, 1973. Pp. 51–102.

Keep America Beautiful, Inc. *Who litters and why*. 99 Park Avenue, New York, New York, 1968.

Kennedy, R. E. Behavior modification in prisons. In W. E. Craighead, A. E. Kazdin, & M. J. Mahoney (Eds.), *Behavior modification: Principles, issues, and applications*. Boston: Houghton Mifflin, 1976. Pp. 321–340.

Kinkade, K. *A Walden Two experiment: The first five years of Twin Oaks Community*. New York: Morrow, 1972.

Kohlenberg, R., & Phillips, T. Reinforcement and rate of litter depositing. *Journal of Applied Behavior Analysis*, 1973, 6, 391–396.

Kohlenberg, R., Phillips, T., & Proctor, W. A behavioral analysis of peaking in residential electrical energy consumers. *Journal of Applied Behavior Analysis*, 1976, 9, 13–18.

Lucero, R. J., Vail, D. J., & Scherber, J. Regulating operant-conditioning programs. *Hospital and Community Psychiatry.* 1968, 19, 53–54.

Luyben, P. D., & Bailey, J. S. Newspaper recycling behavior: The effects of reinforcement versus proximity of containers. Unpublished manuscript, Florida State University, 1975.

Mahoney, M. J., Kazdin, A. E., & Lesswing, N. J. Behavior modification: Delusion or deliverance. In C. M. Franks & G. T. Wilson (Eds.), *Annual review of behavior therapy theory and research.* Vol. 2. New York: Brunner/Mazel, 1974.

Mann, J. H. The effect of inter-racial contact on sociometric choices and perceptions. *Journal of Social Psychology,* 1959, 50, 143–152.

Marholin, D., II, & Gray, D. Effects of group response cost procedures on cash shortages in a small business. *Journal of Applied Behavior Analysis,* 1976, 9, 25–30.

Martin, R. *Legal challenges to behavior modification: Trends in schools, corrections and mental health.* Champaign, Ill.: Research Press, 1975.

McMurtry, C. A., & Williams, J. E. The evaluation dimension of the affective meaning system of the preschool child. *Developmental Psychology,* 1972, 6, 238–246.

Meyers, A. W., Artz, L. M., & Craighead, W. E. The effects of instructions, incentive, and feedback on a community problem: Dormitory noise. *Journal of Applied Behavior Analysis,* 1976, in press.

Milan, M. A., & McKee, J. M. Behavior modification: Principles and applications in corrections. In D. Glaser (Ed.), *Handbook of criminology.* Chicago: Rand McNally, 1974. Pp. 745–776.

Miller, L. K. The design of better communities through the application of behavioral principles. In W. E. Craighead, A. E. Kazdin, & M. J. Mahoney (Eds.), *Behavior modification: Principles, issues and applications.* Boston: Houghton, Mifflin, 1976. Pp. 289–309.

Miller, L. K., & Miller, O. L. Reinforcing self-help group activities of welfare recipients. *Journal of Applied Behavior Analysis,* 1970, 3, 57–64.

Miller, P. M., & Eisler, R. M. Alcohol and drug abuse. In W. E. Craighead, A. E. Kazdin, & M. J. Mahoney (Eds.), *Behavior modification: Principles, issues, and application.* Boston: Houghton, Mifflin, 1976. Pp. 376–393.

O'Leary, K. D., & Drabman, R. Token reinforcement programs in the classroom: A review. *Psychological Bulletin,* 1971, 75, 379–398.

Palmer, M. H., Lloyd, M. E., & Lloyd, K. E. An experimental analysis of electricity conservation procedures. *Journal of Applied Behavior Analysis,* 1976, in press.

Pedalino, E., & Gamboa, V. U. Behavior modification and absenteeism: Intervention in one industrial setting. *Journal of Applied Psychology,* 1974, 59, 694–698.

Pierce, C. H., & Risley, T. R. Improving job performance of Neighborhood Youths Corps aides in an urban recreation program. *Journal of Applied Behavior Analysis,* 1974, 7, 207–215.

Powers, R. B., Osborne, J. G., & Anderson, E. G. Positive reinforcement of litter removal in the natural environment. *Journal of Applied Behavior Analysis,* 1973, 6, 579–586.

Reid, D. H., Luyben, P. L., Rawers, R. J., & Bailey, J. S. The effects of prompting and proximity of containers on newspaper recycling behavior. *Environment and Behavior,* 1976, in press.

Seaver, W. B., & Patterson, A. H. Decreasing fuel oil consumption through feedback and social commendation. *Journal of Applied Behavior Analysis,* 1976, 9, 147–152.

Skinner, B. F. *Walden Two.* New York: Macmillan, 1948.

Stayer, S. J., & Jones, F. Ward 108: Behavior modification and the delinquent soldier. Paper read at the Behavioral Engineering Conference, Walter Reed General Hospital, 1969.

Wheeler, H. (Ed.), *Beyond the punitive society*. San Francisco: Freeman, 1973.

Willems, E. P. Behavioral technology and behavioral ecology. *Journal of Applied Behavior Analysis*, 1974, 7, 151–165.

Williams, J. E., & Morland, J. K. *Race, color, and the young*. Chapel Hill: University of North Carolina Press, 1976.

Winett, R. A., & Nietzel, M. T. Behavioral ecology: Contingency management of consumer energy use. *American Journal of Community Psychology*, 1975, 3, 123–133.

Witmer, J. F., & Geller, E. S. Facilitating paper recycling: Effects of prompts, raffles, and contests. *Journal of Applied Behavior Analysis*, 1976, 9, 315–322.

Wodarski, J. S. The reduction of electrical energy consumption: The application of behavioral analysis. Paper read at the Association for Advancement of Behavior Therapy, San Francisco, December 1975.

BEHAVIOR MODIFICATION
IN COMMUNITY SETTINGS

CLIFFORD R. O'DONNELL

*Department of Psychology
and Social Welfare Development
and Research Center
University of Hawaii
Honolulu, Hawaii*

I. INTRODUCTION

The history of the helping professions can be characterized by the interaction between individual and community oriented approaches. In an excellent presentation of this history, Levine and Levine (1970) point out that the origins of settlement houses, juvenile courts, and child guidance clinics are within a community orientation. These institutions developed in the social reform era of the 1890s to the 1920s, years characterized by social and political concern with community problems in the United States. But following World War I the political climate became more conservative. In an era when the value of individual accomplishment was supreme—and

lack of accomplishment was accordingly blamed on the individual—
an orientation based on individual psychological problems, strongly
influenced by psychoanalytic thinking and the medical model, began
to flourish.

This trend continued until the activist-reform decade of the
1960s, in which an increasing interest in community and behavioral
approaches developed. The community orientation was distinguished
by the use of quasi-institutional settings to facilitate the transition
from institutional to community placement, the treatment of persons in the setting in which problems occur, attention to problems
which affect other members of the community rather than only the
individuals receiving treatment, attempts to identify the sources of
community problems, the use of indirect services through consultation and education rather than direct services, and the promise of
developing means of prevention to replace treatment of behavioral
problems.

A fine overview of these developments has been provided by Zax
and Specter (1974). The influence of community ideas developed in
the reform era prior to World War I is evident in the community
projects they review; however, these projects are now also permeated
with the logic of the medical model. These features are exemplified
by the St. Louis Project (Zax & Specter, 1974, pp. 174–176). This
program provided group therapy for mothers of children with school
problems. When such services were decisively rejected by mothers in
some schools, an additional program was added to educate the
mothers to accept such intervention! The results, based on teacher
ratings, indicated that "all children got worse and that the children in
the experimental groups seemed to worsen more markedly than
controls. The experimenters regarded this finding as positive from
one viewpoint. It conceivably indicated that teachers, as a result of
the program, had become more sensitive to emotional adjustment in
children" (p. 175). The focus on school problems illustrates the
community influence, while the intervention (group therapy for
mothers) reflects the influence of the medical model. The interpretation of negative data to fit preconceptions is also illustrated in this
example.

Another approach within a community orientation stems from
the behavioral tradition. The majority of such research has been in
classrooms and institutions, but an increasing proportion is taking
place in natural settings (Kazdin, 1975a). The purpose of this article
is to review the behavioral research within community settings, i.e.,

within transitional facilities as well as within the settings in which the initial problems occur.

In considering the scope of this review, it is recognized that a distinction between individual and community orientations is to some extent arbitrary. After all, therapists treating individual problems often work with families in the home, teachers at school, employers at work, etc. In addition, concepts of groups, community, and environmental settings are abstractions, and therapeutic efforts made within such a framework must affect individuals if they are to be effective. Nor is a distinction based on the numbers of people served particularly useful. Group therapy, institutional programs, and self-modification interventions can serve large numbers of people without the need to be conceptualized within a community framework. Further, many individuals are placed in special treatment settings, such as hospitals, with intervention continuing in halfway houses after they leave. Others are placed in home settings in lieu of hospitals or prisons. Should such treatment be viewed as individual or community oriented?

Individual and community orientations may be best conceived as forming a continuum rather than separate categories. The community orientation extends on this continuum from the quasi-institutional programs in the psychiatric and correctional areas, through programs in settings such as homes and schools which do not require special facilities, to programs which focus on more general community problems, which traditionally have not been viewed as falling within the province of the helping professions. Consistent with this view, the research reviewed in Section II is presented in the following order: community aftercare programs, correctional programs, family intervention programs, and more general community problems. A review of research in school settings is not included because of the large body of such research, which warrants a separate review (see Copeland & Hall, 1976).

Selection of settings, programs, and specific studies was guided by a focus on outcome data. Traditionally the ultimate justification of these projects has been based on postintervention outcome criteria. One objective of this review is to critically appraise the success to date of community projects on these criteria. In Section II, E it is suggested that perhaps programs should not be primarily evaluated on postintervention outcome criteria and that success will be elusive until the problem of the generalization and maintenance of behavior is resolved. It is argued that perhaps the primary evaluation of whether behavior is maintained should depend on the assessment of postintervention environments and that research in a variety of areas may offer direction for such assessment and evaluation. These research efforts are outlined in Section III.

II. COMMUNITY PROGRAMS

A. Aftercare

1. INTRODUCTION

The rationale behind community aftercare programs rests primarily on the failure of any within-hospital treatment program to affect post-hospital adjustment, whether measured by return-to-hospital rates, employment, or psychosocial functioning. This failure has been documented in a number of recent reviews. Anthony, Buell, Sharratt, and Althoff (1972) used two outcome criteria: (1) recidivism as defined by the percent of discharged patients who are rehospitalized and (2) post-hospital employment defined as the percent of discharged patients who are competitively employed at follow-up or employed full time during the entire follow-up period. They found the base rate for recidivism to be 30–40% at 6 months, 40–50% at 1 year, and 65–75% at 3 to 5 years. Employment figures were 30–50% at 6 months, and 20–30% at 1 year. Further, their review concluded that both traditional hospital treatment and "total push therapy" (token economies and milieu), while improving in-hospital behavior, had no effect on post-hospital adjustment and that work therapy had no effect on community employment. In another review, Erickson (1975) reached the related conclusion that practically any reasonable innovation, including behavior modification, leads to improvement of behavior within the hospital, but there is no relationship between improvement in the hospital and post-hospital adjustment.

Recent studies reporting improved post-hospital adjustment are marred by problems in the methods used to evaluate outcome. Greenberg, Scott, Pisa, and Friesen (1975) compared token and token-milieu groups and found that members of the latter spent more days out of the hospital during the experimental year. Erickson (1975) has characterized such an outcome measure as dated in that it is not necessarily related to patient improvement, since many who spend time out of the hospital later return. Unfortunately, Greenberg *et al.* (1975) did not report data on how many patients were discharged or returned to the hospital during the year. In a nonbehavioral study, Carkhuff (1974) calculated recidivism rate as the number of people released who subsequently return to the institution during the year. He reports a recidivism rate of 16% for the year in which staff were trained in interpersonal skills. This compared favorably with recidivism rates of 25% and 23% during the preceding two years. However, by his method of computation, the rate of recidivism could have been affected by what point in the year discharge occurred; e.g., if everyone were released on the last day of the year, recidivism would be 0%. No data were presented to show that those released during the experimental year were released at a comparable time to those in previous years.

Reviewing token economy studies in hospital settings, Kazdin (1975b) also noted improvements of behavior within the hospital but little evidence of post-hospital improvement. His argument for focusing on behavior within the hospital was that since hospitals exist, programs can mitigate against behavior deterioration in the hospital. Nevertheless, he also noted that the ultimate criterion is extra-hospital adjustment.

Given the lack of influence hospital programs have had on post-hospital adjustment and the developing legal problems of treatment programs within the hospital (Wexler, 1973), increasing interest has focused on community programs.

2. PROGRAMS

Community aftercare programs focus on individuals after they are discharged from hospitals and seek to prevent their return. The Samuels and Henderson (1971) study was one of the first reporting outcome results on the use of a token system within a transitional facility. This program sought to reduce symptomatic behavior and to prepare residents for employment and a return to their homes. The program was compared with traditional state and city facility control groups. Although the initial results appeared favorable for the first 21 men in the program, by the time of follow-up, "the percentage of subjects in the community and in hospitals was similar for the three groups" (p. 267). Further, when all 58 men who had left the program were considered, time in the community, time employed, the percent who worked, and most importantly the percent rehospitalized, differed little from the city facility controls. The state controls did somewhat worse.

Fairweather, Sanders, Cressler, and Maynard (1969) reported on what appears to be the most frequently cited effort within a transitional facility. Their program was based on a lodge concept wherein men discharged from a hospital lived together and worked on jobs provided by the program. With such an arrangement it is not surprising that the men were employed more while they were in the project than their control counterparts. However, when they left the project, approximately two-thirds were unemployed and the remaining one-third were employed for only a median of 47 days. This rate was similar to that of the control group. In addition, there was no effect of the program on association with friends, symptomatic behaviors, drinking, various activities, or rated satisfactions. Most importantly, the recidivism rate (40%) was similar to that of the controls (37%). One of the redeeming findings, however, was that the program could be operated at a lower cost than hospitalization.

Two additional studies, each quite similar to the Fairweather *et al.* program, have been reported. Shean (1973) described a program for women based on the lodge concept. After three years and a total of 25 patients, he cited a recidivism rate of only 12% (three women returned to the hospital). But nine of the 25 women were still living in the transitional facility and no data were provided on the length of time the remaining 13 had been discharged, or how they were functioning. The other program (Atthowe, 1973), called Operation Re-entry, was designed to discharge patients and maintain them in the community. It included a token economy, workshop, self-help ward, discharge to the community as a unit, and living in homes provided by the program. Atthowe also cited a recidivism rate of 12%, based on a total of 59 men who had been discharged from the hospital. But this figure included those who had just been discharged, and rates for those released for 6 or 12 months were not given.

The results of the most recent study (Hudson, 1975) are also disappointing. In this study an attempt was made to continue treatment at home through behavioral intervention. Of 12 consecutive referrals, intervention was not possible in seven cases because of the lack of cooperation from patients or their families; in three other cases there was little success, the patient either discontinued treatment or was rehospitalized; in the remaining two cases some improvement in performing house chores and outside activities was reported.

Finally, Hunt and Azrin (1973) presented a community-reinforcement approach for eight alcoholics who had been hospitalized. The program provided vocational counseling and job finding, marital and family counseling, a social club for nonalcoholic friendships and activities, the initial costs of a telephone, newspapers, magazines, a radio or television, visits by a counselor once or twice a week for the first month to help implement the program and, for nonmarried patients without a parental family, a foster family. Further, family members were instructed to withdraw their contact when the patient drank. The results indicated that while they were in the program, the alcoholics drank less, were employed more, were away from home less, and spent less time in an institution than controls. No follow-up results were reported.

The results of these studies do not alter the Anthony *et al.* (1972) conclusions for aftercare programs: (a) Those who receive aftercare treatment are less likely to recidivate as long as they remain in the program. (b) If they leave the program or it is discontinued, the results are no different from those of no-treatment controls. (c) Aftercare programs do not seem to do worse than hospital programs and can be operated at less cost.

B. Corrections

1. INTRODUCTION

Most of the behavioral research in the correctional field has focused on interventions with juveniles. The seriousness of the juvenile crime problem is reflected in statistics showing that one in nine persons is referred to juvenile courts by his/her eighteenth birthday. The corresponding figures for males only is one in six. In one year alone (1970), 2.8% of children between the ages 10 and 17 appeared before juvenile court for delinquency offenses in the United States (Shah, 1975). In their review, Dean and Reppucci (1974) noted that there were 220 state correctional facilities for juveniles with an average daily population of 42,389 in 1965. Their lengths of stay ranged from 4 to 24 months, with a median of 9 months. The purpose of placing people in correctional institutions is, of course, to deter crime and, especially with juveniles, to prevent future crimes. But is there any evidence that institutional programs affect recidivism rates?

The most frequently cited study of behavioral intervention with an institutionalized juvenile population is the Case II Project (Cohen & Filipczak, 1971). Following the use of a token system, gains of two grade levels on achievement tests and 12.5 points on intelligence tests were reported. Interpretation of these gains is difficult, however, since the students were rewarded for performance on the post-test. Moreover, in a review of such studies, Martinson (1974) concluded that there is no evidence that educational training has any effect on recidivism. Further, the recidivism data reported by Cohen and Filipczak are based on a reduced sample; of 41 persons in the program, follow-up information could not be found on 10, four were dropped from analysis, and 16 others were transferred to other institutions. Thus any comparisons involving the biased sample of the remaining 11 are difficult to interpret.

A similar bias exists in a study reported by Jesness (1975). He compared token economy and transactional analysis groups and noted that the recidivism rates for both groups were 32% after 1 year and 48% after 2 years. These rates apparently compared favorably with the institution's previous yearly rates of 41–49%, as well as those of a control institution (43%). But excluded from the Jesness sample were 24 persons who did not remain in the program at least 3 months, 103 who were transferred to another institution (half for breaches of discipline), and 15 who escaped. Thus 142 youths were not included, a high-risk group that would doubtless have increased the recidivism rate presented. Further, even with this exclusion, 77% of the experimental youths were arrested within 2 years.

The results with adults are no better. A study by the Rehabilitation Research Foundation (1974) found no effect on recidivism for either a token economy or a vocational training program. The latter also had no effect on employment. Martinson (1974), in reviewing all types of programs through 1967, concluded that there is no evidence that any program has an effect on recidivism. These results, similar to those of hospital programs, provide a rationale for community correctional projects.

2. RESIDENTIAL PROGRAMS

The model for behavioral intervention within a community residential setting is Achievement Place. An overview of this program and the results of many process studies have been provided by Braukmann and Fixsen (1975). The process studies have demonstrated the effectiveness of the token system in decreasing the use of

poor grammar and aggressive statements, increasing promptness, academic performance, room cleaning, and in improving employment
interview and police interaction behaviors, among others.

Youth from Achievement Place have been described as follows:
about 13 years old, in the seventh grade but achieving at a third-
grade level, an average IQ of 95, 77% from families with income
under $5,000, 76% suspended from school, 60% failed one or more
grades, 94% classified as school behavior problems, 53% failed probation, and averaging 2.2 police contacts and 1.9 court contacts prior
to entering Achievement Place (Fixsen, Wolf, & Phillips, 1973). The
improvements cited in the process studies are noteworthy with these
youngsters. Given this initial success, homes modeled after Achievement Place are springing up like chain restaurants in many states.
However, the major purpose of placing youth in Achievement Place
is to decrease the likelihood of their committing future crimes.
Although it is reasonable to assume that there may be some relationship between the target behaviors of the process studies and future
criminal violations, no evidence of such a relationship has been
presented to date for Achievement Place youth.

Indeed, the recidivism data presented to date are sketchy at best.
Phillips, Phillips, Fixsen, and Wolf (1973) reported recidivism rates
of 19% for Achievement Place, 54% for probation, and 53% for a
state training school after two years. Harris (1974), in a similar
program for Indian youth, compared 25 youngsters who had completed the program with matched controls from other programs.
After 1 year the experimental group was reinstitutionalized less
frequently (4%) than the matched controls (60%), and also showed a
lower arrest rate (56% vs. 88%). In both of these studies it was noted
that the results were preliminary because of the small numbers and
because youths were not randomly assigned to treatment programs.

Although these preliminary results are favorable, the findings of
both studies raise questions. For example, Eitzen (1975) reported
that there were no differences between Achievement Place and
training school youth in the number of police and court contacts
during follow-up. It is not clear why recidivism rates should be lower
for Achievement Place residents when their police and court contacts
are the same as those in the comparison group. Even less clear is the
fact that only one of 14 arrested experimental youths was reinstitutionalized, while 15 of 22 arrested matched-control youths were
reinstitutionalized (Harris, 1974).

What is clear is that definitive conclusions must await more complete data. Fortunately such an evaluation study, apparently including random assignment to programs, is under way (Nagoshi, 1976, personal communication).

3. NONRESIDENTIAL PROGRAMS

The nonresidential community programs are variations of verbal or written contingency contracting techniques. A description of contracting within the families of delinquents has been provided by Stuart (1971). When these procedures were applied within the families of 79 delinquent youths, however, the data showed no relationship between contract contents, length of treatment, client characteristics, or therapist, and outcome (Stuart & Lott, 1972). The only favorable result occurred when these youths were compared to 15 who had refused treatment and who had declined in school grades and attendance. This result, based on the biased sample of those who refused treatment, cannot be attributed to the contracting process.

Similarly disappointing results have been reported by Weathers and Liberman (1975). In their study, only six of 28 families referred by the probation department completed treatment, and these six showed virtually no improvement. As a result of this frustrating experience, the authors drew negative conclusions about the utility of contingency contracting with multiproblem families.

Overall conclusions may, however, be premature. Positive results *during* contracting intervention with probationers have been reported by Kleinknecht (1969), Fitzgerald (1974), and Polakow and Doctor (1974). In the study by Kleinknecht, drivers who had received at least five traffic citations and violated a driving probation ($N = 182$) were either: (a) issued a restricted driver's license with extension of driving time given every 2 weeks contingent upon a lack of violations and accidents, (b) issued the same license and received the extensions without any contingency, or (c) simply given their regular license back. During the 3-month experiment the contingency group went a significantly longer time without a traffic violation (a mean of 37 days) than either control group (means of 21 and 24 days). A 3-month follow-up after completion of the program, however, showed no differences among the groups.

The results of the two more recent studies (Fitzgerald, 1974; Polakow & Doctor, 1974) demonstrate that shortening time on probation can be an effective reinforcer. Fitzgerald's contracting group worked more hours to pay fines, and thereby shorten their probation period, than those randomly assigned to three control groups. In the Polakow and Doctor study, adults placed on probation for use of dangerous drugs received time off probation for employment, nondrug activity, improved living accommodations, etc. Results showed fewer probation violations and arrests, and more months employed, for those randomly assigned to the contracting group than for those who received traditional probation services.

In addition, Alexander and Parsons (1973) found a lower rate (26%) of what were called *behavioral* offenses (mostly status offenses which would not be crimes if the juveniles were adults) for a group receiving behavioral family treatment including contingency contracting. All comparison groups (client-centered, psychodynamic, and no-treatment controls), as well as county base rates, showed higher recidivism rates (47 to 73%) for such offenses. Those who did not complete treatment were nevertheless included in the analysis. As noted by Weathers and Liberman (1975), however, the variable follow-up period of 6 to 18 months could have biased the comparison rates among groups. More importantly, when *criminal* offenses were evaluated, rates among groups did not significantly differ.

From all of these contracting studies, it appears that greater success is likely when youths contract with probation authorities than with their families. Probation officials have both the authority and the access to a sought-after reward (time off probation) that many of these families lack.

Another approach to contracting with juveniles from multiproblem families has been illustrated by Fo and O'Donnell (1974, 1975). Adapting the triadic model of Tharp and Wetzel (1969), indigenous nonprofessionals were employed as mediators. These mediators (called buddies) were trained in the application of contingency management and worked with the youths on a variety of problem behaviors. This procedure was effective in reducing school truancy and the frequency of various other problems (Fo & O'Donnell, 1974). Although delinquent acts were not directly targeted, only 37.5% of the youths who had committed a criminal offense in the previous year did so during the project year. This rate compared favorably to the rate (64%) of those in a randomly assigned control group (Fo & O'Donnell, 1975). These results with delinquent children are congruent with the above probation studies, which also proceeded independently of the family system.

Nondelinquent youngsters, however, also participated in the project. These youths were referred (mostly by school officials) for what were considered predelinquent behaviors, such as school truancy. A separate analysis indicated that intervention with these juveniles might have been countereffective. Of these program youths who had not committed a major criminal offense in the preceding year, 15.7% did so during the project year. This rate was approximately double that of the control youth (7.2%). It is possible that youngsters with no major offenses in the preceding year formed relationships with those with major offenses. Unfortunately, it was not feasible to assess this possibility. Even so, it might be worth considering whether programs of preventive intervention should also include those who have already committed criminal offenses.

In conclusion, it should be noted that in these studies virtually all of the positive results occurred *during* the intervention program. Only two studies reported follow-up data *after* intervention was terminated. Of these two, Alexander and Parsons (1973) showed an effect for behavioral but not criminal offenses, and Kleinknecht (1969) noted that improvement during intervention was not maintained during the follow-up period. Thus, the Alexander and Parsons study apparently stands alone in finding at least some effect beyond the intervention period. As a result, additional information showing the relationship between length of follow-up and recidivism for each group would be of interest.

4. METHODOLOGICAL PROBLEMS

Serious methodological problems continue to mar evaluation studies in the correctional field. In this review, examples of biased comparisons include the use of a group who refused treatment (Stuart & Lott, 1972), the exclusion of those who did not complete treatment (Jesness, 1975), a comparison group whose members were transferred to another program before release (Cohen & Filipczak, 1971), and nonrandom assignment to groups (Harris, 1974; Phillips *et al.*, 1973). Further, in a recent review of behavioral intervention studies with delinquents, Davidson and Seidman (1974) reported that 82% of the studies reviewed did not use an untreated control group, and only 18% presented follow-up data.

An equally serious problem is that recidivism results can be misleading if the comparison groups are treated differently after intervention (i.e., during a follow-up period). This can occur if recidivism is defined in a way which favors a particular group, or where similar behaviors do not result in a similar recidivism rate for each group. The California Community Treatment Project, for example, has been criticized for the latter (Becker & Heyman, 1972; Lerman, 1968). Although favorable parole revocation rates were presented for the experimental groups in this project, rates of parole suspension and the mean number of delinquent offenses were higher. For the first severe offense, 82% of the control youths, but only 31% of the experimental youngsters, had parole revoked (Beker & Heyman, 1972, Table 1). Such bias led Lerman (1968) to conclude that the positive results reported appear to be more a function of the parole agents' parole-revoking behavior than the delinquents' response to treatment.

None of the studies in this review appears this biased. However, questions can be raised about the lower recidivism rates for Achievement Place youths when they have the same mean number of police and court contacts as the comparison group (Eitzen, 1975). Similar questions occur when 68% of those arrested in the matched control group are reinstitutionalized, compared to only 7% of those arrested in the experimental group (Harris, 1974).

C. Family Intervention

1. INTRODUCTION

Family intervention programs have focused on the modification of children's deviant behavior in the home. The goal of these programs is to reduce such behavior and prevent future problems as these children mature into adults. The need for such intervention has been well documented by Robins (1974). She compared the adult

TABLE I

The Adult Status of Children Referred for Antisocial Problems, Referred for Other Problems, and Not Referred (Controls)[a]

	Males			Females		
Adult status (%)	Antisocial	Other	Control	Antisocial	Other	Control
Arrested	71	30	22	40	10	0
Imprisoned	43	13	0	12	0	0
Divorced	51	30	16	70	31	42
Unemployed[b]	36	14	8	64	37	25
Registered with social agency	37	22	20	55	35	10
Heavy use of alcohol	53	38	29	33	13	14

[a]Abstracted from Robins (1974).
[b]More than 2% of the time within the preceding 10 years.

status of 524 children treated in child guidance clinics with the adult status of 100 nonreferred children of the same age, sex, neighborhood, race, and intelligence. The major findings of this study (abstracted from Robins, 1974, Chapter 3) are presented in Table I. Clearly, the percentage of youths referred for antisocial problems who later experienced various problems as adults is markedly higher than that of children referred for other problems or that of children not referred.

In a model review article, Berkowitz and Graziano (1972) presented the results of intervention studies with antisocial youth through 1971. Most of these results were based on single case studies. Since that time, outcome results of more extensive intervention programs have become available. The remainder of this section presents (a) a brief description and the major findings of these programs, and (b) a critique of these results.

2. PROGRAM DESCRIPTION AND RESULTS

A detailed description of a family intervention program has been provided by Patterson, Cobb, and Ray (1973). Briefly, boys aged 6–13 were referred for high rates of aggressive behavior. The majority of these boys lived in lower socioeconomic families and had at least one sibling. The program sought to exclude severely retarded, psychotic, and brain-damaged children. Parents were first trained in behavioral observation and principles of social learning, and then participated in structured training sessions to design programs and review data. Supervision was provided by telephone, by home visits, and during the group sessions.

Behavioral observations were obtained during 6–10 baseline sessions, during intervention, and during follow-up periods of up to 12 months. These observations by trained observers were coded into 29 categories of behavior, of which 14 were considered deviant. In addition, parent report measures of global perceptions and daily problem behavior occurrences were obtained.

The results of this program have been reported on the first 13 families by Patterson *et al.* (1973), an additional 11 families by Patterson and Reid (1973), and a total of the first 27 families by Patterson (1974b). In the last-mentioned, Patterson reported that the mean *total* deviant behavior score of .75 responses per minute during baseline decreased significantly during intervention to .40. Two of every three boys showed a reduction of 30% or more in deviant behaviors. Further, an analysis of *nontargeted* deviant behavior indicated a trend toward reduction. Data available on 20 families at a

4-month follow-up showed a mean total deviant behavior score of
.34, which was significantly lower than the mean baseline score.
Patterson notes that comparison data suggest that a score of .45 is
maximally efficient in discriminating between referred and nonreferred children. Thus, these postintervention data show mean scores
within the normal range.

Results of the initial outcome study also indicated that the mean
rate of referred problem behaviors, as reported by parents, decreased
from baseline (.59) to intervention (.28), and continued to decline at
follow-up to .17 (Patterson *et al.,* 1973). The global ratings of
parents have also suggested improvement in deviant behavior (Patterson *et al.,* 1973; Patterson & Reid, 1973).

Control groups were not included in the above outcome studies.
Two other studies, however, have reported positive results for this
intervention program in comparison to control groups. Walter and
Gilmore (1973) compared these intervention procedures with a placebo control group whose members did not read the programmed
text or have a therapist present during training sessions. The rest of
the program was similar and behavioral observation and parent
checklist data were obtained. These data indicated that the experimental group decreased in targeted deviant behaviors while the
placebo group did not. In addition, Wiltz and Patterson (1974)
compared an intervention group with a waiting control group. The
data indicated a significant reduction after 5 weeks in targeted
deviant behaviors for the treatment but not the control group.

Finally, Arnold, Levine, and Patterson (1975) have presented
data on the 55 siblings of the 27 boys referred for treatment in the
Patterson (1974b) program. The baseline data for these siblings
showed that their mean total deviant behavior score (.56) did not
significantly differ from that of the referred children. Although these
siblings were not targeted for intervention, an analysis of the behavioral observation data showed a significant decrease in their total
deviant behavior from baseline to termination. This improvement
was maintained through a 6-month follow-up. The authors interpreted this result as indicating a generalization effect and as evidence
that the parents learned child management skills which they applied
to the sibling behaviors.

3. A CRITIQUE OF PROGRAM RESULTS

a. Sample Representativeness. Crucial for interpreting these
results is the representativeness of the sample on which the results
are based. This is especially important in considering the external

validity of these studies. The question is: Are the results based on a representative sample of those who seek help from this program? The answer appears to be that they are not.

Patterson (1974b) reports that of 35 referred families on which baseline data were collected, 27 completed at least 4 weeks of intervention, 21 a 1-month follow-up, 18 a 6-month follow-up, and 16 a 1-year follow-up. Thus, approximately one-fourth of the families dropped out prior to intervention, and little or no follow-up data are available for virtually 50% of the initial sample.

Other studies of similar intervention programs have reported the same problem. Of seven families seen by Ferber, Keeley, and Shemberg (1974), intervention data were available for five, and follow-up data for only one. Johnson and Christensen (1975) saw 64 families for at least one intake interview. Of these families, 22 "remained for extended treatment, representing 34% of the initial sample" (p. 141). Of these 22 families, only 14 participated in follow-up assessments. Thus, follow-up results are based on only 21% of the initial sample and on only 64% of those who completed intervention.

In 3 years of family intervention studies, Bernal (1975) reported dropout rates of 38%, 74%, and 91%. Further, during 1 year in which families were recruited by mailing a description of the program (including home observations) to the parents of kindergarten and first grade boys, only three families volunteered. The dropout rate was lowered to 13% in the fourth year only by stressing prevention and treatment in recruitment and by paying from $50 to $100 for postintervention assessments.

Thus, from all of these studies it appears that intervention results, and especially follow-up findings, are not based on a representative sample of families referred for treatment. Johnson and Christensen (1975) also found that families remaining in the program were rated as more cooperative by their therapists during treatment. Accordingly, any interpretation of these results must be qualified by the evidence that they are based on motivated, cooperative families.

b. Behavioral Observation: Reliability. The commendable efforts to establish the reliability of the behavioral codes used in many of the family intervention studies have been well documented by Jones, Reid, and Patterson (1975). Despite these efforts, questions about the reliability of these behavior codes still remain. Correlations between baseline sessions for the 14 deviant behaviors were below .50 for six behaviors, between .50 and .75 for seven behaviors, and above .75 for only one behavior—"cry," which mothers had rated as the least deviant. For 14 nondeviant behaviors the highest correlation was .67 and 10 were below .50 (Jones *et al.,* 1975, Table 7). Although Johnson and Bolstad (1973) have argued that low reliability is acceptable if the error is unsystematic (since positive results must then be strong effects), it is difficult to determine when experimental error is unsystematic. Experimenter effects, social desirability, and "hello—goodbye" effects, may influence experimental error systematically in these studies.

The high variability in the frequency of occurrence among these behaviors can also create problems. Frequency of behavior can influence reliability (Hawkins & Dotson, 1975) and observer agreement (Johnson & Bolstad, 1973), and can produce variability when the scoring of some behaviors has priority over others (Jones, 1973) as is true in this behavior coding system.

Moreover, the frequency of deviant behavior which is recorded can decrease when observers do not know their reliability is being assessed. In a study by Romancyzk, Kent, Diament, and O'Leary (1973), disruptive behavior decreased 25% under such covert assessment conditions. This can be important when the number of observations, and hence the number of reliability checks, varies among baseline, intervention, and follow-up conditions, as it does in these family intervention studies.

The frequency of behavior is also affected when people know they are being observed (Lipinski & Nelson, 1974; Zegiob, Arnold, & Forehand, 1975), or when parents are asked to present either a good or bad picture of their child (Johnson & Lobitz, 1974). Orne (1970) wisely suggests caution in interpreting situations where people can easily alter their performance when asked to do so.

These studies have demonstrated that behavioral observation is a highly complex process. Serious problems are created when the behavior codes are not high in reliability, when variable frequency behaviors are compared or combined into categories, and when the intrusiveness of the procedures may affect the frequency of the behaviors recorded. It is also possible that these problems may systematically interact with experimental conditions. To the extent that they do, results become increasingly difficult to interpret. Since these problems seem to be present in the family intervention studies, results should be interpreted with caution.

   c. *Behavioral   Observation: Baseline.*   Patterson   (1974b) reported that a total deviant behavior score of .45 was maximally efficient in discriminating between children referred for treatment and those not referred. Using this criterion, it is appropriate to ask if the results are based on boys whose baseline total deviant behavior score exceeded .45. In other words, did the baseline behavioral observations indicate that deviant behavior was a sufficient problem to warrant intervention?

In Patterson's (1974b) sample of 27 families, the baseline score was below this criterion level for 12 boys. Interpretation of behavioral observation data is difficult when baseline observations indicate there was not a sufficient problem to warrant intervention in 44% of the sample.

Other studies in which individual data are presented indicate a similar problem. The baseline data presented by Eyberg and Johnson (1974) show that only seven of 17 boys exceeded the .45 score. This problem also raises questions about the results of the two studies which used control groups. Wiltz and Patterson (1974) did not present individual data, and the data presented by Walter and Gilmore (1973) are for *targeted* rather than *total* deviant behaviors. For these reasons, the extent of total deviant behavior at baseline cannot be determined in either study. Finally, the potentially important finding by Arnold *et al.* (1975) that successful intervention generalized to nontreated siblings becomes questionable when it is noted that the mean total deviant behavior scores of siblings were below criterion in 14 of the 27 families.

An inspection of the family intervention studies in which individual data are presented shows that, in a number of cases, the appropriateness of the intervention may be questioned. This is not to say that the .45 score should be construed as an absolute criterion. For referrals whose baseline scores are below .45, several possibilities might be considered: (a) obtain additional baseline data to determine the stability of the behaviors, (b) obtain baseline data at the times and in the situations for which parents report the occurrence of deviant behavior (cf. Johnson, Christensen, & Bellamy, 1976), (c) deviant behavior in the home is not the reason for referral (cf. Reid & Hendriks, 1973), and (d) the parents' expectation for appropriate behavior is unrealistically high. Without additional information on these possibilities, however, a more accurate and fair evaluation of the intervention program would be possible if the observation results were not based on these boys. The question would then become: Is this intervention effective for the children for whom it is most appropriate?

    d. Behavioral Observation: Intervention. Interpretation of the intervention results is problematic due to the lack of control groups in most of these studies. As Kent (1976) has noted, this makes possible interpretations based on motivation, instrument decay, and the reactivity of the observation procedures. The results of those studies with controls are not convincing. For example, Bernal (1975) reported that two boys for whom data were collected but who did not enter treatment, still showed improvement over 6 to 9 months. Neither Walter and Gilmore (1973) nor Wiltz and Patterson (1974) directly compared their treatment and control groups, but instead reported that the targeted deviant behavior of the treatment group significantly decreased while the targeted deviant behavior of the control group did not. In both of these studies baseline data show the control group with a much higher rate of targeted deviant behavior, making results based on a comparison of these groups less convincing.

An additional problem in the interpretation of intervention results is noted by Patterson (1976). He cites an unpublished study (Taplin, 1974) that showed no significant correlation between children's baseline deviant behavior and their parents' schedules of positive consequences for these behaviors. In addition, reduction in deviant behaviors did not follow reduction in parental reinforcement of these behaviors. But most perplexing, during the initial phases of intervention, children's deviant behavior was decreasing while parental reinforcement of these behaviors was increasing.

Given the absence of well-controlled studies, the possible paradoxical relationship between parent reinforcement and child deviant behavior, and the failure to demonstrate significant changes in behavioral observation data in other studies (Bernal, 1975; Johnson & Christensen, 1975), the question of successful behavior changes during intervention must remain open.

e. Behavioral Observation: Follow-up. Interpretation of follow-up data is hindered by the attrition of families. Kent (1976) has analyzed Patterson's (1974b) data for the 16 families who remained through the 12-month follow-up. He found that these boys were significantly less deviant during baseline than those who left the program and were not significantly different from nonreferred children. In addition, the rate of deviant behavior of these boys did not significantly change during the course of the study.

An additional analysis is also possible. If one only considers the 15 boys for whom baseline data indicated that deviant behavior was a problem, nine of the 15 decreased these behaviors by 30% or more during intervention. If one then averages the follow-up data for the maximum time available for these nine boys, four (cases numbered 15, 18, 31, and 45 in Table I) show an increase from their intervention data of at least 30%. Thus, of the original 35, only five boys remained in the program, decreased deviant behavior by at least 30% during intervention, and maintained this lower rate during follow-up. If a similar analysis is used for their siblings (Arnold *et al.,* 1975), the same pattern emerges. Of the 27 families, mean sibling deviant behavior was higher than the .45 criterion during baseline in 13 families; when intervention was terminated this mean sibling rate had decreased by at least 30% in eight of the 13 families; follow-up data of up to 6 months were available for six of these eight families (cases numbered 14, 16, 25, 27, 31, and 35), for which the rate of deviant behavior increased in every family and the mean rate tripled from .20 at termination of intervention to .60 during follow-up!

These separate analyses suggest that those boys whose deviant behavior warrants intervention are more likely to leave the program. Of all those who remain in the program, a significant reduction in deviant behavior through follow-up does not occur (Kent, 1976). For those whose deviant behavior warrants intervention and who remain in the program, many either do not decrease their deviant behavior during intervention, or subsequently increase such behavior during follow-up. Further, a similar pattern occurs for the siblings of these referred boys. Thus, based on behavioral observations, there is little evidence of a treatment effect once intervention is terminated.

Any final follow-up evaluation of this program, of course, cannot be made until what eventually happens to these boys is determined. Preliminary results, however, are not encouraging. Within two years of termination, seven boys to date have been either placed in foster homes or institutionalized (Patterson, 1976).

f. Parent Reports. In addition to behavioral observations by trained observers, parent reports have been used as outcome measures. They have included global ratings, parent daily reports of symptom occurrence, telephone checks, and parent behavioral observations. In a reply to an objection to the use of such measures to evaluate outcome (Gordon, 1975), Johnson and Eyberg (1975) defended these measures as part of multiple criteria measurement in which each measure "may be best employed to complement, clarify, and correct for the others" (p. 918). But have they complemented and clarified results? Most importantly, are parent reports a valid indicator of the child's deviant behavior? Unless they are valid, they are not useful in the correction of other measures.

Studies to date have indicated that rather than complementing and clarifying, the incongruity of parent report measures and behavioral observations has confused the interpretation of outcome. Both Johnson, Bolstad, and Lobitz (1976) and Bernal, Delfini, North, and

Kreutzer (1976) correlated parent ratings, teacher ratings, home observations, and school observations, and found virtually no relationship among these four measures. The Johnson *et al.* (1976) study illustrates the difficulty when different measures yield contradictory results. In this study, behavioral observations were used to illustrate a possible contrast effect, wherein children treated in one setting *increased* their deviant behavior in the other. However, in the one sample where parent ratings were noted, the parents rated the deviant behavior as *decreasing*. If these parent ratings were selected for interpretation instead of behavioral observations, a generalization rather than a contrast effect would have been illustrated.

Discrepancies between observational and parent report data were also noted in two other studies. Hetherington, Stouwie, and Ridberg (1971) investigated differences in family interactions and parental attitudes in families with either delinquent or nondelinquent adolescents. Correlations showed the behavioral measures of family interactions to be unrelated to parental attitudes. Bernal (1975) found no differences in behavioral observation data from pre- to postintervention. When she switched to asking parents by telephone if certain behaviors occurred, significant differences appeared. But she noted that a similar effect occurred in one of her two control cases, i.e., no difference in observation data, but a significant difference as measured by the telephone report of parents.

In an innovative attempt to resolve the lack of agreement between parent reports and observations, Johnson *et al.* (1976) used audio-tapes to assess intervention with five children. Parent reports indicated improvement, while audio-tape observations based on randomly selected times showed no significant change. However, audio-tape observations based on parent selected times (they could turn on the recorder during problem situations) supported the parent reports. This finding was interpreted as evidence for the validity of parent reports. But it seems equally feasible to interpret the results as showing that measures under the control of parents may indicate change, even when measures not under their control suggest no change.

It is possible to interpret this discrepancy between outcome measures as showing that few children improve their deviant behaviors, but a "hello–goodbye" effect alters the parental reports. The latter may be illustrated by help-seeking parents reporting deviant behaviors prior to intervention, but because of the time, effort, and surveillance required by the program, less cooperative parents drop out and the more cooperative parents terminate the program by reporting improvement. In any case, we would do well to heed the advice of Patterson *et al.* (1973) who observed,

> ... the discrepancy between the level of change reported in some of the parent data and the change indicated by the observer data suggests that, while both forms of data may be necessary for a complete evaluation of treatment effects, greater emphasis should be placed on observer data on targeted behaviors as the primary criterion for judging effectiveness of treatment... As a general strategy during the early stage of effectiveness testing, it is probably better to underestimate the degree of outcome success than to overestimate it (pp. 198–199).

The discrepancy between observational and parent report data might be resolved in favor of the latter if it could be shown that these measures are valid indicators of children's deviant behavior. But studies to date do not indicate such validity.

In one of these studies, Novick, Rosenfeld, Bloch, and Dawson (1966) presented procedures to reduce false endorsements in the construction, administration, and scoring of a deviant behavior inventory. Despite these efforts, and the concreteness of the items, they concluded that errors were of sufficient magnitude to seriously question the value of these inventories. In particular, they note that the use of inventories by mothers as a measure of change in therapy may be misleading and erroneous; moreover, such measures may be valid indicators of the mothers' perceptions but should not be construed to indicate the extent of children's deviant behavior.

In addition, a study by Schnelle (1974) is quite enlightening. Following an intervention program to reduce school truancy for youths, rating scales were collected from 23 of the youngsters' parents. The parents of 78% of these youths reported school attendance as very improved or improved, even though mean attendance actually declined. Of these 18 youths whose parents reported attendance as improved or very improved, attendance had actually increased (by at least 2 days a month) in only four cases. That such problems can exist in the family intervention programs reviewed is apparent from the Walter and Gilmore (1973) study. Parents reported that the children improved even when observation data and the parent checklists showed no improvement.

Finally, a useful comparison of global evaluations and behavioral coding has been provided by Kent, O'Leary, Diament, and Dietz (1974). Subjects trained to code video-tapes were led to expect that there would be either no change or a decrease in disruptive behavior during intervention. This expectation had no effect on behavioral coding but did affect global evaluations congruent with the expectation given.

In conclusion, studies of family intervention programs, especially those of Patterson and Johnson and their colleagues, have made a major contribution toward the development of behavioral observation procedures. Their concern for methodological problems, reports of failures as well as successes, and publication of the data of individual cases, is a model for continued research in this area. However, results based on behavioral observation data show that the initial promise of these programs has yet to be fulfilled. Although parent report data present a more positive picture, the validity of these measures is open to question.

D. Community Problems

1. LITTER CONTROL

One of the first of the more general community problems to which behavior modification procedures have been applied is litter control. A prerequisite for the control of litter is, of course, the availability of litter receptacles. Finnie (1973) has shown that the presence of litter cans reduced the amount of ground litter on highways by 29% and in an urban area by 17%. The distribution of litterbags to children during a Saturday matinee movie increased the amount of litter deposited in trash cans from 19 to 31% (Burgess, Clark, & Hendee, 1971). Prompting procedures have also been shown to be effective in some situations. Written prompts telling people where to dispose of their litter increased appropriate litter disposal (Geller, 1973). The distribution of handbills to people entering a grocery store requesting that they select soft drinks in returnable bottles (rather than nonreturnable ones) increased the proportion of such purchases by 25% (Geller, Farris, & Post, 1973).

Contingent reward conditions, however, have been the most effective of the procedures used. They have been shown to reduce the amount of litter in movie theaters (Burgess et al., 1971), zoo grounds (Kohlenberg & Phillips, 1973), housing projects (Chapman & Risley, 1974), on the grounds of a correctional institution (Hayes, Johnson, & Cone, 1975), and in recreational areas (Clark, Burgess, & Hendee, 1972; Powers, Osborne, & Anderson, 1973).

Two problems appear in the findings to date. The first is the low degree of participation of the general population. In most of the studies, participants have been children or college students. In those studies where others might also have participated, few did so and thus greater effectiveness was noted with younger people. For example, Kohlenberg and Phillips (1973) reported their procedures were most effective with persons 10 to 20 years of age; Powers *et al.* (1973) estimated that only four people per thousand participated, of which 70% were students. Hayes *et al.* (1975) have suggested that paying only for planted, marked items reduces littering, since more litter makes it less likely that a given bag of litter will contain a marked item. But presumably such an effect would be limited to those who participate; thus the low rate of participation (25% in their study) limits the utility of such procedures.

A second problem is the finding that effectiveness is maintained only as long the procedures are in operation (Chapman & Risley, 1974). However, when the cost of these procedures is less than the cost of removing the additional litter, it would be economically feasible to maintain the procedures in continuous operation. This is especially possible when additional personnel are not required (e.g., Powers *et al.*, 1973).

2. ENERGY CONSERVATION

Contingent reward conditions have also been shown to be effective in the conservation of energy by increasing the number of people using buses and by decreasing the use of electricity. Using a reversal design, Everett (1973) demonstrated that receiving a 25¢ payment upon entering a bus increased the number of riders. In a similar study, Everett, Hayward, and Meyers (1974) found the use of tokens with back-up rewards increased the number of riders compared to a control bus. Most tokens were exchanged for bus rides. The authors suggested that these procedures might prove economically feasible by either (a) rewarding every Nth bus rider or (b) thorough savings in costs for roads, traffic personnel, etc.

Winett and Nietzel (1975) compared volunteer households that either received information on procedures to reduce usage of electricity or natural gas, or received such information plus cash payments of up to $5 per week, with bonuses of up to $25, for reducing consumption. The incentive group averaged a 15% greater reduction in electricity, but there was no effect for natural gas users. Apparently, the latter finding was because of the higher correlation of gas usage with temperature and because fewer procedures were available to restrict gas consumption. The best predictor of electricity reduction was use during baseline ($r = .54$). This showed that greater reduction can be achieved with those who initially use more electricity. There was no relationship between reduction and environmental attitudes. When the incentive conditions were terminated, however, the difference between groups declined to 8% within 2 weeks, and a 2-month follow-up showed that the groups did not differ significantly.

3. EMPLOYMENT

The lack of sufficient employment is a major community problem. One approach has involved helping low-income groups in developing self-help and problem-solving skills. Miller and Miller (1970) reported that attendance at self-help meetings increased when specific goods, services, and information were offered for attendance. Even with these rewards, however, less than 20% of group members attended any one meeting. More importantly, no evidence was presented that attending meetings helped participants in any way. Indeed, the lack of attendance may indicate that such meetings were unproductive. In a related study, Briscoe, Hoffman, and Bailey (1975) attempted to teach problem-solving skills to low-income members of a community board. The frequency of problem-solving statements during board meetings increased following training, compared to board members who did not receive training. A follow-up indicated that some members maintained the use of these skills while others did not, leading the authors to suggest that "the maintenance of problem solving skills over time may present major problems" (p. 167). It was also noted that no information was available on whether such training helped the board to accomplish its objectives.

A more direct approach is to help people find and keep jobs. Jones and Azrin (1973) presented a view of the employment process as a job information network, in which those who have early knowledge of openings exchange such information with relatives and friends for social rewards. In a procedure designed for people who do not have access to such a network, they found that a newspaper advertisement offering $100 for information on specific job openings resulted in a higher number of job leads and more applicants hired, than an advertisement which did not offer a reward. In an extension of this idea, Azrin, Flores, and Kaplan (1975) formed a job-finding club. Volunteer members included those who were neither employed nor receiving unemployment compensation. Clients were matched on demographic and socioeconomic variables and randomly assigned to either the club or a control group. The club provided assistance with job leads, resumes, interview skills, transportation, vocational choices, time planning, family understanding, and mutual support.

The results favored the 60 club members. After 3 months the data showed more club members found jobs (92%) than did controls (40%), in less time (a median of 14 compared to 53 days), and at higher average salaries. These results, however, were based only on club members who attended more than four sessions. The number of club members excluded by this process was not reported. Although matched controls were also excluded, this procedure does not control for motivation. Thus interpretation of these results is ambiguous. Also, since these procedures do not create jobs, presumably any increase in the employment rate of club members is accompanied by a decrease in employment rate for other job seekers. This would be an important consideration in any attempt to implement this program on an expanded basis.

Two studies have reported efforts to help people keep jobs by reducing absenteeism. Pedalino and Gamboa (1974) used a poker lottery system whereby a card was drawn for each day of work attendance. Each week an employee in each department with the winning hand received $20. Departments which used this system reduced absenteeism compared to other departments. The results are uninterpretable, however, since absenteeism data were not presented for the comparison departments. Moreover, these departments differed in type of work, shifts, and initial absenteeism. In addition, there were motivational differences, since departments whose managers did not request the system formed the comparison groups. In the other study (Hermann, de Montes, Dominguez, Montes, & Hopkins, 1973), six workers who were chronically late for work improved their arrival time when given a bonus of 2 pesos per day for being on time.

Although there are many problems to solve, these procedures should be considered for use in programs to help people released from correctional institutions and mental hospitals find and keep jobs.

E. Conclusion

The results of studies in the community settings reviewed are remarkably consistent. Although not the emphasis of this review, improvements in behavior have been demonstrated *within* institutional, transitional, and community-based programs. These improvements have been noted with psychiatric, correctional, and more general community problems. Many difficulties have arisen in programs where parents were trained in the management of their children's problems. Even in this area, however, some success has been reported, particularly when people other than parents (e.g., probation officials) have implemented programs for these youth.

More important, however, is that the results of studies with follow-up data are virtually unanimous in showing that the improved behaviors are not maintained after the participants either leave the program or it is terminated. This finding was ubiquitous across all types of programs and areas reviewed. Unfortunately, too few studies presented follow-up data and, therefore, it is not possible to know if a general conclusion, across programs, clients, problems, and settings, is warranted. Additional studies which include follow-up data, whether positive or negative, are needed to determine which behaviors are more likely to generalize to postintervention settings and which will require additional generalization-maintenance strategies.

Other reviewers have reached similar conclusions and offered suggestions for the generalization and maintenance of behavior. For example, Kazdin (1975b), in a review of token economy research, suggested the following procedures: (a) train individuals in self-control so that they may manage their own behavior more successfully, (b) train significant others to help maintain the individual's behavior after they leave a structured program, and (c) increase resistance to extinction through the use of fading and partial or delay of reinforcement techniques during the program. Similarly, Jones (1974) suggested training clients to recognize stimulus—response relationships. Conway and Bucher (1976) recommended training mediators such as parents, teachers, and peers, and the use of cognitions to mediate transfer; Atthowe (1973) advocated that a team of professionals and paraprofessionals be formed and given the task of discharging and maintaining patients in the community.

Although these suggestions are constructive and worthy of continued research efforts, a variety of problems indicates that the usefulness of these procedures may be limited. As O'Leary and Kent (1973) have noted, there are few demonstrations that verbal skills can be used to facilitate generalization with adults and no such evidence with children. A recent review of research in the teaching of language to nonverbal children supported the lack of generalization of these behaviors (Harris, 1975). Attempts to train mediators, especially parents, must face the many problems inherent in the task. In a sense, such attempts also simply beg the question, for it is not clear how mediator behaviors are to be maintained. Finally, procedures designed to increase resistance to extinction may merely postpone the extinction, except in those cases where the nontreatment environment can support the improved behaviors given an increase in the time for transition. To accurately predict such cases, more substantial knowledge of nontreatment environments is required. Levine and Fasnacht (1974) also argue that attempts to increase resistance to extinction will make our programs more complicated and less practical; moreover, the use of token systems may hinder such attempts by decreasing the intrinsic value of the behaviors.

The lack of success as measured by postintervention outcome criteria, despite the fine efforts by many investigators in the areas reviewed, may indicate that the appropriateness of such criteria for these programs should be reconsidered. It is possible that additional studies with follow-up data and programmatic attempts to maintain improved behavior are all that are needed. It is possible, but not likely. The family intervention studies represent one of the most meticulous research efforts to date in the areas reviewed. Both follow-up data and a programmatic attempt to maintain behavior through the training of parents have been included, but success continues to be elusive. There is another possibility. Perhaps we have been asking the wrong question. Is it reasonable to expect that the effect of any intervention will generalize to a postintervention setting and improved behavior will be maintained? Is it reasonable even with efforts to use cognition, train significant others, or increase resistance to extinction? Undoubtedly the answer will depend to some degree on the behavior which is the target of intervention. Nevertheless, perhaps programs should be primarily evaluated on the effects within the program setting and not on the generalization of behavior to other settings or future dates. Indeed, perhaps the primary evaluation of whether behavior has been maintained should depend on the assessment of postintervention environments. Such a reconsideration would not alter the appropriateness of the outcome criteria per se, but would shift assessment on these criteria from program to postintervention settings.

Behavior modifiers have often attributed posttreatment deterioration of behavior to environments with contingencies which do not support the improved behavior, but there have been few attempts to document these assertions by actually assessing the posttreatment environment. Unfortunately, there is not sufficient knowledge of such environments or of how to assess them. Research in a variety of areas, however, may increase our knowledge of these environments, supplement within-program evaluation, and offer direction toward the solution of the central problem of the generalization and maintenance of behavior. These research efforts are outlined in Section III.

III. SUGGESTED DIRECTIONS

A. Stimulus Control and Response Clusters

An examination of the stimuli which precede both high and low rates of the target behavior may suggest how such behavior is maintained, as well as how to alter its frequency. Innovative research on this approach has been reported by Patterson and Cobb (1973). Observation data, obtained from both families with referred boys and families with nonreferred boys, indicated that sibling rather than parent behaviors were important stimuli in the control of socially aggressive behavior in boys. This finding suggests that greater emphasis on sibling interactions may be necessary in family intervention programs. Studies by Patterson (1973, 1974a) illustrate the analysis of stimuli for individual case intervention.

In a related approach, behaviors which covary to form response classes or clusters are examined. It is possible that the generalization and maintenance of targeted behaviors may partially depend on their relationship with some nontargeted behaviors. A number of studies have noted that intervention with a targeted behavior apparently altered other behaviors in directions which were not always positive or understandable. For example, when the deviant behavior of six children with severe problems was ignored, new deviant behaviors occurred for each child (Herbert, Pinkston, Hayden, Sajwaj, Pinkston, Cordua, & Jackson, 1973); when the climbing and rocking of an autistic child was punished, eye contact and the imitation of new behaviors increased (Risley, 1968); eye and physical contact of retarded children also increased in response to the punishment of inappropriate behavior (Lovaas & Simmons, 1969); when the initiated speech of a retarded boy to his teacher was ignored, initiated speech to children and cooperative play increased during free play activities, but so did disruptive behavior in another activity (Sajwaj, Twardosz, & Burke, 1972); improvement of targeted oppositional behaviors has resulted in improvement of nontargeted behaviors, such as stuttering (Wahler, Sperling, Thomas, Teeter, & Luper, 1970) and enuresis (Nordquist, 1971). In addition, Wahler (1975b) reported a case in which, as oppositional behavior decreased at home, it increased at school, while Johnson *et al.* (1976) noted that 10 of 15 children treated in one setting (home or school) increased their deviant behavior in the other.

In all of these studies, it is not clear how the nontargeted behaviors changed (see Evans & Nelson, 1977, for a discussion of some possibilities). Further, Wahler (1975b) reported clusters of behavior both at home and at school for two children which remained stable for as long as 3 years, but which did not seem to be related to environmental stimuli. There are no definitive explanations for this paradox at the present time, but the application of the stimulus analysis procedures developed by Patterson and Cobb (1973) might be fruitful. The outcome of such an endeavor might also be helpful in developing procedures to enhance the generalization and maintenance of behavior.

B. Behavioral Norms

1. INTRODUCTION

Epidemiological studies have been conducted to establish the incidence and prevalence of psychiatric symptoms among the general population (Dohrenwend & Dohrenwend, 1972). The development of intelligence tests was based on normative data. But there is surprisingly little information on behavioral norms for particular groups or the incidence and prevalence of problem behaviors in the general population (cf. Evans & Nelson, 1977). Such information may suggest new methods of intervention and would be particularly helpful in deciding whether intervention was appropriate at all. Behavioral norms may also be crucial for the development of generalization and maintenance strategies for nontreatment environments. The utility of behavioral norms is illustrated in answer to the questions posed below.

2. DOES THE PROBLEM EXIST?

When people are referred, it is commonly assumed that some problem exists or otherwise they would not have been referred. Baseline data are typically obtained to indicate the frequency of the problem behaviors, but rarely are these data compared to the frequency of these behaviors among those not referred. Notable exceptions to this practice are studies by O'Connor (1969, 1972), where teacher referrals and behavioral observations were used to identify social isolates in nursery school. Data on intervention strategies, including a follow-up period, then served in the comparison of isolates with nonisolates. Additionally, in other studies nonreferred families have been recruited to obtain data for comparison with referred families (Delfini, Bernal, & Rosen, 1976; Johnson & Bolstad, 1975; Johnson, Wahl, Martin, & Johansson, 1973; Wahl, Johnson, Johansson, & Martin, 1974). In a Head Start project, Melahn and O'Donnell (1976) gathered normative behavioral data through the academic year. When teachers referred specific children, behavioral observations were obtained on the referred child and compared with the normative data. This procedure proved helpful in reaching decisions to accept, modify, or reject teacher referrals.

3. IS THE PROBLEM SPECIFIC TO TIME OR PLACE?

Although once again baseline data are typically obtained to determine the stability of the behavior in question, rarely is similar information obtained for nonproblem situations. Preschool children, for example, were shown to have stable behavior patterns within a setting, but quite different behaviors in other settings (Rose, Blank, & Spalter, 1975). Information on nonproblem situations might suggest different interventions for the problem situation. Even less frequently considered is the periodicity of behavior (McGrew, 1972, Chapter 9). Not much knowledge is currently available on how behaviors vary over daily or weekly periods. Such knowledge could be useful in deciding the "if, how, and when" questions of intervention.

4. WILL IMPROVEMENT OCCUR WITHOUT
   INTERVENTION?

This is perhaps the most crucial question to answer before implementing any intervention strategy. Unfortunately, not much information is available to guide our answers. Shechtman (1970) reported that data extracted from the files of boys and girls seen at a mental health center indicated that the number of symptoms decreased with age. In an epidemiological study, Shepherd, Oppenheim, and Mitchell (1971) found that after 3 years three-fourths of the children considered the most deviant reported fewer symptoms and one-half reported none at all. For children seen at a child guidance clinic, two-thirds improved markedly even though improvement was not related to the specific treatments. The authors concluded that the persistence of behavior problems appeared to be the exception and suggested that the duration of the problem be considered before beginning treatment. The results of the Robins (1974) study indicate that whether intervention is warranted may depend on the nature of the problem. Intervention for the antisocial behaviors of children may be more necessary than for other problems (see Table I in Section II,C,1).

5. INTERVENTION FOR WHICH BEHAVIOR BY WHOM?

Normative data, such as those obtained in the studies referred to in Section III,B,2, can provide a basis for deciding which behaviors may require intervention. When normative data for peers, parents, teachers, and settings are available, a greater variety of possible intervention strategies exists. For example, knowledge of the rates of teacher approval and disapproval for different behaviors (White, 1975) may suggest the simple intervention of placing a child in a different classroom. Normative data on the activities of people who are neither patients nor criminals (Brail & Chapin, 1973; Chapin & Brail, 1969; Chapin & Logan, 1969) may be useful in both the development of measures of psychosocial functioning and generalization-maintenance strategies. Such information on successful former patients and criminals would be especially valuable.

C. Research Design

The proper evaluation of community projects could contribute to both program evaluation and our understanding of the generalization and maintenance of behavior. However, the problems of conducting well-designed research studies in community settings are well known. The impracticality of random assignment in many community settings becomes apparent all too soon to our graduate students armed with split-plots and latin squares and aspiring to conduct research in this area. Levine (1974) has provided a sophisticated documentation of these problems. As a possible remedy he advocated the use of an adversary model, similar to that used in the legal profession, for clinical and field research. This model would be in addition to the experimental method, with each applied to the types of problems for which they are best suited.

Wortman (1975) has argued that randomization may be inappropriate even when it is possible. Randomization may affect results by indicating to participants that they are in an experiment, or by people assuming they were assigned to a control group because they do not need treatment, or by becoming angry that they are not receiving treatment.

Furthermore, Cronbach (1975), in an outstanding article, has suggested that the experimental method may not provide the advancement of knowledge of human behavior that we expect. The large number of variables which seem to influence human behavior may lead to endless qualification where results continuously interact. Time itself may interact with results and thus nullify the conclusions reached during any one period of time. He notes that perhaps conclusions localized for time and place are the best we can achieve. It is possible, however, that instead of results interacting continuously, a state of diminishing returns might be reached where additional variables would not account for additional variance. In the meantime, as Rimm and Masters (1974, pp. 33–34) have pointed out so well, it is necessary to make simplifying assumptions to reduce the complexity of human behavior.

Fortunately, when "true" experimental designs are not possible, or deemed inappropriate, quasiexperimental designs may well serve the purpose for research in community settings (Campbell & Stanley, 1963). The usefulness of these designs has been explicated by Campbell (1969). Statistical analyses appropriate for quasiexperimental designs have been provided by Kenny (1975b). He has illustrated those cases where assignments have not been random, or where people drop out of groups differentially, or where random assignment still produces groups which differ on pretests or baseline. He recommends different procedures depending on how people were selected for experimental and control conditions.

A quasiexperimental design which may prove to be particularly useful for community research in both program and postintervention settings is cross-lagged analysis (Campbell & Stanley, 1963). Kenny (1975a) has presented a test for spuriousness for cross-lagged panel correlation and suggested that it might be used in determining causal relationships between uncontrolled variables.

Excellent examples of the application of quasiexperimental logic in social evaluation research are the studies of Schnelle and Lee

(1974) and Schnelle, Kirchner, McNees, and Lawler (1975). Their discussion of the sources of bias and their plausibility for interpretation illustrate the ingenuity needed in community research.

D. Economics

Another area which may influence the generalization and maintenance of behavior is economics. Economic theory has already contributed to the accuracy of performance predictions in token systems (Kazdin, 1975b). Specifically, performance has been shown to vary with the level of income, savings, and expenditures (Winkler, 1971, 1972).

Economic conditions also appear to be related to admission to mental hospitals. Brenner (1973) analyzed the relationship between manufacturing employment and admission to mental hospitals in the state of New York from 1914 through 1959. Additional analyses extended back to 1841 and up to 1967. After trends were statistically removed from the data, a remarkably stable pattern emerged through these years. In general, an inverse relationship was shown to exist between manufacturing employment and mental hospital admissions. This relationship tended to be stronger for males between 30 and 69 years of age and to reverse for those over 70. Brenner interpreted these findings in terms of economic stress created by economic recessions for those of working age and by inflation for those over 70. Similar patterns, though not as strong, were found for females. In addition, this inverse relationship appeared, as might be expected, for those of marginal or dependent financial status but not for those of comfortable means (Brenner, 1973, Fig. 17). Overall, the correlations for total admissions and manufacturing employment were −.75 for males and −.60 for females (Brenner, 1973, Appendix II).

There is also increasing interest in the application of economic models to the prediction of crime rates. In simplest terms, crime is conceived as a function of the means of legitimate income, the means of illegitimate income, and the probability of punishment (Becker, 1968). An introduction to this literature, with an extensive bibliography, has been provided by Sullivan (1973). In a good example of this approach, Votey and Phillips (1974) presented an economic analysis of property crimes. This analysis was essentially based on the unemployment rates (means of income) of 18- and 19-year-old males and the rates of offenses cleared by arrest (probability of punishment). Various regression equations yielded R^2's ranging into the .80's. In general, predictions were most accurate for larceny and least adequate for robbery.

This type of research shows that a knowledge of local economic conditions might be useful in the prediction of (a) the numbers of people likely to seek help with behavior problems or require the use of correctional programs, and (b) the need for employment programs to prevent behavior problems and criminal activities. Further, when such knowledge is combined with an assessment of the employment skills of those leaving intervention programs, a more accurate prediction of the likelihood of recidivism is possible. It is hoped that such information would be used to support the need for follow-up programs focusing on employment.

E. Ecology

1. INTRODUCTION

The potential contribution of an ecological approach for the generalization and maintenance of behavior has been detailed by Willems (1974). One of several suggestions he made was that the relationship between behavior and its physical context be studied. The study of this relationship has been incorporated in the community center systems developed by Risley, Clark, and Cataldo (1976). These systems include infant day care, toddler and preschool care, recreational programs for older children, and a center to give advice to families on specific problems. This behavioral–ecological system illustrates how different approaches can be integrated in community settings.

Other ideas from ecology may also eventually be useful in this endeavor. In a scholarly review of the history of human ecology in the social sciences, philosophy, the arts, and related applied disciplines, Young (1974) has abstracted ideas common to these fields. One such idea, diversity and stability, might be especially important in the generalization and maintenance of behavior. In ecology, the diverse system tends to be more stable. Thus the stability of behavior may, for example, depend on the diversity of the stimuli to which it is related, the number and variety of situations in which the behavior occurs, the response class of the behavior, the normative rate of the behavior in each situation, etc.

The potential usefulness of an ecological perspective, however, will not be fully realized until the wide variety of nontreatment environments has been assessed. Only then will a determination of the feasibility of environmental intervention be possible. Toward this end, the remainder of this section presents different procedures of ecological assessment and the limited application, thus far, of this type of assessment to crime research.

2. ASSESSMENT

Craik (1971) has presented an overview of five modes of ecological assessment: (a) physical and spatial properties, (b) organization of material artifacts, (c) behavioral activities, (d) traits of environments as assessed by checklists, ratings, Q-sorts, etc., and (e) institutional attributes, including social climate. Modes (a), (b), and (c) seem particularly compatible with a behavioral approach. Mode (d), although perhaps the most frequently used method of assessment, is subject to all of the problems associated with self-report measures.

Within the fifth mode, social climate measures have been developed by Moos (1974, 1975). These scales were constructed from respondents' data in a wide variety of environmental settings (e.g., school, work, family, correctional, community, etc.). Each scale is composed of subscales to assess personal relationships, areas of personal development or growth, and the emphasis on system maintenance and change for each environmental setting. These paper-and-pencil scales can be administered to various groups within a setting (e.g., residents and staff) to assess differing perceptions and study areas of conflict, or used to compare the social climates of different settings. In discussing the relationship of social climate in correctional settings to postinstitutional outcome, Moos (1975) concluded that "there is very little evidence that institutional climate factors (or for that matter any other institutional characteristics) differentially affect more 'objective' post-institutional outcome indices such as parole performance and recidivism" (p. 175). He suggests that the current community setting may influence behavior more than the previous treatment setting. Although the more behaviorally oriented may question the usefulness of these specific scales, they are likely to be in agreement with this rationale for a lack of generalization from treatment to posttreatment settings. Given an acceptance of this rationale, the need for measures to assess environmental settings is evident.

Historically, one of the most popular means of assessing environments has focused on the density of the population in the environmental setting. In general these studies have supported a correlative relationship between density and social problems (e.g., Galle, Gove, & McPherson, 1972; Harries, 1974; Levy & Rowitz, 1973; Zlutnick & Altman, 1972). Since density is also related to many other variables (e.g., social class, income, ethnicity, education, resources, etc.), interpretation of this relationship is difficult. In an attempt to clarify the effect of density, it has been suggested (see Edney, 1974) that perhaps there is a dynamic relationship between territoriality and social hierarchies. In low-density areas each group is dominant in its own territory, whereas in high-density areas dominance would depend on individual social status. Such a relationship would predict that social problems would increase in high-density areas, where territoriality is less possible and where there is no consensus on a social hierarchy. This prediction could become testable with the development of measures of social hierarchies and their assessment in equally high density areas.

The density of a population within an organization has also been shown to influence the participation of its members. As the size of an organization increases, proportionately fewer members participate in its activities (Gump, 1974; Wicker, 1969). This has been interpreted as meaning that more opportunities for participation exist in smaller organizations, since fewer members are available to carry out organization functions. Wicker, McGrath, and Armstrong (1972) have suggested that greater precision in this relationship could be achieved by also considering organization capacity, the number of applicants for positions, and the minimum number of persons required in the organization.

As noted above, assessments which relate the physical context to the behaviors of participants might be most fruitful in integrating a behavioral–ecological approach. One such procedure is behavioral mapping (Ittelson, Rivlin, & Proshansky, 1970), in which behavior is observed and categorized by physical location. This procedure can be useful in describing what activities occur in which locations, in the comparison of different locations or subpopulations, and in testing predictions of how physical design influences behavior. Sanoff and Coates (1971) have used this procedure to assess the relationship between environmental settings and children's play. They suggested that the greater the variety of behavior in a location, the more ambiguous are the cues for appropriate behavior. Behavior modifiers might find this concept useful in the study of inappropriate behaviors.

Several other investigations have also related the environmental context to behavior. Wolf (1966) reported that assessments of home environments correlated .69 with intelligence and .80 with achievement test scores of children. Similar results have been obtained by Marjoribanks (1971), Jones (1972), and Hanson (1975). Although their data were obtained by interviews, a scale based on the coding of the availability of objects to which the child has access has also been developed (Watts & Barnett, 1973). In other studies, noise levels in both home (Cohen, Glass, & Singer, 1973) and school (Bronzaft & McCarthy, 1975) settings have been negatively related to the academic performance of children. In addition, methodologies for the assessment of towns and cities have been developed. For example, Price and Blashfield (1975) factor-analyzed 43 variables across 455 behavior settings in an entire town; O'Donnell and Lydgate (1976) have developed a procedure for coding the physical resources of a city. Such procedures may eventually be useful in studies relating behavior to its physical context.

The least developed, but perhaps one of the potentially most powerful, means of assessing human habitats is economics. Boulding (1970, Chapter 2) defined a habitat as the relative uniformity of the physical environment and the close interaction of all of the biological species involved. In some human habitats (e.g., sections of cities) certain businesses (e.g., bars) are economically dependent on specific subpopulations (e.g., military personnel). A change in the number of members in the subpopulation affects the number of such businesses, which in turn may influence other activities, including social problems (e.g., crime rates), in the area.

These procedures of ecological assessment represent but a beginning in this young field. Clearly, much work in their development— no less in their application—remains. It may be illustrative, however, to consider the application of this type of assessment in one area; thus, a brief example of such an application follows.

3. APPLICATION: CRIME RESEARCH

The general relationship between geographical location and crime rates has been investigated for many years (see Harries, 1974, for a review of these studies). Recently, several research projects have focused on more specific aspects of this relationship. One aspect investigated is the relationship between the rate of specific crimes and surveillance in an area. Ley and Cybriwsky (1974) ascertained that low-surveillance areas of a neighborhood (institution, vacant houses, empty lots) accounted for 26% of the street frontage, but 56% of the neighborhood's stripped cars. This finding supported those of an exploratory study of housing projects (Newman, 1973). In the housing projects, crime rates were higher in low-surveillance areas (e.g., elevators). Crime rates also increased with the number of units in the housing project. This could be interpreted in terms of surveillance, since it becomes more difficult to distinguish between intruders and residents as the number of units increases.

Another aspect is the relationship among environmental variables, maladaptive behaviors, and recidivism. Scales for the prediction of criminal behavior and recidivism have been validated with a sample of released offenders (Barton & Jenkins, 1973; Jenkins, Barton, deValera, DeVine, Witherspoon, & Muller, 1972). The variables assessed in these scales include employment, education, type of residence, contact with family members and friends, financial status, organizational participation, and maladaptive behaviors. Initial results have indicated that predictive accuracy for law violation and recidivism ranged from 66% to 87% (Jenkins et al., 1972). Using a variation of these scales, Wood (1975) found a positive relationship between time spent behind bars and recidivism. Results using the variables assessed by these scales appear quite promising, but await cross-validation with a variety of offender populations. In addition, several studies have shown that employment is associated with lower recidivism rates among prison parolees (Rehabilitation Research Foundation, 1974), those released from transitional facilities (Social Welfare Development and Research Center, 1974a, 1974b), probationers (Wood, 1975), and juveniles (Schwitzgebel & Kolb, 1964). These results indicate that employment should be a major focus of efforts to reduce recidivism among criminal offenders. It would be worthwhile to evaluate the procedures reviewed in Section II,D,3 (e.g., Herman et al., 1973; Jones & Azrin, 1973; Pedalino & Gamboa, 1974) with this population.

IV. A FINAL WORD

In 1971, Krasner (1971, pp. 518–519) predicted that one extension of behavior therapy research would be toward the social environment; principles and procedures of behavior therapy would extend into the social systems of the community and, by the 1980s, give birth to a newer paradigm. The community studies reviewed in Section II bear witness to the thrust of this prediction. These studies have highlighted the problem of the generalization and maintenance of behavior. Postintervention outcome criteria were used to assess these projects, but the virtually unanimous lack of success may indicate that such criteria are inappropriate for these programs. It was suggested that programs should perhaps be primarily evaluated on the effects within the program setting and not on the generalization of behavior to other settings or times.

It was argued that, instead, postintervention environments should be evaluated on the maintenance of behavior; further, the directions suggested by the research outlined in Section III may eventually help in the resolution of this problem and become integrated with the current research of behavior modification in community settings. It is also apparent that, at the present time, pursuit of these research leads yields more potential and direction than solution. Wahler (1975a) expressed it well in concluding his discussion of the integration of behavior modification with an ecological perspective: "this sort of study is apt to be expensive, complex and at first of low yield in terms of clinically useful outcome. In the long run, however, this work will lead to an expansion of treatment techniques, better means of sustaining their effectiveness, better means of predicting unintended effects and, who knows, maybe even a new paradigm" (p. 9).

REFERENCES

Alexander, J. F., & Parsons, B. V. Short-term behavioral intervention with delinquent families: Impact on family process and recidivism. *Journal of Abnormal Psychology*, 1973, **81**, 219–225.

Anthony, W. A., Buell, G. J., Sharratt, S., & Althoff, M. E. Efficacy of psychiatric rehabilitation. *Psychological Bulletin*, 1972, **78**, 447–456.

Arnold, J. E., Levine, A. G., & Patterson, G. R. Changes in sibling behavior following family intervention. *Journal of Consulting and Clinical Psychology*, 1975, **43**, 683–688.

Atthowe, J. M., Jr. Behavior innovation and persistence. *American Psychologist*, 1973, **28**, 34–40.

Azrin, N. H., Flores, T., & Kaplan, S. J. Job-finding club: A group-assisted program for obtaining employment. *Behaviour Research and Therapy*, 1975, **13**, 17–27.

Barton, M., & Jenkins, W. O. *The Maladaptive Behavior Record (MBR): A scale for the analysis and prediction of community adjustment and recidivism of offenders.* RRF 906. Montgomery, Ala.: Rehabilitation Research Foundation, 1973.

Becker, G. S. Crime and punishment: An economic approach. *Journal of Political Economy*, 1968, **76**, 169–217.

Beker, J., & Heyman, D. S. A critical appraisal of the California differential treatment typology of adolescent offenders. *Criminology*, 1972, **10**, 3–59.

Berkowitz, B. P., & Graziano, A. M. Training parents as behavior therapists: A review. *Behaviour Research and Therapy*, 1972, **10**, 297–317.

Bernal, M. E. Comparison of behavioral and nondirective parent counseling. Paper read at the Association for Advancement of Behavior Therapy, San Francisco, November 1975.

Bernal, M. E., Delfini, L. F., North, J. A., & Kreutzer, S. L. Comparison of boys' behaviors in homes and classrooms. In E. J. Mash, L. A. Hamerlynck, & L. C. Handy (Eds.), *Behavior modification and families*. New York: Brunner/Mazel, 1976. Pp. 204–227.

Boulding, K. E. *Economics as a science*. New York: McGraw-Hill, 1970.

Brail, R. K., & Chapin, F. S. Activity patterns of urban residents. *Environment and Behavior*, 1973, **5**, 163–189.

Braukmann, C. J., & Fixsen, D. L. Behavior modification with delinquents. In M. Hersen, R. M. Eisler, & P. M. Miller (Eds.), *Progress in behavior modification*. Vol. 1. New York: Academic Press, 1975. Pp. 191–231.

Brenner, M. H. *Mental illness and the economy*. Cambridge, Mass.: Harvard University Press, 1973.

Briscoe, R. V., Hoffman, D. B., & Bailey, J. S. Behavioral community psychology: Training a community board to problem solve. *Journal of Applied Behavior Analysis*, 1975, **8**, 157–168.

Bronzaft, A. L., & McCarthy, D. P. The effect of elevated train noise on reading ability. *Environment and Behavior*, 1975, **7**, 517–527.

Burgess, R. L., Clark, R. N., & Hendee, J. C. An experimental analysis of anti-litter procedures. *Journal of Applied Behavior Analysis*, 1971, **4**, 71–75.

Campbell, D. T. Reforms as experiments. *American Psychologist*, 1969, **24**, 409–429.

Campbell, D. T., & Stanley, J. C. *Experimental and quasi-experimental designs for research*. Chicago: Rand McNally, 1963.

Carkhuff, R. R. *Cry twice*. Amherst, Mass.: Human Resource Development Press, 1974.

Chapin, F. S., & Brail, R. K. Human activity systems in the metropolitan United States. *Environment and Behavior*, 1969, **1**, 107–130.

Chapin, F. S., & Logan, T. H. Patterns of time and space use. In H. S. Perloff (Ed.), *The quality of urban environment: Essays on "new resources" in an urban age*. Baltimore: Johns Hopkins Press, 1969. Pp. 305–332.

Chapman, C., & Risley, T. R. Anti-litter procedures in an urban high-density area. *Journal of Applied Behavior Analysis*, 1974, **7**, 377–383.

Clark, R. N., Burgess, R. L., & Hendee, J. C. The development of anti-litter behavior in a forest campground. *Journal of Applied Behavior Analysis*, 1972, **5**, 1–5.

Cohen, H. L., & Filipczak, J. A. *A new learning environment*. San Francisco: Jossey-Bass, 1971.

Cohen, S., Glass, D. C., & Singer, J. E. Apartment noise, auditory discrimination, and reading ability in children. *Journal of Experimental Social Psychology*, 1973, **9**, 407–422.

Conway, J. B., & Bucher, B. D. Transfer and maintenance of behavior change in children: A review and suggestions. In E. J. Mash, L. A. Hamerlynck, & L. C. Handy (Eds.), *Behavior modification and families*. New York: Brunner/Mazel, 1976. Pp. 119–159.

Copeland, R., & Hall, R. V. Behavior modification in the classroom. In M. Hersen, R. M. Eisler, & P. M. Miller (Eds.), *Progress in behavior modification*. Vol. 3. New York: Academic Press, 1976.

Craik, K. H. The assessment of places. In P. McReynolds (Ed.), *Advances in psychological assessment*. Vol. 2. Palo Alto: Science and Behavior Books, 1971.

Cronbach, L. J. Beyond the two disciplines of scientific psychology. *American Psychologist,* 1975, **30**, 116–127.

Davidson, W. S., II, & Seidman, E. Studies of behavior modification and juvenile delinquency: A review, methodological critique, and social perspective. *Psychological Bulletin,* 1974, **81**, 998–1011.

Dean, C. W., & Reppucci, N. D. Juvenile correctional institutions. In D. Glaser (Ed.), *Handbook of criminology.* Chicago: Rand McNally, 1974. Pp. 865–894.

Delfini, L. F., Bernal, M. E., & Rosen, P. M. Comparison of deviant and normal boys in home settings. In E. J. Mash, L. A. Hamerlynck, & L. C. Handy (Eds.), *Behavior modification and families.* New York: Brunner/Mazel, 1976. Pp. 228–248.

Dohrenwend, B. P., & Dohrenwend, B. S. Psychiatric epidemiology: An analysis of "true prevalence" studies. In S. E. Golann & C. Eisdorfer (Eds.), *Handbook of community mental health.* Englewood Cliffs, N.J.: Prentice-Hall, 1972.

Edney, J. J. Human territoriality. *Psychological Bulletin,* 1974, **81**, 959–975.

Eitzen, D. S. The effects of behavior modification on the attitudes of delinquents. *Behaviour Research and Therapy,* 1975, **13**, 295–299.

Erickson, R. C. Outcome studies in mental hospitals: A review. *Psychological Bulletin,* 1975, **82**, 519–540.

Evans, I. M., & Nelson, R. O. The assessment of child behavior problems. In A. R. Ciminero, K. S. Calhoun, & H. E. Adams (Eds.), *Handbook of behavioral assessment.* New York: Wiley, 1977, in press.

Everett, P. B. Use of the reinforcement procedure to increase bus ridership. *Proceedings, 81st Annual Convention, American Psychological Association,* 1973, **8**, 891–892. (Summary)

Everett, P. B., Hayward, S. C., & Meyers, A. W. The effects of a token reinforcement procedure on bus ridership. *Journal of Applied Behavior Analysis,* 1974, **7**, 1–9.

Eyberg, S. M., & Johnson, S. M. Multiple assessment of behavior modification with families: Effects of contingency contracting and order of treated problems. *Journal of Consulting and Clinical Psychology,* 1974, **42**, 594–606.

Fairweather, G. W., Sanders, D. H., Cressler, D. L., & Maynard, H. *Community life for the mentally ill: An alternative to institutional care.* Chicago: Aldine, 1969.

Ferber, H., Keeley, S. M., & Shemberg, K. M. Training parents in behavior modification: Outcome of and problems encountered in a program after Patterson's work. *Behavior Therapy,* 1974, **5**, 415–419.

Finnie, W. C. Field experiments in litter control. *Environment and Behavior,* 1973, **5**, 123–144.

Fitzgerald, T. J. Contingency contracting with juvenile offenders. *Criminology,* 1974, **12**, 241–248.

Fixsen, D. L., Wolf, M. M., & Phillips, E. L. Achievement Place: A teaching-family model of community-based group homes for youth in trouble. In L. A. Hamerlynck, L. C. Handy, & E. J. Mash (Eds.), *Behavior change: Methodology, concepts and practice.* Champaign: Research Press, 1973. Pp. 241–268.

Fo, W. S. O., & O'Donnell, C. R. The Buddy System: Relationship and contingency conditions in a community intervention program for youth with nonprofessionals as behavior change agents. *Journal of Consulting and Clinical Psychology,* 1974, **42**, 163–169.

Fo, W. S. O., & O'Donnell, C. R. The Buddy System: Effect of community intervention on delinquent offenses. *Behavior Therapy,* 1975, **6**, 522–524.

Galle, O. R., Gove, W. R., & McPherson, J. M. Population density and pathology: What are the relations for man. *Science,* 1972, **176**, 23–30.

Geller, E. S. Prompting antilitter behaviors. *Proceeding, 81st Annual Convention, American Psychological Association*, 1973, **8**, 901–902. (Summary)

Geller, E. S., Farris, J. C., & Post, D. S. Prompting a consumer behavior for pollution control. *Journal of Applied Behavior Analysis*, 1973, **6**, 367–376.

Gordon, S. B. Multiple assessment of behavior modification with families. *Journal of Consulting and Clinical Psychology*, 1975, **43**, 917.

Greenberg, D. J., Scott, S. B., Pisa, A., & Friesen, D. D. Beyond the token economy: A comparison of two contingency programs. *Journal of Consulting and Clinical Psychology*, 1975, **43**, 498–503.

Gump, P. V. Big schools—small schools. In R. H. Moos & P. M. Insel (Eds.), *Issues in social ecology: Human milieus.* Palo Alto: National Press Books, 1974. Pp. 276–285.

Hanson, R. A. Consistency and stability of home environmental measures related to IQ. *Child Development*, 1975, **46**, 470–480.

Harries, K. D. *The geography of crime and justice.* New York: McGraw-Hill, 1974.

Harris, S. L. Teaching language to nonverbal children—with emphasis on problems of generalization. *Psychological Bulletin*, 1975, **82**, 565–580.

Harris, V. W. *Centers for youth development and achievement: Alternative treatments for troubled youths.* CYDA 1. Tucson, Ariz.: Centers for Youth Development and Achievement, 1974.

Hawkins, R. P., & Dotson, V. A. Reliability scores that delude: An Alice in Wonderland trip through the misleading characteristics of interobserver agreement scores in interval recording. In E. Ramp & G. Semb (Eds.), *Behavior analysis: Areas of research and application.* Englewood Cliffs, N.J.: Prentice-Hall, 1975. Pp. 359–376.

Hayes, S. C., Johnson, V. S., & Cone, J. D. The marked item technique: A practical procedure for litter control. *Journal of Applied Behavior Analysis*, 1975, **8**, 381–386.

Herbert, E. W., Pinkston, E. M., Hayden, M. L., Sajwaj, T. E., Pinkston, S., Cordua, G., & Jackson, C. Adverse effects of differential parental attention. *Journal of Applied Behavior Analysis*, 1973, **6**, 15–30.

Hermann, J. A., de Montes, A. I., Dominguez, B., Montes, F., & Hopkins, B. L. Effects of bonuses for punctuality on the tardiness of industrial workers. *Journal of Applied Behavior Analysis*, 1973, **6**, 563–570.

Hetherington, E. M., Stouwie, R. J., & Ridberg, E. H. Patterns of family interaction and child-rearing attitudes related to three dimensions of juvenile delinquency. *Journal of Abnormal Psychology*, 1971, **78**, 160–176.

Hudson, B. L. A behavior modification project with chronic schizophrenics in the community. *Behaviour Research and Therapy*, 1975, **13**, 339–341.

Hunt, G. M., & Azrin, N. H. A community-reinforcement approach to alcoholism. *Behaviour Research and Therapy*, 1973, **11**, 91–104.

Ittelson, W. H., Rivlin, L. G., & Proshansky, H. M. The use of behavioral maps in environmental psychology. In H. M. Proshansky, W. H. Ittelson, & L. G. Rivlin (Eds.), *Environmental psychology: Man and his physical setting.* New York: Holt, 1970. Pp. 658–668.

Jenkins, W. O., Barton, M. C., deValera, E. K., DeVine, M. D., Witherspoon, A. D., & Muller, J. B. *The measurement and prediction of criminal behavior and recidivism: The Environmental Deprivation Scale (EDS) and the Maladaptive Behavior Record (MBR).* RRF 905. Montgomery, Ala.: Rehabilitation Research Foundation, 1972.

Jesness, C. F. Comparative effectiveness of behavior modification and transactional analysis programs for delinquents. *Journal of Consulting and Clinical Psychology*, 1975, **43**, 758–779.

Johnson, S. M., & Bolstad, O. D. Methodological issues in naturalistic observation: Some problems and solutions for field research. In L. A. Hamerlynck, L. C. Handy, & E. J. Mash (Eds.), *Behavior change: Methodology, concepts and practice.* Champaign: Research Press, 1973. Pp. 7–67.

Johnson, S. M., & Bolstad, O. D. Reactivity to home observation: A comparison of audio recorded behavior with observers present or absent. *Journal of Applied Behavior Analysis,* 1975, **8**, 181–185.

Johnson, S. M., Bolstad, O. D., & Lobitz, G. K. Generalization and contrast phenomena in behavior modification with children. In E. J. Mash, L. A. Hamerlynck, & L. C. Handy (Eds.), *Behavior modification and families.* New York: Brunner/Mazel, 1976. Pp. 160–188. (a)

Johnson, S. M., & Christensen, A. Multiple criteria follow-up of behavior modification with families. *Journal of Abnormal Child Psychology,* 1975, **3**, 135–154.

Johnson, S. M., Christensen, A., & Bellamy, T. Evaluation of family intervention through unobtrusive audio recordings: Experiences in bugging children. *Journal of Applied Behavior Analysis,* 1976, **9**, 213–219. (b)

Johnson, S. M., & Eyberg, S. Evaluating outcome data: A reply to Gordon. *Journal of Consulting and Clinical Psychology,* 1975, **43**, 917–919.

Johnson, S. M., & Lobitz, G. K. Parental manipulation of child behavior in home observations. *Journal of Applied Behavior Analysis,* 1974, **7**, 23–31.

Johnson, S. M., Wahl, G., Martin, S., & Johansson, S. How deviant is the normal child? A behavioral analysis of the preschool child and his family. In R. D. Rubin, J. P. Brady, & J. D. Henderson (Eds.), *Advances in behavior therapy.* Vol. 4. New York: Academic Press, 1973. Pp. 37–54.

Jones, P. A. Home environment and the development of verbal ability. *Child Development,* 1972, **43**, 1081–1086.

Jones, R. J., & Azrin, N. H. An experimental application of a social reinforcement approach to the problem of job-finding. *Journal of Applied Behavior Analysis,* 1973, **6**, 345–353.

Jones, R. R. Behavioral observation and frequency data: Problems in scoring, analysis, and interpretation. In L. A. Hamerlynck, L. C. Handy, & E. J. Mash (Eds.), *Behavior change: Methodology, concepts and practice.* Champaign: Research Press, 1973. Pp. 119–145.

Jones, R. R. Design and analysis problems in program evaluation. In P. O. Davidson, F. W. Clark, & L. A. Hamerlynck (Eds.), *Evaluation of behavioral programs in community, residential and school settings.* Champaign: Research Press, 1974. Pp. 1–31.

Jones, R. R., Reid, J. B., & Patterson, G. R. Naturalistic observation in clinical assessment. In P. McReynolds (Ed.), *Advances in psychological assessment.* Vol. 3. San Francisco: Jossey-Bass, 1975. Pp. 42–95.

Kazdin, A. E. Characteristics and trends in applied behavior analysis. *Journal of Applied Behavior Analysis,* 1975, **8**, 332. (a)

Kazdin, A. E. Recent advances in token economy research. In M. Hersen, R. M. Eisler, & P. M. Miller (Eds.), *Progress in behavior modification.* Vol. 1. New York: Academic Press, 1975. Pp. 233–274. (b)

Kenny, D. A. Cross-lagged panel correlation: A test for spuriousness. *Psychological Bulletin,* 1975, **82**, 887–903. (a)

Kenny, D. A. A quasi-experimental approach to assessing treatment effects in the nonequivalent control group design. *Psychological Bulletin,* 1975, **82**, 345–362. (b)

Kent, R. N. A methodological critique of interventions for boys with conduct problems. *Journal of Consulting and Clinical Psychology,* 1976, **44**, 297–299.

Kent, R. N., O'Leary, K. D., Diament, C., & Dietz, A. Expectation biases in observational evaluation of therapeutic change. *Journal of Consulting and Clinical Psychology*, 1974, **42**, 774–780.

Kleinknecht, R. A. A program for problem drivers. In R. D. Rubin & C. M. Franks (Eds.), *Advances in behavior therapy, 1968*. New York: Academic Press, 1969. Pp. 211–219.

Kohlenberg, R., & Phillips, T. Reinforcement and rate of litter depositing. *Journal of Applied Behavior Analysis*, 1973, **6**, 391–396.

Krasner, L. Behavior therapy. *Annual Review of Psychology*, 1971, **22**, 483–532.

Lerman, P. Evaluative studies of institutions for delinquents: Implications for research and social policy. *Social Work*, 1968, 13, 55–64.

Levine, F. M., & Fasnacht, G. Token rewards may lead to token learning. *American Psychologist*, 1974, **29**, 816–820.

Levine, M. Scientific method and the adversary model: Some preliminary thoughts. *American Psychologist*, 1974, **29**, 661–677.

Levine, M., & Levine, A. *A social history of helping services: Clinic, court, school and community*. New York: Appleton, 1970.

Levy, L., & Rowitz, L. *The ecology of mental disorder*. New York: Behavioral Publications, 1973.

Ley, D., & Cybriwsky, R. The spatial ecology of stripped cars. *Environment and Behavior*, 1974, **6**, 53–68.

Lipinski, D., & Nelson, R. The reactivity and unreliability of self-recording. *Journal of Consulting and Clinical Psychology*, 1974, **42**, 118–123.

Lovaas, O. I., & Simmons, J. Q. Manipulation of self-destruction in three retarded children. *Journal of Applied Behavior Analysis*, 1969, 2, 143–157.

Marjoribanks, K. Environmental correlates of diverse mental abilities. *Journal of Experimental Education*, 1971, **39**, 64–68.

Martinson, R. What works?—Questions and answers about prison reform. *Public Interest*, 1974, **35**, 22–54.

McGrew, W. C. *An ethological study of children's behavior*. New York: Academic Press, 1972.

Melahn, C., & O'Donnell, C. R. Norm-based behavioral consulting with project Head Start. Unpublished manuscript, 1976. (Available from the Department of Psychology, University of Hawaii.)

Miller, L. K., & Miller, O. L. Reinforcing self-help group activities of welfare recipients. *Journal of Applied Behavior Analysis*, 1970, 3, 57–64.

Moos, R. H. *Evaluating treatment environments: A social ecological approach*. New York: Wiley, 1974.

Moos, R. H. *Evaluating correctional and community settings*. New York: Wiley, 1975.

Newman, O. *Defensible space: Crime prevention through urban design*. New York: Collier, 1973.

Nordquist, V. M. The modification of a child's enuresis. Some response-response relationships. *Journal of Applied Behavior Analysis*, 1971, 4, 241–247.

Novick, J., Rosenfeld, E., Bloch, D. A., & Dawson, D. Ascertaining deviant behavior in children. *Journal of Consulting Psychology*, 1966, 30, 230–238.

O'Connor, R. D. Modification of social withdrawal through symbolic modeling. *Journal of Applied Behavior Analysis*, 1969, 2, 15–22.

O'Connor, R. D. Relative efficacy of modeling, shaping, and the combined procedures for modification of social withdrawal. *Journal of Abnormal Psychology*, 1972, **79**, 327–334.

O'Donnell, C. R., & Lydgate, W. Procedures for the coding of physical resources in an urban environment. Unpublished manuscript, 1976. (Available from the Department of Psychology, University of Hawaii.)

O'Leary, K. D., & Kent, R. Behavior modification for social action: Research tactics and problems. In L. A. Hamerlynck, L. C. Handy, & E. J. Mash (Eds.), *Behavior change: Methodology, concepts and practice*. Champaign: Research Press, 1973. Pp. 69–96.

Orne, M. F. From the subject's point of view, when is behavior private and when is it is public: Problems of inference. *Journal of Consulting and Clinical Psychology*, 1970, 35, 143–147.

Patterson, G. R. Changes in status of family members as controlling stimuli: A basis for describing treatment process. In L. A. Hamerlynck, L. C. Handy, & E. J. Mash (Eds.), *Behavior change: Methodology, concepts and practice*. Champaign: Research Press, 1973. Pp. 169–191.

Patterson, G. R. A basis for identifying stimuli which control behaviors in natural settings. *Child Development*, 1974, 45, 900–911. (a)

Patterson, G. R. Interventions for boys with conduct problems: Multiple settings, treatments, and criteria. *Journal of Consulting and Clinical Psychology*, 1974, 42, 471–481. (b)

Patterson, G. R. The aggressive child: Victim and architect of a coercive system. In E. J. Mash, L. A. Hamerlynck, & L. C. Handy (Eds.), *Behavior modification and families*. New York: Brunner/Mazel, 1976. Pp. 267–316.

Patterson, G. R., & Cobb, J. A. Stimulus control for classes of noxious behaviors. In J. F. Knutson (Ed.), *The control of aggression*. Chicago: Aldine, 1973. Pp. 145–199.

Patterson, G. R., Cobb, J. A., & Ray, R. S. A social engineering technology for retraining the families of aggressive boys. In H. E. Adams & I. P. Unikel (Eds.), *Issues and trends in behavior therapy*. Springfield, Ill.: Thomas, 1973. Pp. 139–224.

Patterson, G. R., & Reid, J. B. Intervention for families of aggressive boys: A replication study. *Behaviour Research and Therapy*, 1973, 11, 383–394.

Pedalino, E., & Gamboa, V. U. Behavior modification and absenteeism: Intervention in one industrial setting. *Journal of Applied Psychology*, 1974, 59, 694–698.

Phillips, E. L., Phillips, E. A., Fixsen, D. L., & Wolf, M. M. Achievement Place: Behavior shaping works for delinquents. *Psychology Today*, 1973, 6, 75–79.

Polakow, R. L., & Doctor, R. M. A behavioral modification program for adult drug offenders. *Journal of Research in Crime and Delinquency*, 1974, 11, 63–69.

Powers, R. B., Osborne, J. G., & Anderson, E. G. Positive reinforcement of litter removal in the natural environment. *Journal of Applied Behavior Analysis*, 1973, 6, 579–586.

Price, R. H., & Blashfield, R. K. Explorations in the taxonomy of behavior settings. *American Journal of Community Psychology*, 1975, 3, 335–351.

Rehabilitation Research Foundation. *The post-prison analysis of criminal behavior and longitudinal follow-up evaluation of institutional treatment*. RRF 910. Montgomery, Ala.: Rehabilitation Research Foundation, 1974.

Reid, J. B., & Hendriks, A. F. C. J. Preliminary analysis of the effectiveness of direct home intervention for the treatment of predelinquent boys who steal. In L. A. Hamerlynck, L. C. Handy, & E. J. Mash (Eds.), *Behavior change: Methodology, concepts and practice*. Champaign: Research Press, 1973. Pp. 209–219.

Rimm, D. C., & Masters, J. C. *Behavior therapy: Techniques and empirical findings*. New York: Academic Press, 1974.

Risley, T. R. The effects and side effects of punishing the autistic behaviors of a deviant child. *Journal of Applied Behavior Analysis*, 1968, 1, 21–34.

Risley, T. R., Clark, H. B., & Cataldo, M. F. Behavioral technology for the normal middle-class family. In E. J. Mash, L. A. Hamerlynck, & L. C. Handy (Eds.), *Behavior modification and families*. New York: Brunner/Mazel, 1976. Pp. 34–60.

Robins, L. N. *Deviant children grown up*. Huntington, N.Y.: Robert E. Krieger, 1974.

Romanczyk, R. G., Kent, R. N., Diament, C., & O'Leary, K. D. Measuring the reliability of observational data: A reactive process. *Journal of Applied Behavior Analysis*, 1973, 6, 175–184.

Rose, S. A., Blank, M., & Spalter, I. Situational specificity of behavior in young children. *Child Development*, 1975, 46, 464–469.

Sajwaj, T., Twardosz, S., & Burke, M. Side effects of extinction procedures in a remedial preschool. *Journal of Applied Behavior Analysis*, 1972, 5, 163–175.

Samuels, J. S., & Henderson, J. D. A community-based operant learning environment IV: Some outcome data. In R. D. Rubin, H. Fensterheim, A. A. Lazarus, & C. M. Franks (Eds.), *Advances in behavior therapy*. New York: Academic Press, 1971. Pp. 263–271.

Sanoff, H., & Coates, G. Behavioral mapping: An ecological analysis of activities in a residential setting. *International Journal of Environmental Studies*, 1971, 2, 227–235.

Schnelle, J. F. A brief report on invalidity of parent evaluations of behavior change. *Journal of Applied Behavior Analysis*, 1974, 7, 341–343.

Schnelle, J. F., Kirchner, R. E., McNees, M. P., & Lawler, J. M. Social evaluation research: The evaluation of two police patrolling strategies. *Journal of Applied Behavior Analysis*, 1975, 8, 353–365.

Schnelle, J. F., & Lee, F. A quasi-experimental retrospective evaluation of a prison policy change. *Journal of Applied Behavior Analysis*, 1974, 7, 483–496.

Schwitzgebel, R., & Kolb, D. A. Inducing behaviour change in adolescent delinquents. *Behaviour Research and Therapy*, 1964, 1, 297–304.

Shah, S. A. Juvenile delinquency: A national perspective. In J. L. Khanna (Ed.), *New treatment approaches to juvenile delinquency*. Springfield, Ill.: Thomas, 1975. Pp. 3–23.

Shean, G. A social learning approach to community living for chronic mental patients. *Proceedings, 81st Annual Convention, American Psychological Association*, 1973, 8, 455–456. (Summary)

Shechtman, A. Age patterns in children's psychiatric symptoms. *Child Development*, 1970, 41, 683–693.

Shepherd, M., Oppenheim, B., & Mitchell, S. *Childhood behaviour and mental health*. New York: Grune & Stratton, 1971.

Social Welfare Development and Research Center. *The Adult Furlough Center: Variables related to successful parole*. No. 137. Honolulu: University of Hawaii, 1974. (a)

Social Welfare Development and Research Center. *Liliha House: An in-community residential program*. No. 131. Honolulu: University of Hawaii, 1974. (b)

Stuart, R. B. Behavioral contracting within the families of delinquents. *Journal of Behavior Therapy and Experimental Psychiatry*, 1971, 2, 1–11.

Stuart, R. B., & Lott, L. A., Jr. Behavioral contracting with delinquents: A cautionary note. *Journal of Behavior Therapy and Experimental Psychiatry*, 1972, 3, 161–169.

Sullivan, R. F. The economics of crime: An introduction to the literature. *Crime and Delinquency*, 1973, 19, 138–149.

Taplin, P. Changes in parental consequation as a function of intervention. Unpublished doctoral dissertation, University of Wisconsin, 1974.

Tharp, R. G., & Wetzel, R. J. *Behavior modification in the natural environment*. New York: Academic Press, 1969.

Votey, H. L., Jr., & Phillips, L. The control of criminal activity: An economic analysis. In D. Glaser (Ed.), *Handbook of criminology*. Chicago: Rand McNally, 1974. Pp. 1055–1093.

Wahl, G., Johnson, S. M., Johansson, S., & Martin, S. An operant analysis of child-family interaction. *Behavior Therapy*, 1974, **5**, 64–78.

Wahler, R. G. The decline and fall of the "operant conditioning" therapies. Paper read at the meeting of the Southeastern Association for Advancement of Behavior Therapy, Atlanta, Georgia, 1975. (a)

Wahler, R. G. Some structural aspects of deviant child behavior. *Journal of Applied Behavior Analysis*, 1975, **8**, 27–42. (b)

Wahler, R. G., Sperling, K. A., Thomas, M. R., Teeter, N. C., & Luper, H. L. The modification of childhood stuttering: Some response-response relationships. *Journal of Experimental Child Psychology*, 1970, **9**, 411–428.

Walter, H. I., & Gilmore, S. K. Placebo versus social learning effects in parent training procedures designed to alter the behavior of aggressive boys. *Behavior Therapy*, 1973, **4**, 361–377.

Watts, J. C., & Barnett, I. C. Observing the child's environment. In B. L. White & J. C. Watts (Eds.), *Experience and environment: Major influences on the development of the young child*. Vol. 1. Englewood Cliffs, N.J.: Prentice-Hall, 1973. Pp. 156–174.

Weathers, L., & Liberman, R. P. Contingency contracting with families of delinquent adolescents. *Behavior Therapy*, 1975, **6**, 356–366.

Wexler, D. B. Token and taboo: Behavior modification, token economies, and the law. *Behaviorism*, 1973, **1**, 1–24.

White, M. A. Natural rates of teacher approval and disapproval in the classroom. *Journal of Applied Behavior Analysis*, 1975, **8**, 367–372.

Wicker, A. W. Size of church membership and members' support of church behavior settings. *Journal of Personality and Social Psychology*, 1969, **13**, 278–288.

Wicker, A. W., McGrath, J. E., & Armstrong, G. E. Organization size and behavior setting capacity as determinants of member participation. *Behavioral Science*, 1972, **17**, 499–513.

Willems, E. P. Behavioral technology and behavioral ecology. *Journal of Applied Behavior Analysis*, 1974, **7**, 151–165.

Wiltz, N. A., & Patterson, G. R. An evaluation of parent training procedures designed to alter inappropriate aggressive behavior of boys. *Behavior Therapy*, 1974, **5**, 215–221.

Winett, R. A., & Nietzel, M. T. Behavioral ecology: Contingency management of consumer energy use. *American Journal of Community Psychology*, 1975, **3**, 123–133.

Winkler, R. C. The relevance of economic theory and technology of token reinforcement systems. *Behaviour Research and Therapy*, 1971, **9**, 81–88.

Winkler, R. C. A theory of equilibrium in token economies. *Journal of Abnormal Psychology*, 1972, **79**, 169–173.

Wolf, R. The measurement of environments. In A. Anastasi (Ed.), *Testing problems in perspective*. Washington, D.C.: American Council on Education, 1966. Pp. 491–503.

Wood, Y. A multi-variate analysis of probation adjustment. Unpublished master's thesis, University of Hawaii, 1975.

Wortman, P. M. Evaluation research: A psychological perspective. *American Psychologist*, 1975, **30**, 562–575.

Young, G. L. Human ecology as an interdisciplinary concept: A critical inquiry. In A. Macfadyen (Ed.), *Advances in ecological research*. Vol. 8. New York: Academic Press, 1974. Pp. 1–105.

Zax, M., & Specter, G. A. *An introduction to community psychology*. New York: Wiley, 1974.

Zegiob, L. E., Arnold, S., & Forehand, R. An examination of observer effects in parent-child interactions. *Child Development*, 1975, 46, 509–512.

Zlutnick, S., & Altman, I. Crowding and human behavior. In J. F. Wohlwill & D. H. Carson (Eds.), *Environment and the social sciences: Perspectives and applications.* Washington, D.C.: American Psychological Association, 1972. Pp. 44–58.

DEMAND CHARACTERISTICS
IN BEHAVIOR MODIFICATION:
THE NATURAL HISTORY OF A "NUISANCE"

DOUGLAS A. BERNSTEIN

Department of Psychology
University of Illinois
Urbana-Champaign, Illinois

AND

MICHAEL T. NIETZEL

Department of Psychology
University of Kentucky
Lexington, Kentucky

I. INTRODUCTION

The fact that most human beings live out their lives in a continuous series of social situations is significant in the develop-

ment, maintenance, and modification of behavior. One of the most important of these consequences is the evolution of *rules*. The literature of psychology, sociology, anthropology, and history makes it clear that, though the specifics vary across time, culture, subculture, geographical locale, and class of behavior, social organization is based upon and results in rules which govern, to some degree at least, the activities of its individual members. From a social-learning perspective, social rules may be thought of as summaries of response contingencies which are illustrated and consequated through modeling, reinforcement, punishment, extinction, and related processes (e.g., Bandura, 1969).

Social-learning theorists (e.g., Staats, 1975; Ullmann & Krasner, 1975) also suggest that the cumulative effect of continued contact with general and specific social rules is the patterning of behavior into social *roles*, or ways of behaving which are appropriate to given individuals at given points in time and space (Neiman & Hughes, 1959; Rosnow & Aiken, 1973; Sarbin, 1954; Sarbin & Jones, 1955). The growing child discovers that behavior which is reinforced in one person or in one context may be punished when displayed by another individual or even by the same person in a different situation. This patterning includes learning not only those behaviors appropriate to the role one is "in," but also learning to recognize and respond to the vast array of obvious, subtle, clear, or ambiguous environmental cues, or discriminative stimuli which signal the appropriateness of "entering" or "leaving" a role.

Further, once "in" a social role, individuals' sensitivity to cues regarding appropriate behavior does not diminish; rather, the role "occupant" uses such cues to refine his/her behavior, often to maximize reinforcement in some sense (e.g., Kelly, 1955; Rotter, 1954). For example, a person who acquires the behavioral repertoire appropriate to the college student role not only becomes responsive to environmental cues discriminative for "entering" that role (such as the presence of a professor), but also learns to pay close attention to subtle verbal and nonverbal cues which may aid in the ongoing adjustment of role behaviors designed to maximize reward (e.g., "Since he underlined that name on the blackboard, it will probably be on the exam; I better get it in my notes").

These considerations are relevant to the problem of bringing about and evaluating changes in human behavior, whether the behavior change tactics employed are medical, psychological, or religious and whether the context is that of clinical treatment or laboratory research, because the to-be-changed individual normally is accorded the status of "patient," "client," or "subject" which, like other social roles, is associated with the display of role-appropriate behavior (e.g., Frank, 1973). The typical medical patient who, usually without question, removes clothing, assumes bizarre positions, surrenders bodily fluids, ingests proffered medication, and otherwise displays compliance provides a clear example of behavior appropriate to a role label. As noted earlier for other role "occupants," the "patient," "client," or "subject" is likely to engage in a continuous process of behavioral adjustment based upon the influence of past role-relevant experience, current social cues, and anticipated contingencies. Often, this adjustment process is observed as an improvement in the problematic behavior or condition which led the person to seek help in the first place and, while behavior change as a function of role learning, social cues, and anticipation may be of considerable benefit to the client (Fish, 1973; Frank, 1973), it poses formidable difficulties for the person attempting to evaluate the effects of ameliorative procedures.

The problem, of course, is that many of the social cues to which "patients," "clients," or "subjects" may respond as stimuli discriminative for the appropriateness of behavior change are embedded in the treatment procedures which the change agent wishes to evaluate, thus casting doubt upon the source of observed improvement. Recognition of this problem has resulted in the labeling of the "active" component of a drug or other intervention as its *specific* effect and its impact as a source of discriminative stimuli for behavior change as its *nonspecific* effect (e.g., Honigfeld, 1964; Paul, 1966; Rosenthal & Frank, 1956; Shapiro, 1971).

A. Demand Characteristics as Nonspecifics

Reviews of research on the influence of nonspecific effects in social learning approaches to behavior modification have employed rather narrow labels to describe more precisely what is meant; the most popular terms have been *expectancy effects* (Borkovec, 1973b; Davison & Wilson, 1973; Emmelkamp, 1975; Lick & Bootzin, 1975; Rosen, 1976; Wilkins, 1971, 1973), and *placebo effects* (Borkovec, 1972; Borkovec & O'Brien, 1976; Lick & Bootzin, 1975). Unfortunately, the environmental sources of these effects have not always been clear, easily observable, or uniform. For example, expectancy effects have been attributed to false physiological feedback, pretreatment instructions, veridical feedback on progress during treatment,

face validity of treatment procedures, characteristics of the treatment setting, personal characteristics of the therapist/experimenter,
and subject motivation and suggestibility. Further, as noted by
Borkovec and O'Brien (1976), placebo and expectancy effects are so
closely related that discrimination between them is difficult and, we
would add, probably irrelevant.

Obviously, a certain amount of semantic confusion has resulted
from previous attempts to specify the meaning of "nonspecifics,"
and a unifying concept appears to be required. We therefore suggest
that, because of its flexibility, its emphasis upon social role-learning,
and its focus on potentially observable discriminative stimuli, Orne's
(1962) concept of *demand characteristics* provides the best way to
refer to the full range of nonspecific influences in behavior modification.

A brief description of this concept and of its comprehensiveness
in relation to other descriptors may clarify the reasons for choosing
it as a means of organizing this article. Because his 1962 paper was
focused on the behavior of subjects in psychological experiments,
Orne's early description of demand characteristics appeared somewhat narrow and did not emphasize the broader implications and
applicability of the notion. Thus, the demand characteristics *of the
psychological experiment* were defined as ". . . the totality of cues
which convey an experimental hypothesis to the subject" (Orne,
1962, p. 779). An implication of this formulation was that experimental demand characteristics include all past and present cues
which: (a) are discriminative for entry into the "subject" role, and
(b) convey information about what specific behaviors are appropriate
in the experimental situation.

Orne (1970) subsequently elaborated on the discriminative
stimulus aspects of demand characteristics and, in addition, hinted at
the breadth of the concept:

Much as a green light on the road communicates directly the appropriate behavior to the
driver, and just as a chair in a waiting room calls forth 'be seated' behavior, so the
experimenter's intentions are communicated through his operations. From the subjects'
point of view, these operations serve to define the appropriate behavior, the "right"
behavior, the way one acts . . . [The subject] is behaving in ways that, unthinkingly, he
perceives as correct and appropriate [p. 225].[1]

―――――――――

[1] The issue of whether these cues typically result in subject compliance, apprehensive-
ness, negativism, or other reactions has received considerable attention (e.g., Argyris, 1968;
Cook, Bean, Calder, Frey, Krovetz, & Reisman, 1970; Masling, 1960; Orne, 1962; Riecken,
1962; Weber & Cook, 1972) but is not central to the present discussion.

From this perspective, demand characteristics may be viewed as a generally applicable label for the cues which define appropriate behavior in any social situation, thus allowing one to speak of the demand characteristics of elevators, supermarket checkout lines, used car lots, libraries, and football stadiums as well as psychological experiments, therapy sessions, faith healing services, and medical examinations. The obvious advantage (for our purposes, at least) of this very generalized use of the demand characteristic concept is that the narrower labels commonly attached to "nonspecifics" can be subsumed under it as special cases, specific examples, or consequences.

For example, Orne (1969) has noted that "what are here termed demand characteristics of the experimental situation are closely related to what the psychopharmacologist considers a placebo effect . . ." [p. 164]. Expanding on this theme in the direction pioneered by Frank (1973), it is not unreasonable to suggest that placebo effects are those behavior changes which occur as a function of the demand characteristics (i.e., cues, or discriminative stimuli) associated directly with the administration of any medical, psychological, or religious treatment. In this analysis, expectancy effects differ from placebo effects only in terms of the source of the demand characteristics which produce them. Thus, expectancy effects may be conceived of as changes in behavior which result from discriminative cues which signal the operation of particular treatment-relevant reinforcement contingencies (Borkovec, 1973b; Goldstein, 1962; Rotter, 1954; Ullmann & Krasner, 1975). Such cues are usually provided by all sorts of prior, socially transmitted information (including "role induction" procedures: Frank, 1973; Heitler, 1976; Orne & Wender, 1968) about the nature of the treatment in question, the appropriateness of receiving treatment, the results of previously treated cases, the reputation of the practitioner (or class of practitioners), and the like, all of which allow the person in the role of "changee" to make overt or covert "if-then" statements (e.g., "If I receive desensitization, I will no longer fear the water").

Both expectancy and placebo effects are thus operative in any behavior modification enterprise, but, by focusing on the more general concept of demand characteristics, the importance of naming such effects or determining their relative influence[2] is reduced and the researcher is free to devote his/her energy to the more fruitful and essential tasks of exploring the specific characteristics and

---

[2] Nietzel (1975) has suggested that this activity be called "Name that Artifact."

sources of relevant discriminative stimuli and of developing techniques for their control and/or exploitation (Borkovec, 1975; McFall, 1971; McReynolds, 1975; Nietzel, 1975). We shall return later to the research implications of our conceptualization of demand characteristics. Our present goal is simply to highlight the breadth of the concept and to make it clear that, in what follows, reference to demand characteristics includes all nonspecific influences.

B. The Status of Demand Characteristics in Behavior Modification

The status of demand characteristics in research on behavior modification and every other area of psychology has always been that of an artifact and, as is the case with other artifacts in science (Boring, 1969; Campbell, 1969; Campbell & Stanley, 1963), is defined as a factor which influences dependent variables but is not part of the experimenter's definition or description of the independent variable. Long before Orne (1959) coined[3] his now familiar term, psychologists had recognized and were wrestling with the problem of setting up stimulus conditions (independent variables) that were free of extraneous social cues which might influence animal (Johnson, 1913, cited in Boring, 1969; Pfungst, 1911) and, particularly, human behavior. For example, in 1921 Boring was concerned about a problem in assessing cutaneous two-point thresholds. "If the subject knows that two points are always being placed on his skin, it becomes difficult for him to report a unitary perceptual pattern. . . . Especially is this difficulty present in naive subjects, like McDougall's primitive people in the Torres Straits who wanted to show off their fineness of perception (McDougall, 1903)" (Boring, 1969, p. 3). Reviews by Gibson (1941) and Goldstein (1962) describe the long history of psychologists' awareness of the potential influence of what we would now call demand characteristics in areas as diverse as visual perception, stuttering, interpersonal perception, psychological testing, recall of written and verbal material, frustration, group behavior, serial addition, attitude formation, recognition thresholds for words, gambling, and the attractiveness of activities.

Since Orne's 1962 paper, recognition of and attempts to evaluate or control the influence of demand characteristics have expanded

---

[3] Actually, it was the literal translation of Lewin's *Aufforderungscharakter*, or valence (Orne, 1970).

dramatically. An unsystematic and far from exhaustive scanning of recent psychological literature revealed studies relating to the effects of demand characteristics on attitude change (e.g., Page, 1974; Page & Yates, 1975; Staats, 1969), psychophysical judgment (Anderson, 1975), hypnosis (e.g., Diamond, Steadman, Harada, & Rosenthal, 1975; Orne, 1970; Orne, Sheehan, & Evans, 1968), ratings of therapy outcome (e.g., Blackwood, Strupp, & Bradley, 1975; Kent, O'Leary, Diament, & Dietz, 1974), self-disclosure (Stone & Gotlib, 1975; Wilson & Rappaport, 1974), dream content (Walker & Johnson, 1974), psychological test responses (e.g., Allen, 1970, Strauss & Marwit, 1970), imitation (Hill, 1971; Peterson & Whitehurst, 1971; Steinman, 1970) fatigue (Snyder, Schultz, & Jones, 1974), verbal conditioning (e.g., Page, 1972), self-recording (Nelson, Lipinski, & Black, 1975), interviewee behavior (Matarazzo, Wiens, & Manaugh, 1975), teacher behavior (e.g., Rosenthal & Jacobsen, 1968), encounter group behavior (McCardel & Murray, 1974), pain tolerance (e.g., Chaves & Barber, 1974; Clark & Goodman, 1974; Kanfer, Cox, Greiner, & Karoly, 1974), altruism (Grusec & Skubiski, 1970), GSR conditioning and extinction (Dawson, 1970; Dawson & Reardon, 1969), marijuana intoxication (Cappell & Pliner, 1973), psychological stress (Becker, Horowitz, & Campbell, 1973), obedience/aggressiveness (e.g., Banuazizi & Movahedi, 1975; Berkowitz, 1971; Holland, 1969; Orne & Holland, 1968), human operant behavior (Kaufman, Baron, & Kopp, 1966; Redd, 1974; Redd & Wheeler, 1973), and sensory deprivation (Orne & Scheibe, 1964).

In behavior modification research, concern over and attention to demand characteristics as artifacts have been so intense that individual references are far too numerous to list. Indeed, by providing plausible rival hypotheses (Campbell & Stanley, 1963), demand characteristics are routinely recognized as standing firmly between behavior modification researchers and their ability to draw cause-effect conclusions about the influence of a given intervention (Paul, 1969).

However, this has not been the only perspective on the status of demand characteristics in behavior modification. As noted by McGuire (1969): ". . . at a given time, one man's artifact may be another man's main effect [p. 13]." Accordingly, the argument has been made that, since demand characteristics alone may produce dramatic and often lasting improvement in physical and behavioral problems (e.g., Shapiro, 1971) and since many technically different but equally effective psychological treatments share common non-specific components, it is the influence of the demand characteristics preceding and accompanying behavior modification tactics, not the tactics themselves, which are responsible for beneficial effects (Fish, 1973; Frank, 1973). Whether this argument applies to any or all of the wide variety of apparently "active" social-learning-based approaches to behavior modification (Bandura, 1969; O'Leary & Wilson, 1975; Rimm & Masters, 1974) has yet to be conclusively determined.[4] But the point is that to some observers, at least, the artifact which creates headaches for the researcher has also attained the status of a potentially valuable tool which may materially aid if not supplant other interventions.

This second, nonartifactual aspect of demand characteristics in behavior modification has had, in Sundberg, Tyler, and Taplin's (1973) words, "a long past and a short history." By this we mean that, though the powerful influence of nonspecifics has long been recognized as the major determinant of early (and some modern) medical treatment, faith healing, voodoo death, and various forms of psychotherapy (Frank, 1973), the notion that demand characteristics may be worthy of study, elaboration, and exploitation as a behavior change tactic is of relatively recent origin (e.g., Borkovec, 1975; Craighead, Kazdin, & Mahoney, 1976, Kanfer & Phillips, 1970; Murray & Jacobson, 1971).

This is probably a function of at least two factors. First, demand-as-artifact, like other artifacts, appeared as an obstacle to an attempt at learning about more "basic" phenomena. Thus, there is an understandable tendency to eliminate "contaminated" data or correct for or prevent artifactual influences (McGuire, 1969) while, in the process, paying only enough attention to the problem to get rid of it.[5] Second, there is in behavior modification research and practice a perceptible though not always clearly articulated assumption that, when behavior changes as a function of nonspecific factors, the change is not "real" and significant and/or provides evidence that the client may not have been "really" distressed in the first place (see

---

[4] For example, confidence in existing analogue therapy data supporting the specific action of variants on systematic desensitization and related anxiety reduction tactics appears to be eroding (e.g., Bernstein & Paul, 1971; Borkovec & O'Brien, 1976; Holroyd, 1973) due mainly to a growing awareness of the influence of demand characteristics. The application of increasingly sophisticated research methodology in the area is required before outcome and process questions can be answered unequivocally.

[5] This was the case for a while with such well-known psychological "nuisances" as individual differences (see Boring, 1950), experimenter bias (Rosenthal, 1966), and transference (Wollheim, 1971).

Ullmann & Krasner, 1975, p. 101). This assumption is noticeable, for example, in the method sections of therapy analogue outcome studies where attention-placebo conditions are sometimes described as controlling for the amount of behavior change attributable *merely* to the influence of hope, expectation, faith in the therapist, and the like.

This bias appears similar to, if not an outgrowth of, the traditional reluctance of physicians to examine and exploit nonspecifics in medical practice. The situation in medicine has been summarized succinctly by Shapiro (1960): "When one considers that the normative history of medical treatment, until recently, has been the history of the placebo effect, one is amazed to find a veritable curtain of silence about it" [p. 114]. Ullmann and Krasner (1975) broaden the same point by noting that, "Those who make the greatest use of the placebo reaction often deny its existence. Most published works on abnormal psychology, psychiatry, and general medicine do not discuss placebo responses, and if they do, it is likely to be in terms of control groups" [p. 100].

The consequence of this state of affairs in medicine was to retard understanding of the role of placebos and to delay recognition of the ways in which such influences could best be integrated into professional practice. Nevertheless, that integration has begun to take place, and it is of interest to note that, despite their power, the usefulness of placebos is limited by practical and ethical considerations.[6] As behavior modification researchers begin to turn their attention to the use of demand characteristics as a class of legitimate influence tactics, a similarly beneficial and comparably limited integration appears likely (Murray & Jacobson, 1971).

Now that the dual status of the demand characteristics concept has been outlined, the remainder of this article will examine research relating to each of its dimensions. As indicated earlier, far more attention has been focused upon the demand-as-artifact side of the coin. Our coverage will reflect this both in terms of the number of references cited and in our suggestions regarding improving "anti-artifact" research designs. However, we shall also devote some space to a discussion of research on the as yet underdeveloped potential of

---

[6] Frank lists three conditions in which use of placebos may be indicated: (a) when an active agent cannot be used or is nonexistent, (b) when patients' anxiety over a physical condition aggravates it, and (c) to keep patients in treatment long enough to employ other techniques.

the nonartifactual aspect of demand. We also will speculate about the directions which future work in this area might take.

II. RESEARCH ON DEMAND-AS-ARTIFACT

The major impetus and primary context for investigating the contaminating influence of demand characteristics in behavior modification have been provided by recent analogue research on the effects and underlying mechanisms of social-learning-based anxiety reduction techniques (e.g., systematic desensitization, modeling, and implosion). This type of research has become associated with a fairly standard overall approach. After a variety of initial recruitment strategies, "fearful" individuals are selected for participation on the basis of a behavioral avoidance test (BAT), which involves engaging in a threatening activity (e.g., speechmaking, snake touching). Subjects are then assigned to one of several groups (usually, a treatment-of-interest group, an alternative-treatment or treatment-component group, a placebo-control group, and a no-contact group), and their posttreatment improvement is assessed by a posttest, procedurally similar or identical to the pretest. It is assumed that elimination of anxiety will be reflected by changes in certain specified behaviors observed at the posttest.

Critical appraisals of this literature (e.g., Bernstein & Paul, 1971; Cooper, Furst, & Bridger, 1969) suggest that the degree of fearfulness displayed by analogue participants can be reliably and significantly influenced by demand characteristics stemming from instructions, assessment procedures, and other sources. Thus, changes in BAT behavior may reflect processes other than anxiety reduction.

This notion has triggered a considerable number of investigations relating to three basic hypotheses about the influence of demand characteristics in behavior modification analogue research. The first of these is that BAT performance can be altered by procedural and situational cues associated with the BAT itself. The second hypothesis is that posttreatment BAT improvement may be, in large measure, a function of changes in demand characteristics preceding and/or accompanying repeated tests. The final hypothesis has been that the potency of demand characteristics' influence interacts with subject variables such as level of fearfulness. Specifically, it has been suggested (Bernstein, 1973) that high-fear subjects will be less strongly influenced by manipulation of demand cues than more moderately fearful subjects.

A. Demand Characteristics and "One-Shot" BAT Performance

While the Lang and Lazovik (1963) BAT procedures have served as a prototype for later analogue researchers, many procedural variations have been introduced. These include mode of instructional presentation (live, taped, or written), timing of instruction presentation ("one-shot" pre-BAT presentation, progressive presentation while the subject attempts a graduated series of BAT tasks, or pre-BAT presentation augmented by written instructions which the subject takes to the BAT), nature of instructions ("approach as close as you can" vs. "do only what is comfortable for you"), phobia criterion (proximity to the target object, touching the object, or holding the object), and experimenter behavior (experimenter present vs. absent; experimenter modeling approach vs. no modeled approach). The implicit assumption made by analogue researchers seems to have been that such variation has little or no effect upon generalizability between analogue studies or between BATs and the clinical problems they are designed to assess. However, differences in the presentation and content of instructions can exert a significant influence on subjects' approach toward a feared object.

Prior to administering an initial BAT, Bandura, Blanchard, and Ritter (1969) provided subjects with information concerning the handling of snakes, snake behavior (e.g., tongue flicking), and the way such animals feel to the touch. Following this introduction, 38% of the subjects previously identifying themselves as "phobic" displayed enough approach behavior to be eliminated from further participation in the study. It is interesting to compare this figure with other reports (Robinson & Suinn, 1969; Lomont & Brock, 1971a, 1971b) indicating that none or very few self-reported "phobics" were eliminated on the basis of BAT screening where no background information about snakes was provided.

The context in which BATs are typically conducted is also likely to provide important cues which affect subjects' behavior. In the first place, subjects are usually aware that the research in which they are asked to participate is designed to evaluate techniques of anxiety modification. They are now contacted after having first identified themselves as fearful of certain objects and then screened on the basis of their performance on a BAT. Some degree of "anxious" behavior is thus virtually guaranteed since subjects: (a) have heard the test characterized as a fear assessment whose purpose is to measure their self-reported fear (Fazio, 1969), and (b) are frequently given instructions for the early termination of the test should they become too uncomfortable. These cues may influence subjects to emit what appears to them to be the most socially acceptable response: a substantial degree of avoidance behavior.

The effects of situational cues on fear assessment have been examined systematically by Bernstein (1973). Sixty-two undergraduate females were given a BAT in which a rat was the target object. The test was administered in either a "clinical" or "laboratory" setting. The "clinical" BAT provided clear clinical fear assessment cues while, in the "laboratory," such cues were excluded by embedding the BAT in a fear-irrelevant experiment. Subjects taking the clinical BAT displayed significantly lower approach scores than did those receiving "laboratory" cues. A verbal report measure (Anxiety Differential; Husek & Alexander, 1963) reflected similar differences.

The influence of demand characteristics stemming from BAT instructions has been confirmed by the results of several other investigations. Kazdin (1973) employed a Solomon four-group design to evaluate the effects of pretesting on posttest BAT performance and also the extent to which approach behavior could be modified by instructions alone. There was no evidence for pretest sensitization, but instructions suggesting little avoidance (at pretest) or improvement in performance (on a second test) resulted in significantly less avoidance by instructed vs. noninstructed subjects.

A more direct comparison of the effects of instructional cues is provided by Bernstein and Nietzel (1973). Allegedly snake-fearful subjects were given BAT instructions in either a "personal" or "impersonal" mode. That is, they either heard "one-shot" tape-recorded instructions and were alone in the test room (impersonal) or heard instructions presented "live" by an experimenter who accompanied the subject to the test room and provided cues for attempting each step in the BAT (personal). Approach scores and the frequency with which subjects touched the snake were significantly associated with mode of presentation ("personal" mode subjects approached more closely and touched more frequently than subjects in the "impersonal" mode).

As part of the same study, half of the subjects within each instructional mode condition heard "high demand" requests for approach ("adequate measurement of physiological responsiveness necessitates handling of the snake"), while the other half received "low demand" approach requests ("since the experiment is concerned with natural fear reactions, termination of the test is permitted at any time"). Results indicated that subjects in the low demand condition took significantly longer to touch the snake and displayed more overt motor fear than those in high demand. There were no significant instructional-mode–demand interactions.

Subsequent research involving a partial replication of the high vs. low demand conditions indicated that subjects run under high demand showed more subjective anxiety, more approach behavior, and less overt fear than low-demand subjects (Bernstein & Nietzel, 1974). In that experiment, 17% more subjects would have been labeled "phobic" (i.e., failed to touch the snake) if low rather than high demand instructions had preceded an actual treatment.

Smith, Diener, and Beaman (1974) reported similar results following manipulation of instructional cues on a pretreatment BAT. Participants were 72 students who had reported a high fear of rats on an initial self-report survey and who indicated motivation for treatment. Subjects were assigned randomly to each of the following four BAT instruction conditions: (a) *traditional,* which attempted to provide the instructional orientation encountered in the typical therapy analogue study; (b) *negative demand,* which suggested that approach behavior was neither expected nor desirable in this situation; (c) *positive demand,* which informed subjects that only if they could touch and pick up the rat would they be eligible for treatment; and (d) *reduced demand,* which told subjects that their BAT performance was irrelevant to the upcoming treatment program. Positive demand subjects displayed significantly more approach behavior than either negative or reduced demand subjects. All positive demand subjects were able to complete the terminal BAT task of picking up the rat. Chi square analysis showed the positive demand group to be significantly superior to the other three groups (which did not differ from one another) in terms of terminal behavior frequency.

Similar results on BATs involving small animal and interpersonal targets have also been reported by Blom and Craighead (1974), Eisler, Hersen, Miller, and Blanchard (1975), and Feist and Rosenthal (1973) and, in conjunction with those studies just outlined, they clearly show that BAT participants who are aware of being tested for fear may be responding, to a significant degree, to the demand characteristics present in such a situation, not just to the fear target. Thus, traditionally employed BAT fear assessment procedures described above are reactive (Webb, Campbell, Schwartz, and Sechrest, 1966) in the sense that they are likely to alter the very behavior they are designed to measure.

B. Demand Characteristics Associated with Repeated BAT Assessment

Orne (1962) has noted that ". . . if a test is given twice with some intervening treatment, even the dullest college student is aware that some change is expected . . ." [p. 779]. As mentioned earlier, a fundamental problem in behavior modification research is the disentanglement of the influence of "active" treatment from that of the demand characteristics usually confounded with it. The potency of demand-change influences alone has been estimated in a number of studies which repeat procedurally identical BATs or which simulate pre- to posttreatment increases in cues for improvement in the absence of treatment.

Data on the effects of repeating a BAT with no programmed increase in demand cues are equivocal. In the analogue therapy literature, no-treatment control subjects typically do not change significantly over time (e.g., Bandura *et al.*, 1969; McReynolds, Barnes, Brooks, & Rehagen, 1973; Rimm & Mahoney, 1969) and test-retest equivalence has also been reported in the context of research on repeated testing itself (Bernstein, 1974; Kazdin, 1973). Yet, significant increases in approach behavior across BATs are not uncommon (Bernstein & Nietzel, 1974; Borkovec & Craighead, 1971; Cotler & Garlington, 1969; DeMoor, 1970; Kimura, Kennedy, & Rhodes, 1972; Miller & Levis, 1971; Saxby, 1973).

Nietzel and Bernstein (1975) have provided evidence on this issue which, while supporting the hypothesis that untreated subjects' approach behavior can be increased over BATs through repeated testing alone, also hints at a possible explanation of heretofore discrepant data. Twenty-five female undergraduates who failed on an initial BAT to touch a snake and who indicated a desire for treatment were randomly assigned to one of four no-treatment control conditions via a phone call which offered one of the following rationales for delayed treatment: *excessive volunteers* (too many subjects to permit immediate treatment); *equipment breakdown* (damage to equipment will require treatment postponement); *veridical no-treatment* (temporary assignment to no-treatment condition will delay treatment); and *motivated no-treatment* (temporary assignment to no-treatment condition with cues to the effect that spontaneous improvement might make treatment unnecessary). Three weeks after the initial assessment, all subjects were administered a BAT under the same conditions prevailing at the pretest. Subjects displayed significantly more approach at BAT 2 than at BAT 1. In addition, individual analyses of the significant groups–time interaction revealed that individuals informed of their no-treatment status (veridical and motivated no-treatment groups) demonstrated greater increases in approach than either of the other groups. There were no significant main or interaction effects on self-report instruments.

Of course, these results cannot lead to the conclusion that no-treatment subjects in existing analogue research do not change because they are deceived (even the deceived subjects in the present study showed more improvement than many comparable groups in the literature reviewed) or that all subjects who are told of (or suspect) their no-treatment status are motivated to improve. The data must be viewed with caution because: (a) the sample size is small, and (b) in two analogue experiments (D'Zurilla, Wilson, & Nelson, 1973; Lick & Bootzin, 1970), no-treatment subjects were correctly informed of their group membership and showed no significant posttest approach change. Nevertheless, these data point to the subtlety of the cues which may influence behavior even in a situation explicitly designed to exclude such influence.

Since it is impossible to entirely eliminate demand characteristics from even the "simplest" condition in behavior modification, researchers have begun to assess the maximal effects (on untreated subjects) of changes in demand for posttest improvement.[7] The results of several investigations on demand-change conditions have been quite clear and indicate that posttest cues for improvement are associated with intrasubject differences across repeated BATs which, in some cases, represent change comparable to that following "active" interventions.

For example, in the Bernstein and Nietzel (1974) investigation mentioned earlier, subjects were exposed to two consecutive BATs in which demand for approach was varied by presenting the test as a measure of avoidance (low demand) or an assessment of physiological reaction requiring subjects to handle the target object (high demand). Half the subjects were tested under the same level of demand each time and half under increased or decreased demand. As already noted, the high-demand condition at BAT 1 resulted in more approach and less overt fear behavior. The main effect of repeated

---

[7] Note that this strategy goes beyond traditional placebo control conditions (and the credibility problems associated with them) since no treatment is involved.

testing was also significant for all behavioral measures, with subjects displaying less fear on the second BAT. The treatment—time interaction was significant for behavioral approach, with subjects in all groups other than the high—low sequence group showing significantly more approach at the second test.

In a study on claustrophobia, Miller and Bernstein (1972) demonstrated similar effects. Each of 28 reportedly fearful subjects was confined in a claustrophobia test chamber after hearing instructions which contained high or low demand cues. After the first BAT, each subject was returned to the instruction room, given the other set of instructions, and then retested. The effect of demand level was significant on time spent in chamber (high-demand subjects tolerated longer confinement). It was reported that 11 subjects would have been defined as "phobic" on the basis of low-demand but not high-demand instructions. In addition, it was found that time in chamber changed significantly in accordance with instructional cues, regardless of the order in which they were presented.

Bernstein (1974) reported data suggesting that significant intra-subject increases in BAT approach behavior can be produced by intensifying the demand characteristics contained in BAT instructions or procedures, and that manipulation of both types of cues is no more influential than altering either alone. Five groups of 15 reportedly snake-fearful female undergraduates were administered two BATs. Four groups were tested first under low demand for approach and then under either the same condition or under increased demand, as mediated by instructions, mode of instruction/test administration (personal vs. impersonal), or both. A fifth group was tested under high, then low demand. As usual, subjects first tested under low demand showed significantly more fear than those first tested under high demand. In addition, subjects in all demand-increase groups showed significant approach increases at the second test, while persons in the demand-decrease group displayed a significant reduction in approach. Subjects in the no-change control group evidenced no significant approach difference.

Borkovec (1973a) described two experiments in which subjects reportedly fearful of snakes were administered repeated BATs, first under low demand and again following instructional cues indicating that more approach behavior was likely (i.e., appropriate). In both studies, a significant increase in approach behavior occurred across tests, which (in Study II) was greater than that shown by a no-demand-change control condition. Comparable results have also been reported by Hicks and Shemberg (1976).

Two therapy analogue studies provide additional data regarding the magnitude of demand-change influences. In the first of these, the effects of a tape-recorded variant on systematic desensitization were compared to those of no treatment or a demand-change condition in which subjects were told that ". . . E wanted to disprove the hypothesis that desensitization was more effective than verbal persuasion and that he would greatly appreciate it if the S would go as far as possible toward the snake during the posttest" [Tyron & Tyron, 1974, p. 5]. The desensitization and demand-change groups improved significantly. In fact, the mean improvement in approach was slightly (though nonsignificantly) greater for the latter. Questions can be raised about the adequacy of the desensitization procedures employed in this experiment, but the technique was no more questionable than that of many other therapy analogue studies which, having failed to include a demand-change group, conclude that a given intervention is specifically responsible for beneficial effects (Bernstein & Paul, 1971).

In the context of a more complex analogue study, Nietzel (1973) also assessed the effects of a demand-change condition (which received no treatment but was pretested under low demand and posttested under high demand) relative to systematic desensitization and a placebo control. This experiment will be described more fully later; the aspect of its results to be emphasized here is that the demand-change subjects showed the largest approach increment across BATs of any group in the study.

C. Demand Characteristics and Subject Variables

Evidence reviewed so far makes it clear that demand characteristics can play a significant role in the determination of subjects' responses in behavior modification research. However, to fully explore the implications of this conclusion one must ask about the degree to which the influence of demand interacts with relevant subject variables.

For the most part, research on this issue has focused upon the relationship between demand influence and subject fearfulness[8] and,

---

[8] Sex of subject is another potentially important variable but, to our knowledge, only one investigation (Speltz & Bernstein, 1976) has looked at it systematically. The results indicated that, though absolute performance differed across sex, the demand–sex interaction effect was not significant.

as noted earlier, on the hypothesis that (usually self-reported) "high fear" subjects are less affected by increases in demand for fearlessness than subjects reporting lower fear intensity. Data on this issue come from only a few studies and are somewhat contradictory. Thus, while several investigators have found low vs. high fear subjects to be about equally responsive to demand manipulations (e.g., Bernstein, 1973; Bernstein & Nietzel, 1974; Speltz & Bernstein, 1976), reviews and data supplied by others (e.g., Borkovec, 1973a, 1973b; Borkovec & Glasgow, 1973; Borkovec & O'Brien, 1976; Conger, Conger, & Brehm, 1976; Kelley, 1976; Wilcoxon & Craighead, 1976) appear to support the notion that the behavior of strongly fearful individuals is less malleable through demand.[9]

In spite of the absence of additional definitive data bearing directly on this question, evidence from other sources supports the view that a demand—fear-level interaction is operating in therapy analogue studies. Two experiments are available to show that, when care is taken to select only those subjects whose fear is extreme, manipulation of demand characteristics is not associated with behavior change. Evans (1972) advertised on radio, television, and in newspapers for snake-phobic individuals in the Chicago area and, in order to insure that only strongly phobic persons would be included in the treatment, all subjects (many of whom had traveled great distances to keep pretreatment interview appointments) were told that touching and handling a snake for at least 15 seconds was a required diagnostic procedure which must precede acceptance into the project. Any subject who complied with this requirement was then eliminated from further formal participation.

For the subjects selected in this stringent fashion, Evans (1972) found minimal therapeutic effects for both symbolic modeling and placebo (t-scope: Marcia, Rubin, & Efran, 1969) treatment conditions. Subjects showed no significant reductions in autonomic activity, increased their approach behavior by only a few points, and reported very small decrements in subjectively perceived distress.

The other relevant analogue experiment was designed to follow up on the implications of previously reported effects of variation in pretreatment fear assessment procedures. Nietzel (1973) reasoned that, given the data reported by Bernstein and Nietzel (1973), analogue studies using impersonal BAT subject selection procedures

---

[9] Variations in the definition of "fearful" in terms of self-report vs. physiological arousal may be at the root of this discrepancy (Borkovec, 1973a).

would choose a larger proportion of low-fear subjects ("false-phobics") than studies using personal-mode selection. Further, on the basis of reviews and data reported by Bernstein (1973), Borkovec (1973a,b), Borkovec and Glasgow (1973), and Evans (1972), it was hypothesized that any treatment which generated cues for increased approach at posttest should result in substantial behavior change by low-fear (impersonally selected) subjects. When personal-mode selection is used, the resulting high-fear subjects should evidence behavior change following only those treatments capable of modifying salient fear components.

To directly investigate the effect that differing pretest procedures would have on conclusions regarding treatment effectiveness, 46 allegedly snake-avoidant subjects were assessed for inclusion in an analogue study under two levels of pretest screening: high demand (personal-mode instructions stressing the importance of completing all approach behaviors) or low demand (impersonal mode instructions stressing the acceptability of terminating the test at any time). Subjects from both demand conditions were then assigned to either systematic desensitization or placebo (t-scope: Marcia et al., 1969) treatment. Increases in approach were found for all low-demand groups (including no treatment), while neither high-demand group changed significantly, suggesting that improvement was related more to pretest assessment procedure (and, by implication, initial fear level) than type of treatment.

These results were consistent with Nietzel's (1973) hypothesis and raised the question of whether the obtained relationship between pretest demand characteristics and treatment outcome is a generalized one. If it is, then the pattern of results reported in analogue therapy literature should be predictable from knowledge of the pretest BAT procedures employed. Specifically, one would expect that, in experiments using the generally less fearful subjects selected through low-demand (e.g., impersonal) BATs, few significant between-treatment differences would emerge since all equally impressive interventions would be likely to produce near-equivalent improvement.[10] On the other hand, the number of significant

---

[10] We are eliminating from consideration here all "placebo" or no-treatment control conditions since, as noted by Bernstein and Paul (1971), treatment, placebo, and no-treatment conditions are usually unequal with reference to credibility. In the present context, "treatment" conditions refer to groups receiving basic therapy packages or variations on them.

between-treatment differences should be larger in studies selecting mainly high-fear subjects (via personal-mode BATs). Such individuals appear less likely to be strongly affected by demand cues stemming from BAT instructions or procedures and, thus, would change only in response to "active" treatments (i.e., those which are differentially effective at altering cognitive, physiological, and behavioral fear components).

In order to address this question, we examined 24 studies reviewed by Borkovec (1973b), Rosen (1976), and Wilkins (1973) which compared anxiety reduction interventions supplemented by varying cues for effectiveness ("expectancy" manipulations). These experiments focused mainly on small animals as fear targets. Pretest BATs were classified as "personal" (selecting mainly high-fear subjects) if instructions were administered progressively during the test and as "impersonal" (selecting both high and moderate fear subjects) if instructions involved "one-shot" presentations of either tape-recorded or written information prior to the test.[11] Further, the outcome of each experiment was classified as having demonstrated a demand (i.e., "expectancy") effect if at least one significant difference appeared in pairwise comparisons between treatment groups.

As shown in Table I, 75% of the studies using "personal" pretests found "expectancy" effects while only 25% of the experiments using "impersonal" BATs found such effects (X^2 = 6.24, p <.02). In an earlier review, Nietzel (1973) presented a similar classification of 39 analogue studies (not all of which focused on "expectancy"; only 13 appeared in both classifications) and showed that a significant relationship existed (X^2 = 16.4, p <.001) between pretest demand and number of intertreatment differences obtained.

D. Some Suggestions for Future Research

The experiments reviewed above have repeatedly demonstrated that demand characteristics may pose serious threats to the internal and external validity of behavior modification research. The challenge presented to experimenters by these data is twofold. First, the environmental sources of demand characteristics which are influen-

---

[11] Fourteen percent of the studies were not easily classified into either mode because of insufficient method descriptions or a combination of elements of both modes in selection procedures.

TABLE I

Outcomes of Expectancy Analogue Studies Classified by Mode of BAT Pretest

Studies demonstrating an expectancy effect	BAT mode	Studies demonstrating no expectancy effect	BAT mode
Efran & Marcia (1967)	Personal	McGlynn, Meliea, & Nawas (1969)	Impersonal
Leitenberg, Agras, Barlow, & Oliveau (1969)	Personal	McGlynn & Mapp (1970)	Impersonal
Marcia, Rubin, & Efran (1969)	Personal	McGlynn & Williams (1970)	Impersonal
Oliveau, Agras, Leitenberg, Moore, & Wright (1969)	Combination of both	Howlett & Nawas (1971)	Impersonal
Parrino (1971)	Personal	Lomont & Brock (1971)	Combination of both
Borkovec (1972)	Impersonal	McGlynn (1971)	Impersonal
Miller (1972)	Personal	McGlynn, Reynolds, & Linder (1971a)	Impersonal
Persely & Leventhal (1972)	Personal	McGlynn, Reynolds, & Linder (1971b)	Impersonal
Rappaport (1972)	No pretest	McGlynn (1972)	Impersonal
Tori & Worell (1973)	Personal	McGlynn, Gaynor, & Phur (1972)	Impersonal
Rosen (1974)	Personal	Wilson & Thomas (1973)	Personal
Evans (1975)	Personal	Lick (1975)	Personal

tial in behavior modification research must be identified and described in clear and measurable terms so that the dimensions of the problem can be better understood. Second, strategies and tactics must be developed which will allow researchers to control for or circumvent the effects of demand characteristics and, thus, increase the interpretability of their data. Though progress is being made on each of these fronts, neither challenge has yet been satisfactorily met.

E. Exploring Demand Sources

The problem of adequately operationalizing the concept of demand characteristics is a difficult, though obviously crucial one since to ignore it is to preclude the possibility of doing scientifically respectable experimental research on this artifact (McFall, 1971; McReynolds, 1975; Nietzel, 1975; Underwood, 1957). Yet, since 1962, there has been a growing tendency to reify demand characteristics in behavior modification and use them as explanations of results (McFall, 1971); it is not uncommon to hear or read the suggestion that demand characteristics (or expectancy or placebo effects) caused a given therapy outcome or intergroup relationship. The analogy between this formulation and the one which argues that "mental illness" is a cause of behavior is disturbingly close. A vital anti-reification process would, it seems to us, be materially aided if the collective attention of behavior modification researchers were directed away from demand characteristics as entities. We hope to have contributed to this enterprise through our earlier suggestion that the term "demand characteristics" be used as an umbrella category inclusive of narrower descriptors like placebo and expectancy effects. Though this would not, in itself, increase the specificity of the term, it may stimulate future researchers to concentrate on identification of those observable environmental stimuli which lead to nonspecific effects instead of attempting to show which effects are operating.

Such an approach, in which the focus of attention is not on reified constructs, but upon measurable antecedents, behavioral consequents, and the functional relationships among them, has already proved itself in dealing with other artifacts in behavioral research. [12]

---

[12] It is also, of course, a hallmark of the social-learning approach to behavior in general.

For example, Rosenthal (1966) attempted to understand (and, thus, avoid reifying) the notion of experimenter bias by investigating the antecedents (mainly experimenter characteristics and behavior) which may affect subjects' responses. Not all the factors investigated were equally measurable but their range provides an idea of the details with which one might be concerned. Rosenthal and his students looked at experimenter sex, anxiety, status, need-for-approval, and familiarity to the subject, and then went on to examine general and specific aspects of experimenter behavior. Their methods ranged from collection of subjects' ratings of experimenters to analysis of films and sound tracks of experimental interactions (Friedman, 1967; Rosenthal, 1966). While this extensive program of research has not provided all the answers with respect to experimenter bias effects (Barber, Calverly, Forgione, McPeake, Chaves, & Bowen, 1969; Barber & Silver, 1968a, 1968b; Levy, 1969; Rosenthal, 1968, 1969), it provides an excellent model for how to ask the questions.

Other examples of the usefulness of this approach for the investigation and definition of artifacts are provided by research on the problems of observer bias and reactivity of observation (see reviews and data supplied by Johnson & Bolstad, 1973; O'Leary & Kent, 1973; O'Leary, Kent, & Kanowitz, 1975). The success of these research programs in enhancing methodological sophistication in their respective areas and, sometimes, illuminating behavioral phenomena which are themselves of interest,[13] argues strongly for abandoning mediational models of demand characteristics (e.g.; Rosnow & Aiken, 1973) and adopting instead an antecedent-oriented approach.

The experiments cited in the preceding sections represent the first steps in this direction, but a great deal more needs to be done. For example, we now know that factors such as instructions, physical settings, and incidental characteristics of assessment and treatment procedures may all provide demand cues in behavior modification research, but the list may be much longer and its components could be specified more precisely. Cataloguing and specifying demand sources is only the beginning. Questions about the relative strength of various cues, the range of behaviors they may alter, and the duration of their influence have yet to be fully dealt with in the

---

[13] For example, Rosenthal (1966) found that the experimenter bias effect was reduced or even reversed when experimenters were paid "excessively" to produce such effects.

context of behavior modification. Further, the difficult problem posed by possible interactions between demand cues and subject variables will require continued research attention.

The search for additional sources of demand cues in behavior modification might profitably be guided by existing research on stimuli known to be influential in social situations in general (e.g., Berkowitz, 1975; Wheeler, 1970) and could be executed without conducting extended and expensive outcome experiments. Much can be learned about the locus and potential influence of demand cues through the use of quasicontrol procedures (Orne, 1969) such as the nonexperiment and the use of simulators (Orne, 1962; Riecken, 1962). Though isolated examples have been reported in which these techniques are used to explore the demand characteristics of behavior modification (Lick & Bootzin, 1970; Nau, Caputo, & Borkovec, 1974), the potential of this strategy is, for the most part, untapped.

Another way in which treatment-relevant demand could be investigated without conducting extensive outcome research would be to focus on the relationship between cues embedded in descriptions (i.e., rationales and predictions of success) of to-be-administered treatments and subjects' subsequent verbal and nonverbal behavior. In the past, behavior modification researchers have tended to assume that an isomorphic relationship exists between what subjects are told about treatment and how those instructions affect them, but this may not always be the case (cf., Borkovec & O'Brien, 1976; Rosen, 1975, 1976). We need to know not only which classes of instructional/descriptive cues are influential and how their effects interact with subject variables, but also how the effects of these cues can be independently assessed. The ecological validity of asking subjects simply to "state their expectancies" or rate the "credibility" of treatment descriptions (e.g., Borkovec & Nau, 1972; Boudewyns & Borkovec, 1974; McGlynn & McDonnell, 1974; Rosen, 1975) would appear less than adequate and, though the use of the nonexperiment (Nau et al., 1974) is certainly better, the development of even less obtrusive tactics would be desirable. For example, it would be of great importance to know that, after having heard varying pretreatment information, subjects behave in correspondingly different ways on treatment-relevant dimensions (such as the amount they are willing to pay for treatment or the way in which they describe to family and friends a treatment's authenticity and probability of success). In addition to aiding in the operationalization of demand characteristics, the data generated by this kind of research would also be vital to the evaluation of behavior modification interventions since, without them, precise equation of the stimulus value of treatment, treatment component, and various control conditions would be virtually impossible (Bernstein & Paul, 1971; Borkovec & O'Brien, 1976).

F. Controlling for Demand

Until relatively recently, attempts to provide experimental control for demand characteristics in behavior modification research were embodied almost entirely in the use of "pseudotherapy" or "attention-placebo" control groups of the type pioneered by Lang, Lazovik, and Reynolds (1965) and Paul (1966). The presence of such groups in outcome research designs is now almost a matter of routine and, ideally, is justified by their contribution of a particular kind of baseline against which to measure the effects of other behavior modification packages. However, they do not and cannot carry the entire demand-control burden.

They often do not provide adequate control because experimenters have not always assured that placebo groups provide all the social cues associated with receiving treatment but do not contain plausible treatment components. As a result, some "placebo" groups described in recent outcome literature are so obviously ineffectual as to eliminate all cues except, perhaps, those indicating that no change is expected. Other "placebo" conditions err in the opposite direction by providing what could be viewed as a programmed treatment along with social cues for behavior change. The problem of developing appropriate placebo controls is a difficult one but, as noted in the last section, may be eased considerably by basic research on the stimulus value of these and other treatment and control groups (Borkovec & O'Brien, 1976).

It is, however, also important to recognize that even the most adequate placebo "treatment" package cannot control for all aspects of the demand artifact. For reasons documented above, if subject selection procedures fail to prevent moderately disturbed individuals from participating in a behavior modification experiment, the meaning of pre—post and intergroup differences may be seriously jeopardized. Thus, the use of high-demand pretests or the inclusion of demand-change control groups has been recommended as a supplement to placebo conditions in outcome research, especially of the analogue variety (Bernstein & Paul, 1971). These strategies are designed to minimize the influence of demand characteristics on subjects' behavior or, at least, provide an estimate of the magnitude of contaminating effects.

Another way of controlling for demand characteristics, suggested by the research of Borkovec (e.g., Steinmark & Borkovec, 1974) and McReynolds (e.g., McReynolds *et al.*, 1973), provides a supplement to the demand-control group approach by attempting to assess demand influences in treatment groups themselves. This is done through affirming the consequent (Sidman, 1960), i.e., asking how demand characteristics would manifest themselves in treatment groups if such cues were a major determinant of behavior change.

Thus, prior to administering "active" or placebo treatment for insomnia, Steinmark and Borkovec (1974) told all subjects that they should not expect any improvement until after the fourth treatment session, at which point dramatic benefits would appear. This "counterdemand" period allowed the investigators to estimate within the treatment groups the degree to which cues for no change would overcome the effects of treatment and to look at the interaction between such cues and the type of treatment administered. The results were clear. Only "active" treatment groups improved during the counterdemand period; at its conclusion the placebo group showed dramatic changes.

McReynolds' tactics are related to Borkovec's but focus on the topography rather than the timing of demand influences on behavior change. McReynolds starts with the assumption that the specific action of a given intervention will influence only treatment-relevant target responses but that *nonspecific* factors will alter a wider range of behaviors. Thus, systematic desensitization should, it totally specific in its action, reduce certain anxiety responses but should not alter, say, eye-blink rate. On the other hand, a treatment whose benefits come about entirely as a function of its nonspecifics (discriminative cues) should produce changes in any response class and in any direction described by the therapist (within limits imposed by plausibility, of course).

This reasoning led to the notion that, the stronger the nonspecific component of a treatment package, the more similar its effects should be on treatment-relevant (target) and treatment-irrelevant (nontarget) behaviors *in the same subjects.* The research tactics suggested by this analysis have been employed by McReynolds in two studies (McReynolds *et al.*, 1973; McReynolds & Tori, 1972) in which a version of systematic desensitization, relaxation training, and placebo "treatments" were compared in terms of their ability to influence both anxiety target responses and frustration tolerance (a nontarget response). While interpretation of the results of these particular experiments with respect to illuminating the nonspecific aspects of systematic desensitization is limited,[14] the research model has considerable potential and should be exploited.

Before concluding this section, two additional tactics for dealing with demand characteristics in behavior modification deserve mention. The first of these is designed to allow assessment of target behaviors under conditions where research-related demand characteristics are minimized, while the second attempts a more general moderation of demand cue potency. In order to assess posttreatment behavior change in a manner which is relatively free of cues for display of improvement, McFall (1971) has suggested the use of unobtrusive measures (Webb *et al.*, 1966). In a series of experiments evaluating the effects of various interventions to increase interpersonal assertion (e.g., McFall & Lillesand, 1971; McFall & Marston, 1970), subjects were telephoned by a "blind" assistant and asked to comply with requests ranging from volunteering to stuff envelopes to lending class notes just before an exam The responses of subjects during these calls were analyzed for assertion. This assessment device cannot, of course, eliminate all demand characteristics (the cues associated with the telephoned requests are clear) but, as long as subjects do not identify the call as being related to the experiment in which they had participated, cues discriminative for behavior change may be absent.[15]

Borkovec (1974) has suggested that the best way to minimize demand influences in behavior modification research is to choose treatment targets which are least susceptible to such influences in the first place. The results of a series of experiments (e.g., Borkovec, Stone, O'Brien, & Kaloupek, 1974a; Borkovec, Wall, & Stone, 1974b) designed to identify such targets resulted in the conclusion that speech and social anxiety are relatively uninfluenced by demand cues and, in addition, meet other essential criteria such as clear clinical significance, high frequency in the general population, and appearance of concomitant physiological arousal. While it is not yet

[14] The problem is that an increase in frustration tolerance might conceivably be a legitimate side effect of desensitization. A more crucial test would have involved a nontarget response which was either totally unrelated to anxiety, or which was scheduled to change in a direction opposite to that predictable from theory. Hopefully, such tests will begin to appear.

[15] McFall (1971) has also suggested a way that the telephone strategy can be used as a source of demand cues which may facilitate generalization of treatment effects. This idea and others related to it are discussed in the next section.

clear that this conclusion is entirely correct with respect to speech anxiety at least (Blom & Craighead, 1974), the goal of identifying significant target behaviors which are robust enough to be resistant to the influence of transient social cues is vitally important and needs to be pursued if the quality of future behavior modification research is to improve.

III. DEMAND CHARACTERISTICS AS CLINICAL TOOLS

Earlier, we made mention of the possibility that demand characteristics can be viewed as clinical tools as well as artifacts. This view has been represented previously in McGuire's (1969) analysis of the three stages in the life of any artifact. In the first, or *ignorance* stage, researchers appear unaware of artifactual influence and may persist in denying its existence despite accumulating data to the contrary. In the second stage, ways of *coping* with the artifact are found since denial of its existence is no longer an alternative; investigators begin to develop procedures which can assess, correct or prevent artifactual contamination (coping research with respect to demand has been reviewed above.) In the final, *exploitation* stage, the artifact is heralded as a variable warranting attention in its own right, and it is this aspect of demand which we shall now explore. If as the research presented above would indicate, demand characteristics are powerful enough to alter individual subjects' behavior and even account for the outcome of therapy analogue studies (see also Nietzel, 1975; Rosen, 1976; Wilkins, 1973), their potential role as a means of planned behavior influence in clinical settings cannot be ignored.

The vision of demand characteristics as clinical tools opens up at least three areas in which such cues could be exploited. These include assessment, behavior modification, and the generalization and maintenance of behavior change.

A. Assessment

Demand characteristics may be used to increase the sophistication of behavioral assessments of clinical targets. As an illustration, Nietzel and Bernstein (1976) applied demand manipulations (previously shown to influence subject fearfulness on small animal BATs) to a standard role-playing measure of assertiveness (e.g., McFall &

Marston, 1970). Self-reported unassertive individuals were administered two tests requiring them to verbally respond to a number of tape-recorded situations in which an assertive response would be considered appropriate but difficult for them to perform. Prior to their participation in the first role-playing test, half the subjects listened to low demand-for-assertion instructions (i.e., "please answer by using the words you would actually use if the situation were actually happening to you"), while the other half heard high demand-for-assertion instructions (i.e., "try to be as assertive as you think the most assertive and forceful person could be"). On the second test, half the subjects heard a shorter version of their initial instructions; the other half heard the opposite set of instructions (thereby receiving either increased or decreased demand for assertiveness).

Among other results, the time–group interaction was significant. A more detailed analysis revealed that: (a) groups first run under low demand had significantly lower assertion scores than high demand groups; (b) significant assertion increases were shown by subjects in the low–high demand sequence; and (c) significant assertion decreases appeared for subjects in the high–low demand order. Neither group run under equivalent demand changed significantly. Finally, on the second test, subjects run under low demand showed significantly less assertion than high-demand subjects.

While these results extend previous research on the effects of demand characteristics in behavioral assessments of anxiety, they also suggest a way to clarify the antecedents of social interaction problems like unassertiveness, speech anxiety, and the like.

If it is correct to assume with Bandura (1969) and other social-learning theorists that a behavioral deficit such as unassertiveness reflects some combination of failure to *acquire* skills and failure to *display* those skills (if they are available), determination of the degree to which each of these factors enters into the appearance of a client's presenting problem would seem to be a valuable guide to treatment planning. The intervention strategy for dealing with an individual who has well-developed but inhibited assertive behaviors in his/her repertoire would probably not need to be as extensive as that associated with a person whose unassertiveness is based upon the total absence of appropriate assertive skills (e.g., Goldsmith & McFall, 1975; McFall & Twentyman, 1973).

The sequential use of low and high demand versions of the standard role-playing test employed in the present experiment and in many other assertion studies might provide vital data on the relevant

(Hersen, Eisler, & Miller, 1973) but usually neglected (MacDonald, 1974) acquisition-performance dimension. This would allow the researcher/clinician to assess not only what the client *will* do in response to situations which warrant assertiveness but also what he/she *can* do under maximal demand in the same situations. Clients who display appropriate assertion only under high demand could then be assigned to treatment oriented toward removal of inhibitory factors. Individuals whose assertion remains inadequate, inappropriate, or absent under both demand conditions could be exposed to skill-building experiences instead of, or as a prelude to, techniques aimed at disinhibition.

B. Behavior Modification

Most clinicians would eschew the use of deliberately fraudulent tricks as a means of altering maladaptive behavior, partly because of concern that such procedures are not "real" treatment and that any behavior change produced would be transitory, situation-specific, and tangential to the development of clients' more generalized coping or problem-solving skills. Unfortunately, the same commendable concerns which protect clients from exposure to trivial or ultimately harmful interventions seem to inhibit exploration of the potential usefulness of demand characteristics as behavior modification tools. This state of affairs arises, in part, from what we see as the failure of clinicians to separate two important dimensions which are descriptive of any intervention package: specificity and effectiveness. Evaluation of the *effectiveness* of a behavior modification enterprise can be accomplished in terms of its ability to induce and maintain generalized benefits (Bandura, 1969) quite apart from the degree to which it is *specific* (e.g., functions through the operation of identified principles of learning). The empirically demonstrated effectiveness of any intervention should not, it seems to us, be evaluated in light of the specificity of the treatment involved, but rather in terms of the level of product possible from the research design employed (Paul, 1969).

Another way to say this is that it seems unduly restrictive to argue at this early point in the history of behavior modification that specific and nonspecific change processes are different in any fundamental way. Indeed, it appears more likely that specific effects are those based upon principles we understand while nonspecific effects are based on principles which are less well known. When, through careful and appropriately controlled research, the operative principles of theoretically inert (but nevertheless effective) treatment packages are revealed, those packages will become specific and the functional relationships upon which they are based can be added to an existing body of knowledge about behavior.[16]

Efforts to understand and exploit demand characteristics as adjuncts to or substitutes for other intervention packages have received encouragement (e.g., Craighead *et al.*, 1976; Fish, 1973), but the requisite research has not yet appeared. In the absence of data directly relevant to this problem, we offer a few examples of research in which the role of demand as a therapy adjunct appears obvious. In the anxiety reduction area, for example, it would be useful to explore ways in which demand characteristics might be programmed to maximize the effectiveness of techniques like participant modeling (Bandura, Jeffery, & Wright, 1974) by prompting strongly avoidant subjects to at least enter the treatment setting and providing social cues making fearless cognitive and motor behavior appropriate and fearful avoidance less acceptable. Our multiple case-study level experience with participant modeling thus enhanced by demand characteristics has been gratifying clinically, but appropriate outcome research is required to support any conclusions.

In cognitive and behavioral skill training programs stemming from a number of theoretical models (e.g., Ellis, 1973; Kelly, 1955; Wolpe, 1973), demand characteristics are clearly if not always deliberately programmed as cues discriminative for the performance of behaviors which, though normally low in probability, are vital to the success of treatment. A related use of demand characteristics appears to be involved in various procedures designed to promote and/or disinhibit those more general client behaviors deemed necessary for enhancement of treatment benefits. Role induction (e.g., Frank, 1973; Heitler, 1976) or group structuring procedures (Bednar, Melnick, & Kaul, 1974) provide relevant examples. In each case, clients are exposed to information which clarifies those individual or group behaviors which are appropriate in the treatment setting. The cues employed to convey this information have included oral instructions,

---

[16] This suggestion parallels that made by Bandura (1969) with respect to differentiating treatments which do or do not result in "symptom substitution": ". . . it would be both more accurate and advantageous to redefine the causal versus symptomatic treatment controversy as being primarily concerned with the question of whether a particular form of therapy chooses to modify conditions that, in actuality, exercise *strong* or *weak* or *no significant control* over the behavior in question" [p.50]. An additional parallel is provided by Sidman's (1960) treatment of the concept of "chance" as a determinant of variability in behavior: "To some experimenters, chance is simply a name for the combined effects of uncontrolled variables. . . . If the uncontrolled variables are actually unknown, then chance is, as Boring has pointed out, a synonym for ignorance" [p. 45].

filmed modeling of desired behaviors, behavioral demonstrations, and behavioral practice of structured group activities followed by performance-related feedback (Bednar & Kaul, 1976; Heitler, 1976). Despite procedural differences in the manipulation of such cues, their converging results suggested the following conclusions (Bednar et al., 1974):

First, the clarity with which clients understand the process of group development, group goals, client and therapist role expectations, and the benefits that can result from meaning-ful group participation represents a general parameter of effective group treatments. Second, pretherapy training in which the therapist deliberately and systematically prepares clients for group participation at both a cognitive and behavioral level is an effective and profes-sionally responsible way of obtaining the benefits that can result from clients understanding their roles in group treatment [p. 33].

The potential value of this application of demand characteristics to individual therapy has also been supported by other data (Frank, 1973; Heitler, 1976) and merits further attention.

Whether the effects of demand manipulations aimed at producing behaviors typically absent from a clients' repertoire are limited to those instances in which the client already possesses at least minimal behavioral competences is an open issue. Though recent literature on impression management (e.g., Braginsky, Braginsky, & Ring, 1969; Watson, 1972) suggests that professionals typically underestimate the ability of psychiatric patients to respond to social cues, it should not be automatically assumed that demand manipulations will be rou-tinely effective in altering the behavior of extremely problematic individuals. For example, Lentz (1975) reported that positive impres-sion management instructions had no significant impact on the quality of interview responses by very impaired, chronic mental patients who had a mean of 19.1 years of accumulated psychiatric hospitalization. Seduction by the patient-uniformity myth (Kiesler, 1966) can best be avoided by specifying which types of clients with what classes of behavior problems will be most affected by demand manipulation procedures and, toward that end, factorial research capable of examining the interaction between treatment-adjunct demand manipulations and client characteristics would be welcome.

C. Generalization and Maintenance of Behavior
Change

In order to be fully effective in clinical terms, a behavior modifi-cation intervention must induce significant behavior change which is not only maintained over time, but is likely to generalize to settings and responses other than those with which it was originally associated (Bandura, 1969). However, it is sometimes the case that changes produced by social-learning-based techniques are short-lived, situation-specific, or trivial (e.g., Bernstein & McAlister, 1976; Cooper *et al.*, 1969; Gruber, 1971; Lazarus, 1971), thus underscoring the often emphasized need for incorporating into treatment packages those components likely to enhance long-term generalized benefits (e.g., Baer, Wolf, & Risley, 1968; Bandura, 1969).

The role of demand characteristics in this regard is rather obvious in the sense that competent clinicians usually employ social cues during treatment as a means of facilitating practice (and, hopefully, reinforcement) of newly acquired, altered, or disinhibited patterns of behavior in situations and variations of ever-increasing breadth. Instructions, encouragement, and descriptions of the value, importance, and potential benefits of such practice provide familiar examples of the application of demand to the problem of treatment durability and generality, but a thought-provoking suggestion by McFall (1971) goes a step further.

After demonstrating the value of nonreactive measures of assertion (discussed earlier), McFall (1971) speculated that by informing treated subjects that their assertiveness might be unobtrusively assessed via telephone or other contacts, laboratory-based increments in assertion would be maintained and transferred to the natural evnironment. Specifically, McFall (1971) hypothesized that because subjects could never be sure that future social interactions requiring assertiveness were not "posttests," they would be more likely to behave as if they were still in the laboratory trying to please the experimenter. Though this creative suggestion for turning demand characteristics to clinical advantage and at the same time obviating the need for deception has not, to our knowledge, been tested empirically, it clearly deserves attention, not only because of its possible usefulness *per se* but also because it provides a model for the kind of clinical research strategy needed to fully exploit demand characteristics as clinical tools.

IV. SUMMARY

Our examination of demand characteristics has revealed three "eras" in the natural history of the concept. Initially, demand

characteristics were viewed as ubiquitous sources of artifactual contamination which obfuscated researchers' attempts at precise understanding of "real" phenomena. This persepective's long experimental
history is exemplified by the numerous empirical investigations of
demand-as-artifact which were reviewed.

The second "era" has been one of transition, in which demand
characteristics have been regarded as a set of viable influencers of
behavior which themselves are worthy of theoretical and research
attention. This view has been associated with conceptualizations of
demand characteristics in terms of discriminative stimuli, social rules,
and instructional control. It was suggested that this perspective
allows the integration of demand characteristics into the general core
of social learning theory.

The attribution of theoretical importance to demand influences
has given rise to a third "era" in which demand characteristics are
envisioned as potential facilitators of therapeutic behavior change.
The use of demand as a clinical tool was explored in three areas.
Demand characteristics may be used, first, to increase the sophistication of clinical assessment by clarifying the etiological contributions
of learning vs. performance deficits in fostering clinical problems. A
second contribution of demand characteristics stems from their usefulness as adjuncts to behavior modification that can prompt, encourage, or describe client behaviors which are normally low in
probability but vital to therapeutic progress. Finally, demand characteristics may be employed as cues designed to promote the generalization and maintenance of therapy-instigated behaviors.

Understanding the history of any phenomenon is usually followed by an appreciation of the errors of the past which should not
be repeated. In the present case, one such error was seen to be the
reification of demand characteristics as unchallenged explanations
for confusing outcomes. In the interest of resisting and reversing such
reification, two general recommendations for future research were
offered. First, we encouraged investigations designed to identify
those specific environmental sources of demand characteristics which
affect various parameters of behavior. Second, we outlined ways in
which efforts at circumventing demand effects in behavior modification research could be organized. Among other points, we suggested
that various demand-control strategies will themselves need to
become the subject of basic research. It is hoped that the pursuit of
these empirical objectives will extend the natural history of demand
characteristics and expand our knowledge of them as artifact, theoretical construct, and clinical tool.

REFERENCES

Allen, G. J. Effect of three conditions of administration on "trait" and "state" measures of anxiety. *Journal of Consulting and Clinical Psychology*, 1970, **34**, 355–359.

Anderson, N. H. On the role of context effects in psychophysical judgment. *Psychological Review*, 1975, **82**, 462–482.

Argyris, C. Some unintended consequences of rigorous research. *Psychological Bulletin*, 1968, **70**, 185–197.

Baer, D. M., Wolf, M. M., & Risley, T. Some current dimensions of applied behavior analysis. *Journal of Applied Behavior Analysis*, 1968, **1**, 91–97.

Bandura, A. *Principles of behavior modification*. New York: Holt, 1969.

Bandura, A., Blanchard, E. B., & Ritter, B. J. The relative efficacy of desensitization and modeling approaches for inducing behavioral, affective, and attitudinal changes. *Journal of Personality and Social Psychology*, 1969, **13**, 173–199.

Bandura, A., Jeffery, R., & Wright, C. Efficacy of participant modeling as a function of response induction aids. *Journal of Abnormal Psychology*, 1974, **83**, 56–64.

Banuazizi, A., & Movahedi, S. Interpersonal dynamics in a simulated prison: a methodological analysis. *American Psychologist*, 1975, **30**, 152–160.

Barber, T. X., Calverly, D. S., Forgione, A., McPeake, J. D., Chaves, J. F., & Bowen, B. Five attempts to replicate the experimenter bias effect. *Journal of Consulting and Clinical Psychology*, 1969, **33**, 1–6.

Barber, T. X., & Silver, M. J. Fact, fiction, and the experimenter bias effect. *Psychological Bulletin*, 1968, **70**, (6, Pt. 2), 1–29. (a)

Barber, T. X., & Silver, M. J. Pitfalls in data analysis and interpretation *Psychological Bulletin*, 1968, **70**, 6, pt. 2), 48–62. (b)

Becker, S. S., Horowitz, M. J., & Campbell, L. Cognitive responses to stress: effect of changes in demand and sex. *Journal of Abnormal Psychology*, 1973, **82**, 519–522.

Bednar, R., & Kaul, T. Empirical and conceptual foundations of group work. In M. S. Garfield & A. Bergin (Eds.) *Handbook of psychotherapy and behavior change*. New York: Wiley, 1976.

Bednar, R., Melnick, J., & Kaul, T. Risk, responsibility, and structure: Ingredients for a conceptual framework for initiating group therapy. *Journal of Counseling Psychology*, 1974, **21**, 31–37.

Berkowitz, L. The "weapons effect," demand characteristics, and the myth of the compliant subject. *Journal of Personality and Social Psychology*, **20**, 332–338.

Berkowitz, L. *A survey of social psychology*. Hinsdale, Ill. Dryden Press, 1975.

Bernstein, D. A. Behavioral fear assessment: Anxiety or artifact? In H. Adams & P. Unikel (Eds.), *Issues and trends in behavior therapy*. Springfield, Ill.: Thomas, 1973. Pp. 225–267.

Bernstein, D. A. Manipulation of avoidance behavior as a function of increased or decreased demand on repeated behavioral tests. *Journal of Consulting and Clinical Psychology*, 1974, **42**, 896–900.

Bernstein, D. A., & McAlister, A. The modification of smoking behavior: Progress and problems. *Addictive Behaviors*, 1976, **1**, 89–102.

Bernstein, D. A., & Nietzel, M. T. Procedural variation in behavioral avoidance tests. *Journal of Consulting and Clinical Psychology*, 1973, **41**, 165–174.

Bernstein, D. A., & Nietzel, M. T. Behavioral avoidance tests: The effects of demand characteristics and repeated measures on two types of subjects. *Behavior Therapy*, 1974, **5**, 183–192.

Bernstein, D. A., & Paul, G. L. Some comments on therapy analogue research with small animal "phobias." *Journal of Behavior Therapy and Experimental Psychiatry*, 1971, **2**, 225–237.

Blackwood, G. L., Strupp, H. H., & Bradley, L. A. Effects of prognostic information on global ratings of psychotherapy outcome. *Journal of Consulting and Clinical Psychology*, 1975, **43**, 810–815.

Blom, B. E., & Craighead, W. E. The effects of instructional demand on indices of speech anxiety. *Journal of Abnormal Psychology*, 1974, **83**, 667–674.

Boring, E. G. *A history of experimental psychology*. (2nd ed.) New York: Appleton, 1950.

Boring, E. G. Perspective: Artifact and control. In R. Rosenthal & R. L. Rosnow (Eds.), *Artifact in behavioral research*. New York: Academic Press, 1969. Pp. 1–11.

Borkovec, T. D. The role of placebo, expectancy, and physiological feedback: Demand characteristics in analogue fear studies with implications for outcome research. Paper read at the Purdue Psychotherapy Symposium, West Lafayette, Indiana, April 1972.

Borkovec, T. D. The effects of instructional suggestions and physiological cues on analogue fear. *Behavior Therapy*, 1973, **4**, 185–192. (a)

Borkovec, T. D. The role of expectancy and physiological feedback in fear research: A review with special reference to subject characteristics. *Behavior Therapy*, 1973, **4**, 491–505. (b)

Borkovec, T. D. Toward improving analogue therapy outcome research. Paper read at the Midwestern Psychological Association, Chicago, May 1974.

Borkovec, T. D. Expectancy: demand for improvement and/or cognitive set. In Douglas A. Bernstein (Chm.), Expectancy effects in behavior change research. Symposium presented at the Association for Advancement of Behavior Therapy, San Francisco, December 1975.

Borkovec, T. D., & Craighead, W. E. The comparison of the two methods of assessing fear and avoidance behavior. *Behaviour Research and Therapy*, 1971, **9**, 285–291.

Borkovec, T. D., & Glasgow, R. E. Boundary conditions of false heart-rate feedback effects on avoidance behavior: A resolution of discrepant results. *Behaviour Research and Therapy*, 1973, **11**, 171–178.

Borkovec, T. D., & Nau, S. D. Credibility of analogue therapy rationales. *Journal of Behavior Therapy and Experimental Psychiatry*, 1972, **3**, 257–260.

Borkovec, T. D., & O'Brien, G. T. Methodological and target behavior issues in analogue therapy outcome research. In M. Hersen, R. M. Eisler, & P. M. Miller (Eds.), *Progress in behavior modification*, Vol. 3. New York: Academic Press, 1976.

Borkovec, T. D., Stone, N. M., O'Brien, G. T., & Kaloupek, D. G. Evaluation of a clinically relevant target behavior for analogue outcome research. *Behavior Therapy*, 1974, **5**, 504–514. (a)

Borkovec, T. D., Wall, R. L., & Stone, N. M. False physiological feedback and the maintenance of speech anxiety. *Journal of Abnormal Psychology*, 1974, **83**, 164–168. (b)

Boudewyns, P. A., & Borkovec, T. D. Credibility of psychotherapy and placebo therapy rationales. *V. A. Newsletter for Research in Mental Health and Behavioral Sciences*, 1974, **16**, 15–18.

Braginsky, B. M., Braginsky, D. D., & Ring, K. *Methods of madness*. New York: Holt, 1969.

Campbell, D. T. Prospective: Artifact and control. In R. Rosenthal & R. L. Rosnow (Eds.), *Artifact in behavioral research*. New York: Academic Press, 1969. Pp. 351–382.

Campbell, D. T., & Stanley, J. C. Experimental and quasi-experimental designs for research on teaching. In N. L. Gage (Ed.), *Handbook of research on teaching*. Chicago: Rand McNally, 1963. Pp. 171–246.

Cappell, H. D., & Pliner, P. L. Volitional control of marijuana intoxication: a study of the ability to "come down" on command. *Journal of Abnormal Psychology*, 1973, **82**, 428–434.

Chaves, J. F., & Barber, T. X. Cognitive strategies, experimenter modeling, and expectation in the attentuation of pain. *Journal of Abnormal Psychology*, 1974, **83**, 356–363.

Clark, W. C., & Goodman, J. S. Effects of suggestion on d' and C_x for pain detection and pain tolerance. *Journal of Abnormal Psychology*, 1974, **83**, 364–372.

Conger, J. C., Conger, A. J., & Brehm, S. Fear level as a moderator of false feedback effects in snake phobics. *Journal of Consulting and Clinical Psychology*, 1976, **44**, 135–141.

Cook, T. D., Bean, J. R., Calder, B. J., Frey, R., Krovetz, M. L., & Reisman, S. R. Demand characteristics and three conceptions of the frequently deceived subject. *Journal of Personality and Social Psychology*, 1970, **14**, 185–194.

Cooper, A., Furst, J. B., & Bridger, W. H. A brief commentary on the usefulness of studying fear of snakes. *Journal of Abnormal Psychology*, 1969, **74**, 413–414.

Cotler, S. B., & Garlington, W. K. The generalization of anxiety reduction following systematic desensitization of snake anxiety. *Behaviour Research and Therapy*, 1969, **7**, 35–40.

Craighead, W. E., Kazdin, A. E., & Mahoney, M. J. (Eds.) *Behavior modification: Principles, issues, and applications.* Boston: Houghton, Mifflin, 1976.

Davison, G., & Wilson, G. T. Processes of fear-reduction in systematic desensitization: Cognitive and social reinforcement factors in humans. *Behavior Therapy*, 1973, **4**, 1–21.

Dawson, M. E. Cognition and conditioning: Effects of masking the CS-UCS contingency on human GSR classical conditioning. *Journal of Experimental Psychology*, 1970, **85**, 389–396.

Dawson, M. E., & Reardon, P. Effects of facilitory and inhibitory sets on GSR conditioning and extinction. *Journal of Experimental Psychology*, 1969, **82**, 462–466.

DeMoor, W. Systematic desensitization versus prolonged high intensity stimulation (flooding). *Journal of Behavior Therapy and Experimental Psychiatry*, 1970, **1**, 45–52.

Diamond, M. J., Steadman, C., Harada, D., & Rosenthal, J. The use of direct instructions to modify hypnotic performance: The effects of programmed learning procedures. *Journal of Abnormal Psychology*, 1975, **84**, 109–113.

D'Zurilla, T. J., Wilson, G. T., & Nelson, L. A preliminary study of the effectiveness of graduated prolonged exposure in the treatment of irrational fear. *Behavior Therapy*, 1973, **4**, 672–685.

Efran, J. S., & Marcia, J. E. Treatment of fears by expectancy manipulation: An exploratory investigation. *Proceedings of the 75th Annual Convention of the American Psychological Association*, 1967, **2**, 239–240.

Eisler, R. M., Hersen, M., Miller, P. M., & Blanchard, E. B. Situational determinants of assertive behaviors. *Journal of Consulting and Clinical Psychology*, 1975, **43**, 330–340.

Ellis, A. *Humanistic psychotherapy.* New York: McGraw-Hill, 1973.

Emmelkamp, P. M. G. Effects of expectancy on systematic desensitization and flooding. *European Journal of Behavioral Analysis and Modification*, 1975, **1**, 1–11.

Evans, M. B. The relative effects of treatment specific and demand characteristic variables in the pre-post behavior therapy outcome research paradigm. Unpublished doctoral dissertation, University of Illinois, 1972.

Evans, M. B. Procedures for a high demand behavioral avoidance test and for a diagnosis/treatment subject expectancy manipulation: brief note. *Behavior Therapy*, 1975, **6**, 72–77.

Fazio, A. F. Verbal and overt-behavioral assessment of a specific fear. *Journal of Consulting and Clinical Psychology*, 1969, 33, 705–709.

Feist, J. R., & Rosenthal, T. L. Serpent versus surrogate and other determinants of runway fear differences. *Behaviour Research and Therapy*, 1973, 11, 483–490.

Fish, J. M. *Placebo therapy.* San Francisco: Jossey-Bass, 1973.

Frank, J. D. *Persuasion and healing.* (Rev. ed.) Baltimore: John Hopkins University Press, 1973.

Friedman, N. *The social nature of psychological research.* New York: Basic Books, 1967.

Gibson, J. J. A critical review of the concept of set in contemporary experimental psychology. *Psychological Bulletin*, 1941, 38, 781–817.

Goldsmith, J. B., & McFall, R. M. Development and evaluation of an interpersonal skill-training program for psychiatric inpatients. *Journal of Abnormal Psychology*, 1975, 84, 51–58.

Goldstein, A. P. *Therapist-patient expectancies in psychotherapy.* New York: Macmillan, 1962.

Gruber, R. P. Behavior therapy: Problems in generalization. *Behavior Therapy*, 1971, 2, 361–368.

Grusec, J. E., & Skubiski, S. L. Model nurturance, demand characteristics of the modeling experiment, and altruism. *Journal of Personality and Social Psychology*, 1970, 14, 352–359.

Heitler, J. B. Preparatory techniques in initiating expressive psychotherapy with lower-class, unsophisticated patients. *Psychological Bulletin*, 1976, 83, 339–352.

Hersen, M., Eisler, R. W., & Miller, P. M. Development of assertive responses: Clinical, measurement, and research considerations. *Behaviour Research and Therapy*, 1973, 11, 505–521.

Hicks, D. A., & Shemberg, K. M. Therapeutic rationale, monetary incentive and fear behavior: a methodological note on analogue research. *Behaviour Research and Therapy*, 1976, 14, 83–84.

Hill, K. T. Social determinants of imitation: the questions of direction and generality of effects. In Determinants of imitation in children: Social learning and control processes. Symposium presented at the Society for Research in Child Development, Minneapolis, April 1971.

Holland, C. H. Sources of variance in the experimental investigation of behavioral obedience. Paper read at the Eastern Psychological Association, Philadelphia, April 1969.

Holroyd, K. Outcome with systematic desensitization: A critical review. Unpublished doctoral dissertation, University of Miami, 1973.

Honigfeld, G. Nonspecific factors in treatment. *Diseases of the Nervous System*, 1964, 25, 145–156.

Howlett, S., & Nawas, M. Exposure to aversive imagery and suggestion in systematic desensitization. In R. D. Rubin (Ed.), *Advances in behavior therapy.* New York: Academic Press, 1971.

Husek, T. R., & Alexander, S. The effectiveness of the Anxiety Differential in examination stress situations. *Educational and Psychological Measurement*, 1963, 23, 309–318.

Johnson, S. M., & Bolstad, O. D. Methodological issues in naturalistic observation: some problems and solutions for field research. In L. A. Hamerlynck, L. C. Handy, & E. J. Mash (Eds.), *Behavior change.* Champaign, Ill. Research Press, 1973. Pp. 7–67.

Kanfer, F. H., Cox, L. E., Greiner, J. M., & Koroly, P. Contracts, demand characteristics and self control. *Journal of Personality and Social Psychology*, 1974, 30, 605–619.

Kanfer, F. H., & Phillips, J. S. *Learning foundations of behavior therapy.* New York: Wiley, 1970.

Kaufman, A., Baron, A., & Kopp, R. Some effects of instructions on human operant behavior. *Psychonomic Monograph Supplements*, 1966, 1, 243–250.

Kazdin, A. The effect of suggestion and pretesting on avoidance reduction in fearful subjects. *Journal of Behavior Therapy and Experimental Psychiatry*, 1973, 4, 213–222.

Kelley, C. K. Play desensitization of fear of darkness in preschool children. *Behaviour Research and Therapy*, 1976, 14, 79–82.

Kelly, G. A. *The psychology of personal constructs*. New York: Norton, 1955. 2 vols.

Kent, R. N., O'Leary, K. D., Diament, C., & Dietz, A. Expectation biases in observational evaluation of therapeutic change. *Journal of Consulting and Clinical Psychology*, 1974, 42, 774–780.

Kiesler, D. Some myths of psychotherapy research and the search for a paradigm. *Psychological Bulletin*, 1966, 65, 110–136.

Kimura, H. K., Kennedy, T. D., & Rhodes, L. E. Recurring assessment of changes in phobic behavior during the course of systematic desensitization. *Behaviour Research and Therapy*, 1972, 10, 279–282.

Lang, P. J., & Lazovik, A. D. Experimental desensitization of a phobia. *Journal of Abnormal and Social Psychology*, 1963, 66, 519–525.

Lang, P. J., Lazovik, A. D., & Reynolds, D. J. Desensitization, suggestibility, and pseudotherapy. *Journal of Abnormal Psychology*, 1965, 70, 395–402.

Lazarus, A. A. *Behavior therapy and beyond*. New York: McGraw-Hill, 1971.

Leitenberg, H., Agras, W., Barlow, D., & Oliveau, D. Contribution of selective positive reinforcement and therapeutic instructions to systematic desensitization therapy. *Journal of Abnormal Psychology*, 1969, 74, 113–118.

Lentz, R. J. Changes in chronic mental patients' interview behavior: Effects of differential treatment and management. *Journal of Behavior Therapy and Experimental Psychiatry*, 1975, 6, 192–199.

Levy, L. H. Reflections on replications and the experimenter bias effect. *Journal of Consulting and Clinical Psychology*, 1969, 33, 15–17.

Lick, J. Expectancy, false galvanic skin response feedback and systematic desensitization in the modification of phobic behavior. *Journal of Consulting and Clinical Psychology*, 1975, 43, 557–567.

Lick, J., & Bootzin, R. Expectancy, demand characteristics, and contact desensitization in behavior change. *Behavior Therapy*, 1970, 1, 176–183.

Lomont, J., & Brock, L. Cognitive factors in systematic desensitization. *Behaviour Research and Therapy*, 1971, 9, 187–195. (a)

Lomont, J., & Brock, L. Stimulus hierarchy generalization in systematic desensitization. *Behaviour Research and Therapy*, 1971, 9, 197–208. (b)

MacDonald, M. L. A behavioral assessment methodology applied to the measurement of assertion. Unpublished doctoral dissertation, University of Illinois, 1974.

Marcia, J. E., Rubin, B. M., & Efran, J. S. Systematic desensitization: Expectancy change or counterconditioning. *Journal of Abnormal Psychology*, 1969, 74, 382–387.

Masling, J. The influence of situational and interpersonal variables in projective testing. *Psychological Bulletin*, 1960, 57, 65–82.

Matarazzo, J. D., Wiens, A. N., & Manaugh, T. S. IQ correlates of speech and silence behavior under three dyadic speaking conditions. *Journal of Consulting and Clinical Psychology*, 1975, 43, 198–204.

McCardel, J., & Murray, E. J. Nonspecific factors in weekend encounter groups. *Journal of Consulting and Clinical Psychology*, 1974, 42, 337–345.

McFall, R. M. Demand characteristics, experimental reactivity, and ecological validity. In The role of expectancy and demand characteristics in behavior modification. Symposi-

158   Douglas A. Bernstein and Michael T. Nietzel

um presented at the American Psychological Association, Washington, D.C., September
1971.
McFall, R. M., & Lillesand, D. B. Behavior rehearsal with modeling and coaching in assertion
training. *Journal of Abnormal Psychology*, 1971, 77, 313–323.
McFall, R. M., & Marston, A. R. An experimental investigation of behavior rehearsal in
assertive training. *Journal of Abnormal Psychology*, 1970, 76, 295–303.
McFall, R. M., & Twentyman, C. T. Four experiments on the relative contributions of
rehearsal, modeling, and coaching in assertion training. *Journal of Abnormal Psy-
chology*, 1973, 81, 199–218.
McGlynn, F. Experimental desensitization following three types of instructions. *Behavior
Research and Therapy*, 1971, 9, 367–369.
McGlynn, F. Systematic desensitization under two conditions of induced expectancy.
Behavior Research and Therapy, 1972, 10, 229–234.
McGlynn, F., Gaynor, R., & Phur, J. Experimental desensitization of snake-avoidance after
an instructional manipulation. *Journal of Clinical Psychology*, 1972, 28, 224–227.
McGlynn, F., & Mapp, R. Systematic desensitization of snake-avoidance following three
types of suggestion. *Behavior Research and Therapy*, 1970, 8, 197–201.
McGlynn, F., & McDonnell, R. Subjective ratings of credibility following brief exposure to
desensitization and pseudotherapy. *Behaviour Research and Therapy*, 1974, 12, 141–
146.
McGlynn, F., Meliea, W., & Nawas, M. Systematic desensitization of snake-avoidance under
two conditions of suggestion. *Psychological Reports*, 1969, 25, 220–222.
McGlynn, F., Reynolds, E. & Linder, L. Systematic desensitization following therapeutically
oriented and physiologically oriented instructions. *Journal of Behavior Therapy and
Experimental Psychiatry*, 1971, 2, 13–18. (a)
McGlynn, F., Reynolds, E., & Lindner, L. Systematic desensitization with pretreatment and
intratreatment therapeutic instructions. *Behaviour Research and Therapy*, 1971, 9,
57–63. (b)
McGlynn, F., & Williams, C. Systematic desensitization of snake-avoidance under three
conditions of suggestion. *Journal of Behavior Therapy and Experimental Psychiatry*,
1970, 1, 97–101.
McGuire, W. J. Suspiciousness of experimenter's intent. In R. Rosenthal & R. Rosnow
(Eds.), *Artifact in behavioral research*. New York: Academic Press, 1969.
McReynolds, W. T. Introduction to social-psychological influences on behavior change. In
Douglas A. Bernstein (Chm.), Expectancy effects in behavior change research. Symposium presented at the Association for Advancement of Behavior Therapy, San Francisco, December 1975.
McReynolds, W. T., Barnes, A. R., Brooks, S., & Rehagen, N. F. The role of attention-
placebo influences in the efficacy of systematic desensitization. *Journal of Consulting
and Clinical Psychology*. 1973, 41, 86–92.
McReynolds, W. T., & Tori, C. A further assessment of attention-placebo effects and
demand characteristics in studies of systematic desensitization. *Journal of Consulting
and Clinical Psychology*, 1972, 38, 261–264.
Miller, B. V., & Bernstein, D. A. Instructional demand in a behavioral avoidance test for
claustrophic fear. *Journal of Abnormal Psychology*, 1972, 80, 206–210.
Miller, B. V., & Levis, D. J. The effects of varying short visual exposure times to a phobic
test stimulus on subsequent avoidance behavior. *Behaviour Research and Therapy*,
1971, 9, 17–22.
Miller, S. The contribution of therapeutic instructions to systematic desensitization, *Behavior Research and Therapy*, 1972, 10, 159–169.
Murray, E. J., & Jacobson, L. I. The nature of learning in traditional and behavioral

psychotherapy. In A. E. Bergin & S. L. Garfield (Eds.), *Handbook of psychotherapy and behavior change*. New York: Wiley, 1971. Pp. 709–747.

Nau, S. D., Caputo, J. A., & Borkovec, T. D. The relationship between credibility of therapy rationale and the reduction of simulated anxiety. *Journal of Behavior Therapy and Experimental Psychiatry*, 1974, 5, 129–133.

Neiman, L. J., & Hughes, J. W. The problem of the concept of role—a re-survey of the literature. In H. D. Stein & R. A. Cloward (Eds.), *Social perspectives on behavior*. Glencoe, Ill.: Free Press, 1959. Pp. 177–185.

Nelson, R. O., Lipinski, D. P., & Black, J. L. The effects of expectancy on the reactivity of self-recording. *Behavior Therapy*, 1975, 6, 337–349.

Nietzel, M. T. The effects of assessment and treatment mediated demand characteristics in a psychotherapy outcome study. Unpublished doctoral dissertation, University of Illinois, 1973.

Nietzel, M. T. Variables associated with expectancy effects in behavior change research. In Douglas A. Bernstein (Chm.), Expectancy effects in behavior change research. Symposium presented at the Association for Advancement of Behavior Therapy, San Francisco, December 1975.

Nietzel, M. T., & Bernstein, D. A. No-treatment control groups: the effect of rationale on subsequent avoidance behavior. Paper read at the Midwestern Psychological Association, Chicago, May 1975.

Nietzel, M., & Bernstein, D. The effects of instructionally-mediated demand upon the behavioral assessment of assertiveness. *Journal of Consulting and Clinical Psychology*, 1976, 44, 500.

O'Leary, K. D., & Kent, R. Behavior modification for social action: research tactics and problems. In L. A. Hamerlynck, L. C. Handy, & E. J. Mash (Eds.), *Behavior change*. Champaign, Ill.: Research Press, 1973. Pp. 69–96.

O'Leary, K. D., Kent, R. N., & Kanowitz, J. Shaping data collection congruent with experimental hypotheses. *Journal of Applied Behavior Analysis*, 1975, 8, 43–52.

O'Leary, K. D., & Wilson, G. T. *Behavior therapy*. Englewood Cliffs, N.J.: Prentice-Hall, 1975.

Oliveau, D., Agras, W., Leitenberg, H., Moore, R., & Wright, D. Systematic desensitization, therapeutically oriented instructions, and selective positive reinforcement. *Behavior Research and Therapy*, 1969, 7, 27–33.

Orne, M. T. On the social psychology of the psychological experiment: With particular *Psychology*, 1959, 58, 277–299.

Orne, M. On the social psychology of the psychological experiment: With particular reference to demand characteristics and their implications. *American Psychologist*, 1962, 17, 776–783.

Orne, M. T. Demand characteristics and the concept of quasi-controls. In R. Rosenthal and R. L. Rosnow (Eds.), *Artifact in behavioral research*. New York: Academic Press, 1969. Pp. 143–179.

Orne, M. T. Hypnosis, motivation, and the ecological validity of the psychological experiment. In W. J. Arnold & M. M. Page (Eds.), *Nebraska symposium on motivation*. Lincoln: University of Nebraska Press, 1970. Pp. 187–265.

Orne, M. T., & Holland, C. H. On the ecological validity of laboratory deceptions. *International Journal of Psychiatry*, 1968, 6, 282–293.

Orne, M. T., & Scheibe, K. E. The contribution of nondeprivation factors in the production of sensory deprivation effects: The psychology of the "panic button." *Journal of Abnormal and Social Psychology*, 1964, 68, 3–12.

Orne, M. T., Sheehan, P. W., & Evans, F. J. Occurrence of posthypnotic behavior outside the experimental setting. *Journal of Personality and Social Psychology*, 1968, 9, 189–196.

Orne, M. T., & Wender, P. Anticipatory socialization for psychotherapy: Method and rationale. *American Journal of Psychiatry,* 1968, **124,** 88–98.

Page, M. M. Demand characteristics and the verbal operant conditioning experiment. *Journal of Personality and Social Psychology,* 1972, **23,** 372–378.

Page, M. M. Demand characteristics and the classical conditioning experiment. *Journal of Personality and Social Psychology,* 1974, **30,** 468–476.

Page, S., & Yates, E. Effects of situational role demands on measurement of attitudes about mental illness. *Journal of Consulting and Clinical Psychology,* 1975, **43,** 115.

Parrino, J. Effect of pretherapy information on learning in psychotherapy. *Journal of Abnormal Psychology,* 1971, **77,** 17–24.

Paul, G. L. *Insight vs. desensitization in psychotherapy.* Stanford: Stanford University Press, 1966.

Paul, G. L. Behavior modification research: Design and tactics. In C. M. Franks (Ed.), *Behavior therapy: Appraisal and status.* New York: McGraw-Hill, 1969. Pp. 29–62.

Persely, G., & Leventhal, D. The effects of therapeutically oriented instructions and of the pairing of anxiety imagery and relaxation in systematic desensitization. *Behavior Therapy,* 1972, **3,** 417–424.

Peterson, R. F., & Whitehurst, G. J. A variable influencing the performance of non-reinforced imitative behaviors. *Journal of Applied Behavior Analysis,* 1971, **4,** 1–9.

Pfungst, O. [*Clever Hans*] (R. Rosenthal, Ed.), New York: Holt, 1965. (Originally published, 1911.)

Rappaport, H. Modification of avoidance behavior: Expectancy, autonomic reactivity and verbal report. *Journal of Consulting and Clinical Psychology,* 1972, **39,** 404–414.

Redd, W. H. Social control by adult preference in operant conditioning with children. *Journal of Experimental Child Psychology,* 1974, **17,** 61–78.

Redd, W. H., & Wheeler, A. J. The relative effectiveness of monetary reinforcers and adult instructions in the control of children's choice behavior. *Journal of Experimental Child Psychology,* 1973, **16,** 63–75.

Riecken, H. W. A program for research on experiments in social psychology. In N. F. Washburne (Ed.), *Decisions, values, and groups.* Vol. 2. New York: Pergamon, 1962. Pp. 25–41.

Rimm, D. C., & Mahoney, M. J. The application of reinforcement and participant modeling procedures in the treatment of snake-phobic behavior. *Behaviour Research and Therapy,* 1969, **7,** 369–376.

Rimm, D. C., & Masters, J. C. *Behavior therapy.* New York: Academic Press, 1974.

Robinson, C., & Suinn, R. M. Group desensitization of a phobia in massed sessions. *Behaviour Research and Therapy,* 1969, **7,** 319–321.

Rosen, G. Therapy set: Its effects on subjects' involvement in systematic desensitization and treatment outcome. *Journal of Abnormal Psychology,* 1974, **83,** 291–300.

Rosen, G. M. Subjects initial therapeutic expectancies towards systematic desensitization as a function of varied instructional sets. *Behavior Therapy,* 1975, **6,** 230–237.

Rosen, G. M. Subjects' initial therapeutic expectancies and subjects' awareness of therapeutic goals in systematic desensitization: A review. *Behavior Therapy,* 1976, **7,** 14–27.

Rosenthal, D., & Frank, J. D. Psychotherapy and the placebo effect. *Psychological Bulletin,* 1956, **53,** 294–302.

Rosenthal, R. *Experimenter effects in behavioral research.* New York: Appleton, 1966.

Rosenthal, R. Experimenter expectancy and the reassuring nature of the null hypothesis decision procedure. *Psychologica. Bulletin,* 1968, **70**(6, Pt. 2), 30–47.

Rosenthal, R. On not so replicated experiments and not so null results. *Journal of Consulting and Clinical Psychology,* 1969, **33,** 7–10.

Rosenthal, R., & Jacobson, L. *Pygmalion in the classroom.* New York: Holt, 1968.

Rosnow, R., & Aiken, L. S. Mediation of artifacts in behavioral research. *Journal of Experimental Social Psychology,* 1973, **3**, 181–201.

Rotter, J. B. *Social learning and clinical psychology.* New York: Prentice-Hall, 1954.

Sarbin, T. R. Role theory. In G. Lindzey (Ed.), *Handbook of social psychology.* Cambridge, Mass.: Addison-Wesley, 1954. Pp. 223–259.

Sarbin, T. R., & Jones, D. S. An experimental analysis of role behavior. *Journal of Abnormal and Social Psychology,* 1955, **51**, 236–241.

Saxby, R. J. Phobic responses and cognitive dissonance arousal. *Behavior Therapy,* 1973, **4**, 230–234.

Shapiro, A. K. A contribution to a history of the placebo effect. *Behavioral Science,* 1960, **5**, 109–135.

Shapiro, A. K. Placebo effects in medicine, psychotherapy, and psychoanalysis. In A. E. Bergin & S. L. Garfield (Eds.), *Handbook of psychotherapy and behavior change.* New York: Wiley, 1971. Pp. 439–473.

Sidman, M. *Tactics of scientific research.* New York: Basic Books, 1960.

Smith, R. E., Diener, E., & Beaman, A. Demand characteristics and the behavioral avoidance measures of fear in behavior therapy analogue research. *Behavior Therapy,* 1974, **5**, 172–182.

Snyder, M., Schulz, R., & Jones, E. E. Expectancy and apparent duration as determinants of fatigue. *Journal of Personality and Social Psychology,* 1974, **29**, 426–434.

Speltz, M. L., & Bernstein, D. A. Sex differences in fearfulness: Verbal report, overt avoidance, and demand characteristics. *Journal of Behavior Therapy and Experimental Psychiatry,* 1976, **7**, 117–122.

Staats, A. W. Experimental demand characteristics and the classical conditioning of attitudes. *Journal of Personality and Social Psychology,* 1969, **11**, 187–192.

Staats, A. W. *Social behaviorism.* Homewood, Ill.: Dorsey Press, 1975.

Steinman, W. M. The social control of generalized imitation. *Journal of Applied Behavior Analysis,* 1970, **3**, 159–168.

Steinmark, S. W., & Borkovec, T. D. Active and placebo treatment effects on moderate insomnia under counterdemand and positive demand instructions. *Journal of Abnormal Psychology,* 1974, **83**, 157–163.

Stone, G. L., & Gotlib, I. Effect of instructions and modeling on self-disclosure. *Journal of Counseling Psychology,* 1975, **22**, 288–293.

Strauss, M. E., & Marwit, S. J. Expectancy effects in Rorschach testing. *Journal of Consulting and Clinical Psychology,* 1970, **34**, 448.

Sundberg, N. D., Tyler, L. E., & Taplin, J. R. *Clinical psychology: expanding horizons.* (2nd ed.) New York: Appleton, 1973.

Tori, C., & Worell, L. Reduction of human avoidant behavior: A comparison of counter-conditioning, expectancy, and cognitive information approaches. *Journal of Consulting and Clinical Psychology,* 1973, **41**, 269–278.

Tryon, W. W., & Tryon, G. S. Desensitization and demand characteristics. Unpublished manuscript, 1974. (Available from Psychology Department, Fordham University, Bronx, New York, 10458.)

Ullmann, L. P., & Krasner, L. *A psychological approach to abnormal behavior.* (2nd ed.) Englewood Cliffs, N.J.: Prentice-Hall, 1975.

Underwood, B. J. *Psychological research.* New York: Appleton, 1957.

Walker, P. C., & Johnson, R. F. Q. The influence of presleep suggestions on dream content: evidence and methodological problems. *Psychological Bulletin,* 1974, **81**, 362–370.

Watson, C. G. The roles of impression management in the interview, self-report, and cognitive behavior of schizophrenics. *Journal of Consulting and Clinical Psychology,* 1972, **38,** 452–456.

Webb, E. J., Campbell, D. T., Schwartz, R. D., & Sechrest, L. *Unobtrusive measures.* Chicago: Rand-McNally, 1966.

Weber, S. J., & Cook, T. D. Subject effects in laboratory research: an examination of subject roles, demand characteristics, and valid inferences. *Psychological Bulletin,* 1972, **77,** 273–295.

Wheeler, L. *Interpersonal influence.* Boston: Allyn & Bacon, 1970.

Wilcoxon, L. A., & Craighead, W. E. The effects of anxiety level and situational instructional demand on speech anxiety. Unpublished manuscript, 1976. (Available from W. E. Craighead, Department of Psychology, Pennsylvania State University, University Park, Pennsylvania.)

Wilkins, W. Desensitization: Social and cognitive factors underlying the effectiveness of Wolpe's procedure. *Psychological Bulletin,* 1971, **76,** 311–317.

Wilkins, W. Expectancy of therapeutic gain: An empirical and conceptual critique. *Journal of Consulting and Clinical Psychology,* 1973, **40,** 69–77.

Wilson, M. N., & Rappaport, J. Personal self-disclosure: expectancy and situational effects. *Journal of Consulting and Clinical Psychology,* 1974, **42,** 901–908.

Wilson, G., & Thomas, M. Self vs. drug produced relaxation and the effects of instructional set in standardized systematic desensitization. *Behavior Research and Therapy,* 1973, **11,** 279–288.

Wollheim, R. *Sigmund Freud.* New York: Viking Press, 1971.

Wolpe, J. *The practice of behavior therapy.* (2nd ed.) New York: Pergamon, 1973.

THE CLINICAL USEFULNESS
OF BIOFEEDBACK[1]

EDWARD B. BLANCHARD
Department of Psychiatry
University of Tennessee Center for the Health Sciences and
Tennessee Psychiatric Hospital and Institute
Memphis, Tennessee

AND

LEONARD H. EPSTEIN
Psychology Department
Auburn University
Auburn, Alabama

I. INTRODUCTION

As has been noted in several recent reviews (Blanchard & Young, 1974; Miller, 1975a; Schwartz, 1973), there has recently appeared on

[1] Preparation of this paper was supported in part by a grant from the National Heart and Lung Institute, HL-18814.

the therapeutic scene a new group of treatment procedures which, collectively, are termed *biofeedback*. This collection of treatment techniques has been hailed by some as the "sure cure" for a diverse group of disorders. Thus, enthusiastic reports have appeared within the past few years in both the lay press and in nonarchival professional journals about the wonders of biofeedback as a treatment modality for many psychosomatic disorders. This enthusiasm has undoubtedly been fed by the numerous advertisements in psychological and psychiatric journals by manufacturers of biofeedback equipment. Typically, the equipment advertisements lay claim to efficacy of treatment for a wide variety of disorders with biofeedback equipment or with *their* biofeedback equipment.

It seems quite appropriate for an article in *Progress in Behavior Modification* to be devoted to clinical biofeedback. In fact, biofeedback can be considered as that subset of behavior modification procedures which focuses primarily on the direct modification of physiological responses as opposed to cognitive or motoric responses. Certainly the operations and terminology from the psychology of learning are at the core of biofeedback training. Moreover, investigators in the field of biofeedback have had a long-term concern with self-control and self-management (as will be detailed later in this article) and thus share this concern with workers in the field of behavior modification.

This article will systematically summarize and evaluate the data on the clinical utility of biofeedback procedures. The review will be organized around bioelectric response systems. For each response system all or most of the studies utilizing changes of that response system will be presented and discussed with regard to the particular clinical problem attacked by that biofeedback procedure. In addition to reviewing the clinical applications of biofeedback, some of the nonclinical work will also be discussed when appropriate. The review will be comprehensive but not exhaustive, and will attempt to bring the Blanchard and Young (1974) review up to date.

This article is organized into several integrated sections: First, there is a brief theoretical integration of the biofeedback, self-control, and self-management literature which includes some important definitions of feedback procedure terms. Next is a brief section describing the "rules" by which the various reports will be evaluated. Then follows the bulk of the article, the evaluative review of the clinical applications of biofeedback by bioelectric response systems (included in this section are summary evaluative comments). Finally, there are conclusions as to the state of the art and speculations as to future directions.

II. BIOFEEDBACK, SELF-CONTROL,
AND SELF-MANAGEMENT

Biofeedback procedures are designed to modify physiological responses. These responses may serve as the direct target response, as in hypertension (Kristt & Engel, 1975), or as a response system that is one of several systems that require modification, as in phobias (Borkovec, 1973). The eventual goal of these techniques is to prevent or reduce the occurrence of the physiological response. This can be accomplished either by (1) attempting to produce a (semi)permanent change in a response system (Sterman & Friar, 1972) or (2) teaching the patient procedures which enable him to regulate the response in his natural environment. This section deals primarily with the latter use, which the authors believe is the more typical case in clinical biofeedback training.

In the great majority of cases, control of the physiological response, to have any long-term utility for the patient, must be accomplished by the patient without external feedback and in the absence of the apparatus utilized in the laboratory setting. Thus, the patient must learn to *self-regulate* the response. The goal of self-regulation has also been expressed by numerous behavioral therapists, and a large body of research on the self-regulation of motoric and cognitive responses has been accumulated (Thoresen & Mahoney, 1974).

A. Self-Management

Self-management, or self-regulation, refers to control of a response by having the patient manipulate factors which reliably influence that response. Thus, self-management and external control of a response are similar in that changes in a target response are a function of manipulating controlling conditions, with the important difference being the agent of control. It is important to recognize that self-management involves the active manipulation of events that influence behavior, in contrast to the common misconception of self-control as a function of will power (Thoresen & Mahoney, 1974). As Skinner (1953) has indicated, the self-control process is often postulated to occur specifically when the controlling mechanisms for a response are not observed. If we cannot tell how someone is controlling a response, it is easy to explain the behavior in terms of self-control. However, if we assume that self-management involves the active management of factors which influence a response, we can then study the self-management process by having the patient manipulate these factors. It should also be clear that, if we do not assume that the target response is a function of specific environmental, cognitive, or motoric events, then the process of self-control for those behaviors will be a capricious affair, and it will be necessary to invoke the construct of will power to explain the presence or absence of behavior.

B. Self-Control

There are numerous components of the self-management of behavior which have been discussed previously (Epstein & Blanchard, 1977). The basic component of management is *self-control.* Self-control can be defined as changes in a response produced by the subject in the absence of external feedback. Ideally, these changes should be bidirectional, i.e., the subject should be able to increase and decrease responding in a system. Brener (1974) has discussed the necessary conditions to exhibit voluntary control of behavior, which is identical to the term self-control as used here. He states that voluntary control can best be studied by instructional control procedures. Instructional control of a response is observed after an instruction is presented, and a response change is reliably observed, but no feedback is available to reinforce any change that has occurred. Thus, self-control can be observed under conditions in which a subject can reliably change a response after being instructed to change without being provided any external assistance. If feedback has been presented to influence response regulation, this procedure has been termed *feedback control* (Epstein & Blanchard, 1977). Feedback control constitutes the bulk of present biofeedback research.

Self-control refers to the process in which a subject reliably changes a response without external feedback. The specific procedures that are required to change the response can be considered tactics which the subjects identify that reliably influence the criterion behavior. For example, when heart rate is increased or decreased, this is not evidence that the person has direct control over the heart per se. Rather, this means that the person has learned to manipulate variables that reliably influence heart rate changes. For example, running in place for several minutes, a motoric response, can reliably increase heart rate. Obrist, Galosy, Lawler, Gaebelein, Howard, and Shanks (1975) and Brener (1974) have indicated that less easily observed somatic activity may be related to heart rate acceleration in feedback studies.

Thus, in clinical studies we may improve self-control by emphasizing change in systems that naturally covary. Both Sroufe (1971) and Epstein and Webster (1975) have attempted to utilize this strategy for the regulation of heart rate by respiratory control, with varying results. The point is again made that self-control is not an internal, motivational, unstudiable process, but rather the control of a response by a subject through actively manipulating variables that exert control over the response.

The degree of self-control may be determined by the extent to which the subject can regulate the response. Procedurally, the degree of control is a function of the quality of instructional control. That is, the subject can either increase or decrease the response when instructed. He also can regulate the degree of increase or decrease. He should be able to accelerate his heart 5 bpm, and then 10 bpm, etc., as well as decelerate it 5 bpm, 10 bpm, etc., and he should be able to produce a steady state when requested. For comparison purposes, a subject who can only comply with the instruction "raise your heart rate 3 bpm" certainly demonstrates less control than one who can comply with instructions to change heart rate, 3, 6, and 9 bpm in either direction.

C. Discrimination

Determining that self-control has been acquired by the subject is not sufficient to ensure that he can regulate the target response in the natural environment. Self-control must be engaged in under the appropriate circumstances, which in most cases is when the problematic physiological response pattern occurs. Thus, the subject must be able to *discriminate* changes in the target behavior. Or, in more precise terms, changes in the target response must exert stimulus control over engaging in self-control tactics.

There are two broad, and probably overlapping, categories of physiological response which one might wish to control. The first, typified by tension headaches, is episodic and it is fairly easy for the patient to identify its presence or absence. The other type, typified by essential hypertension, produces no pain or naturally detectable changes when present.

Discrimination of changes in the target responses is important in both categories of disorders. In the first type, tension headaches, pain may be the result of sustained muscle contraction. This event is easily detected. However, by the time pain is felt, the physiological response probably has been greatly abnormal for a long time, and thus may be more difficult to control than if the response were only slightly abnormal. In the latter case, had slight muscle contraction, rather than the eventual pain, been the signal to exert control procedures, the task would probably have been much easier. This is certainly the case with migraine headaches, which are extremely difficult to control after the vasodilation and edema related to extreme pain are present.

In the second category of responses, discrimination of the abnormal state is much more difficult and, as later sections of this article will reveal, evidence of therapeutic benefits has been much more sparse. In "silent" responses of this category, such as hypertension, it is important for the patient to know when blood pressure is high in order to reliably regulate it to within normal limits. Thus, it can be argued that detection of abnormal levels of a response is necessary for reliable clinical control of the response.

D. Self-Reinforcement

A third component of self-management is *self-reinforcement.* Let us assume that a patient knows when a response is abnormal and that he has a tactic to reliably regulate it. Conditions should be arranged to increase the probability that he does engage in self-control, since demonstrations that he can control it are not sufficient to ensure that he will. It is in the latter area that the importance of self-reinforcement lies.

Some disorders produce pain, and engaging in self-control may be negatively reinforced by removing the pain. In these cases, contingencies are naturally arranged to promote self-control. However, the situation for disorders that do not produce pain, as hypertension or cardiac arrhythmias, is considerably different. While some people may consistently engage in self-control because they want to prevent later cardiovascular or renal damage, a great proportion of people will not work for such a long-range, indefinite goal, and hence, must be externally motivated. To remain consistent with the self-regulation model, this motivating condition should be self-managed. This requires a self-reinforcement procedure in which the subject administers a reinforcing event to himself contingent upon engaging in self-control. Self-reinforcement procedures are often a component of self-management of motoric behavior, and have been demonstrated to produce effects equivalent to external control procedures (Kanfer & Deurfeldt, 1967).

Discrimination may play a role in this area in disorders such as hypertension. Knowledge that one has reduced one's blood pressure, a health benefiting event, may be obtained by discrimination. Such knowledge of change could serve as a reinforcer.

E. Acquisition of Self-Management

The previous discussion identified components of self-management. Studies designed to evaluate procedures for the acquisition of the discrimination or control of these responses have been reviewed by Epstein and Blanchard (1976). However, as detection and control may be interrelated (Brener, 1974), it may not be necessary to teach each of these skills independently, but one may affect the other as McFarland (1975) recently indicated training in heart rate control may influence heart rate discrimination.

At present, no clinical studies have attempted to develop a comprehensive treatment program that teaches each of these skills. In fact, none has demonstrated that subjects had self-control, knew when to engage in self-control, or were provided motivating conditions to ensure that self-control was consistently engaged in. This deficiency may be related to the relatively poor, or at least variable, effects of biofeedback procedures in clinical work. The only data currently available on the relationship between these skills and treatment effects are for tension headaches. Epstein, Abel, and Webster (1974a) provided control training for two patients with chronic headaches. While feedback-control was demonstrated in both cases, discrimination of activity was only present in the subject that improved clinically.

Specific studies dealing with feedback control and self-control, discrimination, and self-reinforcement for individual response systems will be discussed in this article.

III. RESEARCH DESIGN AND
THE BASES FOR EVALUATION

As with any new therapeutic procedure, we believe that the evidence for the clinical efficacy and utility of biofeedback techniques should be evaluated by the same standards one would apply to new drugs or to a new behavioral technique. The studies summarized in this article vary markedly in terms of the experimental procedures used. Since the reliability and validity of conclusions about the efficacy of treatment are directly related to the experimental procedures, these procedures are now briefly summarized, following the format of Blanchard and Young (1974).

Anecdotal Case Report. This term refers to a case report without systematic data. It usually includes a description of the patient's symptoms before and after treatment, as well as some description of the treatment. Although it produces little data of use in evaluating treatment effectiveness (Campbell & Stanley, 1966; Paul, 1969), it can be highly suggestive as to directions for future research and cannot be discounted.

Systematic Case Study. This term refers to a case report in which data are reported from the systematic measurement of some response over several trials, both in a pretreatment and during the treatment condition(s). This represents a quasiexperimental design (Campbell & Stanley, 1966), or an A-B design (Barlow & Hersen, 1973). It yields stronger, more interpretable results.

Multiple Systematic Case Studies. A variant of the above is the report which describes several patients treated in a similar A-B design. Finding similar changes in the target symptom in several patients at a similar point during treatment is fairly strong evidence of the efficacy of a treatment (Barlow & Hersen, 1973).

Controlled Single-Subject Experiment. A better statement of the functional relationship between the treatment and changes in the target response is provided by an A-B-A design (Barlow & Hersen, 1973). In this type of report, systematic data are collected across at least three conditions: baseline or pretreatment, treatment intervention, and then, and most critically, a return to baseline measurement conditions. If changes in the target symptom occur when going from A to B and then revert in going from B to A, this constitutes very strong evidence that B is a causal variable for changes in the symptom. A variation on this design is the A-B-A-B design, which is more powerful than the A-B-A since it contains a second test of the efficacy of B as the agent responsible for change in the target behavior. Unfortunately, this design, although ideally suited for research in clinical biofeedback, has yet to be used.

Single Group Outcome Study. This is a fairly common design and represents the application of some treatment or treatments to a group of similar patients with pre- and posttreatment measurement of target symptoms. Since this type of study lacks any control procedures, such as a second comparable group of patients who are assessed but not treated, it is difficult, on logical grounds, to conclude that the treatment alone is responsible for any changes found. Conclusions drawn from a study of this design can be strengthened if a prolonged series of baseline measurements are taken, making it similar to a series of multiple systematic case studies. Furthermore, it is possible to have a controlled single group outcome study, if, after baseline assessment, some other form of treatment is applied before applying the treatment of interest. This enables one to make within-group comparisons, but conclusions are still not as reliable as those made using a controlled group outcome study.

Controlled Group Outcome Study. This last category represents the strongest design (Campbell & Stanley, 1966; Paul, 1969). The minimum conditions for a controlled group outcome study are an experimental, or treatment, group and an untreated group of comparable patients who are assessed at the same time as the experimental group. This controls for random life events associated with the passage of time, for "spontaneous remission," and for changes due to the measurement operation itself.

A second, even more powerful design (Paul, 1969) includes at least three groups: treatment, attention—placebo control, and no-treatment control. The addition of an attention—placebo group controls for changes in target symptoms due to the attention paid patients in treatment and to various placebo or expectancy effects.

Given the nature of some of the conditions treated by biofeedback, and given the large amount of therapist- and patient-engendered expectancy, the inclusion of an attention—placebo control group is probably mandatory for strong conclusions to be drawn. In fact, Stroebel and Glueck (1973) have speculated that biofeedback may represent the "ultimate placebo."

IV. REVIEW OF UTILITY OF CLINICAL BIOFEEDBACK PROCEDURES

A. Cardiovascular Responses

Cardiovascular responses have been the most studied responses in basic biofeedback research. Thus, numerous studies have been conducted in which subjects were to control their heart rate, blood pressure, or the two in combination. This great attention to cardio-vascular responses is not too surprising given (1) that cardiovascular responses are influenced by both the sympathetic and para-sympathetic branches of the autonomic nervous system and thus are prime examples of "involuntary systems," and (2) that much of psychophysiology has been devoted to studying cardiovascular responses, and hence fairly good measurement techniques have been developed for their responses.

As pointed out in a recent review (Blanchard & Young, 1973), this research has for the most part been conducted on normal subjects, the studies have been of short duration and have achieved relatively small changes in the response studied which were *statistically* but not *clinically* significant.

Since publication of that review, numerous other studies on normal subjects have appeared, the results of which fall into the same general category. A few (Blanchard, Young, Scott, & Haynes, 1974b; Stephens, Harris, & Brady, 1972; Wells, 1973) have shown relatively large changes in heart rate achieved over a number of sessions in several subjects, however. Moreover, some additional clinical applications of feedback for the cardiovascular system have appeared as the field continues to grow.

1. HEART RATE

If one were to survey the nonclinical biofeedback literature, based on sheer frequency with which a response was studied, one would probably conclude that heart rate (HR) was the most important response. Interestingly, HR per se is not a bioelectrical response; rather it is the reciprocal of interbeat interval, the time which elapses between two heart beats. It is the latter function which is usually measured and then converted electronically to HR.

At this point, thanks to the numerous studies of Brener, Engel, Lang, Blanchard and their associates, much is known about the factors which affect the feedback control of HR. Moreover, Blanchard and his associates have demonstrated fairly consistent self-control (as explicitly defined in this article, p. 166) of HR (Blanchard *et al.*, 1974b). Finally, a theoretical model to integrate the research on feedback effects on heart rate has recently been proposed (Lang, 1975; Schwartz, 1975).

Despite all of the above research there are few problems in which heart rate per se is the target clinical problem. Most of the research has involved teaching patients to control HR in an effort to obtain a therapeutic effect on some other clinical problem in the cardio-vascular system.

a. Cardiac Arrhythmias. The first published reports of the use of biofeedback techniques with a cardiovascular problem were those of Engel and his associates working with various cardiac arrhythmias (Engel & Melmon, 1968; Weiss & Engel, 1970, 1971a, 1971b). In a brief communication, Engel and Melmon (1968) noted the successful treatment of arrhythmias such as atrial fibrillation, atrial and ven-tricular tachycardia, and premature ventricular contractions (PVCs) "by means of operant conditioning paradigms." However, since no data were provided on any aspect of the treatment or of the patients, this report must be classified as anecdotal evidence.

Two later brief communications (Weiss & Engel, 1970, 1971a) contained preliminary data on part of a series of eight cases of patients with PVCs, all of whom were treated in approximately the same paradigm. This work was summarized in one of the major papers on clinical biofeedback (Weiss & Engel, 1971b). This study will be discussed in detail since it is one of the most frequently cited clinical applications of biofeedback.

Although the number of patients who completed the various phases of the training procedure varied, the program was more or less standard and consisted of phases of approximately 10 sessions each during which the patient was to accelerate HR, decelerate HR, and then alternately accelerate and decelerate HR for 1–3 minute periods. In the next phase the patient was trained to hold his HR relatively constant within a 10 bpm range. A very important feature of this phase is that the particular feedback arrangement used gave patients direct feedback of the occurrence of PVCs.

Although no rationale was presented for the particular se-quence of feedback conditions, nor for the inclusion of any par-ticular condition, it may be the case that the authors were anticipating Brener's (1974) idea that a demonstration of self-control includes the ability to raise *and* lower the response level as well as to give graded responses upon request. Certainly the direct feedback of the target response, a PVC, should be helpful to patients trying to learn to discriminate its occurrence.

In the final phase, Weiss and Engel instituted a true self-control procedure: While the patient was keeping his HR within the specified *range*, feedback was systematically withdrawn, first 1 minute off and 1 minute on, then 3 minutes off to 1 minute on, and finally 7 off to 1 on. In this fashion patients could learn to control both HR and occurrence of PVCs without the assistance of feedback and thus move from feedback-assisted control to self-control. Sessions lasted 17 or 34 minutes, followed adaptation and baseline HR recording, and were held one to three times daily. Feedback was given by a light which was illuminated when HR was in the appropriate direction as well as by a clock which accumulated the total seconds of the session during which HR was in the correct direction. During the "range" training, two other lights were also available: one came on when HR was faster than the specified range, the other when it was slower. The rapid sequential illumination of these two lights gave the patient feedback of the occurrence of a PVC.

Data were reported in terms of mean HR for a session as well as rate of PVCs for the session. In addition, patients were monitored on the ward by telemetry for rate of PVCs.

Three of the eight cases completed the entire program; one more completed all but the final part of the range-training feedback fade-out and another completed everything through the initial fading out of feedback. Of the other three patients, two had training in accelerating and decelerating HR and holding it within a specified range, and the final patient had training in slowing HR and holding it within a specified range.

The authors were able to obtain follow-up results on all eight cases. In four of five patients who completed 47 or more sessions there was a significant decrease in PVC rate from a pretreatment rate of 10–20 PCVs per minute to a follow-up rate of about 1 PVC per minute. In one other case, for whom there was no demonstrated decrease in PVC rate, the patient claimed to be able to control PVCs at home. For the three cases who had the fewest sessions, there was no evidence during treatment or at follow-up of the patients' learning to control PVCs. By Fisher's Exact Probability Test, there is a significant ($p<.05$) relation between successful treatment and length of treatment.

Because they collected systematic data on the principal dependent variable, rate of emission of PVCs, we are able to determine in which training phase the major reduction of PVCs occurred. For two patients the major reduction occurred during training in alternating HR. For two others the major reduction was during *range* training; however, one patient did more poorly during range training. Finally, for one patient there was a significant reduction during training in HR slowing and a further reduction during training in alternating HR. Thus, unfortunately, there does not seem to be a systematic functional relationship between training phase and decrease in PVC rate.

While this is a laudable piece of research and is certainly highly suggestive of directions for future investigations, there are several methodological flaws which seriously detract from this study's value. First, no baseline trials were run or preintervention data reported. However, since all of the patients had reasonably well-documented histories of PVCs, those results could be considered as baseline data. Under this circumstance each case represents a systematic case study.

In terms of design this study can be considered either as an uncontrolled, single group study in which there was marked improvement in four of eight cases and some improvement in another case, or as a series of systematic case studies. In the former case, the lack of a control group seriously detracts from the study since there is a significant relation between total number of sessions and clinical improvement. In the latter case, since there was no return to baseline, the cases cannot be considered experiments. Moreover, since the major improvement in the dependent variable occurred in different training phases for different patients, the series does not represent a good replication series. These design faults seriously limit this study's value as scientific evidence since alternative explanations in terms of expectancy or placebo effects cannot be ruled out.

In a recent study Engel and Bleecker (1974) reported on the treatment of several more cases of cardiac arrhythmias. One additional patient with PVCs was treated. In-laboratory recordings of PVC rate were made prior to treatment and found to be approximately 15 PVCs per minute. The patient was put through training similar to that described by Weiss and Engel (1971b): first decelerating HR, then accelerating HR, then alternately speeding and slowing HR, and finally holding HR within a specified range. There was a marked drop in PVC rate with training in HR slowing, to 5 PVC per minute, and a further decrease to almost zero during alternation training. At follow-up the patient had no PVCs.

Since there was no return to baseline conditions, this represents a single case A-B design, or systematic case study. It represents a systematic replication (Sidman, 1960) since the order of treatment phases was changed from that used by Weiss and Engel. Interestingly, positive results were achieved in considerably fewer sessions (16) than previously used.

An important replication of these results has recently been completed by T. Pickering (described by Miller, 1975b). Two patients with frequent PVCs have both been trained, via an unspecified biofeedback procedure, to voluntarily suppress PVCs and emit normal sinus rhythm in their ECGs. Although details are lacking in this report, it is very important that the work from Engel's laboratory has been replicated (in the sense of achieving similar results) independently in another setting.

Engel and Bleecker (1974) reported the treatment of several other patients with arrhythmias, including one with supraventricular tachycardia and paroxysmal atrial tachycardia (PAT) and another with PAT and episodic sinus tachycardia. In both cases, experimental design faults, primarily the absence of a stable baseline, limit the reports to the level of systematic case study or anecdotal case report, respectively. Moreover, large-scale changes in HR without feedback training in both cases (as described by Blanchard & Young, 1974) seriously limit the value of these reports. The limited follow-up data seemed to indicate that beneficial clinical results were obtained.

   b. Sinus Tachycardia. In one cardiac arrhythmia, sinus tachycardia, the clinical response is the same as the response for which feedback is given. Thus in this disorder, biofeedback training is aimed at direct modification of the abnormal physiological response.

Engel and Bleecker (1974; also reported in Engel, 1972) treated a 53-year-old woman with a 4-year documented history of chronic sinus tachycardia in which recorded HR averaged 106 bpm. She initially participated in 12 sessions in which she was given binary feedback and instructed to lower her HR. Over the next nine sessions feedback was faded out, first with feedback on for 1 minute and off for 1 minute (three sessions), then on for 1 minute and off for 3 minutes (three sessions), and, finally, on for 1 minute and off for 7 minutes (three sessions). This procedure for transferring from feedback-assisted control to self-control was quite effective. The patient was effective in lowering HR equally with and without feedback.

During treatment, average HR dropped from 86 bpm to 68 bpm, a difference of 18 bpm. Moreover, the patient's HR, as measured independently by her personal physician after treatment, was 75 bpm, indicating that the results had generalized.

This case, although impressive in several ways, has some serious drawbacks due to experimental design considerations. The lack of baseline data and a control (or withdrawal-of-treatment) phase limit the value of this study to that of a systematic case study. The lack of baseline trials is particularly acute in this case since the baseline HR by history is approximately 106 bpm, yet at the first experimental session HR is 86 bpm during a trial on which HR did not decrease in the trial. This 20 bpm drop without treatment limits the value of the results. Moreover, the steady decline over trials leads one to suspect that habituation or some other process, rather than the feedback training, was responsible for the drop in HR. There was some evidence from the in-session data that the patient was learning to consistently lower her HR.

Independent confirmation of the value of biofeedback training in the treatment of chronic sinus tachycardia was provided by Scott, Blanchard, Edmundson, and Young (1973). In both of the clinical cases reported, a stable baseline HR was initially established in the laboratory and measured after a 20-minute adaptation period. For the first case, a 46-year-old male with a 20-year history of tachycardia, 26 trials on one conditioning procedure led to essentially no change from the baseline HR of 89 bpm. Introduction of a different shaping procedure combined with binary visual feedback of HR for 18 trials led to a reduction in HR to the normal range. A final phase of this case included a return to baseline conditions for six more trials. This led to only a partial recovery of baseline values, with HR increasing to 77 bpm.

Other clinical improvement noted in this patient, concomitant with the decrease in HR, was the patient's seeking and obtaining employment after being on disability compensation for his tachycardia for 18 months. Moreover, he decreased his dosage of minor tranquilizers and also reported much less anxiety. An 18-month follow-up revealed that the patient was still employed.

In the second case, baseline HR was 96 bpm. Nineteen feedback trials on the shaping procedure led to a reduction in HR to 80 bpm. Eight trials in a return-to-baseline phase led to no recovery of baseline values; instead HR stabilized at 78 bpm. Clinical improvement was also noted in this patient in that he reported feeling less anxious and was able to do more chores around the house; however, he did not return to gainful employment.

These two cases represent "true" experiments since (1) a stable baseline was established and (2) a return to baseline conditions was included as a control phase to complete the A-B-A design. However, the failure to find a complete recovery of baseline HR values during the return to baseline precludes drawing any definite conclusions from Scott *et al.*'s data and suggests that some process other than their experimental procedure might account for the results.

c. Heart Rate Control and Fear Responses. It has long been known that subjects' reports of fear or anxiety are frequently accompanied by increases in HR or HR variability (Lang, 1969; Leitenberg, Agras, Butz, & Wincze, 1971; Prigatano & Johnson, 1974; Watson, Gaind, & Marks, 1971). Furthermore, several investigators have noted that some subjects who achieved high levels of cardiac acceleration with the aid of biofeedback reported feeling tense and anxious (Headrick, Feather, & Wells, 1971; Scott *et al.*, 1973). Moreover, as Lang (1969) and others have noted, fear or anxiety is frequently measured by responses in three different domains, verbal or cognitive, motoric, and physiological, which may or may not covary. Extrapolating from these observations, several investigators have sought to determine if intervening directly in one part of the physiological response, namely HR, through teaching fearful or anxious patients to control HR with biofeedback training, would have beneficial effects on other response modes such as verbal report of fear or motoric avoidance.

In a prototypical analogue experiment, Sirota, Schwartz, and Shapiro (1974) provided two groups ($N = 10$) of normal female subjects with feedback, rewards, and instructions either to increase or decrease HR while they were undergoing similar series of shock and no-shock trials. The shocks were 2-second peripheral electrical shocks in a range previously determined to be from uncomfortable to painful. Subjects were asked to rate the painfulness of each shock after it occurred.

Although the authors claimed to have demonstrated control of HR, this claim is somewhat suspect, despite the fact that the increase-HR and decrease-HR groups were different in the appropriate direction by about 11 bpm by the end of the experiment ($p < .001$). The subjects who were to increase HR showed no control of HR, i.e., the mean HR for this group never appreciably deviated from the baseline level. The subjects who were to decrease HR showed a steady decrease in HR. However, because of the very short adaptation period (5 minutes), the changes seen in this group could well be due to simple adaptation rather than learning control of HR. The changes did, however, persist when feedback was withdrawn for the final 12 trials.

Regardless of whether feedback control of HR was shown or not, the subjects with the lowered HR allegedly rated the shocks as significantly less painful than the subjects whose HR remained at baseline levels. The term *allegedly* is used because the F value reported, 3.986, *is not significant with the degrees of freedom the authors report* (1,16). To reach the .05 level of significance the F value must equal or exceed 4.49 (Winer, 1962, p. 644). There was only a *nonsignificant trend* for the decrease-HR subjects to rate the shocks as less painful than the increase-HR subjects. Thus, despite the authors' claims, this study provides only minimal support for the premise that teaching subjects HR control could "serve as a behavioral strategy for changing anxiety and fear reactions" (Sirota *et al.*, 1974, p. 261).

Another study involving biofeedback training of HR was reported by Prigatano and Johnson (1972). In a first experiment, they demonstrated that when fearful subjects are exposed to the feared object they show an increase in HR variability. In a second experiment, spider-fearful college students were assessed as to level of fear both by self-report and behavioral approach (motoric) tests, and then assigned either to a condition in which they were trained in two 60-minute sessions via a visual feedback procedure to keep their HR relatively stable and to maintain this stability in the presence of the feared object, or given a comparable focused attention control procedure.

In terms of experimental design this study is a controlled group outcome study with treatment group and attention—placebo group. As such it represents the highest level of scientific evidence. The clinical problem, response to a feared object, spiders, while not especially important per se, is a good analogue.

The results of a posttreatment assessment of fear of spiders showed similar decreases in degree of fear of spiders as measured by both motor response and verbal self-report measures for the two groups. Moreover, the biofeedback-trained subjects did not show any greater control of HR variability than the untrained subjects.

Thus, while this study was adequate in terms of experimental design, and while it is an interesting application of biofeedback procedures, it tells us little of clinical importance. It may be the case that better or longer biofeedback training would show a difference, or that mere prolonged exposure to pictures of the feared object was sufficient to reduce fear (Agras, 1972), or it may be that the basic hypothesis of reducing autonomic arousal to reduce other fear-related response systems is not tenable.

In a related study, Nunes and Marks (1975) systematically added and withdrew biofeedback training in HR lowering to the treatment of 10 phobic women through the use of prolonged in vivo exposure to the feared object. During 2-hour in vivo exposure sessions, patients received feedback of HR and instructions to lower HR for 30-minute periods alternated with equal-length no-feedback periods. The order of feedback and no-feedback periods was counterbalanced with five patients receiving one order and the other five patients the other. Two to four prolonged exposure sessions were held.

The results showed that the patients' HRs were significantly lower during feedback periods than during no-feedback periods (mean difference 3.0 bpm, $p<.02$). However, there were *no* differences in spontaneous GSR fluctuations, nor, more importantly, in reports of subjective anxiety during feedback versus no-feedback periods.

Thus, while patients could learn to lower HR in the face of a phobic object, this training did nothing to enhance the treatment of the phobics through prolonged exposure, nor did it lead to any decrease in reported subjective discomfort during treatment. Therefore, in this report biofeedback training of HR lowering was successful (unlike the Prigatano and Johnson study) but it did not increase the efficacy of the treatment (like the findings of Prigatano and Johnson).

Another recent case report by Blanchard and Abel (1976) demonstrates the use of biofeedback training to counteract cardiac acceleration which typically accompanies anxiety. The patient, a 30-year-old female with a 16-year history of "fainting spells," had had numerous medical work-ups for her condition, a psychophysiological cardiovascular disorder. She had been raped at age 14 and become pregnant because of the rape. Her current problem turned out to be an episodic tachycardia triggered by thoughts of the rape incident or many other sexually related ideas. The tachycardia was typically followed by a bradycardia and a subsequent "fainting spell."

In order to elicit the problem behavior, audio tapes were developed that captured the ideation that triggered the spells. This was confirmed during baseline sessions during which the patient showed a consistent cardiac acceleration over a 10-minute trial with HR reaching levels of 140 bpm. After four baseline sessions, the patient was taught to lower her HR using the binary visual feedback described by Scott *et al.* (1973), while also listening to a neutral audio tape. After eight training sessions, she was reexposed to the HR-accelerating rape-tape while receiving feedback. This continued for 25 sessions until the patient could consistently lower her HR while listening to the tape. She was then returned to baseline conditions (i.e., listening to the rape-tape with no feedback).

This return to baseline made the study a single-subject experiment, and also enabled the authors to demonstrate some true self-control of HR since feedback had been withdrawn. After the six baseline sessions in which the patient was consistently able to lower her HR, five generalization sessions were run in which the patient listened to a new stressful rape audio tape and controlled her HR without the benefit of feedback.

Follow-up sessions at 2 and 4 months showed that the patient had retained her HR control. The patient's clinical course showed marked improvement; her "spells" disappeared during the training sessions in which feedback was paired with the stressful audio tape. Moreover, she became generally less anxious and was able to engage in activities she had avoided because of her fears.

This single-subject experiment is a clear-cut example of the use of HR biofeedback to overcome the cardiac acceleration which accompanies approach to fearful situations and of the subsequent beneficial clinical effects of such a treatment. The direct modification of the physiological response led to changes in motoric and cognitive responses. In other patients for whom the cognitive or self-report responses or the motoric or avoidance responses predominant, direct modification of the physiological response may have no effect. Certainly, the three response systems seem to have differing degrees of interrelation and importance in different patients. It may be the case that direct treatment of the physiological component of fear and anxiety is most efficacious when it constitutes the main clinical problem. Only further research can answer this issue.

d. Heart Rate Control and Cardiac Neurosis. The last report (Wickramasekera, 1974) concerns the biofeedback treatment of a 55-year-old male with a "cardiac neurosis" of 5 years duration. The problem started when the patient experienced shortness of breath and palpitation. He panicked and was rushed to the local hospital emergency room. The physical examination and laboratory tests were negative, however.

Since this incident, the patient had had over 25 similar "panic" attacks. Moreover, his job performance and marital relationship had deteriorated seriously and he was refraining from sexual relations with his wife for fear of another "heart attack." These attacks were characterized by the patient's noticing an increase in his HR and his shortness of breath. These physiological cues served to set off the whole maladaptive behavior chain. The patient had been treated for this condition with psychotherapy, hypnosis, and chemotherapy, in addition to numerous complete physical work-ups.

Treatment consisted of initially having the patient read some lay articles about biofeedback. Then he was given visual feedback of his HR and asked to learn to lower it while relaxing his body. After six sessions the patient could reliably lower his HR. Next, the patient presented himself scenes from a hierarchy concerned with incidents either involving or anticipating palpitations, etc., the cues which usually set off a "panic attack." He was told to continue to monitor his HR and keep it from increasing more than 10 bpm. In the latter event he was to "switch off" the scene. Next, the therapist verbally flooded the patient with anxiety-inducing scenes as well as presenting stimuli designed to elicit a startle reaction (sudden loud noises, etc.). The patient continued to monitor his HR. Although he would frequently experience brief cardiac accelerations of 15 to 35 bpm, he learned (1) that he did not pass out, and (2) he could bring his HR back to its normal level by relaxing and using the feedback.

During treatment the patient ceased having "panic attacks" and recovered much of his former behavior patterns, such as aggressively taking on his job and resuming sexual relations with his wife. At follow-ups 6 and 12 months after discharge, the patient remained free of panic attacks and continued his mental and vocational improvement.

This report represents a systematic case study in which the chief dependent variable involved "panic attacks." After a 5-year history of having up to five attacks per year, they ceased abruptly and permanently with the treatment. The data on the bioelectric response (HR) is admittedly poor but available. Moreover, the case contains elements of systematic desensitization with the hierarchy presentation. However, despite its limitations, this approach combining biofeedback training and "reality testing" certainly seems to warrant further investigation with this type of problem.

e. *Nontherapeutic Applications of Biofeedback Training to Patients.* Several studies have used patients with some cardiac disorder as subjects to be trained in HR control through biofeedback. However, the purposes of the biofeedback training in these studies was not treatment of the disorders but instead to obtain a better understanding of cardiac mechanisms. The basic notion in all of these studies is that HR can be treated as an independent variable, to be manipulated behaviorally through biofeedback training, rather than pharmacologically.

For example, Weiss and Engel (1975) attempted to teach three patients with third-degree (complete) heart blocks to speed their ventricular rate (VR) using their previously described binary visual feedback. Although exercise consistently increased VR in each patient, none of the patients was successful in speeding VR with only feedback, thus indicating that some neural pathways from the sinus pacemaker must be intact for operant conditioning of HR to be effective.

In another study, Bleecker and Engel (1973b) trained six patients with atrial fibrillation to control VR. The patients were taught to speed VR, slow VR, and finally to alternately speed and slow VR. This study was useful in identifying cardiac mechanisms; however, there were no long-lasting therapeutic effects due to the training in VR control.

Bleecker and Engel (1973a) have also reported on one case of Wolff–Parkinson–White syndrome (WPW) which they studied by conditioning techniques. The patient showed two types of cardiac impulse conduction: both normal and WPW. The patient had training in HR slowing, then HR speeding, and finally alternate speeding and slowing of HR. In each phase there was some learning of HR control. The patient was then given direct feedback of WPW conduction by monitoring the ECG from a position such that the QRS deflection for normal beats was in one direction and for WPW beats in the other. With this feedback arrangement, the patient was reliably taught to increase and decrease WPW and normal conduction. Finally, he learned to increase normal conduction as feedback was faded out.

This report is at best a systematic case study, in that the experimental conditions were spelled out clearly. However, since no overall clinical effects were noted and no systematic data reported on the principal dependent variable, its value is limited. Moreover, no baseline data were taken. This study is more like a case report or anecdotal data. Its chief value, like the others described in this section, probably lies in its contributions to the overall understanding of the functioning of the cardiovascular system. Furthermore, it demonstrates that it is possible to treat autonomic responses as independent variables, to be manipulated directly rather than via pharmacological agents.

The final study of this kind to be discussed here was conducted by Troyer, Twentyman, Gatchel, and Lang (1973). Comparisons were made of the abilities of patients with ischemic heart disease and those of normal college students to speed HR for one session and to slow HR for three sessions. Although both groups slowed HR, the patients were unable to increase HR when given visual feedback of HR. Also, the students showed both greater increases and decreases in HR than the patients in the appropriate conditions.

Since so few training sessions were given, it is not possible to ascertain if the results were due to the patients' inability to learn HR control or merely to their requiring more trials to learn the response. Also, the patients were significantly older than the student group so that differences obtained may have been due to age rather than the presence of ischemic heart disease.

f. Comment. There are several obvious methodological flaws present in the work on the clinical applications of biofeedback techniques in HR, such as frequent lack of a measured baseline, lack of adequate control conditions for either a single-subject experiment or a group-outcome experiment, and the occurrence of the therapeutic effect at different stages of treatment for different patients. Nevertheless, there are several conclusions we may tentatively draw on the work with cardiac arrhythmias: (1) In the work on PVCs, Engel's nine cases taken as a whole, along with the reported replication by Pickering, indicate that a therapeutic effect can be achieved through biofeedback. (2) In the studies on sinus tachycardia, the work of Scott *et al.,* in combination with the case reported by Engel and Bleecker, indicates that a therapeutic effect can also be achieved with this disorder. (3) Most of the work in this area is fairly marginal as regards quality of scientific evidence; it is at the level of anecdotal report or systematic case study. The two cases by Scott *et al.,* although "true" experimental analyses of behavior, still present problems of interpretation because of the failure to find a reversal in the return to baseline.

In the work on the use of biofeedback to lower HR as a means to counteract fear and anxiety, the results are mixed. Several controlled group outcome studies provide little evidence on the efficacy of this approach. However, all of these studies are marred by the brevity of biofeedback training. In the one single-subject experiment (Blanchard & Abel, 1976) in which adequate biofeedback training was given, positive results were obtained. The successful case of cardiac neurosis provides similar evidence on the need for adequate (i.e., enough training trials so that the response is learned) biofeedback training to obtain clinically meaningful results.

The biofeedback work with patients in which the aim is to study cardiac mechanisms seems very fruitful and has been brought to a high level by Engel. If one grants that it is desirable and useful to study cardiac mechanisms in patients who, as a result of naturally occurring disease, exhibit some sort of cardiac anomaly, and who give their informed consent to such research, then producing temporary voluntary changes in these patients through psychological means (biofeedback training) seems preferable to inducing changes by means of drugs such as beta-blockers, etc.

2. BLOOD PRESSURE

The second cardiovascular response that has received major attention is blood pressure (BP), due in large part to the large-scale health problem represented by hypertension, particularly essential hypertension. Technically, there is no bioelectric response of BP. Like HR, it is an indirectly measured response. The pressure in the major arteries varies moment to moment between two values: the highest pressure, or systolic BP, and the lowest pressure, or diastolic BP. Although BP can be measured directly by inserting a cannula attached to a pressure tranducer into an artery, this is rarely done. Instead, most BP measurements are done indirectly with an occluding cuff. The pressure in the cuff, which is sufficient to occlude all blood flow in the artery, is called the systolic BP. It is measured as the pressure at which blood just begins to flow in the vessel as detected by the *onset* of the Korotkoff sounds (as pressure is gradually reduced from above the occlusion point). The pressure at which these sounds *disappear* is termed the diastolic BP.

In BP, in contrast to the work with HR, the physiological response itself is the clinical response of interest. The World Health Organization has defined hypertension as BP in excess of 140 mmHg for systolic and in excess of 90 mmHg for diastolic.

Numerous studies, summarized for the most part by Blanchard and Young (1973), have been reported in which normotensive subjects were taught to increase or decrease BP through various biofeedback training techniques. Interestingly, most of this research came from a limited number of investigators, probably because of the technical problems involved in giving feedback of BP as opposed to the ease with which feedback of HR may be obtained.

The earlier review listed four studies in which BP was both the clinical response and the biological response for which feedback was given. These four studies, plus the four additional studies of direct biofeedback training of BP, are all summarized below.

The first (and in some ways one of the best) study of BP feedback in hypertensive patients was that conducted by Benson, Shapiro, Tursky, and Schwartz (1971), utilizing the BP feedback system developed by the Harvard group (Shapiro, Tursky, Gershon, & Stern, 1969; Tursky, Shapiro, & Schwartz, 1972). Seven patients were initially run in baseline sessions, during which time they sat comfortably relaxed until their systolic BP measured in the session showed no further decrease for five consecutive sessions. Next, feedback training to lower systolic BP was introduced and continued until systolic BP again showed no further decrease over five consecutive sessions.

Results showed that one patient was not hypertensive during baseline. Five of the seven subjects showed marked (16 mmHg or greater) decreases in systolic BP from baseline to the end of treatment. Two of the six hypertensive patients reduced systolic BP to the normotensive range ($<$ 140 mmHg). For the group, the change in BP was highly significant ($p < .02$).

Several features of this study are noteworthy: First, a very stable baseline was established before treatment was begun. Only one other study (Kristt & Engel, 1975) has baseline data with this degree of stability. Obtaining a stable baseline is important when one considers that four of the seven patients required 15 or more sessions to reach stability. Second, marked decreases in BP were achieved in five of seven subjects. In two cases, BP was reduced to the normotensive range.

The study's shortcomings are in terms of experimental design: (1) As a group study, although there is a significant decrease in BP, the lack of a control group hinders interpretation of the results. (2) An alternative way of viewing the study is as a series of systematic case reports of the A-B nature. This being the case, the series is impressive but lacks the strength of the single-subject experiment. (3) The failure to include return-to-baseline sessions, or any other follow-up data, also limits the value of the study. Inclusion of the former would have turned the study into a series of experiments.

Schwartz and Shapiro (1973) conducted a similar study on a second group of seven hypertensive patients. There were several differences in this study: (1) Diastolic BP was the response monitored and the response for which feedback was given. (2) Subjects were run for a fixed number of trials in each of three conditions. Results showed that average diastolic BP in baseline was 102 mmHg. Unfortunately, there was no overall decrease in any subsequent condition, despite the fact that decreases in BP of up to 5 mmHg occurred within individual sessions during the feedback conditions.

This study is a single group outcome study. No individual data are presented. Although in terms of design the lack of a control group is a problem, the major difficulty for this study is the lack of overall significant changes in diastolic BP. Thus the study is of little clinical importance.

As an aside, this study seemed to mark the end of the Harvard group's efforts at clinical studies of BP. Shapiro (1974) reported on a single case of a hypertensive patient treated in his laboratory. Although the patient could show reductions in BP to 135/85 in the laboratory, his BP was measured by his physician as 160/110 mmHg both before treatment and at the conclusion. Results like these seem to have led Shapiro to abandon this work. Likewise, Benson (personal communication, May 1975) found his hypertensives treated by biofeedback returned to their previously high levels when he followed them up informally. Benson apparently has abandoned biofeedback as a nonpharmacological strategy for dealing with hypertension and moved to trying to teach patients to use the "relaxation response" (Benson, Rosner, & Marzetta, 1973), a meditation-like practice.

Miller (1972) has reported on the treatment of one case of hypertension. During baseline the patient's diastolic BP varied from 75 to 115 mmHg with a mean of 97 mmHg. She was trained both to raise and lower BP in the experimental sessions, which were conducted both in the hospital and, after discharge, on an outpatient basis. Her diastolic BP at the end of training was 76 mmHg and relatively stable; moreover, she had been withdrawn from antihypertensive medication and diuretics.

This work represents a very good systematic case study; however, it cannot be considered as experimental evidence to support the efficacy of biofeedback procedures since no control conditions were run. Miller himself noted that other factors may have been responsible for the changes.

Interestingly, in a later report, Miller (1975b) noted that the above patient "lost voluntary control" of her BP during a series of emotional stresses and had to be restarted on antihypertensive drugs. Later, biofeedback training led to some degree of recovery of control of BP. Miller (1975b) also reported that similar training procedures with 27 other hypertensive patients had "produced considerably poorer, not really promising, results." He too (Miller, personal communication, May 1975) has more or less abandoned seeking to treat hypertensives through biofeedback.

One controlled group outcome study of the use of BP feedback with hypertensives has been completed (Elder, Ruiz, Deabler, & Dillenkoffer, 1973). Three groups of "hypertensive patients" were run in the study. After one baseline session, the experimental subjects were given seven sessions of feedback of diastolic BP. One experimental group received only feedback while the other received the same feedback plus social reinforcement for success. An interesting technical feature of this study was that BP was measured and feedback given only once every 2 minutes as contrasted to the beat-by-beat feedback used in the other three studies.

Results, expressed as a percent of baseline BP rather than actual BP values, showed no significant between-group effects on systolic BP. On diastolic BP, however, the group that received feedback and social reinforcement showed a 20% decrease in diastolic BP and was significantly lower than the no-feedback or feedback-only group. The latter group was significantly lower than the no-feedback group for the last session. Follow-up data were collected 1 week later on those subjects who were available. However, the differential dropout rate was so great that the results were inconclusive.

At first glance this study seems highly encouraging since large-scale decreases in diastolic BP were obtained in a controlled group outcome trial. However, several features of the methodology present serious problems. (1) There were apparently instructional differences between the feedback-plus-reinforcement group and the feedback-only group; the former subjects were asked to try to lower BP and to try to relax whereas it is not clear what the latter subjects were told. In defense of Elder *et al.* (1973), however, regardless of instructional differences, the results seem to confirm the efficacy of their procedure. (2) Unfortunately, only one baseline session was conducted. Since Benson *et al.* (1971) have elegantly documented that BP may continue to decrease for as many as 16 daily sessions, it could be that the results were entirely due to differential adaptation rates in the hospital. (3) Only the BP values for the baseline session are given. These reveal that one no-feedback subject was normotensive at the start of the study and two were only borderline hypertensive. It might well be the case that these patients with lower (and hence more nearly normal) BPs at the start of the study showed less adaptation, and hence less percentage decrease, than the two feedback groups. (4) Finally, some unspecified number of subjects were on minor tranquilizers.

On the whole, the Elder *et al.* (1973) study seems to hold out promise but has enough questionable methodology to warrant withholding wholesale adoption of the results. What is needed is a replication to confirm or contradict these interesting results.

The study by Shoemaker and Tasto (1975) is a small-scale controlled group outcome study comparing BP feedback, relaxation training, and no-treatment (except BP monitoring) as strategies for lowering the BP of "hypertensive patients." The results show greater lowering of both systolic and diastolic BP by the relaxation training group than for the BP biofeedback group or the control, both within sessions and across sessions. As a group, the relaxation training subjects reduced both systolic and diastolic BP by about 7 mmHg. The biofeedback group also showed a small (1.2 mmHg), but statistically significant, decrease in diastolic BP in comparison to the control group. No follow-up data were obtained.

There are two major problems with this study: First, the subjects, with one exception, *were not hypertensive;* they were normotensive or at least borderline hypertensive. Thus the study becomes more nearly one involving changing BP in a nonhypertensive population. Second, the BP biofeedback procedure was not refined. In fact, the results show that it was ineffective for the most part. Thus the study becomes one of comparing Jacobsonian relaxation [which has been shown several times before, e.g., Jacobson (1939), to be effective at lowering BP] with an ineffective procedure and no treatment. The BP biofeedback therefore becomes an attention–placebo condition!

Blanchard, Young, and Haynes (1975b) provided data on the treatment of four hypertensive patients with a novel, yet simple, feedback technique. It was an open-loop feedback system in which the systolic BP of each subject was determined once per minute. This value was read by the experimenter and then plotted on a graph visible to the patient. By using both baseline and feedback conditions, Blanchard et al. (1975b) treated each patient as a single-subject experiment. Two were A-B-A experiments and the other two were A-B-A-B.

In each instance systolic BP was lowered into the normotensive range. Changes ranged from 9 to 55 mmHg. Follow-up data at 1 or 2 weeks after the last feedback session showed that systolic BP was remaining low.

Because of the experimental design used, it was clear that the biofeedback procedure was responsible for the lowering of BP. Moreover, stable initial BP baseline values were obtained.

The study has several faults, however. (1) Only one of the patients was clearly hypertensive; the other three were borderline hypertensive. (2) No measurements of BP outside of the laboratory were obtained. Thus it was not possible to determine if the effects generalized to the patient's natural environment. If they did not, they are interesting but trivial. (3) The follow-up data were woefully inadequate.

The BP biofeedback procedure developed by Blanchard and his associates has been shown (in graph comparison studies) to be effective at helping normotensives lower BP (Blanchard, Young, Haynes, & Kallman, 1974a; Blanchard, Haynes, Kallman, & Harkey, 1975a). However, this procedure awaits a controlled group outcome study with hypertensive patients to adequately assess its value.

Kleinman and Goldman (1974) reported on seven newly diagnosed hypertensive patients who were treated with biofeedback training for nine sessions using the Harvard apparatus. All patients were drug free. No baseline measurement sessions were run.

Over the nine training sessions, average systolic BP dropped from 167.4 mmHg to 145.1 mmHg at session 5 but had returned to a level of 161.1 mmHg by session 9. Consistent within-session decreases in BP of 8.0 mmHg were found. Diastolic BP dropped from an initial level of 108.6 mmHg to a value of about 94 mmHg by session 5 or 6 and remained there.

The lack of a control group, combined with the lack of any baseline or adaptation session, as well as little or no in-session adaptation, lead one to speculate that these results were little more than adaptation or habituation effects. Perhaps there was a real decrease in diastolic BP; however, the grouped data curve looks very much like an adaptation curve. In any event, this study seems to point towards failure of the Harvard beat-by-beat BP apparatus to produce clinically meaningful results.

The final BP biofeedback study is by Kristt and Engel (1975) on five hypertensive patients. All five had 10-year documented histories of hypertension, and all were on antihypertensive medication. Following Engel's typical paradigm for teaching HR control, all subjects were first taught to raise BP, then lower BP, and finally to alternately raise and lower BP using a feedback procedure like that of the Harvard group (Tursky et al., 1972), which gives beat-by-beat feedback.

A valuable feature of this study is that the patients were taught to take their own BPs at home and run in a 7-week baseline period during which time they took their BP four times a day and mailed in the results daily to the experimenter. This gave the study very good baseline data, gathered in the patient's own environment under stable conditions.

The in-laboratory training data seem to show that all subjects learned to lower BP in the laboratory (usually by about 10 to 20 mmHg) and four of five to raise BP. All subjects also learned the alternation. (One could question the author's use of statistics in this experiment as all of the tests were done separately on data from a single subject. However, the graphical displays of mean values collapsed across sessions seem to bear out the statistical findings.)

After training, the subjects continued to monitor their BP at home and send in daily reports. More importantly, they also were instructed to practice lowering their BP at home. The important results of this study highlight comparisons of baseline data with data from the posttraining follow-up at home. Unfortunately, baseline data were not available on one patient. For the other four there were decreases in systolic BP for each patient, ranging from 9 to 36 mmHg, and averaging 18 mmHg. For two of the four subjects there were significant decreases in diastolic BP (7 and 20 mmHg, respectively). Three of the patients were also able to lower their antihypertensive medication schedules as a result of training.

This study demonstrates fairly well that subjects learned BP control while in the laboratory and that their BP at posttraining follow-up for 3 months was lower than baseline (pretraining). However, for two reasons this study does not enable us to say if these two sets of events are related: (1) Subjects were not asked to lower BP during baseline and were asked to do so during follow-up. That alone might account for the difference. (2) Failure to collect subject-read BP during the training sessions while the patients were in the laboratory is a methodological inadequacy. Inspection of the pre- and posttraining for the four subjects on whom it is available reveals that two patients clearly had lower systolic BP after training and two had had marginal changes. On diastolic BP, one had a clearly lower BP, one marginally lower, and two seemed unchanged.

Because of the failure to hold conditions constant during pre- and posttraining, the data from the pre- and posttraining measurement become good systematic case studies but are not single-subject experiments. (The data from the laboratory do represent true experiments, however.) As a series of systematic case studies, the changes which did occur seem related to the biofeedback training, but could be due to the 3-week hospitalization. Certainly, they are provocative and warrant following up. Also, an interesting aspect of this report is that three of the patients had evidently learned "true" self-control of BP since they could demonstrate it to neutral examiners, in the absence of any feedback.

   a. Additional Studies of Biofeedback Training to Lower Blood Pressure. Although we stated earlier that this review is organized around bioelectric responses for which feedback is given, in this section we are going to deviate from that organization by reviewing several studies in which the clinical response of interest is BP but in which the bioelectric response for which feedback was given was different.

In the first study of a series performed in England, Patel (1973) treated 20 hypertensive patients for three 30-minute sessions per week for 3 months. All but one patient were on antihypertension medication; 17 of the 20 cases were diagnosed as essential hypertension. All had been diagnosed as hypertensive for at least 1 year.

Treatment consisted of a combination of passive relaxation training and biofeedback of skin resistance (galvanic skin potential, similar to GSR). In relaxation, the patient was instructed to attend mentally to the various parts of his body, to make them limp and relaxed, and also to focus attention on his regular breathing. He was taught phases similar to those from autogenic training (Schultz & Luthe, 1969) and also similar to yoga exercises. Patients were instructed to practice relaxation at home and were told their BP values for each session.

The biofeedback signal was a tone which increased in pitch as skin resistance increased. Supposedly, this signal was directly related to sympathetic nervous system activity; thus as the tone decreased in pitch or was turned off, sympathetic arousal was decreasing.

Results showed that 16 of 20 patients had some decrease in BP. Group results were expressed as mean BP (diastolic plus 1/3 pulse pressure); group mean BP decreased from 121 to 101. (Fortunately Patel gave complete data on all subjects so that we can calculate the results. Systolic BP decreased an average of 24.7 mmHg; diastolic BP decreased an average of 14.3 mmHg). Five patients were able to stop antihypertensive medication altogether, while seven more decreased dosages of antihypertensive medication from 33 to 60%. There were no changes in respiration rate, HR, or body weight.

This single group outcome study certainly provides some intriguing possibilities. The lack of stable baseline measurements as well as follow-up data limit the study somewhat, as does the lack of a control group. Moreover, the fact that the experimenter took the BP measurements is also a weakness in methodology. However, the real strength of the study is the magnitude of the results and the large number of patients who had positive responses.

The second study in the series (Patel, 1975a) represents an exact replication of the first study with two added benefits: 12-month follow-up data are presented as well as data on a control group.

Two groups of 20 patients each, matched closely for age, sex, and initial BP comprised the subject sample. The experimental group received the same treatment as previously described: passive relaxation training akin to yoga exercises and autogenic training and biofeedback of skin resistance as an indication of sympathetic tone. The control subjects received the same number of physician contacts for the same duration. However, they merely rested in a supine position. Again, the experimenter took all of the BP measurements. Follow-up measurements were made at 3, 6, and 12 months.

Results showed significant ($p < .001$) decreases in both systolic BP ($\Delta = 20.4$ mmHg) and diastolic BP ($\Delta = 14.2$ mmHg) while the controls showed no change on systolic and a 2.1 mmHg decrease (nonsignificant) on diastolic BP. These results are comparable to those of the first study.

During the 1-year follow-up, BP for the experimental subjects and controls remained unchanged. The therapeutic gains from training were maintained. Subjects had been instructed to practice relaxation at home during training and after the experiment as a way of maintaining and enhancing gains.

Drug dosage was reduced in 12 patients by 33 to 100%. These reduced dosages were maintained in 10 of 12 patients throughout the year. This study answers two of the three previous criticisms. A control group which received an attention–placebo treatment was included and follow-up data were obtained. Moreover, calculations of changes in BP were made from the readings at the first three sessions, giving something of a baseline. There remains only the issue of the experimenter doing the measurement, which is resolved in the next study.

The third study in this series (Patel & North, 1975) represents a systematic replication of Patel's earlier work. Three pretreatment assessments of BP were made on separate visits on the total sample of 34 hypertensive patients. Then, for the first phase of the study, patients were randomly assigned to either the biofeedback and yoga treatment or to a control condition. Treatment was reduced to twice-weekly sessions for 6 weeks. The yoga and biofeedback treatment involved instructions and practice in passive relaxation and meditation as well as biofeedback. In the first 6 sessions feedback of skin resistance was given. For the later sessions, EMG feedback from an unspecified site was administered to further aid relaxation. Patients were urged to practice relaxation twice a day and to incorporate the relaxation into their daily lives. Control subjects were seen for the same length of time and frequency of sessions. During these sessions they rested quietly on a couch. Most important, all BP measurements were done by a third party, a nurse, who was "blind" as to group assignment. Again, medications were held constant.

Results showed a mean decrease, from pretreatment levels of BP of 26.1 mmHg systolic and 15.2 mmHg diastolic for the experimental group and 8.9 mmHg systolic and 4.2 mmHg diastolic for the controls. Changes for the experimental subjects were significantly ($p < .005$) greater than those for the controls. During the 3-month follow-up, the experimental group's BP rose slightly from 141.4 to 148.8 systolic and from 84.4 to 87.9 diastolic. Rises in the control group were substantially higher: 160.0 to 176.6 systolic and 96.4 to 104.3 diastolic.

In the very important second phase of the study, the control group was then given the same treatment the experimental group received in phase 1. This "half-crossover design," or exact replication of treatment on the controls provides a very powerful test of the efficacy of the treatment since it had already been established that patients in the phase 1 control group did not respond to repeated contacts, attention, or periods of simple relaxation.

The results of this study were that the newly treated group showed decreases in BP comparable to those shown by the experimental group in phase 1. Systolic BP was decreased by 28.1 mmHg and diastolic BP by 15.0 mmHg. The phase 1 experimental subjects continued to show lowered BP values.

This study seems to show conclusively that the combination of passive relaxation and meditation (modeled after several yoga exercises) and of biofeedback of skin resistance for lowered sympathetic tone is very effective. The three studies taken together are very impressive and are of the highest quality in terms of scientific merit.

Only two questions remain: (1) Is biofeedback training necessary for the success of the procedure? (2) Are the results replicable by another independent investigator? On the first point it may be the case that yoga exercises alone are the active ingredient in the treatment. Datey, Deshmukh, Dalvi, and Vinekar (1969) reported on 47 hypertensive patients who were trained in the yoga exercise ("Shavasan") for 3 weeks and then instructed to continue practicing it. It consists of passive relaxation and breathing exercises similar to those used by Patel. Datey et al. (1969) found significant ($p < .05$) decreases in BP for the 10 nonmedicated hypertensives. The change in mean BP (diastolic plus 1/3 pulse pressure while recumbent) was 27 mmHg; significant decreases occurred in nine of 10 patients. In the medicated subjects, little change in BP occurred.

However, in 13 of the 22 well-controlled patients, significant (33% or more) decreases were made in medication levels.

Patel (1975b) performed another interesting experiment on the subjects from Study 3. Before training began, and at the completion of phase 1 training, all subjects were exposed to two stressful situations to see the effects on BP and the time necessary for BP to recover to prestress level. The two stresses were an exercise test and the "cold pressor" test for which essential hypertensives usually show a dramatic rise in BP.

The treated subjects showed significant ($p < .05$ or better) reductions in BP rise to stress and in time of recovery after treatment. Moreover, in seven of eight comparisons, they showed less BP reaction than the control subjects after the former had completed their training. This is another indication of the strength of the training effects.

A second series of studies has been conducted by Love and his associates. In the first study (Moeller & Love, 1974), six patients who had had a diagnosis of essential hypertension for at least 3 years and who were on antihypertensive medication took part in a 15-session training program which combined autogenic training with EMG feedback. Initially, the EMG feedback was from the forearm, but later it was from the frontalis muscles. BP measurements were made manually at the beginning of each session.

Results showed that five of six subjects had meaningful decreases in BP. Average systolic BP dropped from 153 mmHg to 135 mmHg while diastolic dropped from 100 mmHg to 88 mmHg ($p < .10$), decreases of 12%.

In a second, larger-scale study (Love, Montgomery, & Moeller, 1974), three treatment conditions, all of which utilized EMG feedback for frontalis muscle, were used. In two of the treatment conditions, subjects were given relaxation training which was a blend of Jacobsonian progressive relaxation and autogenic training. Also, they were instructed to use tapes to practice at home twice daily. These two groups differed in terms of one receiving two sessions per week and the other one session. A fourth group, the controls, had BP monitored in the laboratory twice weekly for 4 weeks. Experimental subjects were run for 12 weeks.

Unfortunately, there were differential dropout rates and much lost data, so that from 10 to 40% of subjects' data were not available. There were no differences among the three experimental groups so that the data on all three were combined.

A comparison of BPs at the end of the control period (4 weeks) showed significantly greater decreases in the combined treatment groups than the controls for diastolic BP (Δ = 9.8 mmHg) and a trend for systolic BP (Δ = 12.7 mmHg). Further comparisons of pre- and posttreatment BP's for the treated subjects showed significant (p < .01) decreases at the end of treatment for systolic (Δ = 14.7 mmHg) and diastolic (Δ = 12.7 mmHg) BP.

A 9-month follow-up (Montgomery, Love, & Moeller, 1975) on 23 of the 32 subjects who completed the EMG feedback training showed further decreases in BP. At the end of 1 year after training began, BP had decreased by 27.5 mmHg systolic and 17.7 mmHg diastolic.

Although the loss of subjects detracts from this study, particularly for the treated subjects, the results do seem to indicate that EMG feedback training is an effective procedure for dealing with elevated BP.

Russ (1974), in a preliminary report, found statistically significant decreases in systolic BP in a group of five borderline hypertensive patients who received a combination of progressive relaxation for two sessions followed by frontalis EMG feedback for nine sessions. Both systolic and diastolic BP dropped an average of 8 mmHg. Three hypertensive subjects run in a direct BP feedback similar to that of Elder *et al.* (1973) showed little or no change.

b.   Other Related Studies of Blood Pressure Lowering. Three other studies of interest have recently been completed, in which the clinical response was the lowering of BP in hypertensive patients. In the first study, Deabler, Fidel, Dillenkoffer, and Elder (1973) treated six hypertensive patients who were free of medication and nine who were on stable doses of antihypertensive medication, with a combination of Jacobsonian progressive relaxation and hypnosis. Six other hypertensives not on medication constituted the control group. The latter subjects were seen as frequently as the experimental subjects and had BP measurements taken in the same manner, but received no other treatment.

The treated subjects were first put through progressive relaxation training and then given hypnosis training in the same session to deepen the relaxation. BP measurements were made after the relaxation training and after the hypnosis training in each session.

In analyzing their results, the authors treated their data in a somewhat unorthodox manner. Repeated BP measurements for experimental subjects were treated *as if* they were obtained on separate groups of subjects. These statistical manipulations led the authors to conclude that both hypnosis and relaxation training resulted in greater decreases in BP than the control procedure for both systolic and diastolic BP in both groups, but that hypnosis was superior. Such claims do not seem warranted by the data, especially in view of the confound of hypnosis always coming later in the session after the patient had been in a relaxed state for a longer period of time.

What does seem clear is that the combination of relaxation and hypnosis led to significant decreases in systolic BP of about 17%, in diastolic BP of about 20% in the drug-free group, and 10% in the group on drugs. Although no follow-up results were presented, the relatively sizeable decreases in BP over the short training period certainly are encouraging and warrant further investigation. Whether hypnosis training is needed is not at all clear.

In the second study, Benson *et al.* (1973) examined the effects of regularly practicing a relaxation procedure like meditation in 30 hypertensive patients on stabilized doses of antihypertensive medication. Initially, stable levels of BP were obtained over a 6-week period, with measurements taken about once a week and repeated in the session until they showed no further decrease. Then, after they were given instructions in the meditation procedure, subjects were asked to practice it twice a day.

Posttraining measurements of BP were made after 3, 6, and 9 weeks. Systolic BP showed significant decrease from a pretreatment level of 150.2 to posttreatment values of 142.1, 140.1, and 135.2 mmHg, respectively. Diastolic BP *did not change significantly.* Nine of the subjects stopped the meditation practice after the experiment was completed. Within 4 weeks their BPs had returned to pretraining levels.

This constitutes a good single-group study. The discontinuation of meditation by nine of the subjects enabled the authors to obtain single-subject experimental data on these since measurements were obtained during the return-to-baseline condition. Interestingly, during the return to baseline, the continued practice of relaxation was shown to be the causal agent in the BP decrease since BPs returned to the original levels.

The final study, by Brady, Luborsky, and Kron (1974), examined the effects of metronome-conditioned relaxation on the diastolic BP of four labile hypertensive patients. Each subject constituted a single-subject experiment in either an A-B-A or A-B-A-B design.

The BP measurements were made daily at times different from the relaxation sessions. Thus, the dependent variable measurement was more conservative than in most of the other studies reported in this section. The latter consisted of half-hour sessions in which patients relaxed in a prone position while listening to tape recordings designed to facilitate relaxation. One subject made all of his own BP recordings and practiced the relaxation at his own initiative.

After allowing BP to stabilize over a 2 to 4 week period, relaxation was introduced for 18 to 75 sessions. There was then a return to baseline conditions for 14 to 22 sessions and a final return to relaxation for another 6 months, with the last 50 sessions being used for data.

Three of the four subjects showed clear decreases in diastolic BP while practicing relaxation and returns to baseline levels when it was discontinued. Decreases ranged from 3 to 13 mmHg.

Although the study, because of the use of a single-subject experimental design, clearly demonstrates the role of relaxation training in decreasing diastolic BP, this same feature leads one to question its long-term clinical utility. Diastolic BP returned to baseline levels in as little as 2 weeks despite as many as 75 training sessions. It would seem that the patient would have to continue relaxation training with the same faithfulness that he took his antihypertensive medication!

c. Comment. At this point the research on BP biofeedback is not impressive. A truly solid study with adequate controls, adequate baseline, and good follow-up data has yet to be done. Results with the beat-by-beat feedback device, developed by the Harvard group, have been mixed. One study (Benson *et al.*, 1971) found significant reductions in systolic BP, but later informal follow-up (Benson, 1975) found that the results did not persist. Two other group studies were failures. Miller (1975b) has also failed to replicate the initial success (Miller, 1972) found with his feedback procedure.

Feedback of a more intermittent basis has shown some degree of success (Blanchard *et al.*, 1975b; Elder *et al.*, 1973), but no meaningful follow-up data have been available. Other similar attempts (Shoemaker & Tasto, 1975) were clear-cut failures.

Only Krist and Engel's (1975) study has both adequate baseline and adequate follow-up. Although their sample size is small, for some patients their rigorous training program, which contained many self-control elements and follow-up practice, seems to have been truly beneficial.

When one leaves direct feedback of BP and looks instead at feedback of some other response, the results are more encouraging. Patel's series of studies represents a hallmark in the area. He has moved from single group study to a controlled outcome study and then to a second, better controlled group outcome study with a replication. In each case he has achieved large-scale, clinically significant decreases in BP. The main issue in his work is whether the biofeedback training (of skin resistance to aid relaxation) adds anything to his basic passive relaxation procedure. Love and his colleagues have demonstrated that relaxation training assisted by EMG feedback has a clinically significant effect which holds up over a 1-year follow-up. Other studies involving relaxation training without biofeedback have yielded good results. However, effects do not tend to persist once training is discontinued.

At this point it would seem that relaxation training, preferably of a passive nature like autogenic training rather than progressive relaxation, can have clinically significant effects on the blood pressure of hypertensive patients, especially if the patients continue to practice the relaxation exercises and adapt it to their everyday life. Biofeedback seems to aid in the initial relaxation training, but this point is not definitely confirmed at present.

A key issue in the psychological treatment of hypertension may be how to get the patient to practice his relaxation regularly and how to get him to use it in his day-to-day routine. In a word, "patient compliance" may be as much of an issue in psychological treatment as in pharmacological treatment.

Regardless of the compliance problems, psychological treatment, based generally on relaxation, would seem to warrant a major trial since its side effects are much less of a problem than those of any medication. Moreover, the growing literature on self-control and self-regulation may aid in obtaining higher degrees of patient compliance. Finally, there may be an overall global benefit in "self-esteem" or patient morale since a patient using relaxation would be more likely to attribute success to his own efforts than one on medication.

B. Electromyographic Responses

The electromyogram, or EMG, response is a measure of muscle activity which has been demonstrated to be useful in numerous clinical applications. The EMG serves as the target response in biofeedback research for several different types of disorders. In one major category, muscle activity serves as the primary target for a particular clinical effect. This is the case with muscle retraining of stroke patients. Movement of a limb in a hemiplegic patient is very dependent upon demonstration that the controlling muscle fibers can move, as EMG activity and voluntary movement are interdependent. (Passive movement of a muscle does not produce EMG activity.) A second category of disorders utilizes modification of the EMG response to produce change in another response system. An example of this is tension headache research, in which the forehead or neck muscle is changed to produce changes in self-report of pain. Demonstrations of reliable EMG changes without changes in self-report of headaches would not be sufficient for clinical success. Other types of disorders that are treated by utilizing EMG change to produce modification in another response system include: (1) reducing subvocal speech to improve reading speed and comprehension, and (2) overall reduction in EMG as a means of producing relaxation to reduce self-reports of anxiety.

1. MUSCLE RETRAINING

Changes in muscle activity as the primary focus of treatment involve two separate uses: to increase activity in a dormant muscle, as in hemiplegic or foot drop; or to decrease activity in an overactive muscle, as in spastic movement or torticollis.

a. Increasing Muscle Activity. The initial report of feedback effects in increasing muscle activity was presented in an anecdotal case report by Marinacci and Horande (1960). They presented clinical case data on feedback effects to teach voluntary EMG control in several types of disorders, including hemiplegia, reversible physiological block due to edema, muscle atrophy as a function of causalgia, muscle control after nerve injury by giant motor unit compensation, substitution of normal muscles for paralyzed ones, and control of paralysis due to Bell's palsy and polio. Since each of the patients treated suffered from the above disorders for a considerable time prior to the treatment, which involved direct auditory feedback of muscle activity, remarkable clinical effects that had not been obtainable by standard physical therapy procedures were demonstrated.

Several other demonstrations of the successful treatment of hemiplegia have been reported. In a series of systematic case reports, Andrews (1964) utilized visual feedback to increase upper extremity muscle functioning in 20 hemiplegics. Training involving a single 5-minute feedback trial was associated with strong, voluntarily controlled activity of the paretic muscle in 17 of 20 patients. Brudny, Korein, Levidow, Grynbaum, Lieberman, and Friedmann (1974b) used visual and auditory feedback to increase functioning of upper extremities for 13 hemiplegics, nine of whom had the disorder for more than 9 months. Results indicated some improvement in seven of the nine with maximal improvement in four of the nine. Treatment durations for these patients ranged from 4 to 6 weeks of thrice weekly, half-hour sessions. The maximum duration of treatment for any patient was 12 weeks.

Johnson and Garton (1973) and Basmajian, Kukulka, Narayan, and Takebe (1975) have demonstrated successful rehabilitation of patients suffering from foot drop, a paralytic condition involving the tibias anterior muscle in the lower extremity. Johnson and Garton (1973) used a two-step training procedure for 10 patients in a single group outcome design. The first stage involved visual feedback using a diagnostic EMG machine, while the second phase utilized a portable EMG unit that provided both auditory and visual feedback. Patients were requested to practice for two half-hour sessions a day over a duration of 2 to 16 weeks. Clinical results, determined by assessment of functional levels of foot dorsiflexion, indicated better than fair improvement (on the Georgia Warm Springs Foundation measurement system; Hines, 1965) for seven of the 10 patients, while each patient showed some change. Basmajian *et al.* (1975) compared standard physical rehabilitation procedures with these procedures plus biofeedback using both auditory and visual feedback for two groups of 10 patients with chronic foot drop. Results indicated improvement in both range of motion and muscle strength tests. The effects of biofeedback were approximately twice as great as standard physical training alone. Also, better changes in functional movement were apparent for the patients receiving biofeedback. This study is notable for the extensive measurement employed, as well as the follow-up gait measurement, conducted from 4 to 16 weeks posttreatment, which showed no decreases in function.

An interesting use of feedback to increase muscle functioning was reported in a systematic case study by Booker, Rubow, and Coleman (1969) in a woman who had lost voluntary function in left-sided facial muscles following damage to the left facial nerve in an automobile accident. An initial surgical intervention performed to activate facial nerves by trapezius and sternomastoid muscle movement was not successful in producing acceptable functional and cosmetic control of facial muscles. Prior to feedback training, the patient could produce some left facial changes by exaggerated left shoulder movements. Training involved having the subject produce EMG activity to match oscilloscope signals generated either by a computer or by the muscles on the right side of her face. This latter implementation was critical as concurrent regulation of muscles in both sides of the face was necessary for cosmetic purposes to assure symmetry during normal activity. Training effects were reported to be positive, with some regression at 4-month follow-up which was easily reversed by 3 days of booster training.

   Comment. In summary, the use of biofeedback procedures to produce movement in paralyzed muscles produces striking clinical effects. This effect is particularly notable since many of the patients described in the above studies had the disorders for long durations and other attempted therapeutic procedures had been unsuccessful. Finally, consistent with the results of Basmajian, there are strong indications that biofeedback plus physical training is superior to physical training alone. The consistency of results in these studies indicates that biofeedback procedures are associated with positive outcome in accelerating muscle activity in numerous dysfunctions. However, no studies have demonstrated that the feedback procedures per se are critical to the success. On the one hand, no studies have provided data on the relationship between feedback and the actual EMG, which is necessary to demonstrate the importance of feedback. An interesting approach might be to provide patients noncontingent feedback prior to contingent feedback to rule out placebo effects which might be attributable to the feedback equipment or to provide feedback for a different muscle group in a multiple baseline design. Also, none of the studies provides quantitative EMG data to indicate the changes in muscle activity. Of course, it can be argued that changes in functional movement, as measured by Johnson and Garton (1973) and Basmajian *et al.* (1975), are more important than simple EMG changes, since an EMG change without resultant change in functional movement would not be clinically important.

   b. Decreasing Muscle Activity. A decrease in muscle activity can also serve as the target response. Several single group outcome studies have been done with torticollis, which requires decrease in muscle activity of a hypertrophied muscle of one side of the body, while functioning is increased in the opposite, atrophied muscle. Both auditory and visual feedback were used by Brudny, Grynbaum, and Korein (1974a) to produce equal amounts of muscle activity from sternocleidomastoid muscles on both sides of the neck when the head was kept in a neutral position. The EMG data presented indicated that successful feedback control was achieved by each patient for at least 30 minutes. Self-control of EMG and the attendant positive clinical effects were shown in six of the nine patients for periods of several hours. Three patients eventually required some posttreatment boosters. Brudny *et al.* (1974b) replicated these procedures with four more patients, and demonstrated self-control of neutral head position for at least 30 minutes in three of the four patients. In addition, four other dystonic subjects were treated for torticollis; self-control of normal head position was obtained for only one subject for several hours but no clinically significant changes were observed for the other three patients. Cleeland (1973) reported the use of auditory and visual feedback plus shock contingent on increase of muscle activity in 10 torticollis patients. Eight of the patients demonstrated feedback-influenced control, while six of these also maintained self-control of clinical effects after treatment. However, the combination of treatments makes it difficult to isolate the specific effects of biofeedback. The report did indicate that contingent shock plus feedback was consistently better than feedback alone, however.

Visual feedback designed to relax the gastrocnemius muscle was used to facilitate foot dorsiflexion by Amato, Hermsmeyer, and Kleinman (1973). They designed a portable EMG apparatus for the client to use at home. He was instructed to practice twice a day over a 2-month period. The use resulted in self-controlled change in dorsiflexion and improvement in gait. Similar voluntary inhibition of muscle activity was reported by Brudny et al. (1974b) in two patients with facial spasms. Finally, Jacobs and Felton (1969) indicated that visual feedback of the trapezius muscle was successful in producing feedback-influenced control in patients with neck injuries; furthermore, these patients could later demonstrate levels (compared to a prior no-feedback condition) of instructional control comparable to those of normal subjects provided with feedback. Regrettably, no clinical or follow-up data have been reported.

Comment. The results of decreasing muscle activity are equally impressive with those reported for increasing muscle activity. However, an actual report of EMG activity was provided in only one of these studies. Moreover, there was only one demonstration of the relationship between feedback and response changes (Jacobs & Felton, 1969) in a nonclinical investigation. Thus, while clinical effects of muscle control are potentially great, research is needed to clearly identify whether EMG feedback is necessary to produce such changes. This will serve not only to increase the scientific merit of these investigations but also to improve training procedures.

c. Muscle Regulation. In muscle retraining the target response is the EMG, as changes in striate musculature and EMG activity are synonymous. However, there are numerous problems in which the target response is not EMG, but changes in EMG may be critical in modifying the target. These problems do not involve diseased or damaged muscles; rather, they involve muscles which are poorly regulated or hyperresponsive to environmental stimuli. Three different types of problems in which feedback of the EMG response have been used will be discussed. These are modifications of speech muscle activity to effect silent reading performance, controlling forehead and neck muscles to reduce tension headache pain, and regulation of muscle activity to reduce self-reports of anxiety.

i. Subvocalization. Hardyck, Petrinovich, and Ellsworth (1966) attempted to modify vocal muscle activity which they identified as subvocalization during silent reading. They assumed that reductions in subvocalization might be clinically useful in increasing reading speed. The procedure involved presenting auditory feedback when EMG responses recorded from laryngeal muscles exceeded a set threshold. Results in a single group outcome report from 17 subjects indicated reliable control during silent reading after only one training session. McGuigan (1967) indicated that chin EMG could also be controlled during silent reading with a similar procedure with one subject. However, he also provided data on control subjects who were not given feedback, but who showed similar EMG changes. These data suggest that EMG changes reported by Hardyck *et al.* (1966) may not have been a function of the feedback.

Hardyck and Petrinovich (1969) replicated their procedures on college and high school student subvocalizers. To identify feedback effects, they included a control group in the college student sample which received no feedback. The results indicated effects of feedback with no EMG changes for the control group. Control subjects were then provided feedback training with reliable effects. The procedures worked differentially for the high school students, suppressing EMG only for average or above-average IQ subjects during silent reading, with no effects on below-average IQ subjects. The authors report no consistent effects of reducing subvocalization on reading speed; however, reducing vocal EMG led to decreases in fatigue associated with long periods of reading. Finally, in a complex report of EMG feedback, Aarons (1971) also indicated that subvocal speech could be reduced after training, but this had no effect on mathematical problem solving.

In summary, these reports indicate that subvocal speech may be modified, but that this has little demonstrated effect on reading performance. One beneficial reported side effect has been reduction of fatigue after long reading, but no hard data to substantiate this claim were reported.

The only attempt at a controlled clinical investigation was by Hardyck and Petrinovich (1969), who indicated that the feedback group showed greater EMG reduction than a no-feedback control. However, this result does not indicate that feedback was essential, as the critical component of the procedure may have been simply attending to a sound when reading. While the post-feedback self-control demonstrated by Hardyck and Petrinovich (1969) and Aarons (1971) is interesting, procedures to adequately demonstrate feedback effects have not been utilized. These could include use of noncontingent feedback during which no EMG change occurs, or a condition in which feedback is parametrically varied according to schedules of reinforcement.

A problem in measurement arises when one considers that subvocalization is defined by throat EMG activity. Certainly, a person could be simply trained to emit significant throat EMG activity under conditions other than subvocalization. Under these circumstances, it is only possible to functionally describe subvocalization in terms of reading speed, which already has been shown to be independent of throat EMG activity. An interesting project might be to increase reading speed and assess whether throat EMG activity is modified. Better functional, as opposed to correlational, relationships between throat EMG and reading speed or performance are necessary to establish the credibility of this potential applied research area.

ii. Muscular contraction headache. The use of feedback for EMG activity has certainly produced the best clinical psychiatric results of any response system. The target response in muscular contraction headaches includes both a reduction in frontalis (forehead) or trapezius (neck) muscle tension and a reduction in self-report of headache frequency and intensity. Since the concordance between these systems is variable (Epstein & Abel, 1977; Mathews & Gelder, 1969), the sufficient condition to determine success is change in self-report, while control of EMG is assumed to be necessary. Thus, treatment would probably be considered successful if a subject reported a sustained decrease in headaches, an increase in ability to work, but no systematic change in EMG activity. The headache research reported to date has taken a unitary approach that systematic changes in EMG will lead to headache reduction.

The initial report that frontalis EMG could be reliably controlled by feedback was by Budzynski and Stoyva (1969). The results of this investigation indicated that "true" feedback was superior to irrelevant feedback or instructions to relax. In a second single group outcome study (Budzynski, Stoyva & Adler, 1970), the training procedure plus home relaxation was useful in controlling tension headaches of five subjects. Results showed a decrease in both laboratory EMG activity and extralaboratory headaches as a function of treatment. Post-follow-up trends were continued for each subject, with booster training sessions and continuation of home relaxation required for two clients.

A further evaluation of this procedure is provided by Budzynski, Stoyva, Adler, and Mullaney (1973). Using a controlled group outcome design, they compared the effects of "true" feedback plus relaxation training, irrelevant feedback plus relaxation training, and a no-feedback, no-relaxation control for three groups consisting of six tension headache subjects. Results indicate that the contingent-feedback—relaxation group was superior in terms of reducing headache reports, with four of six patients headache-free. The noncontingent-feedback—relaxation group had one subject with remission of symptoms. It is interesting that the two subjects who were not headache-free in the contingent group did not practice relaxation at home, while the one patient in the noncontingent group who improved practiced relaxation regularly. The experimental design of this study does not permit assessment of the role of relaxation in headache control. However, several reports (Epstein, Abel, & Webster, 1974; Tasto & Hinkle, 1973) indicate that relaxation training alone is often a sufficient treatment for tension headaches.

Recently, Cox, Freundlich, and Meyer (1975) have reported on a controlled group outcome study comparing EMG feedback combined with regular home practice in relaxation, training in progressive relaxation with regular home practice, and a medication placebo condition in the treatment of chronic tension headaches. All subjects were initially seen for two weekly pretreatment assessment sessions. Then the biofeedback and relaxation groups were seen twice a week for 4 weeks of treatment. The medication placebo group was seen only once a week. Follow-up data were collected 4 months after the last treatment session.

On all of the dependent measures (self-report of headache activity, EMG readings, self-report of medication), both the EMG feedback group and the relaxation group showed significantly greater improvement than the medication placebo group, which did not change. Moreover, these gains were maintained at the 4-month follow-up. The biofeedback group and the relaxation group did not differ on any measure. From these results one must conclude that

EMG biofeedback training added little to the instruction in, and regular practice of, relaxation training.

Wickramasekera (1973a) also utilized EMG feedback and relaxation training to reduce reports of headache frequency and intensity of five tension headache clients. The specific relationship between relaxation and feedback is obscured by the sequential implementation of relaxation followed by feedback. Since the data indicated the headache and EMG curves were both decreasing prior to feedback implementation, the effects may have been a function of relaxation training alone.

Epstein, Hersen, and Hemphill (1974b) used EMG contingent music in the treatment of a chronic headache patient. During a hospitalization phase, feedback was reliably associated with a decrease in headache and EMG activity, evaluated by an A-B-A-B withdrawal design. Headaches returned after discharge from the hospital, but were suppressed again with additional booster training. However, measurement during these sessions indicated that EMG reduction was a feedback-influenced effect, and not a function of self-control. Thus, when feedback training was stopped in the final A phase of the outpatient A-B-A withdrawal, headaches returned. Headaches were finally controlled after relaxation training with no return of symptoms over a 7-month follow up.

Epstein and Abel (1977) attempted to evaluate whether subjects learn self-control of EMG activity as a function of contingent feedback training (evaluated in a series of single case experiments). Six chronic tension headache subjects were provided 16 training sessions which included baseline, contingent feedback, and self-control phases. No relaxation training was provided. Laboratory results indicated reliable feedback-influenced EMG control, with no evidence for sustained self-control. In addition, no relationship was observed between EMG activity and headache reports in the laboratory. However, clinical results indicated reduction in headache reports for three of the subjects, with maintenance of effects for up to an 18-month follow-up. These positive effects were observed for subjects with the lowest initial EMG activity.

Comment. In summary, it appears that EMG feedback plus home relaxation results in a reliable decrease in both laboratory EMG activity and reported tension headaches. The important research question of whether biofeedback is necessary for this effect seems to have been answered in the negative by Cox *et al.* (1975). This is not too surprising since it has already been demonstrated that relaxation training alone is sufficient to bring about headache abatement (Tasto & Hinkle, 1973). It is quite possible that reduction in headaches is not necessarily dependent upon EMG changes. On the one hand, biofeedback results in better EMG control than relaxation (Haynes, Moseley, & McGowan, 1974; Reinking & Kohl, 1975). Thus, it is not expected that relaxation would be sufficient solely on the basis of reducing EMG activity. Even though EMG is influenced during feedback, extended EMG training does not necessarily result in self-control of EMG (Epstein & Abel, 1977). Also, it is clear that reports of muscle tension and EMG activity are not concordant (Epstein & Abel, 1977; Mathews & Gelder, 1969; Reinking & Kohl, 1975), so changes in EMG may not be reflected in changes in headache reports such that headache changes may occur with minimal EMG changes. A better understanding of the variables that influence headache reports is necessary, as it is probable that headaches are a function of both muscle changes and environmental contingencies.

These speculations do not affect the evidence that biofeedback plus relaxation is good treatment for some tension headache patients. The specific role that biofeedback plays is not yet known.

iii. Biofeedback-assisted relaxation. The use of EMG feedback technology to produce a relaxation response has been discussed by Leaf and Gaarder (1971) and Green, Walters, Green, and Murphy (1969). The basic idea is that after a person is trained to relax he can inhibit or reduce feelings of anxiety, hence, EMG feedback can assist in the relaxation process. Thus, the target responses for this form of training are measures of anxiety.

Raskin, Johnson, and Rondestvedt (1973) in a single group outcome study provided 10 anxious patients with frontalis EMG feedback training. The patients' problems included anxiety symptoms, insomnia, and tension headaches. Results indicated good clinical effects for only the headache and insomnia symptoms. There was little or no reduction in overall self-report of anxiety. Townsend, House, and Addario (1975) attempted to compare a 2-week trial of EMG biofeedback-assisted relaxation with group therapy in two groups of 15 patients. The chief dependent variable was anxiety ratings on an adjective checklist. The results indicated that EMG and anxiety reports decreased more for the feedback-assisted relaxation than for the control group. Thus, the results of these two clinical studies are divergent.

To the extent that reports of anxiety are a function of EMG activity, biofeedback should produce better changes than relaxation alone (Haynes *et al.*, 1974; Reinking & Kohl, 1975). However, there are several points that must be considered in using EMG feedback to treat anxiety symptoms. First, Alexander (1973) has demonstrated that feedback effects are specific to the muscle being trained. Thus, a generalized relaxation response does not follow training in frontalis EMG control. Second, verbal reports of relaxation are not dependent upon EMG changes (Alexander, 1973; Reinking & Kohl, 1975). And probably most important, anxiety cannot be defined simply by muscle activity, but must include changes in motoric, cognitive, and physiological responses (Epstein, 1976). Research on concurrent measurement of these three systems consistently indicates that they are not concordant, i.e., they may change independently (Lang, Rice, & Sternbach, 1972; Rachman, 1975). Thus, there is little reason to expect that changes in EMG produced by feedback training add appreciably to the efficiency of relaxation training, as the potential effect of EMG reduction greater than that produced by relaxation alone is probably unrelated to changes in reports of anxiety.

2. ADDITIONAL USES

Any behavior that involves muscle activity may be modified by better regulation of EMG activity. For example, Basmajian and Newton (1974) attempted to improve the efficiency of clarinet players by improving regulation of the upper and lower buccinator muscle. The authors note that performance was not affected by consciously regulating EMG responding, but the goal would be to improve performance by better control of various muscles.

An additional use of EMG control is to regulate jaw muscle activity to reduce jaw pain. Budzynski and Stoyva (1973) indicated that masseter muscle activity could be reliably controlled by EMG feedback in normal subjects. In addition, Mulhall and Todd (1975) reported the use of a portable EMG feedback apparatus in the modification of a subject suffering from jaw pain and headaches as a function of jaw clenching (bruxism). While no EMG or self-report data are presented in this case, the approach seems viable for facial pain caused by jaw clenching.

C. Electroencephalogram

The electroencephalogram (EEG) represents the measurement of electrical activity of the cortex. Although it has long been used as a diagnostic tool in neurological disorders and to identify levels of sleep and wakefulness, it was considered an involuntary response system. It was work by such pioneer biofeedback researchers as Barbara Brown (1970) and Joe Kamiya (1968) that showed that aspects of the EEG, particularly the alpha activity (8–13 Hz), could be operantly conditioned or brought under feedback control. These studies were classic examples of bringing responses, which had previously been thought to be involuntary, under voluntary control.

1. ALPHA ACTIVITY

In a previous review, Blanchard and Young (1974) indicated that there was no published evidence on the efficacy of feedback of alpha activity on clinical problems. Since then several additional studies have appeared in which biofeedback of EEG alpha activity was used for clinical purposes. These studies are summarized below.

Gannon and Sternbach (1971) speculated that, since yogis undergoing what should be a very painful experience (walking on hot coals) show high levels of alpha in their EEG, production of a high alpha state in a patient might inhibit pain in that patient. Thus they treated a patient suffering from frequent, very painful headaches, which had resulted from several instances of head trauma, with approximately 70 sessions of alpha feedback training. As a result of this training, the patient gradually learned to produce a fairly high percentage of alpha in his EEG, both with his eyes closed and with his eyes open. However, alpha training "was able to make him feel better when he felt normal, but had no effect when he was already experiencing pain" (p. 212). His headaches gradually decreased in frequency but this had occurred before.

Since no systematic data were given on the clinical response, this becomes an anecdotal case report in terms of design. More importantly, there was no significant clinical benefit to the patient despite his learning some control of the bioelectric response.

Following the same reasoning that high alpha state might inhibit pain, McKenzie, Ehrisman, Montgomery, and Barnes (1974) conducted a controlled group outcome study of the treatment of tension headaches with alpha biofeedback. The control group received relaxation training by tape recordings. After 1 week of baseline recording of headache frequency and duration, both groups were given 5 weeks of twice weekly sessions.

No statistical comparisons were made between groups. The biofeedback group was reported to have an average reduction in hours of headache per week of 79.4%. At 1-month and 2-month follow-ups, this percentage reduction had held up well (77.4%). No details of how this percentage was calculated were given nor was any indication given of its level of significance. The authors noted that the relaxation group also showed reduction in symptoms. However, they claimed the biofeedback group showed "earlier symptom reduction" and "earlier production of alpha." Some anecdotal data were given about the increase in alpha activity found in the experimental subjects.

This study, while a controlled group outcome study, has two major faults: the data analysis, or lack thereof, does not allow meaningful conclusions to be drawn; second, the biofeedback treatment was not significantly more effective than a relaxation procedure. Thus, there is no evidence for the efficacy of EEG biofeedback training.

Mills and Solyom (1974) reported on the treatment of five patients having obsessive ruminations with alpha biofeedback training. The two patients who showed the most evidence of "learning," i.e., an increased percentage of time in the treatment session during which alpha was being emitted, discontinued treatment early. For the three who remained for the full 20 sessions, there was little evidence of increased alpha.

Four of the five patients reported an absence of ruminations during their feedback-assisted alpha state while the fifth patient had a marked decrease in ruminations. Although no baseline data on frequency of rumination were obtained, the authors claim it was very high. Therefore, within treatment sessions, the patients were much improved. Unfortunately this did not generalize at all outside of the treatment sessions.

This study represents five anecdotal case reports. The lack of systematic data on the clinical response of interest seriously reduces the value of the findings. However, the greatest problem with this study is the complete lack of transfer of any therapeutic result outside of the biofeedback laboratory. In this respect it is similar to the finding of Gannon and Sternbach (1971). Perhaps what is needed is a way to teach patients to "turn on" alpha outside of the laboratory, or some true self-control.

Glueck and Stroebel (1975) reported on the most ambitious program of research to date into the clinical application of alpha biofeedback training. Groups of psychiatric in-patients at a well-known private psychiatric hospital, The Institute of Living, were assigned to one of three conditions: relaxation training by autogenic training (N = 12), alpha EEG biofeedback (N = 26), and transcendental meditation (TM) (N = 187).

Some interesting results were obtained. Patients in the relaxation training group all complained after 2 to 3 weeks that the procedure was boring and asked to stop. All did by the fourth week. Twenty-six patients completed 15 sessions of alpha biofeedback training. Although they developed some ability to increase alpha density while receiving feedback, they had much difficulty in demonstrating any self-control. The authors state: "For a number of patients in the alpha biofeedback group, the attempts to produce alpha resulted in an increase in tension and anxiety because of the uncertainty about the results and did little to promote the relaxation and tranquility that were the primary goals of the technique. We therefore terminated the alpha biofeedback phase of the project after 26 patients had been through this type of biofeedback training" (Glueck & Stroebel, 1975, p. 307).

The subjects receiving TM did very well. Of 96 patients who completed more than 8 weeks of training, 83 were discharged. Comparisons of these patients with non-TM-trained patients from the general population, matched for sex, age, and MMPI profile, revealed significantly greater improvement and discharge rates than the controls ($p < .001$). In fact, patients trained in TM did better than the hospital population as a whole ($p < .05$).

Although the diagnostic groupings of the patients were not given, and the method of evaluation of improvement is somewhat unclear, the global impression remains that TM training helped the patients' hospital course appreciably while alpha biofeedback training was ineffective at best and possibly detrimental. The control procedures and other methodology in this study are somewhat poor. However, the overall finding is clear; alpha training did not help. This is in direct contrast to an earlier preliminary report by Stroebel.

By way of contrast, Weber and Fehmi (1975) report on the use of alpha biofeedback training as the principal treatment, or as an adjunct, in psychotherapy with 10 outpatients. Diagnoses were mainly neurosis and personality disorder with some psychophysiological reactions. Eight of the 10 were much improved after 20 feedback training sessions.

This constitutes a series of anecdotal case reports. However, the consistency of clinical benefit seems to indicate that the treatment does aid some psychiatric outpatients. The results certainly are interesting enough to warrant further, more controlled investigation.

In a study to be described in more detail later, Andreychuk and Skriver (1974) treated groups of patients with migraine headaches by temperature biofeedback training, hypnosis, and alpha biofeedback training in a controlled group outcome study. All three groups showed significant reduction in headache activity (27.7%, $p < .025$ for the alpha biofeedback group) but no differences in improvement on pairwise companions of treatment groups.

Thus for migraine headaches, alpha biofeedback training had a significant clinical effect, equivalent to that of the best known feedback training, for this problem.

Johnson and Meyer (1974), in a good systematic case study, presented the case of a patient suffering from severe grand mal seizures who was treated with alpha biofeedback. During the 2 years prior to treatment the patient had been on a stable dose of antiseizure medication but continued to have seizures at the rate of 2.8 per month.

Initially she was given relaxation training, some sessions of which utilized EMG feedback. She was then given 36 EEG feedback training sessions over a 1-year period starting with two a week, then weekly, and finally every 2 weeks. She started on alpha training, i.e., learning to produce alpha; then she was supposed to produce a mixture of alpha and theta, and finally just theta. She had been instructed to try to practice relaxation exercises daily and had also been told to relax and stay calm, as if she were in a feedback situation, when she experienced the aura which preceded her seizures. These instructions seemed designed to develop self-control of the feedback-controlled response based on a loose stimulus control paradigm.

Her rate of seizures decreased during the year of treatment to an average of 1.5 per month. For a 3-month follow-up, her seizure rate was down to one per month. The patient was able to return to public school.

This represents a systematic case study. It would have been better had month-by-month seizure frequencies been given. Then one could determine if reduction coincided with, or closely followed, the onset of training or onset of alpha control. In any event, given the stable baseline and the long history of the disorder, it would appear that the EEG biofeedback training probably led to the reduction in frequency of seizures.

Rouse, Peterson, and Shapiro (1974) have also reported on the treatment of one patient with a history of grand mal seizures. He was on a stable dose of antiseizure medication and had a seizure rate of approximately one per month.

The alpha biofeedback training in this case attempted to develop entrainment of the alpha activity from several frequencies to one dominant rhythm in the alpha range. The patient had shown a distinct bimodal display of frequencies. Over the 4 months of treatment he began to display a dominant rhythm in session which eventually persisted overnight between sessions. Seizures were eliminated for the last 1½ months of training and for 3 months of follow-up. The authors noted, however, that he had been seizure-free for up to 6 months before. This is a systematic case study. However, the clinical benefit is somewhat suspect because of the short follow-up time.

Comment. The evidence for the clinical utility of alpha EEG biofeedback training remains very unclear, much like the whole field of alpha biofeedback training. In the latter, there is fairly good evidence that the environment in which training and measurement of alpha are carried out exerts stronger effects than the feedback training itself (Paskewitz & Orne, 1973). It also seems fairly well established that alpha index (or percentage of time during which alpha is present in the EEG) does not exceed baseline levels when baseline is measured under appropriate conditions.

More recently, Walsh (1974) has shown that subjects experience positive affects during the alpha state only if they have previously been given the appropriate set and have been taught to produce alpha. Thus the positive affect associated with alpha seems largely to be an acquired or learned response.

Several types of studies, case reports, systematic case studies, and controlled group outcome studies have combined to show little or no clinical benefit to a variety of neurotic and psychosomatic patients despite the fact that these patients did show increases in alpha activity. In the area of relief of headaches, alpha biofeedback training has been shown to be of significant benefit to patients suffering from tension headaches (McKenzie *et al.,* 1974) or migraine headaches (Andreychuk & Skriver, 1974). However, in neither case do the effects of biofeedback training surpass those of control conditions utilizing relaxation and suggestion.

Finally, alpha feedback may be useful in helping to suppress seizures, particularly grand mal seizures. Two case reports, both of the systematic case study variety, have shown reduced seizure activity. Again this could be due to teaching the patient to relax and to the relatively low frequency of seizures. In order to truly demonstrate its utility for seizure control, studies of alpha biofeedback will require longer follow-up and a control condition in which relaxation training is applied.

Thus, on balance, the experimental evidence on the clinical efficacy of alpha biofeedback training is weak at best and lacking in any control studies.

2. SENSORIMOTOR RHYTHM

Sterman and his associates (Sterman, 1973; Sterman & Friar, 1972) have reported a novel biofeedback procedure which seems promising as a treatment for various kinds of seizure disorders. The procedure involves teaching patients to increase the occurrence of a 12–14 Hz rhythm recorded over the sensorimotor cortex (the so-called sensorimotor rhythm, SMR) by giving them feedback training of its occurrence both in the laboratory and at home.

Sterman (1973) has presented data on four cases: (1) a 7-year-old boy with a mixed seizure disorder, i.e., major motor seizures, plus petit mal variant; (2) a 23-year-old woman with a focal major motor disorder; (3) an 18-year-old youth with a mixed seizure disorder plus petit mal variant; (4) a 46-year-old man with adult petit mal seizures. In all four cases there was (1) significant clinical improvement in terms of reduced seizure frequency and periods when the patient was seizure-free, and (2) significant changes in both the clinical EEG in terms of decreases in abnormal (i.e., spike and slow wave) activity and increases in density of SMR recorded in the laboratory.

Detailed data on frequency of seizure were presented in only one case (Sterman & Friar, 1972) and systematic data from training sessions on emission of SMR were not presented. Nevertheless, three of the cases represent informal single-subject experiments because feedback training was discontinued after 6 months for a 9-week period. During this time, which constitutes the withdrawal, seizure activity showed marked increase from the previously established low levels after 4 to 6 weeks. Reintroduction of SMR biofeedback training to complete the A-B-A-B design rapidly returned patients to their improved clinical state.

Since Sterman's reports, three other teams of investigators have attempted to replicate and extend his work on the treatment of seizure disorders by SMR training.

By far the most impressive work has been that of Lubar and his associates (Lubar & Bahler, 1976; Seifert & Lubar, 1975). The eight patients had a variety of seizure disorders and had been selected by an attending neurologist to represent cases with frequent seizures, difficulty in seizure control, and high doses of anticonvulsant drugs. Included were psychomotor seizures, as well as grand mal, petit mal, and other forms of seizures. All had had documented seizure disorders for at least 4 years and most for over 11 years.

After baseline EEG measurements and the establishment of baseline seizure frequency counts, all patients were given three sessions a week of SMR feedback training as well as binary feedback of the presence of epileptiform spike activity or slow waves.

Results were that six of the eight patients had marked reduction in seizure frequency as well as reduction in levels of medication in some cases. In addition, the severity of the seizures that were experienced was also reduced in many cases. For the two cases for which there was no appreciable decrease in seizure frequency, the seizures experienced tended to be of lesser severity and shorter duration.

In four cases, single-subject experimental analyses of behavior were conducted due to patients discontinuing treatment during vacations (10 to 30 days). These "natural reversals" enabled the experimenter to conduct A-B-A-B designs. In three of the four cases, seizure frequency decreased from initial baseline levels when treatment was instituted and increased when it was discontinued. Reintroduction of SMR training led to a decrease in seizure frequency in three of four cases. Lubar and Bahler (1976) also provided data on the incidence of the SMR in the patients' EEGs as recorded during the baseline portion of each session. These data were reported in terms of ratio of feedback sessions SMR to pretreatment SMR incidence. Four of the six successful patients showed increasing incidence of SMR in their EEGs as did one of the unsuccessful cases. In the other three cases there was variation around the baseline level, but no overall trend towards change.

These results provide very strong evidence for the efficacy of this form of biofeedback training, especially since the patients were selected to represent severe seizure disorders which were poorly controlled by medication. Certainly, the systematic case studies and single-subject experiments provide solid evidence, in terms of experimental design, for the efficacy of the treatment. The lack of perfect correspondence between SMR changes in the EEG and the seizure frequency casts some doubt on the mechanism of change. Perhaps it was the feedback of seizure activity itself that was used by some patients rather than the SMR feedback.

Finley, Smith, and Etherton (1975) have also reported on one case of frequent epileptic seizures treated by SMR biofeedback training. Prior to treatment, the 13-year-old male patient was having approximately 75 atonic seizures per 10 hours of wakefulness. His SMR percentage was 10% in baseline recordings.

He was initially given 34 sessions of SMR feedback with the result that his seizure frequency was reduced to about one per hour and his SMR percentage was up to 65%. He then received 45 more sessions in which feedback of epileptiform EEG activity was given. This seemed to reduce the variability in the data somewhat but led to no overall changes.

The authors, in an attempt to do a single-subject experiment, gave the subject false feedback for three sessions (trials 29–31), before returning to the true feedback training (a B-A-B design). Results of the single-subject experimental phase of treatment are difficult to interpret. There is marginal evidence of an increase in seizures and a decrease in SMR incidence during the reversal, with corresponding changes after the return to treatment. However, there is so much variability in the data that one cannot be sure that changes occurred in the dependent variables coincident with changes in treatment.

Thus the study becomes a systematic case study. As such it seems to confirm the efficacy of SMR training for the reduction of seizure frequency. It may well be that the reversal phase was not long enough (three sessions or approximately 1 week) for the changes to occur. Sterman (1973) reported that from 4 to 6 weeks were required for his reversals to lead to changes. In any event, this report gives additional evidence on the efficacy of SMR feedback training.

One report (Kaplan, 1973) has failed to confirm the efficacy of SMR feedback training for the treatment of epilepsey. Kaplan treated two epileptics for 3 months with feedback of the SMR. Neither showed any improvement in seizure rate or any evidence of learning to produce SMR although a technique similar to Sterman's was used.

Kaplan then switched paradigms to some extent. She added two new patients to one of the original two who did not drop out and began to give feedback training for the central mu rhythm, or wicket rhythm, which is a synchronous activity of 9±2 Hz recorded over the central cortex. With this change in procedure, positive results were obtained: (1) Seizure incidence was reduced in all three patients in spite of a medication reduction in one patient. (2) There were changes towards normalization in the clinical EEG of two patients. However, Kaplan notes that there was no evidence of learning a new EEG pattern; instead, she regards changes as being due to an overall reduction in level of arousal.

Her systematic case studies thus throw some doubt on Sterman's procedure. However, her failure to obtain positive results could be due to (1) slight modifications in the procedure, including a sharper filtering system to isolate the 12–14 Hz activity than that used by Sterman; (2) the idiosyncracies of different seizure patients and of their electrophysiology (i.e., what might work for one patient might not work for another, as Lubar had shown); (3) training may not have been long enough.

Comment. The picture on the clinical efficacy of SMR feedback training is fairly clear. Investigations in two separate laboratories, both a systematic case study and a series of systematic case studies and single-subject experiments, have confirmed Sterman's initial findings. Kaplan's (1973) failure to replicate the finding, while somewhat disquieting, could be due to any of a number of factors. On the whole, it would seem that massive SMR feedback training, 40-plus sessions over a 6-month interval, is a very promising technique for treating a variety of seizure disorders.

3. OTHER EEG STUDIES

Sittenfeld (1972) reported on the utility of theta (4–7 Hz) feedback training for sleep onset insomnia. Of the seven patients treated, four reportedly benefited. This brief report must be considered anecdotal data at this point.

Miller (1969) reported on an unspecified number of patients with abnormal EEGs who, when given feedback of the occurrence of paroxysmal spikes in the laboratory, showed an in-laboratory reduction of abnormal EEG activity. No data were given on transfer outside of the laboratory or of clinical improvement. Thus this anecdotal report must await further elaboration.

Comment. The picture on the utility of EEG biofeedback training has changed somewhat over the past few years. Several new studies have appeared in which alpha biofeedback training has been applied. With the exception of relieving both tension and migraine headaches, and possibly as an adjunct in the outpatient treatment of psychiatric patients, alpha training still seems to have little clinical utility. The work on the use of SMR feedback training for the treatment of seizure disorders has received validation in studies and single-subject experiments. At this point this procedure seems worthy of a controlled group outcome trial.

D. Skin Temperature

One of the chief responses used in clinical biofeedback work has been surface or skin temperature. Measurement of skin temperature is principally influenced by two factors: the air temperature around the subject and the degree of vasodilation of peripheral blood vessels. The latter is under the control of the autonomic nervous system. Thus, in discussing feedback of skin temperature we are indirectly referring to the vasomotor response or degree of vasodilation or vasoconstriction. Snyder and Noble (1968) have shown that the latter response can be brought under feedback control in normal subjects.

1. MIGRAINE HEADACHES

Most of the clinical biofeedback work in control of skin temperature has been with patients suffering from migraine headaches. These headaches, as contrasted to tension headaches, are considered to be vascular in origin, tend to be less frequent and much more severe than tension headaches, and result from dilation of vessels in the head and subsequent edema.

The use of temperature training was originated by a team from the Menninger Clinic. In a recent review, Blanchard and Young (1974) noted that "Feedback training for skin temperature in treating migraine headaches has, because of a lack of control procedures, produced questionable evidence from which no substantive conclusions on therapeutic efficacy can be drawn" (p. 587). In the 2 years since that review was written, several additional studies have appeared which somewhat strengthen the case for the efficacy of temperature training as a treatment for migraine.

The first published report on the use of "autogenic feedback training" (Sargent, Green, & Walters, 1972) described a procedure which combined features of autogenic training (Schultz & Luthe, 1969), relaxation training, and feedback of the difference in temperature between fingertip and forehead. Typically, the patient learned the autogenic phrases and then went through a period of passive relaxation and self-instruction, repeating phrases such as: "I feel quite quiet ... I am beginning to feel quite relaxed" and, later, "My hands are warm " After some practice sessions in the laboratory with the temperature feedback device, the patient is switched to practice at home with a portable device.

The "treatment package," to use a term coined by Gordon Paul (1969), consists of suggestion, passive relaxation training, self-instruction, temperature feedback training, and other elements from autogenic training.

Of the 75 patients studied, the investigators were able to confirm some degree of clinical improvement in 29% to 39% of the sample. The treatment of the data and the methods of data collection were so poor that the study, although seemingly a single-group outcome study, was really an anecdotal case report. As such it was highly suggestive, *and certainly highly influential* as judged by the proliferation of temperature training devices and reports of the treatment of migraine patients. The lack of adequate baseline data, the variability in the data which prevented it from reaching statistical significance, and the lack of interjudge agreement on outcome were all problems which hindered interpretation of the results.

In terms of shifting the patients from feedback control to self-control of the response, however, the authors used several commendable steps: (1) self-instructions which aided the process were taught (a way possibly of achieving stimulus control of the behavior with the SD being under the control of the subject); (2) after early training on a daily basis with feedback, no-feedback sessions were alternated with feedback sessions; (3) requirements for regular practice at home to augment laboratory trials; (4) a gradual "thinning" of the schedule of the laboratory trials from daily to weekly to monthly.

Two other anecdotal reports of the successful use of differential temperature training with migraine patients were summarized by Blanchard and Young (1974): Peper (1973) reported three cases, in which temperature training was the main treatment for two and an adjunct to intensive psychotherapy for the third. Weinstock (1972) reported the successful treatment of seven patients suffering from tension headaches and/or migraine headaches by the use of relaxation training, EMG feedback, differential temperature training, and psychotherapy.

Eight more reports of the use of differential temperature training have recently appeared. Peper and Grossman (1974) reported on the successful treatment of two children, ages 9 and 13, with migraine headaches. Again these are anecdotal reports but give some idea of the range of the treatment.

The Menninger group (Sargent, Green, & Walters, 1973) have presented a second report on their work involving 28 patients, 20 of whom had definite migraine headaches, six of whom had tension headaches, and two of whom had "questionable migraine" attacks. It is not clear from the report whether these are new patients or a subset of those reported in the first article (Sargent et al., 1972).

Training followed essentially the same regimen described previously. Differential temperature training sessions were held daily with contact between the staff and patient held to approximately once weekly after the initial instruction. Again, procedures to develop self-control of the response were instituted by shifting the patient to alternate days with or without feedback.

The results were evaluated in a somewhat unusual fashion; one member of the team conducted clinical evaluations without access to the patient's records on headache activity, drug usage, or temperature training results. Two other members evaluated the patient solely on the basis of these data. Fortunately, they took the conservative approach of counting as improved only those patients for whom there was agreement. However, it would seem that a more systematic method of evaluating results could be obtained.

One patient was dropped because of insufficient data. Of the 27, there was agreement on 19 patients. For migraine headaches, 12 of 19 (63%) were rated as improved. For tension headaches, two of six (33%) were noted as improved. As in the previous paper, no statistical analyses of the data were reported.

This report can be classed as an uncontrolled single group outcome study. Unfortunately, no pretreatment or posttreatment data on headache frequency or intensity or on medication were given. The lack of baseline data is particularly distressing. Furthermore, no follow-up data were available and patients had varying lengths of treatment. A major fault of the study involves the reliance on uncorroborated "clinical judgment." This is notoriously open to experimenter bias effects (Rosenthal, 1966). A much better procedure would have been to use a second, independent clinical assessment.

The second major fault, and one which this group will hopefully correct, is the absence of a control group. As will be noted later in this section, such a lack is particularly telling in dealing with headache patients.

Fortunately, some of the later reports do include control conditions. Wickramasekera (1973b) described the treatment of two patients with migraine headaches by the differential temperature biofeedback procedure. Both patients had long histories (10 years plus) of migraine headaches and of previous unsuccessful treatment using medications and psychotherapy. Fortunately for this report, each had also undergone an extensive course of frontalis EMG feedback training (16 and 18 sessions, respectively) without success. This previous treatment with a proven procedure serves as a control phase for the experiments and helps to rule out attention–placebo effects.

After 3 weeks of baseline recording of headache intensity and frequency and change in hand temperature, feedback training began on a once-a-week basis. Within 3 to 4 weeks both patients were able to generate sizeable (4° and 5°) increases in hand temperature. Roughly coincident with mastering the hand warming technique, headache frequency and intensity began to show marked decreases. In one case it was essentially absent by the 11th week, while in the other it was at very low levels for weeks 11 to 14. At 3-month follow-up, consumption of analgesics was markedly reduced.

These two systematic case studies provide very strong evidence of the value of the differential temperature training procedure. Of special importance is the fact that autogenic training was deliberately omitted from the treatment of these two cases. Moreover, these patients already had a prolonged course of relaxation training with no benefit.

Johnson and Turin (1975) reported on a single case of migraine which was treated in a systematic case study with interesting control features. After baseline assessment of frequency and duration of headaches and medication use, the patient was first taught to lower the temperature of her hands for 6 weeks while receiving strong positive expectancies that it would help. Next she was shifted to hand warming for 6 weeks. Feedback sessions were held daily and consisted of 20 minutes in which visual feedback of hand temperature, *rather than differential temperature*, was given. She was also instructed to practice at home and to use the procedure to inhibit headaches.

Frequency and duration of headaches increased over baseline levels during the hand-cooling phase. In the hand-warming phase there was a return to at least baseline levels. Because of the overlapping distributions it is not clear that the patient was improved in the hand-warming phase over her condition during the last 4 weeks of baseline. Thus the data suggest but do not confirm the efficacy of hand warming via biofeedback training for treatment of migraine.

In a later paper, Turin (1975) reported on seven migraine patients treated with hand warming alone in the absence of autogenic training. Three of the patients were trained in hand cooling, similar to that described in Johnson and Turin (1975), to control for expectancy effects. All seven patients had fewer headaches as a result of temperature training. This, of course, is another anecdotal report, in the absence of any hard data on headaches. However, it does serve something of a confirmatory function.

Diamond and Franklin (1975) presented data from a large series of studies conducted with headache patients (292) treated with EMG and temperature biofeedback. By their clinical ratings, approximately 85% of patients with exclusively migraine (or vascular) headaches improved. The temperature training was modeled after that of the Menninger group and included autogenic training. Although this paper primarily consists of a large series of anecdotal reports, the sheer numbers begin to be impressive in the absence of any experimental control procedures or systematic data.

In the final analysis, only controlled group outcome studies can confirm the degree of efficacy, if any, of a procedure. Fortunately, one controlled group outcome study of biofeedback treatment of migraine headache sufferers has been completed (Andreychuk & Skriver, 1974). Eleven migraine patients were randomly assigned to each of three conditions: (1) a temperature training group in which patients received autogenic training and then training in hand warming with binary auditory feedback of finger temperature, not differential temperature; (2) EEG alpha enhancement training using auditory feedback; and (3) instructions and practice in self-hypnosis and relaxation.

Baseline headache activity was collected on all patients for 6 weeks prior to the beginning of treatment. Treatment involved once a week sessions for a 10-week period. The basic data analysis was a comparison of average baseline headache activity with headache activity (duration times intensity) during the *last* 5 weeks of treatment.

Two subjects from each feedback group dropped out, as did one hypnosis subject. Results showed significant ($p < .025$ or better) improvement in each group. More importantly, there were *no* pairwise differences among the groups in degree of improvement. No follow-up data were reported. Thus, all three treatments were equally effective at the end of treatment. An interesting aspect of the study was that hypnotic susceptibility of all subjects was determined prior to treatment. A post hoc analysis showed significantly ($p < .025$) higher degree of improvement in highly suggestible as opposed to less suggestible subjects (71% vs. 41%). Also, the temperature feedback condition had a clear majority of highly suggestible subjects while the other groups did not. This study certainly is a valuable contribution to the temperature biofeedback literature.

Comment. It seems fairly clear now, in contrast to several years ago, that some form of temperature biofeedback training involving hand warming has beneficial effects with migraine headaches. However, it is not at all clear what the active treatment components are. Wickramasekera (1973b) and Turin and his associates (Johnson & Turin, 1975; Turin, 1975) have shown improvement in migraine headaches in reasonably well-controlled case studies *in the absence of* autogenic training. Andreychuk and Skriver (1974) and Turin (1975) have shown that changes in hand temperature per se, rather than changes in the difference between hand and forehead, are effective.

Additionally, in the only controlled group outcome study, temperature training and autogenic training, though effective, were no more effective than training in alpha enhancement or training in self-hypnosis and relaxation. Moreover, in a controlled outcome study, Mitchell and Mitchell (1971) found significant reduction in migraine activity when relaxation training was combined with other behavioral techniques such as systematic desensitization and assertive training. Mitchell (1971) and Lutker (1971) have replicated these effects with smaller samples.

It may be that the "active ingredient" is relaxation training of a passive nature, as opposed to the progressive relaxation of Jacobson, and in which peripheral vasodilation is the final common pathway. Whether peripheral vasodilation (the cause of the hand temperature increase) is a cause, effect, or accompaniment of passive relaxation is yet to be determined. Thus there may be two routes to the particular state which, when practiced regularly, leads to decrease in frequency and/or intensity of migraine headaches. Further research is obviously warranted.

Certainly, what is needed now are additional controlled group outcome studies with long-term follow-up in which passive relaxation, possibly via autogenic training, is compared with temperature training and some appropriate attention–placebo condition.

2. RAYNAUD'S DISEASE

Raynaud's disease is a functional disorder of the peripheral cardiovascular system in which the patient experiences painful episodes of vasoconstriction in the hands, and possibly the feet, which leave the extremities cold to the touch. Biofeedback treatment of this disorder could proceed through either surface temperature training or direct training in peripheral vasodilation. As noted below, both approaches have been used successfully.

Schwartz (1972) reported two cases of Raynaud's disease treated with biofeedback of blood volume in a peripheral member. In the first case, a male with Raynaud's disease in his feet, blood volume was recorded from both big toes. The patient was given binary feedback of increases in blood volume for one toe, in a manner similar to that used in the BP biofeedback work of Shapiro and the Harvard group. Over 10 sessions the patient began to show "large increases in blood volume, particularly for the left foot." Feedback was then switched to the right foot, which showed similar responses. The patient reportedly was symptom-free after treatment for 1½ years and then requested booster treatments. Interestingly, the patient claimed to have developed certain imagery which enabled him to warm his feet outside of treatment at his own initiation.

The second case, a female with more typical Raynaud's disease in her hands, showed no meaningful bioelectric response and no symptomatic relief in the fewer than 10 sessions in which she participated. These two anecdotal reports provide conflicting evidence that biofeedback of peripheral vasodilation, or blood flow, can be useful in the treatment of Raynaud's disease.

Peper (1973) reported the unsuccessful treatment of one woman with Raynaud's disease using temperature biofeedback training. The details of training were not articulated. Failure was attributed to psychological problems on the part of the patient, such as "saying she did not want to get well."

Surwit (1973), in a thorough summary of the biofeedback work with Raynaud's disease existing at the time, described the treatment of one severe case of the disorder treated by himself and two colleagues. The patient, a 21-year-old female who had been suffering from the disease for about 5 years, had undergone two sympathectomies in efforts to relieve the painful vasospasms.

An elaborate, computer-controlled shaping program was used to give the patient auditory and visual feedback of hand surface temperature over the three 10-minute trials in each session. In addition, the patient had received instruction in relaxation and autogenic imagery prior to the biofeedback treatment. Initially, she attended 14 treatment sessions over a 3-week period; a month later she resumed treatment for 32 more sessions on a twice weekly basis; finally, she received one session a week for another 6 months.

After a year's training the results were such that (1) her basal skin temperature had increased from 23.0°C to 26.6°C; (2) she was able to go outdoors in Montreal in the winter without elaborate protective garments; (3) her frequency of Raynaud's attacks were markedly decreased; and (4) her hand color was much improved. Unfortunately, the patient suddenly lost all ability to control her hand temperature shortly after the end of treatment. There is a suggestion that placebo and expectancy effects were much in operation with this patient. This good anecdotal report demonstrates that there can be some symptomatic improvement coincident with physiological change. However, the final outcome was not very promising.

Jacobson, Hackett, Surman, and Silverberg (1973) reported one case of Raynaud's disease treated by a combination of hypnosis and biofeedback. The patient, a male in his early 30's, had a 3-year history of the disease. He was put on drugs, primarily reserpine, with no alleviation of Raynaud's symptoms and many side effects. He was then given three sessions of training in hypnosis, including self-hypnosis. Learning to relax and to develop imagery which would lead to hand warming was emphasized. Fingertip temperature was monitored during this time but yielded little evidence of hand warming; the best response was an increase of $0.75°C$. He was then given five sessions of biofeedback training, using the differential temperature between fingertip and forehead and an auditory signal. No change occurred during the first session. During the next four sessions the patient was able to achieve a consistent increase in fingertip temperature of $3.9°$ to $4.3°C$.

Much clinical improvement accompanied these laboratory changes, such as being able to touch cold objects without a painful vasospasm. The patient reported much practice of his "hand warming" skill outside of the laboratory and seemed to have gained self-control of the response through the use of certain imaginal cues. He remained symptom-free after 7½ months.

This report is a good systematic case study in that another therapeutic technique was introduced before the biofeedback treatment. The failure of the former treatment to relieve the symptoms helps confirm that it was the biofeedback training rather than the placebo effects that were responsible for the success in this case.

Blanchard and Haynes (1975) treated one female patient with moderate Raynaud's disease in a single-subject experiment. Visual feedback was given of the difference between hand temperature and forehead temperature. After baseline recording, sessions during which the patient tried to increase hand temperatures without feedback were alternated with feedback sessions in an A-B-A-B design.

Results (on maximum change in hand temperature for each session) showed clearly the superiority of feedback sessions over instructed, no-feedback sessions. Follow-up sessions were held at 2, 4, and 7 months and included self-control sessions and feedback-assisted control booster sessions. Ability to show at least a 2°F increase in hand temperature was reestablished each time.

Basal temperatures of finger surface, collected at the beginning of each session, showed an increase of 12°F from the initial baseline to the end of training. At the follow-ups, basal hand temperature was still at least 7.8°F higher than baseline temperatures. Clinically, the patient reported less difficulty with her condition and the ability to warm both her hands and, to some extent, her feet with certain imagery and self-instruction. This single-subject experiment seems to clearly demonstrate the efficacy of biofeedback training, in the absence of any other form of treatment, for the treatment of Raynaud's disease.

Comment. Research on the use of temperature biofeedback training for Raynaud's disease seems to have been demonstrated at three levels; anecdotal case reports, systematic case study, and single-subject experiment. Although only half of the six cases reported were clear-cut successes, it does appear that this is a treatment which merits further use. Because of its relative rarity, it seems unlikely that controlled group outcome studies of this form of treatment will be done. However, one could, with three cases, conduct a multiple baseline experiment across subjects, thus further solidifying the evidence.

E. Gastrointestinal Responses

In this section we deviate somewhat from our usual procedure of organizing the review sections around bioelectrical response systems. Instead, we review here all of the clinical biofeedback studies which have dealt with some aspect of the gastrointestinal system. The signals used in this area of biofeedback research are usually transduced physical signals, such as pH level or sphincter pressure, rather than bioelectric signals.

1. FUNCTIONAL DIARRHEA

Furman (1973) described the biofeedback treatment of five patients suffering from what he termed "functional diarrhea" or, more technically, "functional enterocolonopathies." These include disorders commonly known as "irritable colon," "spastic colon," "colonic neurosis," or "emotional diarrhea," and are defined by the "clinical features of periodic abdominal pain and intermittent irregularity of bowel habit, usually constipation or constipation alternating with periods of normal rhythm" in the absence of specific organic pathology.

The five cases were treated using auditory feedback of amplified bowel sounds (borborygmi). After an initial session, in which the patient was introduced to listening to bowel sounds, she received a series of half-hour sessions in which she was asked alternately to increase or decrease bowel sounds, for four trials (per session). The experimenter delivered social reinforcement in the form of praise for successful following of instructions. The experimenter rated the degree of success of the patient at following the instructions on a scale of 0 to 4+ for each trial.

The experimenter claimed that all five cases showed noticeable clinical improvement by "now enjoying normal bowel function" and no longer being "virtually toilet bound." All cases also showed some degree of control of intestinal motility within five training sessions. Improved clinical course was noted either shortly before or shortly after laboratory control of bowel sounds was achieved.

One patient went from being "toilet-bound," and hence unable to work, to having fairly regular, one-a-day bowel movements and being able to work. She had experienced only three mild episodes of abdominal cramping and diarrhea since biofeedback training. This study represents an anecdotal case report. Little or no systematic data are given on the bioelectrical response or the clinical response. However, it certainly points the way for further clinical research.

2. FECAL INCONTINENCE

Another gastrointestinal disorder to be treated with biofeedback is fecal incontinence, resulting from a lack of control of the external rectal sphincter. Engel, Nikoomanesh, and Schuster (1974) reported on six adults and one child who had experienced daily fecal incontinence for 3 to 8 years.

In all cases the initial stage of the treatment consisted of measurement of the external sphincter reflex closure to stimulation from a balloon inserted in the rectum that was rapidly inflated. Normal reflex response to this stimulation is contraction of the external sphincter and relaxation of the internal sphincter. Baseline recordings from these patients, obtained from Sanborn pressure transducers, showed the reflex to be absent or very slight.

In the second phase of treatment, a description of the normal response and how it appeared on the polygraph recording was initially given the patient. Then the patient was given an unspecified number of sessions, each of which contained about 50 trials. During the trial the patient viewed his polygraph record directly and was encouraged to try to produce a "normal" response; he was also informed when he had responded inappropriately. Sessions were about 3 weeks apart and patients were encouraged to practice at home between sessions.

During the third phase the patient was again given immediate visual feedback and asked to refine control of his external sphincter response to an appropriate magnitude and to coordinate it with the relaxation of the internal sphincter. Also, feedback was withheld on some trials in a manner similar to the fading out of feedback in the Weiss and Engel (1971b) study.

Results were assessed by patients' reports of continence between sessions and at follow-ups scattered over several years. Four patients were completely successful, with no incontinent episodes following training. Two patients showed marked improvement and one withdrew from treatment very early.

This report constitutes a series of systematic case studies. Since improvement always occurred coincident with treatment, and since there was a long baseline of symptomatic behavior which had proved refractory to other treatments, one can be fairly confident in attributing the improvement to the treatment package. However, it is not clear if the final stage of treatment was necessary. Further research, possibly using the multiple baseline design across subjects, might be useful.

3. NONCLINICAL STUDIES ON GASTROINTESTINAL
    FUNCTION

The next two studies are attempts to demonstrate the effects of biofeedback training on gastrointestinal functioning in patients and normal subjects. However, in neither of the studies were there attempts at clinical treatment.

a. Lower Esophageal Sphincter. Nikoomanesh, Wells, and Schuster (1973) studied the ability of three normal subjects and six patients with esophageal reflux to control lower esophageal sphincter pressure (a smooth muscle innervated entirely by the ANS) when given feedback of the amount of pressure exerted by that smooth muscle. The lower esophageal sphincter is the "valve" which controls entrance into the stomach from the esophagus; patients with esophageal reflux disorders typically have lower esophageal sphincter pressure.

Pressures were recorded simultaneously from three sites: esophagus, lower esophageal sphincter, and stomach. The results showed that both normal subjects and patients showed increases in esophageal sphincter pressure when given feedback (average increase for normal was 5.5 mmHg; for patients, 1.5 mmHg, significantly lower than for the normals). Moreover, increases were independent of increases in other pressure measures or respiratory maneuvers. Normal subjects showed continued ability to control the pressure when feedback was discontinued.

    b. Stomach Acid pH. Welgan (1974) reported two studies in which patients with confirmed duodenal ulcers were able to control their gastric acid secretions. In both studies, gastric secretions were continuously aspirated. The pH, the hydrochloric acid concentration, and the total volume of stomach secretions were continuously monitored.

In the second study ($N = 10$), the baseline recording phase was asked alternately to increase pH (lower acid concentration) and rest. Feedback of the pH of stomach contents was provided continuously during increase pH trials.

Results showed a significant ($p < .05$) increase in pH from the baseline period to the second of three experimental periods. No other significant differences were noted. Decreases in acid concentration were found from baseline to each experimental period and one rest period. Similar results were found for volume of gastric secretions. There were no differences between experimental (feedback plus instructions) periods and rest (no feedback plus contrary instructions) periods.

In the second study ($N = 10$), the baseline recording phase was doubled in length. The 10 subjects were divided into two groups and given the following sequence of 15-minute conditions: (I) rest, increase pH-1, increase pH-2; (II) increase ph−1, rest, increase pH-2. Feedback was again given only during increase pH trials.

Results showed a significant increase in pH from baseline to the second experimental trial ($p < .01$). Also, group I had a significantly higher pH at the last period than group II. Differences were found between groups in different conditions on acid concentration and volume of acid secretion, with feedback and instructions leading to a lower acid concentration.

Overall, the study seemed to provide indications that ulcer patients can gain some control over stomach pH in a therapeutic (higher pH) direction when given feedback and instructions. Moreover, feedback seems to provide some increment over mere instructions but not consistently. However, despite these results, feedback trials (based on one author's experience, EBB) are so traumatic that little therapeutic benefit accrues from this procedure. This experiment provides some interesting results but little of therapeutic value for the ulcer patient.

There have also been two other studies of biofeedback training of normal subjects to control stomach acid pH. Gorman and Kamiya (1972) reported on biofeedback training of nine normal subjects in controlling stomach acid pH on three separate days. Results showed appropriate differences in trials in which subjects were to increase pH and decrease pH for four of six trials. On the other two, no difference or reverse effects were obtained. However, the overall degree of control was slight.

Whitehead, Renault, and Goldiamond (1975) first taught four subjects to easily swallow a nasogastric tube. They were then run for a number of baseline sessions (6–13) until stability was achieved with a pH electrode *in the stomach.* They were then given binary feedback of pH and instructions. Three of the four subjects could show regular and reliable decreases in pH, i.e., increases in acid secretion. One of them could also achieve some degree of increase in pH, but only to baseline levels after a decrease.

An interesting aspect of this study was the systematic difference between in vivo measures of stomach acid pH and pH determinations of aspirated stomach contents. The correlation between these variables was relatively low, casting some doubt on Welgan's (1974) results. This study also casts doubts on the utility of biofeedback training in pH control for ulcer patients.

Finally, Deckner, Hill, and Bourne (1972) reported on the biofeedback control of gastric motility. Four normal subjects were given both visual and auditory feedback of the electrogastrogram (EGG), a measure of gastric motility. Subjects were instructed to increase and decrease motility during four sessions. Results showed that by the fourth session three of the four subjects could reliably increase and decrease motility on command with the aid of feedback. Since there is some degree of relation between increased gastric motility and increased stomach acid secretion, this technique may provide a practical way of using biofeedback training with ulcer patients.

4. COMMENT

Although there is relatively little work in the area of biofeedback control of gastrointestinal responses (as compared to other response systems), some significant publications have appeared. The Engel *et al.* (1974) procedure of teaching control of the rectal sphincter has provided beneficial effects. The study by Furman (1973) on treatment of spastic colon and functional diarrhea, while promising and certainly indicating the direction for new clinical research, represents only preliminary data.

The remainder of the studies are all nonclinical. They indicate that subjects, both patients and normals, can change stomach acid pH. Moreover, repeated practice seems to help. However, to date no practical application of this work has been carried out. In our opinion, it will not prove practical to give feedback of pH directly because of the invasive and traumatic form such monitoring takes. Feedback of gastric motility, on the other hand, a relatively benign measurement operation, may prove to be useful.

F. Penile Erection

Although there has been considerable research using degree of penile erection (tumescence) as a dependent variable in the behavioral treatment of male sexual deviates (see Abel & Blanchard, 1976), there has been relatively little work on the biofeedback control of penile responses.

1. STUDIES ON NORMAL SUBJECTS

Two studies have been performed on normal subjects. In one (Rosen, 1973), groups ($N = 10$) of normal males listened to erotic audio tapes designed to elicit erection responses. After one baseline session, three groups received instructions to suppress their erection for the following three sessions while a fourth only listened. One of the suppression groups received contingent binary feedback of small increases in erection. A second group received false feedback while the third received no feedback. Results, expressed as percentage time during which the subject responded with more than the criterion erection, were that only the group receiving accurate feedback demonstrated any suppression of erection. They were significantly ($p < .01$) more successful than the other three groups, which did not differ.

In the second study, Price (1973) investigated the effects of feedback on producing erections in two groups of eight normal males. Both groups listened to erotic audio tapes. One group received binary visual feedback of erection and instructions to increase tumescence. The other group received no feedback and no instructions to increase tumescence. The feedback group showed a shorter latency to maximum erection than the no-feedback group. However, the other dependent measures, such as degree of erection and self-report of sexual arousal, were not different between the groups. The different instructions given the two groups are a confound of such magnitude that the results are practically meaningless with regard to biofeedback effects.

2. CLINICAL APPLICATIONS

a. Increasing Sexual Arousal. Two studies have been published in which a biofeedback procedure was used to help generate increased sexual arousal. As is fairly customary in behavioral research in the sexual area (Abel & Blanchard, 1976), we equate sexual arousal and degree of erection. Although it is quite possible to have an erection without sexual arousal (as in priapism) and sexual arousal without erection (as in impotence), the two show a very high correlation in most males (e.g., Mavissakalian, Blanchard, Abel, & Barlow, 1975).

In the first study (Herman & Prewett, 1974), a homosexual male was given trials in which he was alternately shown slides of males and females, given binary visual feedback of increasing penile tumescence, and instructed to try to generate an erection. Next, feedback was made noncontingent; finally, to complete the single-subject experiment, feedback was made contingent. The therapeutic objective in this study seemed to be to increase sexual arousal to either sex.

Erection responses, measured at independent probe sessions, were greater to both male and female images when feedback was contingent, showed partial reversal when it was noncontingent, and another sustained increase when it was made contingent again. Thus the study adequately demonstrated that contingent feedback led to increased erection. Also, there was increased sexual arousal to both males and females and increased masturbatory activity. Follow-up revealed that the patient established several homosexual relationships and engaged in some sexual activity. However, after 7 months his behavior had deteriorated and he was little different from his presenting condition.

The other direct clinical application of biofeedback of penile tumescence is that of Barlow, Agras, Abel, Blanchard, and Young

(1975). Three homosexual males were shown slides of nude females and simultaneously given visual analogue feedback of degree of erection. The patients were asked to generate erection responses to these slides, using feedback as an aid. Independent assessments of degree of sexual arousal to male and female images were also made. While there was good evidence that the patients could generate a fairly large degree of penile tumescence in feedback sessions, particularly when they were also reinforced for showing increased erection responses, evidence of transfer of sexual arousal to female stimuli in the separate probe sessions was not at all straightforward. In one patient there was no transfer; in the second patient there was a slight increase in heterosexual arousal; a still larger increase was noted in the third patient. In the latter two cases, however, control conditions in the single-subject experiments seemed to point to an overall exposure effect rather than any particular benefit from biofeedback of penile tumescence per se. This has been documented elsewhere (Herman, Barlow, & Agras, 1974).

Through this careful use of control conditions in the single-subject experiments, and the use of probe measurements independent of the feedback sessions, it was possible to show that feedback was not the active component of treatment. Failure to use these procedures could have led to erroneous conclusions, thus endorsing the use of biofeedback for generating heterosexual response in homosexuals.

   b.   Reduction of Sexual Arousal.   Rosen (1974) described the use of biofeedback of erection response as part of "a self-control training program." A 45-year-old married male had a history of cross dressing and exposing himself. As part of his total treatment, the patient was videotaped while cross dressed and masturbating. Baseline measurement of erection response to viewing this videotape showed a great deal of arousal. (The number of baseline sessions was not given.) The patient was then shown the videotape repeatedly while being asked to suppress his erection. He was given feedback in the form of an audio recording of his alarm clock, which was activated whenever his erection exceeded a criterion level. Intensity of feedback sound was increased with increasing erection. The patient was also shown heterosexual films during the treatment and his erection response to them was assessed.

After 12 treatment sessions the patient showed complete suppression of his erection to the transvestite film. His response to the heterosexual material, on the other hand, remained virtually unchanged.

This procedure is suggestive of a punishment, in which the noxious stimulus was an aversive sound which was contingent on erection response. Since no control procedures or actual data were given, it must be considered an anecdotal case report.

Abel (1975, personal communication) described the treatment of an exhibitionist by a biofeedback technique. After four baseline probes of sexual arousal to deviant (exhibitionistic) and nondeviant stimuli, the patient received 20 sessions of biofeedback treatment to suppress arousal to deviant cues. Treatment consisted of playing an erotic deviant audiotape and giving the patient feedback of his erection response while he tried to suppress his arousal. Over the 20 sessions, arousal to deviant cues, as measured at independent probe sessions, decreased from 25% to about 12%, while arousal to non-deviant cues remained unchanged at about 30%. Card sorts and other self-report measures showed no change. This is another anecdotal case report of the effects of biofeedback on suppression of arousal.

Comment. At this point it seems fairly well documented by single-subject experiments that biofeedback is of little value for increasing sexual arousal to formerly nonarousing stimuli. However, it may be of value for teaching self-control of deviant arousal to sexual deviates. The two case reports by Rosen (1974) and Abel (1975, personal communication) suggest the need for further investigation in this area.

G. Other Responses

In this section we include reports on responses for which only a very limited number of papers have been published.

1. GALVANIC SKIN RESPONSE (GSR)

One of the principal autonomic responses studied by psycho-physiologists is the GSR. Procedures for measuring it and the basic mechanisms involved in it have been described in great detail (Edelberg, 1972). At present it is considered to be a result of sympathetic nervous system activation. GSR was also one of the first responses to be used in biofeedback studies (Kimmel, 1974). However, the clinical applications of GSR feedback have been fairly limited.

Toomim and Toomin (1975) described the use of GSR feedback as an adjunct to "dynamically oriented psychotherapy." Their procedure consists of attaching a GSR monitoring device to patients during psychotherapy sessions. The GSR is then converted to an audio signal which both the patient and therapist can hear. The patient is taught the meaning of changes in the feedback signal, primarily in terms of being relaxed and being aroused.

Feedback is subsequently used for two purposes: (1) to confirm for patient and therapist that some arousing topic is being discussed and possibly needs further exploration; and (2) to help the patient learn to relax and reduce arousal. The data on this use are entirely anecdotal. Moreover, there seems to be little biofeedback training involved; rather, the feedback signal is used primarily as a monitor of arousal.

Javel and Denholtz (1975) described a similar use of GSR feedback in the treatment of a spider phobic. After a brief course of imaginal systematic desensitization had failed to bring about much improvement, a form of desensitization accompanied by GSR biofeedback was instituted. The patient was shown a series of slides of spiders and instructed to remain relaxed and keep off the audio signal from the GSR feedback device. Later, she was to handle jars containing live spiders while receiving GSR feedback. The author reports that with eight sessions of exposure to slides and in vivo exposure, the patient had overcome her fear as evidenced by her approach behavior and self-report.

The GSR feedback served as a cue to the patient when she was becoming aroused and, hence, when she should institute relaxation. Failure of the patient to improve with standard desensitization in imagination lends some credibility to the idea that a combination of GSR biofeedback and vicarious and in vivo exposure led to improvement. It is not clear what role biofeedback really played since the exposure itself has been shown to be effective in phobias (Marks, 1972).

Tamayo, Standley, and Treon (1973) presented the case of a stutterer treated with GSR biofeedback. The patient was given a number of trials on which he read aloud, either with GSR feedback or without. When feedback was available, the patient was instructed to keep the signal low, i.e., to keep his level of "anxiety" or sympathetic arousal low. Over a number of trials this led to his having half as many "blocks" with feedback as without. This is, of course, an anecdotal case report but does yield an interesting finding.

By far the most impressive work has been that of Patel (Patel, 1973, 1975a; Patel & North, 1975) on the use of GSR feedback and passive relaxation in the treatment of hypertension. This work was reviewed earlier in detail.

Comment. In most clinical biofeedback training, the basic notion has been to teach the patient to learn to control a certain response. The effects of this learned control are then evaluated. In GSR biofeedback training the emphasis has not been on learning to control the response; instead, the biofeedback signal has been used to alert the patient to his increased level of sympathetic arousal. In this sense it has been used for discrimination training.

2. ELECTROOCULOGRAM (EOG)

Ballard, Doerr, and Varni (1972) reported the treatment of one case of essential blepharospasm (a disorder consisting of involuntary clonic and tonic spasms of the eyelids and associated musculature) using a biofeedback training procedure. Blink rate was recorded from the EOG during several conditions: baseline, massed practice, an avoidance procedure in which the patient received a mild peripheral shock if she blinked during the delay intervals, and a biofeedback procedure. In the latter, a tone was generated by each blink and the patient was taught to delay the tones, first for 1 second, then for 2 seconds.

The design used failed to include adequate control phases; therefore, it represents a good systematic case study rather than a single-subject experiment. There was, however, marked reduction in blink rate as measured at independent probes. Moreover, continued home practice by the patient led to a full recovery (i.e., absence of spasms at a 9-month follow up).

This single systematic case study provides very provocative evidence on a possible treatment for a most disabling eye disorder. Certainly it warrants further follow-up and replication, especially since this disorder responds so poorly to other forms of treatment, including surgery.

3. VAGINAL CONTRACTIONS

Varni (1973) reported briefly on a case of vaginismus treated by biofeedback. The patient had persistent vaginismus (a painful spasm of the vagina due to local hyperesthesia) to the point of not being able to insert the smallest tampon without extreme pain. Sexual intercourse was not possible.

The patient was given visual and auditory feedback of pressure of vaginal contractions from a pressure transducer. She gradually learned to control the pressure exerted by these muscles with the aid of feedback. After 13 sessions she not only reported decrease in anxiety over the thought of sexual intercourse but had experienced successful sexual intercourse. This anecdotal case report thus suggests that biofeedback may be a useful tool in the treatment of vaginismus.

4. RESPIRATORY RESISTANCE

Levenson, Manuck, Strupp, Blackwood, and Snell (1974) have presented data on a system designed to give feedback of respiratory resistance so that subjects could learn to change airway resistance. (The system has been described separately by Levenson, 1974.) Such changes have potential value in the treatment of asthma. In addition to presenting data on normal subjects showing that some changes in airway resistance could be learned with the aid of feedback, they attempted the treatment of four patients with asthma.

Two of the patients dropped out early. For the other two patients, there was consistent evidence of their being able to decrease airway resistance within a trial as a result of feedback training. Moreover, there was some evidence of the patients' learning this control in the absence of feedback. In fact, patients could show within-session decreases in airway resistance of 50%. Unfortunately, in both patients there was no evidence of transfer effects from session to session. Thus, airway resistance was the same at the end of training as at the beginning.

These two systematic case studies seem to mark a good beginning in this area. The failure to find consistent improvement, while disappointing, may mean that the treatment could be used episodically during periods of increased airway resistance when bronchial dilating drugs are typically used.

V. CONCLUSIONS AND FUTURE DIRECTIONS

When one surveys the wide array of clinical problems on which there is at least some evidence (admittedly of fairly poor quality in some instances) that biofeedback can be of benefit, it becomes possible to begin to believe in a "new panacea" for all psychosomatic disorders. The field continues to grow and new applications continue to be found.

Fortunately, some investigators are beginning to conduct the hard but necessary controlled studies to determine how well biofeedback treatments compare with no-treatment or attention–placebo treatment. This latter work will finally determine if biofeedback has a rightful place in the therapeutic world.

One theme that seems to emerge from this review is that biofeedback can frequently be shown, with good reliability and validity, to be a valuable treatment modality when such feedback is tied very closely to the clinical response in question. Thus, in such areas as EMG feedback for muscle retraining and anal sphincter pressure feedback for chronic fecal incontinence, a biofeedback treatment has been successful after standard therapies have failed. In fact, in areas such as these, a biofeedback treatment may become the treatment of choice.

Conversely, when the response for which feedback is given is far removed from the clinical problem, the biofeedback approach seems to be less successful. Thus, in areas such as alpha feedback for pain, EMG feedback for chronic anxiety, and perhaps peripheral fingertip temperature for migraine headaches, the evidence of clinical efficacy is less convincing. It seems that attempting to train a response which may play some mediating role in the clinical problem has little therapeutic result.

Another theme of this review is that relaxation, broadly conceived, may account for many of the clinical effects. By relaxation we mean both active tension release, as found in Jacobsonian progressive relaxation, and passive relaxation, as found in autogenic training. Relaxation, or something akin to Benson's (1975) "relaxation response," may be the needed antidote to the chronic stress underlying many psychosomatic disorders.

In any event, the few direct comparisons of relaxation training with biofeedback training, such as for BP in hypertensives (Shoemaker & Tasto, 1975), tension headaches (Cox *et al.*, 1975), or migraine headaches (Andreychuk & Skriver, 1974), seem to show that relaxation training is equivalent or superior to biofeedback training. What is needed are studies in which biofeedback is compared with relaxation training. Also needed are studies in which biofeedback training is systematically added to relaxation training to determine if biofeedback does, in fact, contribute anything to the treatment.

As for future directions, more well-controlled clinical trials should be conducted. Good small-scale studies to demonstrate the efficacy of biofeedback treatment are greatly needed. These could be done economically (in terms of subjects) by using the methodology from the experimental analysis of behavior. In particular, the "multiple baseline design across subjects" (Baer, Wolf, & Risley, 1968) is a means of producing very reliable, convincing results with as few as three to four subjects. This design has an additional advantage over the A-B-A design in that effects need not be transitory, or solely demonstrable while treatment is taking place.

There should be greater emphasis, during a biofeedback treatment, on issues of self-management or self-regulation. The work on PVCs by Weiss and Engel (1971) and by Cox et al. (1975) on tension headaches suggest how to build self-control and self-management into a treatment program, rather than merely giving training on a response and then hoping it will "magically" transfer to the natural environment. Generalization training must be an integral part of treatment.

Another possible future direction would involve comparisons of biofeedback treatment with medication. At present, a pharmacological approach is the treatment of choice. However, should comparisons of biofeedback training with optimal doses of medication show the psychological approach to be as effective, then biofeedback training could become the treatment of choice because of the absence of side effects. Even the most benign pharmacological treatment, such as aspirin for headaches, can have unwanted side effects. At this point, no deleterious side effects of biofeedback, other than frustration, have been noted. And fortunately, the shibboleth of "symptom substitution" seems to have been laid to rest.

A final issue is the possibility of Federal regulation of biofeedback training. The FDA has recently declared biofeedback equipment to be "medical devices," and as such, subject to its regulation. Such regulation could stifle this burgeoning field. However, the requirement of demonstrated efficacy of training, similar to such requirements for new drugs, could bring some much-needed, well-controlled research to this area.

Federal regulation would probably mean that biofeedback would ultimately come under medical regulation. While this seems onerous to nonmedical practitioners, it may be a blessing in disguise. Certainly, the nonphysician practitioner, dealing with psychosomatic patients, needs to maintain close liaison with a physician to avoid missing major physical causes of symptoms (e.g., a tumor causing chronic headaches or a cancer causing chronic gastrointestinal upset). Our position is that a partnership needs to be established between the nonphysician biofeedback trainer and the physician for the ultimate benefit of the patient.

REFERENCES

Aarons, L. Subvocalization: Aural and EMG feedback in reading. *Perceptual and Motor Skills,* 1971, 33, 271–306.

Abel, G. G., & Blanchard, E. B. The measurement and generation of sexual arousal in male sexual deviates. In M. Hersen, R. M. Eisler, & P. M. Miller (Eds.), *Progress in behavior modification.* Vol. 2. New York: Academic Press, 1976. Pp. 99–136.

Agras, W. S. *Behavior modification: Principles and clinical applications.* Boston: Little, Brown, 1972. pp. 151–153.

Alexander, A. B. Generalization to other muscles during EMG biofeedback training of the frontalis. Paper read at the Society for Psychophysiological Research, Galveston, October 1973.

Amato, A., Hermsmeyer, C. A., & Kleinman, K. M. Use of electromyographic feedback to increase inhibitory control of spastic muscles. *Physical Therapy,* 1973, 53, 1063–1066.

Andrews, J. M. Neuromuscular re-education of the hemiplegic with the aid of the electromyograph. *Archives of Physical Medicine and Rehabilitation,* 1964, 45, 530–532.

Andreychuk, T., & Skriver, C. Hypnosis and biofeedback in the treatment of migraine headache. Paper read at the Biofeedback Research Society, Colorado Springs, Colorado, February 1974.

Baer, D. M., Wolf, M. M., & Risley, T. R. Some current dimensions of applied behavior analysis. *Journal of Applied Behavior Analysis,* 1968, 1, 91–97.

Ballard, P., Doerr, H., & Varni, J. G. Arrest of a disabling eye disorder using biofeedback. *Psychophysiology,* 1972, 9, 271.

Barlow, D. H., Agras, W. S., Abel, G. G., Blanchard, E. B., & Young, L. D. Biofeedback and reinforcement to increase heterosexual arousal in homosexuals. *Behaviour Research and Therapy,* 1975, 13, 45–50.

Barlow, D. H., & Hersen, M. Single-case experimental designs: Uses in applied clinical research. *Archives of General Psychiatry,* 1973, 29, 319–325.

Basmajian, J. V., Kukulka, C. G., Narayan, M. G., & Takebe, K. Biofeedback treatment of foot-drop compared with standard rehabilitation technique: Effects on voluntary control and strength. *Archives of Physical Medicine and Rehabilitation,* 1975, 56, 231–236.

Basmajian, J. V., & Newton, W. J. Feedback training of parts of baccinator muscle in man. *Psychophysiology,* 1974, 11, 92.

Benson, H. *The relaxation response.* New York: Morrow, 1975.

Benson, H., Rosner, B. A., & Marzetta, B. R. Decreased systolic blood pressure in hypertensive subjects who practiced meditation. *Journal of Clinical Investigation,* 1973, 52, 8a.

Benson, H., Shapiro, D., Tursky, B., & Schwartz, G. E. Decreased systolic blood pressure through operant conditioning techniques in patients with essential hypertension. *Science,* 1971, 173, 740–742.

Blanchard, E. B., & Abel, G. G. An experimental case study of the biofeedback treatment of a rape-induced psychophysiological cardiovascular disorder. *Behavior Therapy*, 1976, **7**, 113–119.

Blanchard, E. B., & Haynes, M. R. Biofeedback treatment of a case of Raynaud's disease. *Journal of Behavior Therapy and Experimental Psychiatry*, 1975, **6**, 230–234.

Blanchard, E. B., Haynes, M. R., Kallman, M. D., & Harkey, L. A comparison of direct blood pressure feedback and electromyographic feedback on the blood pressure of normotensives. Paper read at the Southeastern Psychological Association, Atlanta, May 1975. (a)

Blanchard, E. B., & Young, L. D. Self-control of cardiac functioning: A promise as yet unfulfilled. *Psychological Bulletin*, 1973, **79**, 145–163.

Blanchard, E. B., & Young, L. D. Clinical applications of biofeedback training: A review of evidence. *Archives of General Psychiatry*, 1974, **30**, 530–589.

Blanchard, E. B., Young, L. D., & Haynes, M. R. A simple feedback system for the treatment of elevated blood pressure. *Behavior Therapy*, 1975, **6**, 241–245. (b)

Blanchard, E. B., Young, L. D., Haynes, M. R., & Kallman, M. D. A simple feedback system for self-control of blood pressure. *Perceptual and Motor Skills*, 1974, **39**, 891–898. (a)

Blanchard, E. B., Young, L. D., Scott, R. W., & Haynes, M. R. Differential effects of feedback and reinforcement in voluntary acceleration of human heart rate. *Perceptual and Motor Skills*, 1974, **38**, 683–691. (b)

Bleecker, E. R., & Engel, B. T. Learned control of cardiac rate and cardiac conduction in the Wolff-Parkinson-White Syndrome. *New England Journal of Medicine*, 1973, **288**, 560–562. (a)

Bleecker, E. R., & Engel, B. T. Learned control of ventricular rate in patients with atrial fibrillation. *Psychosomatic Medicine*, 1973, **35**, 161–175. (b)

Booker, H. E., Rubow, R. T., & Coleman, P. J. Simplified feedback in neuromuscular retraining: An automated approach using electromyograph signals. *Archives of Physical Medicine and Rehabilitation*, 1969, **50**, 621–675.

Borkovec, T. D. The role of expectancy and physiological feedback in fear research: A review with special reference to subject characteristics. *Behavior Therapy*, 1973, **4**, 491–506.

Brady, J. P., Luborsky, L., & Kron, R. E. Blood pressure reduction in patients with essential hypertension through metronome-conditioned relaxation: A preliminary report. *Behavior Therapy*, 1974, **5**, 203–209.

Brener, J. A general model of voluntary control applied to the phenomena of learned cardiovascular change. In P. A. Obrist, A. H. Black, J. Brener, & L. V. DiCara (Eds.), *Cardiovascular psychophysiology*. Chicago: Aldine, 1974. Pp. 365–391.

Brown, B. B. Recognition aspects of consciousness through association with EEG alpha activity represented by a light signal. *Psychophysiology*, 1970, **6**, 442–452.

Brudny, J., Grynbaum, B. B., & Korein, J. Spasmodic torticollis: Treatment by feedback display of the EMG. *Archives of Physical Medicine and Rehabilitation*, 1974, **58**, 403–408. (a)

Brudny, J., Korein, J., Levidow, L., Grynbaum, B. B., Leiberman, A., & Friedmann, L. W. Sensory feedback therapy as a modality of treatment in central nervous system disorders of voluntary movement. *Neurology*, 1974, **24**, 925–932. (b)

Budzynski, T. H., & Stoyva, J. M. An instrument for producing deep muscle relaxation by means of analog information feedback. *Journal of Applied Behavior Analysis*, 1969, **2**, 231–237.

Budzynski, T., & Stoyva, J. M. An electromyographic feedback technique for teaching voluntary relaxation of the masseter muscle. *Journal of Dental Research,* 1973, **57**, 116–119.

Budzynski, T., Stoyva, J., & Adler, C. Feedback-induced muscle relaxation: application to tension headache. *Journal of Behavior Therapy and Experimental Psychiatry,* 1970, **1,** 205–211.

Budzynski, T. H., Stoyva, J. M., Adler, C. S., & Mullaney, D. J. EMG biofeedback and tension headache: A controlled outcome study. *Psychosomatic Medicine,* 1973, **6,** 509–514.

Campbell, D. T., & Stanley, J. C. *Experimental and quasi-experimental designs for research.* Chicago: Rand McNally, 1966.

Cleeland, C. S. Behavioral techniques in the modification of spasmodic torticollis. *Neurology,* 1973, **23,** 1241–1247.

Cox, D. J., Freundlich, A., & Meyer, R. G. Differential effectiveness of electromyograph feedback, verbal relaxation instructions, and medication placebo with tension headaches. *Journal of Consulting and Clinical Psychology,* 1975, **43,** 892–898.

Datey, K. K., Deshmukh, S. N., Dalvi, C. P., & Vinekar, S. L. "Shavasan": A yogic exercise in the management of hypertension. *Angiology,* 1969, **20,** 325–333.

Deabler, H. L., Fidel, E., Dillenkoffer, R. L., & Elder, S. T. The use of relaxation and hypnosis in lowering high blood pressure. *American Journal of Clinical Hypnosis,* 1973, **16,** 75–83.

Deckner, C. W., Hill, J. T., & Bourne, J. R. Shaping of gastric motility in humans. *Proceedings, 80th Annual Convention, American Psychological Association,* 1972, 759–760.

Diamond, S., & Franklin, M. Indications and contraindications for the use of biofeedback therapy in headache patients. Paper read at the Biofeedback Research Society, Monterey, California, February 1975.

Edelberg, R. Electrical activity of the skin: Its measurement and uses in psychophysiology. In N. S. Greenfield & R. A. Sternbach (Eds.), *Handbook of psychophysiology.* New York: Holt, 1972. Pp. 367–418.

Elder, S. T., Ruiz, Z. B., Deabler, H. L., & Dillenkoffer, R. L. Instrumental conditioning of diastolic blood pressure in essential hypertensive patients. *Journal of Applied Behavior Analysis,* 1973, **6,** 377–382.

Engel, B. T. Operant conditioning of cardiac function: A status report. *Psychophysiology,* 1972, **9,** 161–177.

Engel, B. T., & Bleecker, E. R. Application of operant conditioning techniques to the control of cardiac arrhythmias. In P. A. Obrist, A. H. Black, J. Brener, & L. V. DiCara (Eds.), *Cardiovascular psychophysiology.* Chicago: Aldine, 1974. Pp. 456–476.

Engel, B. T., & Melmon, L. Operant conditioning of heart rate in patients with cardiac arrhythmias. *Conditional Reflex,* 1968, **3,** 130.

Engel, B. T., Nikoomanesh, P., & Schuster, M. M. Operant conditioning of rectosphincteric responses in the treatment of fecal incontinence. *New England Journal of Medicine,* 1974, **290,** 646–649.

Epstein, L. H. Psychophysiological measurement in assessment. In M. Hersen & A. S. Bellack (Eds.), *Behavior assessment: A practical handbook.* New York: Pergamon, 1976, in press.

Epstein, L. H., & Abel, G. G. An analysis of biofeedback training effects for tension headache patients. *Behavior Therapy,* 1977, in press.

Epstein, L. H., Abel, G. G., & Webster, J. S. Feedback assisted control and discrimination of EMG activity in the treatment of tension headaches. Paper read at meeting of AABT, Chicago, December, 1974.

Epstein, L. H., & Blanchard, E. B. Biofeedback, self-control and self-management: An integration and reappraisal. *Biofeedback and Self-Regulation,* 1977, in press.

Epstein, L. H., Hersen, M., & Hemphill, D. Music feedback in the treatment of tension headache: An experimental case study. *Journal of Behavior Therapy and Experimental Psychiatry,* 1974, 5, 59–63. (b)

Epstein, L. H., & Webster, J. S. Instructional pacing, and feedback control of respiratory behavior. *Perceptual and Motor Skills,* 1975, 41, 895–900.

Finley, W. W., Smith, H. A., & Etherton, M. D. Reduction of seizures and normalization of the EEG in a severe epileptic following sensorimotor biofeedback training. *Biological Psychology,* 1975, 2, 195–209.

Furman, S. Intestinal biofeedback in functional diarrhea: A preliminary report. *Journal of Behavior Therapy and Experimental Psychiatry,* 1973, 4, 317–321.

Gannon, L., & Sternbach, R. A. Alpha enhancement as a treatment for pain: A case study. *Journal of Behavior Therapy and Experimental Psychiatry,* 1971, 2, 209–213.

Glueck, B. C., & Stroebel, C. F. Biofeedback and meditation in the treatment of psychiatric illnesses. *Comprehensive Psychiatry,* 1975, 16, 303–321.

Gorman, P. J., & Kamiya, J. Operant conditioning of stomach acid pH. Paper read at the Biofeedback Research Society, Boston, February 1972.

Green, E. E., Walters, E. D., Green, A. M., & Murphy, G. Feedback technique for deep relaxation. *Psychophysiology,* 1969, 6, 371–377.

Hardyck, C. D., & Petrinovich, L. V. Treatment of subvocal speech during reading. *Journal of Reading,* 1969, 1, 3–11.

Hardyck, C. D., Petrinovich, L. F., & Ellsworth, D. W. Feedback of speech muscle activity during silent reading; rapid extinction. *Science,* 1966, 154, 1467–1468.

Haynes, S. N., Moseley, D., & McGowan, W. T. Relaxation training and biofeedback in the reduction of muscle tension. Paper read at Biofeedback Research Society, Colorado Springs, February 1974.

Headrick, M. W., Feather, B. W., & Wells, D. T. Unidirectional and large magnitude heart rate changes with augmented sensory feedback. *Psychophysiology,* 1971, 8, 132–142.

Herman, S. H., & Prewett, M. An experimental analysis of feedback to increase sexual arousal in a case of homo- and heterosexual impotence: A preliminary report. *Journal of Behavior Therapy and Experimental Psychiatry,* 1974, 5, 271–274.

Hines, T. F. Manual muscle examination. In S. Licht (Ed.), *Therapeutic exercise.* New Haven, Conn.: Elizabeth Licht, 1965.

Jacobs, A., & Felton, G. S. Visual feedback of myoelectric output to facilitate muscle relaxation in normal persons and patients with neck injuries. *Archives of Physical Medicine and Rehabilitation,* 1969, 50, 34–39.

Jacobson, A. M., Hackett, T. P., Surman, O. S., & Silverberg, E. L. Raynaud phenomenon: Treatment with hypnotic and operant technique. *Journal of the American Medical Association,* 1973, 225, 739–740.

Jacobson, E. Variation of blood pressure with skeletal muscle tension and relaxation. *Annals of Internal Medicine,* 1939, 12, 1194–1212.

Javel, A. F., & Denholtz, M. S. Audible GSR feedback and systematic desensitization: A case report. *Behavior Therapy,* 1975, 6, 251–253.

Johnson, H. E., & Garton, W. H. Muscle re-education in hemiplegia by use of EMG device. *Archives of Physical Medicine and Rehabilitation,* 1973, 54, 320–325.

Johnson, R. K., & Meyer, R. G. Phased biofeedback approach for epileptic seizure control. *Journal of Behavior Therapy and Experimental Psychiatry,* 1974, 5, 185–187.

Johnson, W. G., & Turin, A. Biofeedback treatment of migraine headache: A systematic case study. *Behavior Therapy*, 1975, **6**, 394–397.

Kamiya, J. Conscious control of brain waves. *Psychology Today*, 1968, **1**, 57–60.

Kanfer, F. H., & Duerfeldt, P. H. Effects on retention of externally or self-reinforced rehearsal trials following acquisition. *Psychological Reports*, 1967, **21**, 194–196.

Kaplan, B. J. EEG biofeedback and epilepsy. Unpublished doctoral dissertation, Brandeis University, 1973.

Kimmel, H. D. Instrumental conditioning of autonomically mediated responses. *American Psychologist*, 1974, **29**, 325–335.

Kleinman, K. M., & Goldman, H. Effects of biofeedback on physiological and cognitive consequences of essential hypertension. Paper read at the Biofeedback Research Society, Colorado Springs, February 1974.

Kristt, D. A., & Engel, B. T. Learned control of blood pressure in patients with high blood pressure. *Circulation*, 1975, **51**, 370–378.

Lang, P. J. The mechanics of desensitization and the laboratory study of human fear. In C. M. Franks (Ed.), *Behavior therapy: Appraisal and status*. New York: McGraw-Hill, 1969. Pp. 160–191.

Lang, P. J. Acquisition of heart rate control: Method, theory and clinical implications. In D. C. Fowler (Ed.), *Clinical applications of psychophysiology*. New York: Columbia University Press, 1975.

Lang, P. J., Rice, D. G., & Sternbach, R. A. The psychophysiology of emotion. In N. S. Greenfield & R. A. Sternbach (Eds.), *Handbook of psychophysiology*. New York: Holt, 1972. Pp. 623–643.

Leaf, W. B., & Gaarder, K. R. A simplified EMG feedback apparatus for relaxation training. *Journal of Behavior Therapy and Experimental Psychiatry*, 1971, **2**, 39–43.

Leitenberg, H., Agras, W. S., Butz, R., & Wincze, J. Relationship between heart rate and behavior change during the treatment of phobias. *Journal of Abnormal Psychology*, 1971, **78**, 59–68.

Levenson, R. W. Automated system for direct measurement and feedback of total respiratory resistance by the forced oscillation technique. *Psychophysiology*, 1974, **11**, 86–90.

Levenson, R. W. Manuck, S. B., Strupp, H. H., Blackwood, G. L., & Snell, J. D. A biofeedback technique for bronchial asthma. Paper read at the Biofeedback Research Society, Colorado Springs, February 1974.

Love, W. A., Montgomery, D. D., & Moeller, T. A. Working paper number 1. Unpublished manuscript, Nova University, Ft. Lauderdale, Florida, 1974.

Lubar, J. F., & Bahler, W. W. Behavioral management of epileptic seizures following EEG biofeedback training of the sensorimotor rhythm. *Biofeedback and Self-Regualtion* 1976, **1**, 77–104.

Lutker, E. R. Treatment of migraine headache by conditioned relaxation: A case study. *Behavior Therapy*, 1971, **2**, 592–593.

Marinacci, A. A., & Horande, M. Electromyogram in neuromuscular re-education. *Bulletin of the Los Angeles Neurological Society*, 1960, **25**, 57–71.

Marks, I. M. Flooding (implosion) and allied treatments. In W. S. Agras (Ed.), *Behavior modification*. Boston: Little, Brown, 1972. Pp. 154–213.

Mathews, A. M., & Gelder, M. G. Psychophysiological investigation of brief relaxation training. *Journal of Psychosomatic Research*, 1969, **13**, 1–12.

Mavissakalian, M., Blanchard, E. B., Abel, G. G., & Barlow, D. H. Subjective and erectile responses to complex erotic stimuli in homosexual and heterosexual males. *British Journal of Psychiatry*, 1975, **126**, 252–257.

McFarland, R. A. Heart rate perception and heart rate control. *Psychophysiology,* 1975, **12,** 402–405.

McGuigan, F. J. Feedback of speech muscle activity during silent reading: Two comments. *Science,* 1967, **157,** 579–581.

McKenzie, R. E., Ehrisman, W. J., Montgomery, P. S., & Barnes, R. H. The treatment of headache by means of electroencephalographic biofeedback. *Headache,* 1974, **14,** 164–172.

Miller, N. E. Visceral learning and other additional facts potentially applicable to psychotherapy. *International Psychiatry Clinics,* 1969, 294–309.

Miller, N. E. Postscript. In D. Singh & C. T. Morgan (Eds.), *Current status of physiological psychology: Readings.* Monterey, Calif.: Brooks, Cole, 1972. Pp. 245–250.

Miller, N. E. Applications of learning and biofeedback to psychiatry and medicine. In A. M. Freedman, H. I. Kaplan, & B. J. Sadock (Eds.), *Comprehensive textbook of psychiatry.* (2nd ed.) Baltimore: Williams & Wilkins, 1975. Pp. 356–365. (a)

Miller, N. E. Clinical applications of biofeedback: Voluntary control of heart rate, rhythm, and blood pressure. In H. I. Russek (Ed.), *New horizons in cardiovascular practice.* Baltimore: University Park Press, 1975. Pp. 239–249. (b)

Mills, G. K., & Solyom, L. Biofeedback of EEG Alpha in the treatment of obsessive ruminations: An exploration. *Journal of Behavior Therapy and Experimental Psychiatry,* 1974, **5,** 37–41.

Mitchell, K. R. Note on treatment of migraine using behavior therapy techniques. *Psychological Reports,* 1971, **28,** 171–172.

Mitchell, K. R., & Mitchell, D. M. Migraine: An exploratory treatment application of programmed behavior therapy techniques. *Journal of Psychosomatic Research,* 1971, **15,** 137–157.

Moeller, T. A., & Love, W. A. A method to reduce aterial hypertension through muscular relaxation. Unpublished manuscript, Nova University, Ft. Lauderdale, Florida, 1974.

Montgomery, D. D., Love, W. A., & Moeller, T. A. Working paper number 2. Unpublished manuscript, Nova University, Ft. Lauderdale, Florida, 1975.

Mulhall, D. J., & Todd, R. W. Deconditioning by the use of EMG signals. *Behavior Therapy,* 1975, **6,** 125–127.

Nikoomanesh, P., Wells, D., & Schuster, M. M. Biofeedback control of lower esophageal sphincter contraction. *Clinical Research,* 1973, **21,** 521.

Nunes, J. S., & Marks, I. M. Feedback of true heart rate during exposure in vivo. *Archives of General Psychiatry,* 1975, **32,** 933–936.

Obrist, P. A., Galosy, R. A., Lawler, J. E., Gaebelein, C. J., Howard, J. L., & Shanks, E. M. Operant conditioning of heart rate: Somatic correlates. *Psychophysiology,* 1975, **12,** 445–455.

Paskewitz, D. A., & Orne, M.T. Visual effects on alpha feedback training. *Science,* 1973, **181,** 360–363.

Patel, C. H. Yoga and biofeedback in the management of hypertension. *Lancet,* 1973, **2, ii,** 1053–1055.

Patel, C. H. 12-Month follow-up of yoga and biofeedback in the management of hypertension. *Lancet,* 1975, **i,** 62–67. (a)

Patel, C. H. Yoga and biofeedback in the management of "stress" in hypertensive patients. *Clinical Science and Molecular Medicine,* 1975, **48,** 171–174. (b)

Patel, C. H., & North, W. R. S. Randomized controlled trial of yoga and biofeedback in management of hypertension. *Lancet,* 1975, **ii,** 93–99.

Paul, G. L. Behavior modification research: Design and tactics. In C. M. Franks (Ed.), *Behavior therapy: Appraisal and status.* New York: McGraw-Hill, 1969. Pp. 29–62.

Peper, E. Frontiers of clinical biofeedback. In L. Birk (Ed.), *Seminars in psychiatry:* Vol. 5. New York: Grune & Stratton, 1973.

Peper, E., & Grossman, E. R. Preliminary observation of thermal biofeedback training in children with migraine. Paper read at the Biofeedback Research Society meeting, Colorado Springs, February, 1974.

Price, K. R. Feedback effects on penile tumescence. Paper read at the Eastern Psychological Association, Washington, D. C., May 1973.

Prigatano, G. P., & Johnson, H. J. Biofeedback control of heart rate variability to phobic stimuli: A new approach to treating spider phobia. *Proceedings, 80th Annual Convention, American Psychological Association,* 1972, pp. 403–404.

Prigatano, G. P., & Johnson, H. J. Autonomic nervous system changes associated with spider phobic reaction. *Journal of Abnormal Psychology,* 1974, **83**, 169–177.

Rachman, S., & Hodgson, R. Synchrony and desynchrony in fear and avoidance. *Behaviour Research and Therapy,* 1974, **12**, 311–318.

Raskin, M., Johnson, G., & Rondestvedt, J. W. Chronic anxiety treated by feedback-induced muscle relaxation. *Archives of General Psychiatry,* 1973, **28**, 263–267.

Reinking, R. H., & Kohl, M. L. Effects of various forms of relaxation training on physiological and self-report measures of relaxation. *Journal of Consulting and Clinical Psychology,* 1975, **53**, 595–600.

Rosen, R. C. Suppression of penile tumescence by instrumental conditioning. *Psychosomatic Medicine,* 1973, **35**, 509–513.

Rosen, R. C. The control of penile tumescence in the human male. Paper read at the American Psychological Association, New Orleans, August 1974.

Rosenthal, R. *Experimenter effects in behavioral research.* New York: Appleton, 1966.

Rouse, L., Peterson, J., & Shapiro, G. EEG Alpha entrainment reaction within the biofeedback setting and some possible effects on epilepsey. Paper read at the Biofeedback Research Society, Colorado Springs, February 1974.

Russ, K. L. Effect of two different feedback paradigms on blood pressure levels of patients with essential hypertension. Paper read at the Biofeedback Research Society, Colorado Springs, February 1974.

Sargent, J. D., Green, E. E., & Walters, E. D. The use of autogenic feedback training in a pilot study of migraine and tension headaches. *Headache,* 1972, **12**, 120–125.

Sargent, J. D., Green, E. E., & Walters, E. D. Preliminary report on the use of autogenic feedback training in the treatment of migraine and tension headaches. *Psychosomatic Medicine,* 1973, **35**, 129–135.

Schultz, J. H., & Luthe, W. *Autogenic Therapy.* Vol. 1. New York: Grune & Stratton, 1969.

Schwartz, G. E. Clinical applications of biofeedback: Some theoretical issues. In D. Upper & D. S. Goodenough (Eds.), *Behavior modification with the individual patient: Proceedings of third annual Brockton Symposium on behavior therapy.* Nutley, N. J.: Roche, 1972. Pp. 35–56.

Schwartz, G. E. Biofeedback as therapy: Some theoretical and practical issues. *American Psychologist,* 1973, **28**, 666–673.

Schwartz, G. E. Biofeedback, self-regulation, and the patterning of physiological processes. *American Scientist,* 1975, **63**, 314–324.

Schwartz, G. E. & Shapiro, D. Biofeedback and essential hypertension: Current findings and theoretical concerns. In L. Birk (Ed.) *Biofeedback: Behavioral medicine.* New York: Grune & Stratton, 1973. Pp. 133–143.

Scott, R. W., Blanchard, E. B., Edmundson, E. D., & Young, L. D. A shaping procedure for heart-rate control in chronic tachycardia. *Perceptual and Motor Skills,* 1973, **37**, 327–338.

Seifert, A. R., & Lubar, J. F. Reduction of epileptic seizures through EEG biofeedback training. *Biological Psychology,* 1975, 3, 157–184.

Shapiro, D. Operant-feedback control of human blood pressure: Some clinical issues. In P. A. Obrist, A. H. Black, J. Brener, & L. V. DiCara (Eds.), *Cardiovascular psychophysiology.* Chicago: Aldine, 1974. Pp. 441–455.

Shapiro, D., Tursky, B., Gershon, E., & Stern, M. Effects of feedback and reinforcement on control of human systolic blood pressure. *Science,* 1969, 163, 588–590.

Shoemaker, J. E., & Tasto, D. L. The effects of muscle relaxation on blood pressure of essential hypertensives. *Behaviour Research and Therapy,* 1975, 13, 29–43.

Sidman, M. *Tactics of scientific research.* New York: Basic Books, 1960.

Sirota, A. D., Schwartz, G. E., & Shapiro, D. Voluntary control of human heart rate: Effect on reaction to aversive stimulation. *Journal of Abnormal Psychology,* 1974, 83, 261–267.

Sittenfeld, P. The control of the EEG theta rhythm. In D. Shapiro *et al.* (Eds.), *Biofeedback and self-control, 1972.* Chicago: Aldine, 1972. Pp. 506–507.

Skinner, B. F. *Science and human behavior.* New York: Free Press, 1953.

Snyder, C., & Nobel, M. Operant conditioning of vasoconstriction. *Journal of Experimental Psychology,* 1968, 77, 263–268.

Sroufe, L. A. Effects of depth and rate of breathing on heart rate and heart variability. *Psychophysiology,* 1971, 8, 648–655.

Stephens, J. H., Harris, A. H., & Brady, J. V. Large magnitude heart rate changes in subjects instructed to change their heart rates and given exteroceptive feedback. *Psychophysiology,* 1972, 9, 283–285.

Sterman, M. B. Neurophysiological and clinical studies of sensorimotor EEG biofeedback training: Some effects on epilepsy. In L. Birk (Ed.), *Biofeedback: Behavioral medicine,* New York: Grune & Stratton, 1973. Pp. 147–165.

Sterman, M. B., & Friar, L. Suppression of seizures in an epileptic following sensorimotor EEG feedback training. *Electroencephalography and Clinical Neurophysiology,* 1972, 33, 89–95.

Stroebel, C. F., & Glueck, B. C. Biofeedback treatment in medicine and psychiatry: An ultimate placebo? In L. Birk (Ed.), *Biofeedback: Behavioral medicine.* New York: Grune & Stratton, 1973. Pp. 19–33.

Surwit, R. S. Biofeedback: A possible treatment for Raynaud's disease. In L. Birk (Ed.), *Biofeedback: Behavioral medicine.* New York: Grune & Stratton, 1973. Pp. 123–130.

Tamayo, F. M. V., Standley, S. M., & Treon, M. A. The use of amplitude GSR biofeedback in the modification of stuttering frequency. Paper read at the Western Psychological Association, April 1973.

Tasto, D. L., & Hinkle, J. E. Muscle relaxation treatment for tension headaches. *Behaviour Research and Therapy,* 1973, 11, 347–349.

Thoresen, C. E., & Mahoney, M. J. *Behavioral self-control.* New York: Holt, 1974.

Toomin, M. K., & Toomin, H. GSR biofeedback in psychotherapy: Some clinical observations. *Psychotherapy: Theory, Research and Practice,* 1975, 12, 33–38.

Townsend, R. E., House, J. F., & Addano, D. A comparison of biofeedback-mediated relaxation and group therapy in the treatment of chronic anxiety. *American Journal of Psychiatry,* 1975, 132, 598–601.

Troyer, W. G., Twentyman, C. T., Gatchel, R. J., & Lang, P. J. Learned heart rate control in patients with ischemic heart disease. *Psychophysiology,* 1973, 10, 213.

Turin, A. Biofeedback for migraines. Paper read at the Biofeedback Research Society, Monterey, California, February 1975.

Tursky, B., Shapiro, D., & Schwartz, G. E. Automated constant cuff-pressure system to measure average systolic and diastolic blood pressure in man. *IEEE Transactions in Bio-Medical Engineering*, 1972, 19, 271–276.

Varni, J. G. The use of biofeedback in the treatment of vaginismus. Paper read at the Society for Psychophysiological Research, Galveston, 1973.

Walsh, D. H. Interactive effects of alpha feedback and instructional set on subjective state. *Psychophysiology*, 1974, 11, 428–435.

Watson, J. P., Gaind, R., & Marks, I. M. Prolonged exposure: A rapid treatment for phobics. *British Medical Journal*, 1971, i, 13–15.

Weber, E. S. P., & Fehmi, L. G. The therapeutic use of EEG feedback. Paper read at the Biofeedback Research Society, Monterey, California, February, 1975.

Weinstock, S. A. A tentative procedure for the control of pain: Migraine and tension headaches. In D. Shapiro *et al.* (Eds.), *Biofeedback and self-control*. Chicago: Aldine, 1972. Pp. 510–512.

Weiss, T., & Engel, B. T. Voluntary control of premature ventricular contractions in patients. *American Journal of Cardiology*, 1970, 26, 666.

Weiss, T., & Engel, B. T. Operant conditioning of heart rate in patients with premature ventricular contractions. *Psychophysiology*, 1971, 8, 262–264. (a)

Weiss, T., & Engel, B. T. Operant conditioning of heart rate in patients with premature ventricular contractions. *Psychosomatic Medicine*, 1971, 33, 301–321. (b)

Weiss, T., & Engel, B. T. Evaluation of an intracardiac limit of learned heart rate control. *Psychophysiology*, 1975, 12, 310–312.

Welgan, P. R. Learned control of gastric acid secretions in ulcer patients. *Psychosomatic Medicine*, 1974, 36, 411–419.

Wells, D. T. Large magnitude voluntary heart rate changes. *Psychophysiology*, 1973, 10, 260–269.

Whitehead, W. E., Renault, P. F., & Goldiamond, I. Modification of human gastric acid secretion with operant-conditioning procedures. *Journal of Applied Behavior Analysis*, 1975, 8, 147–156.

Wickramasekera, I. The application of verbal instructions and EMG feedback training to the management of tension headache-preliminary observations. *Headache*, 1973, 13, 74–76. (a)

Wickramasekera, I. Temperature feedback for the control of migraine. *Journal of Behavior Therapy and Experimental Psychiatry*, 1973, 4, 343–345. (b)

Wickramasekera, I. Heart rate feedback and the management of cardiac neurosis. *Journal of Abnormal Psychology*, 1974, 83, 578–580.

Winer, B. J. *Statistical principles in experimental design*. New York: McGraw-Hill, 1962.

PARENTS AS BEHAVIOR THERAPISTS

ANTHONY M. GRAZIANO

Psychology Department
State University of New York at Buffalo
Buffalo, New York

I. INTRODUCTION

A. Parent Training and Mental Health Politics

The main focus of this article will be on the technology of training parents in behavior therapy. Initially however, several significant nontechnical issues must be addressed. The major issue is neither new nor startling but has been largely ignored, i.e., that the development of effective, socially useful applied health services depends on heavy social supports that extend far beyond science and technology. These social supports, which are necessary to translate scientific concepts into social programs, are created and maintained primarily through political, rather than scientific, processes. The politics of health programming are no less important than the science that supposedly bears the major weight.

Mental health professionals generally seem to accept the notion that political decisions are to some degree involved in science, and often denounce the disproportionately great influence that nonscientific individuals seem to have in those political decisions. However, clinicians have not: (1) sufficiently recognized the degree of power that political action has over science, (2) accepted the general idea that, in a democracy, political action is proper in *all* areas of public concern, and (3) admitted how much the behavior of "professionals" and "scientists" is, in fact, political. In this writer's opinion, a major problem in our field is our still muddy perception of these points.

Mental health services for children are still of doubtful effectiveness, limited availability, and exorbitant in cost (e.g., Berlin, 1975; Colby, 1964; Graziano, 1969, 1974; Hersch, 1968; Joint Commission, 1969; Levitt, 1957; Silver, 1963; Smith & Hobbs, 1966). This writer has maintained (Graziano, 1969, 1975) that those pronounced failures of service may be due more to the professions' political constraints than to the limitations of our scientific knowledge or technical skills. Thus called into question is not only the effectiveness of therapeutic techniques, but also the wisdom and direction of professional politics that seem to have relegated children's services to the lowest levels of professional priorities.

Mental health services are determined by the service-givers and the political decision-makers (i.e., the clinical–managerial level of professionals and the elected officials and bureaucrats). The problem is not that these people make significant policy decisions, but, rather, that the mental health consumers do not. In the decision-making process the goals of the professionals are not tempered by an equally weighted clients' consideration of their own goals. Traditionally the only decision allowed to clients has been to accept services or not. If not, they are free to consult another clinic where, in any event, the services are much the same. We believe this has been particularly true of children's services—where the parents have been passive, even docile consumers.

It is on that point, the parents' quiet buying of services that they do not fully understand, cannot evaluate, and in which they have little directive input, that the current serious exploration of parent training in behavior therapy may have its greatest impact. Such training may help reduce some of the ill-defined but no less real social distance (Graziano, 1969) between professionals and consumers that helps bestow higher status to the former but only implies their greater skill. Behavior therapists are beginning to bring parents into the therapeutic situation, not as passive buyers of service but as active participants and, often, as cotherapists.

In numerous cases, as recently reviewed by Berkowitz and Graziano (1972), Graziano (1975), Johnson and Katz (1973), O'Dell (1974), and Tavormina (1974), parents are being taught some measure of heretofore professional skills, are being maintained in more continual contact with their child's treatment than is traditionally the case, are being taught to monitor and evaluate the professional's effectiveness, and finally are being given a position of effective input in the therapy paradigm.

If this development is cultivated, parents may become active paraprofessionals in clinic settings, collectively as well as in individual cases, making several technical contributions (e.g., providing another source of personnel or having access to the child's natural environment). Whatever their technical potential, an equally important contribution lies on the *policy* making level. As we have noted elsewhere:

Although professionals are concerned with the welfare of the children under their care, an element of impersonality must invariably creep in; simply, the professional's commitment to the child cannot be as strong as that of the parents.

The bureaucratization and politicizing of mental health programs have fostered that impersonality by rewarding the professional's commitment to his agency (and profession) for more than his commitment to his client. . . . We do not argue that the professional must have the same intensity of emotional commitment as the parents, but clearly a realignment of values is badly needed in the field so that we will value the child's welfare above that of the (agency). The parents' emotional commitment to their children, given weight in the development of programs, provides another element in the decision-making mix that might be of sufficient influence to pull the professional system toward that realignment of values (Graziano, 1974, pp. 281–282).

An inherent, major objective of mental health technology is its own escalation to large-scale, powerful, and significantly effective social services. Otherwise, what is its point? Such escalation of technology, to be consistent with democratic ideas, must be carried out in an overt, publically observable manner subject to open review, and remain consistent with prevailing public value systems and procedures. Simply, social programming for mental health services is properly a public policy concern.

As argued above, however, most of the public—and most importantly, that portion of the public that makes up the mental health consumers—has been barred from mental health policymaking. Training parents in therapeutic skills, a general area previously limited to closed-rank professionls, is a concrete development, a very real change in professional procedure that may force a realignment of policymakers by bringing the parents into the therapeutic paradigm. The point to be made here is that such parent training is far more than a technological development. It has long-range, perhaps even revolutionary, implications for professional conduct and for policy-making. It may have a profound effect upon the field, and it cannot be denied that the field needs profound change. We suggest that this seemingly small step by parents, from one side of the professional line to the other, may very well be the most important single development that has thus far occurred in mental health treatment of children. There are many important implications of this change, and not all of them will occur. But the potential for major change is present and this writer is willing to label this parent-training focus as a major, historically important development.

B. Basic Dimensions of Parent-Training Models

The emergence of parent behavioral training involves at least three major dimensions, each of which contrasts sharply with prevailing child therapy practice. The *therapist* (1) directly and actively trains *parents* (2) in *behavior therapy* (3) which they are to implement in the child's natural environment. Although the integrated totality of this shift in practice, and all its implications are new and important, none of its individual components is new.

Instructions in "better parenting" or managing children's problems are certainly not novel. Child-rearing manuals and even advice-giving newspaper columns have been published for years, although it cannot be claimed that they have been particularly systematic, well grounded, or sharply evaluated. By and large, most of the parenting literature, until very recently, has been popularizations of "common-sense" and frequently conflicting "certainties."

Lightner Witmer, beginning about 1896, was probably the first clinician to train nonprofessional staff, including adult patients as trainers, teachers and (as one reviews their actual work), psychotherapists (see Brotemarkle, 1931; Levine & Levine, 1970; Sarason, 1972; Sarason, Levine, Goldenberg, Cherlin, & Bennett, 1966). It is not clear, however, if Witmer trained parents to work with their own children, as he trained so many others.

Freud has been credited with the first use of a parent as a psychoanalytic agent. In the case of "Little Hans," Freud's only child analysand, the child's father, supervised by Freud, was the analytic agent (Freud, 1909). Kubie (1937) reported treatment of a child's phobia, also using the father as psychoanalytic agent. Other psychoanalysts included mothers as observers in their children's sessions (e.g., B. Bornstein, 1935; S. Bornstein, 1935, Burlingham,

1935; Elkish, 1935; Kolansky, 1960; Schwarz, 1950), and have also used mothers as active therapeutic agents in the home (e.g., Furman, 1957; Gero-Heymann, 1955; Rangell, 1952; Ruben & Thomas, 1947).

Client-centered counseling approaches have also been used to treat children through their parents as agents (e.g., Baruch, 1949; Fuchs, 1957; Guerney, 1969; Moustakas, 1959; Pechey, 1955). Fuchs (1957), for example, was supervised by her father, Carl Rogers, and successfully treated her infant daughter's serious problem of constipation. Many variations of family therapy also involve parents directly and actively (Jackson, 1968; Levine, 1964; Love, 1966; MacGregor, Ritchie, Serrano, & Shuster, 1964; Minuchin, 1965).

Parent discussion groups dealing with the management of child behavior problems have been reported by Davis (1947), MacNamara (1963), Munro (1952), but none of these papers reported substantial data although it was believed that parent discussion groups were helpful for the children.

The articles cited above were case studies in which only descriptive clinical discussions were presented. However, it is clear that long before the reemergence of behavior therapy in the 1960s (see Graziano, 1971, 1975) many professionals of different therapeutic models were well aware of the value of parents' direct and active involvement in their children's therapy. But, despite those early clinical excursions, most child treatment has continued to routinely exclude parents from direct involvement in anything other than mandatory collateral treatment for themselves and, of course, paying the bills. The newly accelerated movement towards parent behavioral training in active therapeutic responsibility is in very sharp contrast with the norms of current practice.

Likewise, behavior therapy (the second important major dimension noted above of parent training) is only apparently new. Although generally perceived to be a development of the last decade, behavior therapy first clearly emerged in the 1920s. It was soon overshadowed by Freud's successful revival and popularization of the intrapsychic focus of 100 years earlier, a development that has been termed "Romantic Psychiatry" (Graziano, 1975).

Finally, the current fashion of treating the child in the "natural environment" is often mistakenly perceived as another new development of the 1960s. Aside from some thus far unapproached problems of definition (e.g., why is the classroom considered to be any more "natural" than the clinic?), we seem to have ignored Witmer's clinical work with children in which he trained a variety of nonprofessionals to carry out therapeutic and educational programs with child clients, work that he began more than three-quarters of a century ago. Around 1894 Witmer began to develop his psychoedu- cational approach to children in complete contrast to the dominant psychiatry which focused on the supposed organic pathology of hospitalized adults. Witmer emphasized the normal, adaptive behav- ior of the child. He utilized systematic, detailed, and programmatic teaching techniques, and enlisted the aid of significant adults in the child's environment to implement a variety of creative remediation programs. Descriptions of Witmer's work have an up-to-date, 1970s cast, but unfortunately are largely ignored by contemporary clini- cians.

This new clinical strategy, one we have already appended with the term "revolutionary," is actually the current coalescing of at least three "old" dimensions. The importance of this clinical develop- ment lies not in the "newness" or originality of its major concepts but in the stark contrast of this parent-behavior-training approach against the background of clinical practice. The contrast exists not only in one respect but in each of its major underlying conceptual dimensions. It is this contrast, this marked difference from prevailing approaches, that provides its current importance and promise.

C. Implicit Criticisms of Traditional Child Therapy

The current explorations in parent behavioral training are attempts to overcome the major limitations of traditional treatment. Traditional therapy is seen as an "artificial" situation, occupying only a samll portion of the child's life and possibly having only incidental relation to it (Graziano, 1971) and in which the therapist's observations of parent–child interactions or of the problem behavior are grossly limited (Hawkins, Peterson, Schweid, & Bijou, 1966), as summarized by Berkowitz and Graziano (1972):

The therapist's data, then, are usually limited to his one-hour, weekly cross sectional slice of the total reality of the young client's life, and to the retrospective and often unreliable reports of parents not trained in (direct) behavioral observation. Further . . . the therapist rarely makes usuful, practical suggestions, (believing) this to be of less importance than psychodynamic material and, not knowing relevant environmental details, his suggestions may be so technical or general that parents, teachers and even other therapists are unable to translate them into specific behavior. Some parents, overwhelmed and unable to cope with the demands of a disturbing child receive little practical guidance from the therapist and find no ebbing of their feelings of helplessness, rage and literal hate (Holland, 1969; Patterson, McNeil, Hawkins and Phelps, 1967). . . . Such intense parental feelings may occasion significant further disorganization in the family's life. Thus, the direct and practical coping with the everyday realities of the disorganized family situation may be an important therapeutic need currently unmet by psychodynamic therapists who deal with inferences and not behavior (p. 298).

The parent behavior training approaches focus largely on the overt problems within the family system, and assume that a child's maladaptive behavior has been acquired in his natural (i.e., family) environment and can best be changed with the changes maintained by modifying that environment.

Direct parent involvement in child treatment is not new or limited to behavioral models. As noted above, psychodynamic and client-centered therapists have explored the area. With the reemergence of behavior modification in the early 1960s and its more pronounced focus on an *action* orientation that is highly sensitive to environmental as well as personal behavior details, both the behavioral model and more practical strategies became available. As a result, training parents as therapists has become far more possible than before. Most parent training has occurred in the past decade, as part of the behavior modification field.

In summary, training parents as active agents in their own children's treatment has been explored for many years and by therapists from various theoretical orientations. The reemergence of behavior therapy in the late 1950s and 1960s added considerable impetus and the vast majority of the literature has emerged in the past decade, as parent behavioral training. This constitutes a true clinical innovation with important implications not only for the techniques of child therapy, but also for ethical issues, professional political issues, and for public health policymaking. Seriously utilizing parents as cooperative change agents and training them in therapeutic skills may be the single most important development in the child therapy field.

II. REVIEW OF THE LITERATURE

A. Overview

Having introduced the area and discussed nontechnical issues, major technical and methodological issues will now be considered. (For earlier reviews, see Berkowitz & Graziano, 1972; Johnson & Katz, 1973; O'Dell, 1974; Tavormina, 1974.)

Two of the earliest descriptions of parental involvement in a child's behavior therapy were presented by Weber (1936) and Williams (1959). Weber successfully treated a 19-month-old-girl with a strong fear of her shadow. In what would now be described as a contact desensitization procedure, Weber (1936) cast shadows with a doll and other familiar objects while the child was gradually moved from the reassurance of her father's lap to the floor. Williams (1959) instructed parents in simple extinction of their 21-month-old son's crying. Crying behavior was successfully eliminated in 19 daily extinction trials and no further problems were reported in a 2-year follow-up.

Most of the parent training literature has been published since 1965, with the field showing a marked increase in both publication volume and methodological sophistication. As reviewed by Berkowitz and Graziano (1972), parent training approaches have been applied in considerable variety to virtually all child behavior problems. Parents have been trained individually and in groups, through lectures, assigned readings, programmed materials, group discussions, modeling, and direct coaching. The children involved have been mostly boys. In most papers: (1) mothers and not fathers were the primary objects of training, bearing the major responsibility for implementing the home programs; (2) training consisted primarily of operant approaches to contingency management (except for the direct treatment of enuresis, techniques based on respondent paradigms were reported in but a few papers); (3) home programs have been aimed mostly at reduction of maladaptive surplus such as aggressive and hyperactive behavior.

Respondent-based models are seldom used in parent training, except for the treatment of enuresis, using Mowrer (1938) type conditioning devices. Graziano (1974) used a reciprocal inhibition paradigm based on earlier work (Graziano & Kean, 1968) and described four cases in which mothers were taught to train their psychotic children in muscular relaxation. Clement (1970a, 1970b) discussed two cases in which mothers were instructed in a combination of operant and respondent approaches.

B. Problem Behaviors

Many behavioral strategies have been developed in clinical settings and, as noted by Brown (1971), have been applied to a wide variety of childhood behavior disorders. The development of parent behavioral training has involved the transfer of many of these clinical strategies from professional to parental control. An abundance of child behavioral treatment strategies for virtually all behavior problems are thus being made available to parents and, as concluded by O'Dell (1974) in his review, "There does not appear to be any class of overt child behavior that parents cannot be trained to modify" (p. 421).

Our problem-behavior categories are deliberately broad and there is thus some overlap.

1. PROBLEMS INVOLVING SOMATIC SYSTEMS

Many functional disorders of children are related to somatic systems. In the organic brain conditions, for example, biological variables produce functional as well as biological problems (e.g., a brain-damaged child, with perceptual difficulties, may become a major discipline problem in class). In psychophysiological reactions the interaction is in the other direction (i.e., functional variables help produce somatic problems). The psychophysiological reactions ordinarily involve a single organ system that is usually under the control of the autonomic nervous system and, as listed by Verville (1967) and Finch (1972), include stomach aches, accident proneness, manipulative motor habits such as nail biting, thumb sucking, and tics, obesity, skin disorders and elimination problems such as enuresis, encopresis, and functional constipation. Some of the more physically serious, sometimes life-threatening, psychophysiological reactions include bronchial asthma, ulcerative colitis, and anorexia nervosa. In each condition an observed or inferred somatic problem exists, apparently caused largely by functional variables.

Consistent with a model of biological causation, nearly all treatment of the somatogenic conditions have been medical, particularly pharmacological. Psychological or educational treatment or remediation have been considered secondary to what is assumed to be the major somatic problem. Likewise, psychophysiological reactions have been treated medically or, when approached psychologically, through the psychodynamic model which assumes that the somatic problems are symptoms, the results of complex, repressed emotionality. Consistent with that model, psychodynamic treatment has sought to uncover the repressed material and thus to reduce the psychic tension that created the somatic symptoms.

More recently, as reviewed by Graziano (1975), both respondent and operant conditioning models have been applied to somatogenic and psychophysiological conditions of childhood. For example, a striking paper by Wright, Nunnery, Eichel, and Scott (1968) describes their successful conditioning treatment of tracheostomy addiction in young children following tracheal surgery—a severe, life-threatening disorder in which the child is unable to breathe without a tube implanted in the trachea. Asthma, which may be "the leading cause of chronic illness among persons under seventeen years of age" (Colemen, 1972, p. 501), has been successfully alleviated by a number of investigators using relaxation training, assuming asthma to be an anxiety-mediated response (Alexander, Miklich, & Hershkoff, 1972; Moore, 1965; Sargeant & Yorkston, 1969; Walton, 1960). Other papers in which conditioning treatment was successfully applied to asthmatic responding include Alexander, Chai, Creer, Miklich, Renne, and Cardoso (1973), Creer (1970), Kushner (1968), and Neisworth and Moore (1972).

The last-mentioned paper reports the successful use of operant conditioning to reduce asthmatic responding of a 7-year-old boy. It is of particular interest here because the boy's mother, after brief instruction in operant conditioning, carried out the treatment program at home, which essentially consisted of differential reinforcement of the boy's being "well" and withdrawal of reinforcement for his "sick," asthmatic, behavior. All gains were maintained at an 11-month follow-up, with no negative concurrent effects.

There is increasing agreement that asthma is a common and serious illness. Conditioning approaches are promising, and there is some indication that they can be implemented at home by parents. However, extensive research is needed to justify large-scale training of parents to treat their asthmatic children. Nevertheless, these approaches represent a potentially significant public health development.

Several other somatic-related problems have been successfully approached with parents receiving behavioral training or instructions and carrying out portions of the treatment programs at home. These have included: seizures (Gardner, 1967; Peine, 1969; Zlutnick, 1972); self-injurious behavior (Allen & Harris, 1966; Graziano, 1974; Risley, 1968), eating problems (Bernal, 1973), and wearing dental braces (Hall, Axebrod, Tyler, Grief, Jones, & Robertson, 1972).

A problem area for which parent behavior training appears to be extremely appropriate is childhood obesity, and yet there has been extremely little investigation in this area. Two of the few studies that report parent and child behavior training to reduce childhood obesity are both doctoral dissertations (Gillick, 1974; Grace, 1975). Grace's (1975) study is particularly interesting since she utilized a self-control model, teaching children to self-monitor their own physical exercise and food intake, using parental assistance and comparing the children's self-monitoring with the parents' monitoring. Grace reported that the experimental subjects lost significantly more weight than control subjects and, on a 2-month follow-up, maintained the weight loss. However, as with many adult weight reduction studies, while the loss was statistically significant, there is doubt that it was sufficient to be of real personal or clinical value. The two dissertations open research in a new clinical area, treatment of childhood obesity through training both children and parents in behavioral techniques. As with the possibilities of controlling asthma discussed above, these studies suggest a possibly significant area with public health value. Again, much more research is needed.

A set of childhood problems with a high rate of occurrence involves encopresis, enuresis, and functional constipation. These are relatively common problems that have long been considered to be symptoms of complex psychodynamic activity requiring extensive "indirect" psychotherapy. More recently they have been successfully treated by direct conditioning methods, much of which has been increasingly carried out at home by parents. For example, there has been considerable use of commercially available Mowrer-type (Mowrer, 1938) conditioning devices. Although the evaluation of unsupervised use of commercial apparatuses is limited by lack of controls, data on 887 cases are available (Martin & Kubly, 1955; Jones, 1960), indicating remission rates ranging from 56 to 88% permanent cures. Lovibond (1964), in his major review of systematic studies (totaling 512 cases), concluded that while many studies fail to report sufficient procedural details, their evidence strongly supports the effectiveness of direct conditioning methods. Further, there is no evidence of symptom substitution following treatment.

DeLeon and Mandell (1966) employed visiting nurses to supervise mothers' use of a conditioning pad to train their enuretic children. Both frequency and severity of bed-wetting were more effectively and quickly reduced with the nurse-supervised conditioning apparatus than with either psychotherapy or no treatment. In 4-year follow-ups (DeLeon & Sacks, 1972; Sacks & DeLeon, 1973), half of the original subjects were still available and 81% of them were "symptom free" (no wets or one wet in the past year). For those still wetting, the rate was "significantly down." The conditioning success had been rapid and the effects well maintained over a lengthy period.

To overcome the common problem of high relapse rates, estimated by Young (1969) to be about 30%, Young and Morgan (1972a) used an "overlearning" tactic with a parent-supervised buzzer alarm. Overlearning with 61 cases significantly reduced the relapse rate and the improvements were maintained during follow-ups of, in some cases, more than 2 years.

Using another tactic, parental reinforcement of successively longer periods of retention, Paschalis, Kimmel, and Kimmel (1972) reported (1) significant improvement in 23 out of 31 enuretic children who "had never experienced a dry night," and (2) no relapses in a 3-month follow-up.

Parental effectiveness has also been reported in behavioral treatment of encopresis (Barrett, 1969; Conger, 1970; Edelman, 1971) and constipation (Lal & Lindsley, 1968).

A particularly interesting development is the rapid toilet training procedures of Foxx and Azrin (1973). The techniques are applicable at home, by parents of normal as well as exceptional children. The authors have described their training procedures in a book, *Toilet Training in One Day*, and present data to support the notion that such training can, indeed, be carried out in one day.

2. PROBLEMS GROUPED IN COMPLEX "SYNDROMES"

Many children are referred to clinics because of complex, severely disturbed, or markedly deficient and highly generalized behavior. They are often labeled as retarded, brain-damaged, schizophrenic, or autistic (all labels implying some common behavioral syndrome, characteristics of which are supposedly shared by all members of each class). In these cases, although the clinician's focus may be discrete behavior, it is seldom limited to a single behavior category. Unlike, for example, the direct treatment of enuresis in otherwise "normal" children, treatment in the present categories involves multiple and highly generalized surplus and deficit behavior. An underlying physiological base might be assumed by the clinician, but the treatment approaches are, in the main, functional.

Most behavioral treatment of children in these diagnostic categories has been conducted in the past 15 years in special settings such as hospitals, homes, day-care facilities, and special schools and clinics. A brief historical review of the development of behavioral training in these diagnostic categories can be found in Graziano (1975).

Increasingly, parental training for treatment and education of the child at home has been utilized. For many years, predating the advent of behavioral treatment in the early 1960s, workers in mental retardation urged parents to assume active training and educational roles for their children. With the techniques of behavior modification, the implementation of parental responsibility has increased. Denny (1966), for example, suggested 2-week workshops to train parents of retarded children in behavioral approaches. In addition, a number of studies of behavioral training or counseling of parents of retarded children have appeared (e.g., Cone & Sloop, 1971; Galloway & Galloway, 1970; Lasser, 1970; Morrey, 1971; Seitz & Hoekenga, 1974; Tavormina, 1975; Walder, Cohen, Breiter, Daston, Hirsch, & Liebowitz, 1969).

Tavormina (1975) compared the effectiveness of behavioral and reflective group counseling for parents of retarded children. The multiple-success outcome criteria included parent attitude scales, behavior problem checklists, direct observation of mother–child interactions in the clinic, target behavior ratings by parents, frequency counts at home, and parents' verbal reports. Tavormina found that behavioral counseling was more effective than reflective counseling, and both treatment groups improved more than non-treated controls.

A great deal of behavioral programming has been conducted with children labeled psychotic, schizophrenic, or autistic, following the early conditioning attempts by Anthony (1958) and Ferster and DeMyer (1962). Many behavioral programs now exist under a variety of sponsorships (see Graziano, 1975) such as residential hospital environments (e.g., Lovaas, Koegel, Simmons, & Long, 1973), day-care and school environments (e.g., Graziano, 1974), and classroom settings (e.g., Fischer & Glanville, 1970; Koegel & Rincover, 1974; Rutter & Bartak, 1973).

Throughout this development the importance of home programming has become evident. Numerous investigators included some degree of parent training, particularly in preparation for the child's return home. Virtually all behavioral investigators now accept the importance of parent training and the careful development of post-treatment environments inasmuch as such strategies are routinely applied. Clancy and McBride (1969) clearly emphasize the family system: "Autism can be understood better as a developmental process operating within a social system, the family, [which has] many dimensions and levels of organization, all interrelated and controlled by feedback mechanisms" (p. 233).

Nordquist and Wahler (1973) present a single case study in which the parents of a 4-year-old autistic child, whose multiple problem behaviors were of such severity that institutionalization had been repeatedly advised, successfully carried out a home treatment program. Success was reported in developing verbal and nonverbal imitation and in decreasing tantrums, whining, crying, and ritualistic behavior. Although limited because it is a single case study (reported no baseline data, no descriptions of parental training or parental changes, and no follow-ups), this paper makes two important points: (1) the treatments for an autistic child were totally carried out by parents at home, and (2) it was noted that "weak reinforcers" at home may have been critical in the child's behavior problems. In our own work with seriously disturbed children over a number of years (summarized in Graziano, 1974) we have made the same observation that a major factor in the child's disturbed behavior at home may be the weak reinforcing value of the parents. This observation suggests that a possibly critical variable on which to focus is the systematic development of generalized reinforcing value of the parents. This may be as critical in successful parent-administered programs as the precision of contingency management that is generally emphasized. It has been our clinical observation that development of parents' general reinforcing value can perhaps be brought about relatively quickly through direct assertion of control, such as the confrontations that occur in forcing a time-out contingency on severely disturbed children. These observations are worth empirical testing.

Other investigators who have included family systems as treatment settings for psychotic children include: Wolf, Risley, and Mees (1964), Wetzel, Baker, Roney, and Martin (1966), Wolf, Risley, Johnston, Harris, and Allen (1967), Gardner, Pearson, Bercovici, and Bricker (1968), Risley (1968), Peine (1969), Graziano (1970, 1974), Pinkston and Herbert (1971), Webster, McPherson, Sloman, Evans, and Kuchar (1973), Howlin, Marchant, Rutter, Berger, Hersov, and Yule (1973), and Lovaas et al., (1973). Two reports (Graziano, 1974; Lovaas et al., 1973) indicate that, upon leaving their respective structured program, autistic children whose parents had been trained in behavioral management skills maintained their gains while those whose parents had not been trained, or who were discharged to nonbehavioral programs, regressed.

It appears that in such severe conditions where the disturbed behavior is so powerfully overlearned and so thoroughly generalized, a total, 24-hour daily programming may be necessary. Further, training parents for home programming in order to maintain gains posted in special treatment settings is also of critical importance. However, the tentative nature of those conclusions is clearly indicated by the discussions of Browning (1971), Lovaas et al. (1973), and Graziano (1974). Lovaas and Graziano both note the disappointing results with some children despite hundreds of hours of detailed programming. Browning (1971) reported the results of a "total behavior modification program" for five autistic children. A variety of professionals and paraprofessionals carried out intensive individual-child behavioral programming in a residential setting. Family therapy was provided for any parents requesting it, and all parents agreed to a contract to be continuously involved in the program to an eventual maximum of 20 hours per week. As the child progressed through the program, parents' home programming responsibility increased to its maximum upon the child's full discharge. Programming was intensive and included hefty parental involvement as therapists.

After 3 years of the intensive behavior modification program that encompassed the entire day of each child, the results were very disappointing. Although improvements were observed, Browning (1971) noted that they were able, "at best . . . to train [the] children to perform as variably tractable, but severely retarded and socially dependent children" (p. 326). Further, the maintenance of gains after discharge would require such intensive, highly structured, individual daylong programming as to make it virtually impossible for parents to implement.

Those three reports discuss complex behavioral programming of several years' duration, and they concur that even with intensive programming the gains are hard-won and often of such small measure as to raise the question of the social worth of such high-cost programs.

The task is no less for trained parents as it is for trained professionals. Indeed, it is undoubtedly greater. At least at this point in time it appears that training parents to work with severely behaviorally disturbed children, such as autistic children, promises limited effectiveness for maximum effort. It might be, as suggested by Graziano (1974), that parents' strong emotional commitment to their children can provide a good basis for sustaining great efforts in many cases.

3. NEGATIVISTIC, NONCOMPLIANT, OPPOSITIONAL, AND AGGRESSIVE BEHAVIOR

A large portion of behavioral parent training has focused on the reduction of oppositional, noncompliant, negativistic, and aggressive behavior. Adults are more disturbed by children's active oppositional behavior than by more withdrawn or deficit functioning. Children in this category display high rates of surplus behavior that are highly disruptive, aversive, and demandingly intrusive in the lives of adults, involving repeated, often prolonged direct struggle between the child and the adult. It is no wonder that so much professional attention has been directed there, both by the demands of the parents and by the discreet nature of the behavior suggesting ease in bringing it under control.

Most of the papers report single-case studies, with a few reporting two or three cases. Some of the more recent papers attempt controlled, group comparisons. Most of the studies reported on instructing parents, mainly mothers, to implement fairly simple contingencies that were developed by the therapist.

Parents have been instructed to successfully implement a range of home programs that was determined by the therapists, and that dealt with problems of excessive crying (Williams, 1959), hyperactivity and extreme aggressive behavior (Bernal, 1969; Hawkins et al., 1966; Johnson & Brown, 1969; Lavigueur, Peterson, Sheese, & Peterson, 1973; O'Leary, O'Leary & Becker, 1967; Peine, 1969; Sloane, Johnston, & Bijou, 1967; Russo, 1964), manipulative behavior (Wagner, 1968), and fire-setting (Holland, 1969). A series of papers by Hanf (1968, 1969) and by Forehand, Cheney and Yoder (1974), Forehand and King (1974), and Forehand, King, Peed, and Yoder (1975) have focused on noncompliant behavior in young children. Noncompliance refers to a child's failure to initiate a response to a parental command or failure to inhibit a number of deviant behaviors such as fighting or screaming. It is a large category of behavior and a relatively common problem. Reduction of severe aggressive behavior in boys through parent-applied programs has been reported in multiple case studies (Patterson, Cobb, and Ray, 1972; Patterson, Ray, & Shaw, 1968; Patterson & Reid, 1973; Wahler, 19690; Wahler, Winkel, Peterson, & Morrison, 1965).

In most of these cases the children were still young enough to be reasonably well contained, although difficult to manage. A still more serious level of behavior within the present category is juvenile delinquency, considered here to be a more extreme form of oppositional behavior.

Most of the studies in Davidson and Seidman's (1974) excellent review of behavior modification in juvenile delinquency were conducted in special settings such as schools and correctional institutions, with only a minority of studies centered on community or neighborhood groups (e.g., Fo & O'Donnell, 1974; Schwitzgebel, 1964, 1967, 1969; Schwitzgebel & Kolb, 1964) and families (Alexander & Parsons, 1973; Alvord, 1971; Rose, Sundel, DeLange, Corwin & Palumbo, 1970; Stuart, 1971; Tharp & Wetzel, 1969). According to the reviewers, most studies entailed the strengthening of prosocial skills (e.g., improving educational performance in school settings and increasing a variety of cooperative social behavior in correctional programs). A minority of studies were aimed at the direct modification of illegal or delinquent behaviors and included programs in the homes of the adolescents.

The reviewers noted that the effectiveness of behavior modification techniques with this population has been well demonstrated. However, the specific manipulations accounting for improvements have not yet been clearly identified, and the generalizability of improvements to other settings and their maintenance over time are still in question. In general, this is a promising area of behavioral application, but, as with so much of the behavior modification literature, serious limitations (to be discussed in Section IV) require better designed research.

Many articles on family involvement using parent training have been single or multiple case studies, many of which involved contracting, a procedure suggested by Sulzer (1962). When considering ways to deliver better psychotherapy service, Sulzer suggested that a clear businesslike contract between therapist and client be drawn up in order to explicitly state the "exchange of reciprocal benefits between the two parties" (Ayllon & Skuban, 1973, p. 20). Stuart (1971) used contracting in a case study with a 16-year-old delinquent girl. The contract specified both responsibilities and privileges of the girl and her parents. Stuart reported compliance by all parties, termination of the court wardship, and cessation of delinquent activities. Tharp and Wetzel (1969) reported a large project of consultation to families of delinquents, helping them specify and carry out contingency management procedures for specific problems. The authors found that in some families the relationships had so deteriorated that productive verbal interactions were virtually impossible. In several cases, in order to initiate treatment plans a formal contract was negotiated, drawn up, and signed by the families and their children. The authors conducted follow-ups and reported maintained reductions of delinquent behaviors in many cases. Other successful multiple-case studies of behavioral consultations and counseling have been reported by Rose et al. (1970) and by Alvord (1971). The latter also employed contracting procedures between children and their parents.

Alexander and Parsons (1973) and Parsons and Alexander (1973) reported a controlled group comparison of different therapeutic approaches to delinquents. They assigned 46 families to a "short term behavioral intervention program," 19 families to a client-centered family groups program that was "representative of treatment in many juvenile centers," 11 families to a psychodynamic family group program that "represented exactly the form of treatment that a significant proportion of teenagers [in the county] receive," and 10 families to a no-treatment control condition.

In the behavioral group, the investigators applied behavioral tactics within a systems model of family interaction for "systematically extinguishing maladaptive interaction patterns and instituting reciprocity instead" (Alexander & Parsons, 1973, p. 221). They applied contingency contracting, modeling by therapists, social reinforcement and, in some families, token economies and a training manual (a modification of Patterson & Gullion, 1968).

The behavioral intervention group was the most successful when compared with the discussion groups (verbal interactions in group sessions) on process and outcome measures (recidivism 6 to 18 months later), showing a significantly lower recidivism rate (25%). The client-centered and no-treatment controls were equivalent (47% and 50%), while the psychodynamic group showed a 73% recidivism rate. There were some design limitations such as grossly unequal N's (e.g., 46 families in the behavioral group and 11 in the psychodynamic), reporting percentages for such small numbers (e.g., with eight cases of 11 presented as a 73% recidivism rate), and no attempt to control for the experience and ability of the therapists (i.e., the critical differences might not have been in the therapy models, but perhaps were accounted for by the experience and skill of the therapists or the amount and quality of supervision).

Overall, despite these limitations, the study provides evidence that carefully detailed, short-term behavioral intervention with delinquents and their families is more effective than traditional client-centered and psychodynamic treatments. The assignment of subjects to a real therapy program (the psychodynamic treatment already existing in the community rather than a laboratory analog) adds some power to the demonstration.

4. REDUCTION OF CHILDREN'S FEARS

As we have noted in an earlier paper (Graziano, 1975), in contrast to the vast amount of professional effort that behavior therapists and researchers have devoted to the fears of adults, children's fears have been largely neglected. Adults seem to minimize the importance of children's fears and to view such fears as a common, expected, transitory and thus not particularly serious part of normal development. However, childhood fears may be neither transient nor benign (Graziano, 1975; Jersild, 1968; Marks & Gelder, 1966; Miller, Barrett, Hampe, & Noble, 1972). In any event, ". . . the psychological suffering of a fearful child, even if [the suffering] spontaneously improves in a few years, is at least as worthy of professional concern as is the suffering of adults . . . and there are good reasons, then for urging more activity by behavior therapists in the study and alleviation of children's fears" (Graziano, 1975, p. 248).

This behavioral problem, like childhood obesity, seems particularly suited for parent-administered treatment at home. Unlike psychotic, retarded, or other seriously disturbed children, those who suffer from a variety of fears may have no other serious problems of communication, affect, or relationships. Thus, the treatment of fearful behavior may be relatively uncomplicated, and well within the possibility of reasonable training and supervision of parents. However, as with the problem of childhood obesity, there has been little research and clinical investigation into children's fears and, more specifically, into the effectiveness of training parents to treat their own children's fears.

Parents have been involved in treatment of school phobia. In several cases, as reviewed by Hersen (1971), parents were trained to various degrees of responsibility for contingency management (e.g., Ayllon, Smith, & Rogers, 1970; Hersen, 1968, 1970; Kennedy, 1965; Patterson, 1965; Smith & Sharpe, 1970). Kennedy (1965) reports on the rapid treatment of 50 school phobics, in which the parents were given the treatment rationale and were carefully instructed on the necessity for firmness in insuring that the child return to school—by force if necessary—on the first treatment day. Other cases, involving the integration of "systems" (i.e., home and parents, school, client) have been discussed by Bolman (1970), and Graziano, Hastrup, and Pearlson (1975). In the latter case study, four major treatment dimensions were integrated: reduction of positive reinforcement for staying at home, graded reintroduction to school, reciprocal inhibition, and cognitive self-control training to maintain the behavioral gains. The parents, particularly the mothers, were involved in the first dimension, carrying out fairly simple contingencies by maintaining scheduling limits at home that had been set up by the therapists.

Parents in these school phobia cases were involved in crucial aspects of the treatments, primarily in carrying out relatively simple management strategies. The greatest common demand on the parents in these cases was to become firm and consistent in maintaining behavioral limits at home. In virtually all cases, this was a change in the parents' behavior, and that change was brought about relatively easily through direct discussions with the therapist. None of these parents was required to master sophisticated knowledge of behavioral treatment. For these reasons, despite the limitations of using case reports as evidence, these cases do suggest that this particular child-hood fear—school phobia—can be relatively quickly treated by professionally supervised parents who apply relatively simple behavioral strategies.

Parents have been somewhat peripherally involved in other fear treatment for their children, e.g., a bodily injury phobia (Ollendick & Gruen, 1972) and a young child's fear of her shadow (Weber, 1936). Two cases of greater parental involvement were described by Tasto (1969) in which the parents conducted in vivo desensitization trials (following both relaxation training and desensitization hierarchies in the therapist's office) to treat a 4-year-old boy's severe fear of sudden, loud noises. Bentler (1962) described a mother's successful treatment of her child's severe aquaphobia by exposing the child to increasing amounts of water while in close physical contact with the child, who was surrounded by highly prized, floating toys.

There is a very small literature on treatment of children's fears in clinic and laboratory settings (see the review by Graziano, 1975). A number of approaches have been used with apparent success which seem to be easily transferred to parents. For example, live modeling (see Bandura, Grusec, & Menlove, 1967) and contact desensitization (see Bentler, 1962; Murphy & Bootzin, 1973; Ritter, 1968; Weber, 1936) have been used. Parents could conduct both modeling and contact desensitization sequences, the common element being their own calm, quiet, sequenced approach (with physical contact with the child in the contact desensitization). It is reasonable to believe that most parents of phobic children could be trained to conduct and monitor such treatment. However, nearly all the research in this area consists of case studies and, here again, a highly promising area is in need of well-controlled research.

5. LANGUAGE AND SPEECH DISORDERS

Few papers in the behavioral literature describe parent training to treat children's language disorders. Barron and Graziano (1968) described their training of parents in clinical settings to conduct collateral speech training at home for their retarded children. An interesting aspect of the paper is the suggestion that parent training (if it accomplishes little else) might be valuable in mitigating the negative effects that untutored parents might have had through their embarrassed, concerned, reactions to their children's speech limitations in addition to their frustrated imposition of highly unrealistic speech demands.

Several single-case studies involving parents in some aspects of speech training have been reported with autistic children (Hewett, 1965; Risley & Wolf, 1966), with a "disturbed" and illiterate child (Mathis, 1971), and with cases of elective mutism (Nolan & Pence, 1970; Wulbert, Nymon, Snow, & Owen, 1973).

Although parents of retarded, autistic, and other speech-impaired children have been urged by clinicians to assist in their children's language development, the skills needed to train language acquisition or even to correct relatively minor speech problems are, at present, both complex and not well-known. Before transferring detailed and complex skills to parents, the effectiveness of behavioral language training for disturbed and retarded children must be established. Beyond training parents in relatively straightforward contingency management to support the increase or improvement of already existing speech in their children, more severe speech disorders such as those found in retarded and autistic children seem beyond the present techniques of parent behavior training. Perhaps at this point the most reasonable use of parents with regard to language and speech development is as ancillary support at home in cases of speech problems where there is no other serious, grossly interfering involvement.

Well-designed, controlled, group comparison-research is needed to establish the effectiveness of parent training in improving even minor speech problems.

6. COMMON BEHAVIOR PROBLEMS IN THE HOME

Parent behavior training has thus far been a clinical, therapeutic endeavor, in which the behavior problems have had a clear "pathological" weighting. A few investigators have begun to examine parent training to cope with less traditionally clinical or "emotional" disorders, and more common issues at home. Hall *et al.* (1972) reported four case studies in which fairly mild and commonly occurring behavior problems were treated at home by parents, who recorded baseline observations and applied social and token reinforcement. The target behaviors included wearing an orthodontic device, regularly cleaning up a bedroom, a child's persistent whining and shouting, and a 5-year-old girl's mean time of 3 hours and 10 minutes to dress herself in the morning.

Knight and McKenzie (1974) reported the elimination of bedtime thumbsucking for three children whose parents made bedtime reading to them immediately contingent on non-thumbsucking. Daytime thumbsucking also was eliminated in two of the cases without additional contingencies.

It appears to us that to whatever degree such "rational" and relatively objective contingent reinforcment techniques can reduce the often sharp conflicts that occur in virtually all homes, they are of social value and potentially useful particularly in terms of prevention of behavioral problems.

C. Complexity and Severity of Problems Treated by Parents

Like the behavior modification literature in general, most of the earlier parental training reports involved mild or highly discrete, single-problem behaviors such as tantrums or enuresis. Beginning in the last half of the 1960s, parent training focused increasingly on more severe and multiple problem behaviors (e.g., Alexander & Parsons, 1973; Eyeberg & Johnson, 1974; O'Leary, O'Leary, & Becker, 1967; Patterson & Brodsky, 1966; Patterson & Reid, 1973; Peine, 1969; Sloane, Johnston, & Bijou, 1967; Tavormina, 1975; Walder, Cohen, Breiter, Daston, Hirsch, & Leibowitz, 1969; Zeilberger, Sampen, & Sloane, 1968). The research by Tharp and Wetzel and by Alexander and Parsons, for example, included very severe and complex behavior of juvenile delinquents. Hanf (1968, 1969), Bernal (1969), and Tavormina (1975) are among several who have focused on complex mother–child interactions rather than limiting their investigations to discrete behavior of children. Tavormina (1975), Forehand and King (1975), and Peed, Roberts, & Forehand (1975) have conducted investigations of attitude and behavior change in *parents* as a result of training. These studies indicate a shift from single-problem, discrete, and relatively simple issues in parent training to more severe and complex behavior problems and more complex social interaction.

III. TRAINING

A. Selection of Parents for Behavioral Training

As noted by Berkowitz and Graziano (1972), in virtually all of the parent training reports, the mothers were trained, fathers being involved in only a minority of cases. Holland (1969), for example, instructed both parents with the father being largely responsible for implementing strategies to eliminate his son's fire-setting. In several of the school phobia cases reviewed earlier, fathers were instructed to assume the firm, authority role in returning the child to school. Patterson, Shaw, and Ebner (1969) described a case in which the father was specifically instructed to carry out contingency management procedures with his son. In an earlier paper, Lindsley (1966) reported training 14 fathers of retarded children in group sessions, and indicated some success with nine. Generally, in the larger and more sophisticated parent training programs (e.g., Alexander & Parsons, 1973; Patterson, McNeal, Hawkins, & Phelps, 1967; Tharp & Wetzel, 1969) more attention was paid to complex family interactions. Fathers appeared more involved, although only Tharp and Wetzel give much space to discussion of fathers' roles in several cases.

On the whole, however, mothers have received most of the training and have carried out virtually all of the home programming. Several investigators have reported detailed assessments of mother–child interactions (e.g., Bernal, 1969; Forehand & King, 1974; Johnson & Brown, 1969; Tavormina, 1975; Wahler et al., 1965) but few have given equal attention to father–child interactions (e.g., Patterson, 1959).

Our social biases seem reflected in the nearly exclusive focus on the mother as the parent in each case who is expected to bear most of the child-rearing responsibility and, now we have added, also the child-*treatment* responsibility. This, of course, reflects social reality—the father is still the major economic provider while the mother generally remains at home, largely to take care of the children. But this reality, as we are increasingly reminded, is itself partly a product of social biases. Our parent training may be a new technology, but it is being implemented with full deference to some quite traditional and increasingly questionable conditions.

Parent trainers may be omitting crucial factors by not examining father–child interactions, comparing skill levels of fathers with those of mothers, and not routinely utilizing these "other" parents.

There is little information on the characteristics of mothers who are trained, and virtually no attempts have been made to relate parent characteristics to outcome. Some investigators have commented upon the differential response associated with economic status. For example, Salzinger, Feldman, and Portnoy (1970) and Patterson *et al.* (1972) have noted difficulty in training low-socioeconomic-status parents, perhaps because of the parents' limited education. On the other hand, Hirsch and Walder (1969) and Mira (1970) found that training success was not related to parents' educational or socioeconomic levels. O'Dell (1974) has suggested that in the latter two papers the investigators tended to minimize verbal skills in training and, instead, emphasized more "direct" teaching.

There are few data on effects of parents' adjustments on outcome. Wiltz (1969) and Patterson (1965) excluded parents who appeared psychotic. Bernal (1973) suggested screening out families in which there is sharp marital discord. Tharp and Wetzel (1969) commented on the near impossibility of working with some families where there was extreme conflict or excessive rigidity on one parent's part. In one case. Webster *et al.* (1973) had to discontinue parent training and family intervention because of the mother's "fragile psychiatric state." It is reasonable to expect that the training task will be made more difficult if more than one family member exhibits emotional or behavioral problems. However, no systematic study of the relationship between parent characteristics and training success—either training of the parent or the parent's training of the child—has been conducted. The parameters for predicting high and low success parents are yet to be identified.

B. Training Settings and Methods

As discussed by Walder *et al.* (1969), the major training settings have been individual consultations, controlled learning environments, and educational groups.

Parent training began as a clinical endeavor. This is reflected in most of the papers, particularly the earlier case studies in which training was carried out in individual parent–therapist interactions, much like other therapy settings. The therapist might not see the child at all (e.g., Welsh, 1966) or might visit and observe in the home (e.g., Peed *et al.*, 1975; Zeilberger *et al.*, 1968). In these cases, individual supervision of the parents and a detailed focus on that particular child and family were followed.

Even more systematic and detailed approaches have developed within laboratory-like controlled learning environments where the parents' behavior is systematically shaped by the therapist (sometimes in predetermined training sequences). Audio communications, one-way vision screens, light and sound signals, and video taping have all been used (e.g., Bernal, Duryea, Pruett, & Burns, 1968; Johnson & Brown, 1969; Patterson & Brodsky, 1966; Terdal & Buell, 1969; Toepfer, Reuter, & Maurer, 1972; Wahler, 1967). Some investigators have begun by modelling appropriate behaviors for parents and then shaping the parents' imitation of the modeled behavior (Engelm, Knutson, Laughly, & Garlington, 1968; Hewett, 1965; Johnson & Brown, 1969; Wagner & Ora, 1970). A particularly interesting development has been reported by Johnson and Katz (1973). Referring to two unpublished papers (Ora, 1971; Wagner & Ora, 1970), they point out that previously trained parents are obligated, as part of their own training, to serve as trainers for parents newly involved in the program. Parent-to-parent consultation in that controlled learning setting is becoming a major aspect of the program.

Perhaps the most systematic investigations in controlled learning environments are those reported by Hanf (1968, 1969) and Bernal, Delfini, North, and Kreutzer (1974). Hanf (1968, 1969) has developed parent training programs and has altered specific interactions between mothers and their noncompliant young children in a controlled learning setting. While each mother interacts with the child, the observing therapist shapes the mother's behavior through a now fairly standardized, sequenced, two-stage program. Hanf's research was not limited to single, discrete behaviors but attempted to analyze and modify more generalized mother–child interaction systems. The level of parental involvement was high, and mothers were trained to analyze their own as well as their children's behavior.

In their literature review, Berkowitz and Graziano (1972) noted that none of Hanf's training was conducted in the home—it was apparently assumed that proper generalization to the home would occur. There was no reporting of clinical material or specification of how the mothers' presenting complaints changed as a result of training, and no reports of baseline to posttreatment comparisons of child behaviors, reinstatements of pretraining conditions, or follow-ups. Therefore the value of Hanf's training methods to alter clinical problems outside of the training setting was not demonstrated.

In a recent series of studies, Forehand and his associates have further investigated Hanf's training program (particularly its generalization value and its effects on the parents) and have begun to meet many of these criticisms (Forehand & King, 1974, 1975; Peed, Roberts, & Forehand, 1975). The latter study (Peed *et al.*, 1975), a controlled group comparison, employed direct behavioral observations in both the clinic and homes, together with parent attitude measures. It was reported that parents' attitudes and mother–child interactions in the clinic improved and that the improved interactions generalized to the homes. These data support the effectiveness of Hanf's programming not only for its immediate effects in the clinic, but also its generalization to the homes and changes in mothers' behaviors and attitudes.

The Hanf–Forehand studies constitute an important programmatic research effort. It would be useful if the investigators were to eventually provide data on the training program's cost–gains efficiency, its relative effectiveness in training fathers as well as mothers, its value for even wider generalization (such as to schools as well as homes), and its power to effect changes in more severe clinical populations.

Training parents in groups has ranged from relatively unstructured group discussions through comprehensive and fairly well structured classes. Effective group training has been reported by Rose (1969), Walder *et al.* (1969), Peine and Muno (1970), Salzinger *et al.* (1970), Lindsley (1970), Mira (1970), Cohen (1970), Hall *et al.* (1972), and Patterson *et al.* (1972). The use of groups is ostensibly more efficient, provides multiple-*N* groups for research purposes, and may provide important peer support. As yet there are no clear, controlled comparisons of individual and group training procedures.

Several investigators have combined group and individual training (Engelm *et al.*, 1968; Patterson *et al.*, 1972; Salzinger *et al.*, 1970; Wahler, 1969a).

In individual or group settings, a "consultation" or structured learning environment, a variety of training methods are employed. Common to all, of course, is the assumption that parents are able to learn specific behavioral techniques and, when necessary, general behavior therapy concepts. Parents may be observed and coached by the trainer as they work with their children. Radio communication, light and buzzer signals, and video taping for later review and discussion with parents have been used. Lectures, films, programmed texts, daily and weekly assignments to carry out at home, and detailed discussions of specific cases have provided the content of training sessions. Frequently the trainer had modeled behavior to be taught, such as shaping procedures, so the parents can observe, imitate, and rehearse it under supervision.

Although prescribing systematic operant procedures for application to the children, only a minority of trainers have applied the same procedures to support the parents' behavior. It appears that positive reinforcement is generally assumed to occur during use of programmed texts (i.e., as immediate feedback on each item) and as the child's problem behavior improves. It is also assumed that the trainer will, as a matter of course, provide sufficient verbal reinforcement throughout the training. Most parent trainers, then, seem to rely on the assumption that the process of training is inherently reinforcing to the parents.

Some investigators see need for more systematic reinforcement of the parents' efforts (e.g., Rose, 1969). Some have applied specific contingencies to parents' behavior such as reducing clinic fees contingent upon parents' attendance or completion of assigned work (e.g., Hirsch & Walder, 1969; Patterson, McNeal, Hawkins, & Phelps, 1967; Peine, 1971; Peine & Munro, 1970; Redd, 1969). Walder et al. (1967) and Mira (1970) required completion of assigned work in order to be admitted to the next scheduled meeting with the therapist. Patterson et al. (1969) offered to treat the parents to a steak dinner when the father earned a specified number of points working with his son.

The use of written contracts with parents, specifying the target behaviors and the agreed upon involvement of parents, has been discussed by Walder et al. (1969), Stuart (1970), and Peine (1971).

Whatever the setting, specific techniques, complexity, or sophistication of the training package, therapists have aimed at teaching parents to specify target behaviors, control conditions, and to use contingency management and monitor results.

C. Levels of Parental Involvement

In each case, a decision must be made concerning the degree of involvement and responsibility that parents will assume. If the parents assumed full responsibility for working with the child, they would not be seeking professional assistance. The parent–therapist relationship, then, involves a shared responsibility, and their respective involvement will depend upon many factors (Graziano, 1971, 1974).

In their review, Berkowitz and Graziano (1972) categorized the literature in terms of increasing task complexity. The studies were arranged along dimensions of (1) the nature and complexity of parental involvement (2) the level of knowledge and sophistication in learning theory principles required of the parents, and (3) the level of rigor and sophistication of the methodologies employed. They reported a considerable range of parental involvement. At its least complicated level there was minimal and brief technique-oriented involvement, where parents implemented the therapist's instructions in simple contingency management to control discrete and relatively uncomplicated problem behaviors. At the level of greatest parental involvement, parents were taught not only specific strategies but also behavior principles in an attempt to develop greater generalized parenting skills. Parents were instructed to observe and record behavior, to plan, carry out, and monitor sequenced programs, thus becoming increasingly independent of the therapists. The programs described by Walder *et al.* (1969) and Paterson *et al.* (1969) are examples in which greatest parental involvement was demonstrated. The exploratory parent-to-parent consultation, described by Wagner and Ora (1970) and Ora (1971) seems potentially significant in this regard.

IV. EVALUATION ISSUES

A. Social Standards

At minimum, any therapeutic approach must demonstrate that it is feasible, is consistent with prevailing moral, ethical, and legal standards, and results in at least some stated client satisfaction. These are minimum social standards that are necessary but far from sufficient conditions and which have been met by virtually all modern therapy systems. In this regard, parent behavior training fares at least as well as any other approach. Therapists and researchers have amply demonstrated the feasibility of parent behavior training applied to a variety of childhood problems, and many parents report satisfaction with the results. Ethical issues regarding behavior modification in general are currently debated, but these issues do not discriminate among the various therapy systems. Rather, they apply as well to all modern therapy (see Graziano, 1975, Chapter 1).

Parent behavior training has joined the variety of other face-valid clinical approaches and, at this level of evaluation, parent behavior training is at least equal to any other approach.

B. Research Standards

Feasibility, ethical consistency, and apparent client satisfaction are the very least to be expected of any therapy approach. When more demanding criteria of effectiveness are applied, parent behavior training shows mixed results, but considerable promise. The available evidence suggests that continued, expanded, research is well justified.

The major methodological issues involved in behavior therapy research (e.g., Baer, Wolf, & Risley, 1968; Paul, 1969) and those specific to parent training (Johnson & Katz, 1973; O'Dell, 1974) have been frequently discussed elsewhere. Basically, the criteria demand clear, replicable demonstration of control over selected variables. Generally, in parent training research, control has been adequately demonstrated over only a limited portion of the important variables (i.e., over targeted behavior of children) while other important variables are still unexplored. Thus, there has been reasonably good demonstration that certain problem behaviors of children have improved after parent training, but much is yet to be done to determine reliability of measurements, replication of results, generalization and maintenance of the improved behavior, parent characteristics, changes in parent behavior, and clear specifications of the antecedent operations (e.g., parent training procedures and child therapy manipulations) in order to determine if they are, indeed, responsible for the observed improvements.

Those issues seem to cluster around several main factors: (1) assessment of change, (2) replicability, and (3) relative effectiveness.

1. ASSESSMENT OF CHANGE

A modern psychotherapeutic approach must at least demonstrate that (see Paul, 1969, p. 41):

(a) The client's distressing problems have changed significantly in the desired direction.

(b) New problems have not been created [see Graziano & Fink's (1973) discussion of negative second-order effects of treatment].

(c) The improved behaviors have generalized and become stable outside the treatment setting.

(d) The improved behaviors are maintained over a substantial time period.

We propose the above as the minimum level criteria for therapy validation. Necessary to these criteria is the clear specification of target behaviors and their reliable measurement at least at pre- and posttreatment and at follow-up.

Overall, parent behavior trainers have done quite well in specifying targeted child behaviors, thus establishing a good basis for the needed assessment of change. This is particularly true with discrete problems such as enuresis (e.g., DeLeon & Mandell, 1966; Lovibond, 1964), self-injury (Allen & Harris, 1966), and thumbsucking (Knight & McKenzie, 1974). Their discreteness minimizes problems of definition, quantification and reliability, and assessment of generalization and maintenance.

Thus, with many discrete problems, parent training has met this minimum level of validation fairly well, showing good specificity of problem behaviors, demonstrating change, some generalization and its maintenance over quite long periods. In the enuresis literature, for example, follow-ups for as long as 3 years (Lovibond, 1964) and 4 years (DeLeon & Sacks, 1972) have been reported in fairly large group studies, and 6 years (Graziano, 1974) in a case study.

Specificity of problem behavior has been generally good and the problems of obtaining reliability may be less in behavior modification than in other approaches because of behavioral specificity. However, no matter how clearly the target behavior might be defined, measurement reliability is also needed and, although often reported, has not been consistently demonstrated (O'Dell, 1974). Johnson and Katz (1973), for example, noted that slightly less than one-third of the parent-training studies they reviewed reported reliability estimates.

When reported, reliability estimates usually entail calculating the percentage of agreement, often exceeding 90% between two or more trained, independent observers. One continuing problem involves the periodic retraining of observers to prevent reliability from drifting downward. Stability of parent observations over time or agreement between parent and professional observations has not been sufficiently studied. Likewise, there has been little investigation of agreement between parent and child observations. Grace (1975) is an exception and reports high parent–child agreement.

Overall, the parent trainers can be commended for their specificity in defining target behaviors, but can also be rightly criticized for not routinely reporting reliability data on their behavioral observations. It is clear that reliability estimates can be easily obtained and there should be no great difficulties involves in including reliability measures routinely in future studies (even in case histories and single-subject designs).

The specificity of target behaviors and the existence of easily applied reliability measures provide an excellent base for subsequent demonstrations of effectiveness. Pre- and post-measures of behavior, showing improvements, are common in this literature. What has been demonstrated, thus far, is that many problem behaviors of children have, indeed, been improved through parent behavior training.

However, the remaining criteria at this minimum level of research validation have been less completely met. (Are the observed changes significant in a psychological or personal sense? Have they been achieved without creating new problems? Do they generalize beyond the training setting? Are they durable?)

Psychological significance and avoidance of unintended negative effects are difficult to assess and, by and large, have not been adequately dealt with by any current therapeutic model. In psychotherapy research, "significance" has been defined in statistical terms and, when demonstrated, has been equated with clinical effectiveness. Lick (1973) and Lick and Unger (1975) have pointed out that, although an experimental manipulation in a factorial design may be significantly more effective according to statistical criteria, it is not necessarily adequate in accomplishing its clinical goal. Those authors argue that the "discovery" or "exploratory" phase of research (Miller, 1972) has been insufficiently developed and requires greater attention from psychotherapy researchers, while the ". . . literature is filled with studies employing multiple control groups and reporting very weak (but statistically significant) treatment effects" (Lick, 1973, p. 34). Parent behavioral training is still largely in this exploratory or discovery phase and it might be valuable for it to remain there for some time. However, there is need to focus on the development of parent training "packages" for relatively homogeneous subject populations. More importantly, there is the need to show that behavioral changes are both of large magnitude and of clinical significance before moving on to more sophisticated validation of what might be personally unimportant effects. Parent training packages dealing with enuresis provide examples of large and clinically important changes. But, as discussed by Berkowitz and Graziano (1972), there are still numerous problems involved in clearly specifying the precise variables involved in the treatments.

Negative, second-order, or unintended effects of psychotherapy must always be guarded against but, as discussed by Graziano and Fink (1973), therapists and researchers have not paid sufficient attention to this issue. In behavior therapy, "symptom substitution" as a direct result of behavioral treatment does not routinely occur and, until it is demonstrated, is not a serious issue. However, consistent with the argument by Graziano and Fink, there may be numerous possible *negative* effects of intervening in the complicated ecology of a family or the relationships between a mother and her child. Papers by Wahler (1969a), Sajwaj, Twardosz, and Burke (1972), and Herbert, Pinkston, Hayden, Sajwaj, Pinkston, Cordua, and Jackson (1973) suggest adverse side effects of behavioral training in several cases. The last-mentioned authors studied six mother–child pairs, training the mothers in contingent use of differential attention to reduce maladaptive behavior in their children. Contrary to previous findings, differential attention did not reduce the maladaptive behavior. In fact, for four of the six children, deviant behavior actually increased in a "substantial and durable manner." More to the point of this present section, the authors reported negative "side effects" for all of the children that included: (1) the emergence of new, deviant behavior that had not been in evidence during the baseline evaluations, and (2) for four children, decreases in the appropriate behavior that had been monitored.

The above study clearly cautions against the possible overgeneralization of even "basic" contingency management in family settings, and the assumption that a therapy enterprise is always benign. Thus, although behavioral change associated with parent training has been demonstrated, we have not yet sufficiently demonstrated that those improvements are either clinically or personally significant, or that they have been brought about without creating new problems. Those issues must be dealt with before we invest more confidence in our parent-training "packages."

This field also lacks consistent data on the generalization of observed improvements and their maintenance over time. On the latter point, as discussed by Johnson and Katz (1973), many studies have no follow-ups, few exceed 8 months, and "most were conducted infrequently, informally and indirectly" (p. 195). The longest follow-ups, as noted earlier, are reported in studies of enuresis.

Generalization of change can be measured in terms of generalizing new behavior (parent's or child's) from one problem to another or from the training setting to other settings. Recent research by Bernal *et al.* (1974), Wahler (1969a), Martin (1974), and Johnson, Bolstad, and Lobitz (1974) strongly caution against the assumption that disturbed behavior, or improved behavior after behavioral training, necessarily generalizes from one setting to others, Generalization of improved behavior, then, must be empirically demonstrated, and not merely assumed to occur. Patterson *et al.* (1972) found that neither skills taught to parents nor behavior improvements brought about in children necessarily generalize from one child problem to another. Even the most careful research (e.g., Hanf's parent training in controlled learning environments) does not attempt to evaluate the generalization of either parent or child behavior changes. More recently, however, Forehand and King (1974, 1975) and Peed, *et al.* (1975) reported generalization of improved mother–child interactions from the clinic training setting to the home. Overall, neither generalization nor maintenance of the improved child behavior has yet been consistently established.

We must conclude that parent behavioral training only incompletely meets the criteria at even this minimum level of validation. Desirable and predicted changes in well-specified problem behavior has been repeatedly demonstrated, but reliability of measurement, the personal significance of the changes, their generalization and maintenance, and the lack of negative effects have not yet been well established. At this level, the strongest part of the literature is that dealing with highly discrete problems (such as enuresis) where definitional and observational difficulties are minimized. That is no small gain, for ameliorating such problems can be of considerable personal value to the children and their families. It is clear that a great deal of research is still needed at this essentially exploratory, minimum level of validation.

2. REPLICABILITY

The minimum criteria proposed above leave many other issues unresolved, issues that cluster mainly around replicability. If uniformly met, those minimum criteria would provide evidence that significant, generalizable, stable behavior changes (without negative side effects) follow various parent training packages. Those criteria do not help to isolate the variables responsible for the observed changes, do not allow for replicability of the studies, and leave no basis for judging the generalizability of the methods to individuals and groups beyond those already studied. Continued research must:

(A) specify therapeutic operations both in the professionals' training of the parents and the parents' training of their children, and specify changes in parents' behavior, so as to:
    (1) demonstrate that those operations were responsible for the observed improvement, and
    (2) make replications possible;

(B) specify both demographic information and child and parent characteristics, so as to:
   (1) generalize the approaches to different client groups, and
   (2) make predictive statements within client groups (i.e., discriminate between and predict successful and unsuccessful clients).

Basic, here, is the clear specification of training and therapeutic operations of demographic, behavioral, and personal characteristics of parents and children. Without such specificity, the necessary demonstrations of control over dependent variables, replications, and generalizations to other groups cannot be made. Overall, when evaluated in accordance with these criteria, parent behavior training does not fare too well.

Two of the major criticisms by O'Dell (1974) are: (1) the marked lack of specific descriptions of the parent-training procedures used, and (2) the lack of data on parent behavior changes. In addition, there is little information provided on parent characteristics (see Section III, A).

Johnson and Katz (1973) noted that about 65% of the studies they reviewed presented "clear" descriptions of parent training operations. Overall, however, despite their clarity, they presented global rather than specific and operationalized descriptions. Until parent training procedures are clearly operationalized, replication of the research will not be possible, leaving a string of only vaguely comparable research.

As we noted earlier, some of the more recent studies (e.g., Herbert & Baer, 1972; Patterson et al., 1972; Peed et al., 1975; Tavormina, 1975) have included measures of parent changes. But these have been relatively minor parts of each study, and some were limited to changes in attitude measures. It is still to be adequately demonstrated that parents' behavior does change through training, that their new behavior is both generalized and stable over time, and that it is, indeed, responsible for improved child behavior.

In addition to the basic and severe limitation of poor specification of training procedures, design weaknesses further reduce the possibility of replications and demonstrations of control over dependent variables. Each of the three earlier reviews cited throughout this chapter noted that most of the studies have been uncontrolled case reports providing virtually no demonstration of control over dependent variables. Johnson and Katz (1973) concluded that in approximately 64% of the studies they reviewed, treatment operations were "hopelessly confounded" with extraneous, uncontrolled variables, precluding the "unambiguous interpretation of results" (p. 195).

Experimental control has been demonstrated in a number of studies (e.g., Hall & Broden, 1967; Hall, Cristler, Cranston, & Tucker, 1970; Wahler, 1969a). These have included single-subject or small-sample, single- or multiple-baselines reversal studies. A general problem in many of these studies is the limitation in generalizing from the experimental to the clinical situation (see Section IV, B, 1). Further, some studies (e.g., Risley, 1968; Wahler, 1967) have introduced successive, multiple treatments, without return-to-baseline conditions, making it impossible to sort out cumulative from individual treatment effects.

A major problem common to all of the single-subject and small-sample case studies and experiments is their limited sampling, making it impossible to draw inferences about populations. As O'Dell (1974) points out, the sampling procedures throughout this literature are weak, often consisting of volunteers or clinic referrals. Systematic, unbiased sampling procedures, adequate sample size, and information concerning demographic characteristics are needed.

3. RELATIVE EFFECTIVENESS

If all of these criteria were met, the effectiveness of various specific parent-training procedures (with known populations) would be well established. However, tests against other criteria would still be necessary to determine the social value of the procedures (i.e., if these procedures are effective, what are the costs, and, are they any more effective than other, currently available therapeutic approaches to children?).

Neither of these two issues has been systematically studied, but, as reviewed by Johnson and Katz (1973), some estimates are available of the time required to train parents (e.g., Alexander & Parsons, 1973; Herbert & Baer, 1972; Mira, 1970; Patterson et al., 1967, 1969; Tahmisian & McReynolds, 1971; Wahler & Erickson, 1969). Overall, the investment of time in each parent-training case seems surprisingly small, and suggests good efficiency. But, with severely disturbed or psychotic children, as we have discussed in Section II, B, 2, a vast expenditure of professional time is required to bring about even minor gains. The difference suggests that what is required to adequately evaluate efficiency is a careful analysis of the distribution of time (over many cases, grouped by problem behavior) and demographic variables. Data are needed fon the professional time required to train parents and the parents' time required to train children. Further, the total time must be gauged against the magnitude and personal or clinical significance of the observed behavioral gains (see Section IV, B, 1), a difficult assessment that requires the comparison of very different classes of events. Finally, an analysis of time required by different therapeutic approaches is needed.

The data are yet too sparse to permit clear assessment of the efficiency of parent behavior training, and the field is still very far from answering that question. The same holds for its effectiveness relative to other therapeutic approaches (e.g., psychodynamic behavior modification in direct child therapy). Approaches based on different models might be compared directly in factorial designs, or indirectly, against some known standard of "natural" improvement of specific behavior problems. Few investigators have made such comparisons, and when they do, there are often design problems that seriously limit the conclusions.

Walder et al. (1967, 1969) compared behavioral and psychodynamic parent counseling, but did not adequately specify training and therapy procedures or behavioral data on children and parents. DeLeon and Mandell (1966) reported that an automated buzzer conditioning device applied by parents with minimal professional supervision or training was superior to professional psychodynamic psychotherapy in treating enuresis. The design problems included grossly unequal group size of the two treatment conditions, uncontrolled parent—child interactions, and failure to specify the psychotherapy procedures (making it difficult to attribute the observed improvements solely to the superiority of the conditioning apparatus).

More recent papers by Alexander and Parsons (1973), Parsons and Alexander (1973), and Tavormina (1975) provide more complete, better designed group comparisons, but their results, too, are somewhat equivocal (see Section II, B, 3).

Tavormina's investigation of behavioral and reflective parent counseling appears to be the best of these comparative studies. Like the others, Tavormina concludes that behavioral parent counseling is more effective than the other approaches.

The data available, with all of their design limitations, tend to support the greater effectiveness of parent behavioral training. However, as with nearly all other evaluation issues, the field is still a long way from clear, unequivocal answers.

V. CONCLUSIONS

In this writer's judgment, parent behavior training, as a child psychotherapy approach, is a highly promising area that might prove to be one of the most important developments in the child mental health field. On evaluation, this increasingly used set of approaches, like other major current therapies, is feasible and ethically acceptable but has, thus far, met only the minimum criteria of scientific evaluation. In this respect, it appears to be at about the same level of validation as other major, and far older, approaches.

One of the field's strengths is that improvements in child behavior (associated with parent behavioral training, across a wide variety of problems and with numerous children) have been repeatedly demonstrated. However, the personal and clinical significance of those improvements and their generalization and maintenance, the replicability of results, demonstrations of control over dependent variables, generalization of methods to other populations, cost efficiency, and comparative effectiveness have not been satisfactorily established.

These weaknesses are not limited to parent behavior training but are common to all models throughout the field. A necessary condition for acceptable research validation is the clear specificity of therapy goals and the therapeutic operations used to achieve them. With those specified, other research issues (such as those listed above) become more readily solved technical problems. In this regard, behavior therapy (including parent behavior training) has potential because of its focus on specificity. Many of the research limitations in parent behavior training have been approached and met in individual studies, but not reliably or consistently across the field. What this suggests is that solutions to many of the validation problems have been developed and demonstrated, but are scattered throughout the literature. Most of the necessary elements are available for a major, integrative, research attempt. It appears possible that, over the next decade, highly effective, efficient child treatment approaches will be developed and validated.

However, we must emphasize that a great deal of careful research yet to be done separates us from those truly exciting prospects. The present reality consists of scattered elements in an essentially research endeavor that offers little clinical validation and demands continued caution against uncritical, overgeneralized, clinical applications.

REFERENCES

Alexander, A. B., Chai, H., Creer, T. L., Miklich, D. R., Renne, C. M., & De. A. Cardoso, R. R. The elmination of chronic cough by response suppression shaping. *Journal of Behavior Therapy and Experimental Psychiatry*, 1973, 4, 75–80.

Alexander, J. F., Miklich, D. R., & Hershkoff, H. The immediate effects of systematic relaxation training on peak expiratory flow rates in asthmatic children. *Psychosomatic Medicine*, 1972, 34, 388–394.

Alexander, J. F., & Parsons, B. V. Short-term behavioral intervention with delinquent families: Impact on family process and recidivism. *Journal of Abnormal Psychology*, 1973, 81, 219–225.

Allen, K. E., & Harris, F. R. Elimination of a child's excessive scratching by training the mother in reinforcement procedures. *Behaviour Research and Therapy*, 1966, 4, 79–84.

Alvord, J. R. The home token economy: A motivational system for the home. *Corrective Psychiatry and Journal of Social Therapy*, 1971,17, 6–13.

Anthony, E. J. An experimental approach to the psychopathology of childhood: Autism. *British Journal of Medical Psychology*, 1958, 31, 211–225.

Ayllon, T., & Skuban, W. Accountability in psychotherapy: A test case. *Journal of Behavior Therapy and Experimental Psychiatry*, 1973, 4, 19–30.

Ayllon, T., Smith, D., & Rogers, M. Behavioral management of school phobia. *Journal of Behavior Therapy and Experimental Psychiatry*, 1970,1, 125–138.

Baer, D. M., Wolf, M. M., & Risley, T. R. Some current dimensions of applied behavior analysis. *Journal of Applied Behavior Analysis*, 1968, 1, 91–97.

Bandura, A., Grusec, J. E., & Menlove, F. L. Vicarious extinction of avoidance behavior. *Journal of Personality and Social Psychology*, 1967, 5, 16–23.

Barrett, B. Behavior modification in the home: Parents adapt laboratory-developed tactics to bowel-train a 5.5 year old *Psychotherapy: Theory, Research and Practice*, 1969, 6, 172–176.

Barron, D. P., & Graziano, A. M. Parent participation in speech therapy *Speech Journal*, 1968, 3, 46–50.

Baruch, D. *New ways in discipline*. New York: McGraw-Hill, 1949.

Bentler, P. M. An infant's phobia treated with reciprocal inhibition therapy. *Journal of Child Psychology and Psychiatry*, 1962, 3, 185–189.

Berkowitz, B. P., & Graziano, A. M. Training parents as behavior therapists: A review. *Behaviour Research and Therapy*, 1972, 10, 297–317.

Berlin, I. N. (Ed.) *Advocacy for child mental health*. New York: Brunner/Mazel, 1975.

Bernal, M. E. Behavioral feedback in the modification of brat behaviors. *Journal of Nervous and Mental Disorders*, 1969, 148, 375–385.

Bernal, M. E. Preliminary report of a preventive intervention project. Paper read at the Rocky Mountain Psychological Association, Las Vegas, Nevada, May 1973.

Bernal, M. E., Delfini, L. F., North, J. A. & Kreutzer, S. L. Comparison of boys' behaviors in homes and classrooms. Paper read at the Banff International Conference on Behavior Modification, Banff, Canada,00 1974.

Bernal, M. E., Duryea, J. S., Pruett, H. L., & Burns, B. J. Behavior modification and the brat syndrome. *Journal of Consulting and Clinical Psychology*, 1968, 32, 447–455.

Bolman, W. M. A behavioral systems analysis of the school refusal syndrome. *American Journal of Orthopsychiatry*, 1967, 37, 348–349.

Bolman, W. M. Systems theory, psychiatry and school phobia. *American Journal of Psychiatry*, 1970, **127**, 25–32.

Bornstein, B. Phobia in a two-and-a-half-year-old child. *Psychoanalytic Quarterly*, 1935, **4**, 93–119.

Bornstein, S. A child analysis. *Psychoanalytic Quarterly*, 1935, **4**, 190–225.

Brotemarkle, R. A. (Ed.) *Clinical psychology: Studies in honor of Lightner Witmer*. Philadelphia: University of Pennsylvania Press, 1931.

Brown, D. G. *Behavior modification in child and school mental health: An annotated bibliography on applications with parents and teachers*. DHEW Publication No. (HSM) 71–9043. Washington, D. C.: National Institute of Mental Health, 1971.

Browning, R. M. Treatment effects of a total behavior modification program with five autistic children. *Behaviour Research and Therapy*, 1971, **9**, 319–327.

Burlingham, D. T. Child analysis and the mother. *Psychoanalytic Quarterly*, 1935, **4**, 69–92.

Christopherson, E. R., Arnold, C. M., Hill, D. W., & Quilitch, H. R. The home point system: Token reinforcement procedures for application by parents of children with behavior problems *Journal of Applied Behavior Analysis*, 1972, **5**, 485–497.

Clancy, H., & McBride, G. The autistic process and its treatment. *Journal of Child Psychology and Psychiatry*, 1969, **10**, 233–244.

Clement, P. W. Elimination of sleepwalking in a seven-year-old boy. *Journal of Consulting and Clinical Psychology*, 1970, **34**, 22–26. (a)

Clement, P. W. Please mother, I'd rather you did it yourself: Training parents to treat their own children. Paper read at the Western Psychological Association, Los Angeles, April 1970. (b)

Cohen, H. C. *The P.I.C.A. project. Year 2, Project interim report: Programming interpersonal curricula for adolescents*. Silver Springs, Md.: Institute for Behavioral Research, 1970. (ERIC Document Reproduction Service No. ED 044 717)

Colby, K. M. Psychotherapeutic processes. *Annual Review of Psychology*, 1964, **15**, 347–370.

Coleman, J. C. *Abnormal psychology and modern life*. Glenview, Ill.: Scott, Foresman, 1972.

Cone, J. D., & Sloop, E. W. Parents as agents of change. In A. Jacobs & W. W. Spradlin (Eds.), *Group as agent of change* Chicago: Aldine, Atherton, 1971.

Conger, J. C. The treatment of encopresis by the management of social consequences. *Behavior Therapy*, 1970, **1**, 386–390.

Creer, T. L. The use of a time-out positive reinforcement procedure with asthmatic children. *Journal of Psychosomatic Research*, 1970, **14**, 117–120.

Davidson, W. S., & Seidman, E. Studies of behavior modification and juvenile delinquency: A review, methodological critique and social perspective. *Psychological Bulletin*, 1974, **81**, 998–1011.

Davis, A. B. L. Some experiences with two small groups of mothers in a child guidance clinic. *British Journal of Psychiatric Social Work*, 1947, **1**, 16–22.

DeLeon, G., & Mandell, W. A comparison of conditioning and psychotherpy in the treatment of functional enuresis. *Journal of Clinical Psychology*, 1966, **22**, 326–330.

DeLeon, G., & Sacks, S. Conditioning functional enuresis: A four-year follow-up. *Journal of Consulting and Clinical Psychology*, 1972, **39**, 2, 299–300.

Denny, M. R. A theoretical analysis and its application to training the mentally retarded. In N. R. Ellis (Ed.), *International review of research in mental retardation*. Vol. 2. New York: Academic Press, 1966.

Edelman, R. I. Operant conditioning treatment of encopresis. *Journal of Behavior Therapy and Experimental Psychiatry*, 1971, **2**, 71–73.

Elkisch, P. Simultaneous treatment of a child and his mother. *American Journal of Psychotherapy*, 1935, **7**, 105–130.

Engelm, R., Knutson, J., Laughly, L., & Garlington, W. Behavioral modification techniques applied to a family unit—A case study. *Journal of Child Psychology and Psychiatry*, 1968, **9**, 245–252.

Eyeberg, S. M., & Johnson, S. M. Multiple assessment of behavior modification with families: Effects of contingency contracting and order of treatment problems. *Journal of Consulting and Clinical Psychology*, 1974, **42**, 594–606.

Ferster, C. B. Positive reinforcement and behavioral deficits of autistic children. *Child Development*, 1961, **32**, 437–456.

Ferster, C. B., & DeMyer, M. K. A method for the experimental analysis of the behavior of autistic children. *American Journal of Orthopsychiatry*, 1962, **32**, 89–98.

Finch, S. M. Psychophysiological disorders of children. In A. M. Freedman & H. I. Kaplan (Eds.), *The child: His psychological and cultural development*. Vol. 2. New York: Atheneum, 1972. Pp. 144–159.

Fisher, I., & Glanville, B. Programmed teaching of autistic children. *Archives of General Psychiatry*, 1970, **23**, 90–94.

Fo, W. S., & O'Donnell, C. R. The buddy system: Relationship and contingency conditions in a community intervention program for youth with non-professionals as behavior change agents. *Journal of Consulting and Clinical Psychology*, 1974, **42**, 163–169.

Forehand, R., Cheney, T., & Yoder, P. Parent behavior training: Effects on the non-compliance of a deaf child. *Journal of Behavior Therapy and Experimental Psychiatry*, 1974, **5**, 281–283.

Forehand, R., & King, H. E. Pre-school children's non-compliance: Effects of short-term behavior therapy. *Journal of Community Psychology*, 1974, **2**, 42–44.

Forehand, R., & King, H. E. Noncompliant children: Effects of parent training on behavior and attitude change. Unpublished manuscript, University of Georgia, 1975.

Forehand, R., King, H. E., Peed, S., & Yoder, P. Mother-child interactions: Comparison of a non-compliant clinic group and a non clinic group. *Behaviour Research and Therapy*, 1975, **13**, 79–84.

Foxx, R. M., & Azrin, N. H. Dry pants: A rapid method of toilet training children. *Behaviour Research and Therapy*, 1973, **11**, 435–442.

Freud, S. Analysis of a phobia in a five year old boy. *Collected Papers*. Vol. 3. New York: Basic Books, 1959. (Originally published in *Jahrbuch für Psychoanalytische und Psychopathologische Forschungen*, **8**, 1909.)

Fuchs, N. R. Play therapy at home. *Merrill-Palmer Quarterly*, 1957, **3**, 89–95.

Furman, E. Treatment of under-fives by way of their parents. *Psychoanalytic Study of the Child*, 1957, **12**, 250–262.

Galloway, C., & Galloway, K. C. Parent groups with a focus on precise behavior management. Institute on Mental Retardation and Intellectual Development. *Imrid Papers and Reports*, 1970, **7**, 1.

Gardner, J. E., Pearson, D. T., Bercovici, A. N., & Bricker, D. E. Measurement, evaluation and modification of selected social interactions between a schizophrenic child, his parents, and his therapist. *Journal of Consulting and Clinical Psychology*, 1968, **32**, 537–542.

Gardner, J. M. Behavior modification in mental retardation: A review of research and analysis of trends. In R. D. Rubin, H. Fensterheim, A. A. Lazarus, & C. M. Franks, (Eds.), *Advances in behavior therapy*. New York: Academic Press, 1971. Pp. 37–59.

Gardner, W. I. Behavior therapy treatment approach to a psychogenic seizure case: *Journal of Consulting Psychology*, 1967, **3**, 209–212.

Gero-Heymann, E. A short communication on a traumatic episode in a child of two years and seven months. *Psychoanalytic Study of the Child,* 1955, **10,** 376–380.

Gillick, S. Training mothers as therapists in treatment of childhood obesity. Unpublished doctoral dissertation, State University of New York at Buffalo, 1974.

Grace, D. Self-monitoring in the modification of obesity in children. Unpublished doctoral dissertation, State University of New York at Buffalo, 1975.

Graziano, A. M. A description of a behavioral day-care and treatment program. Report to the Connecticut State Department of Mental Health, Division of Children's Services, 1963.

Graziano, A. M. Clinical innovation and the mental health power structure: A social case history. *American Psychologist,* 1969, **24,** 10–18.

Graziano, A. M. A group treatment approach to multiple problem behaviors of autistic children. *Exceptional Child,* 1970, **36,** 765–770.

Graziano, A. M. (Ed.) *Behavior therapy with children.* Vol. 1. Chicago: Aldine, Atherton, 1971.

Graziano, A. M. *Child without tomorrow.* New York: Pergamon, 1974.

Graziano, A. M. *Behavior therapy with children.* Vol 2. Chicago: Aldine, 1975.

Graziano, A. M., & Fink, R. Second-order effects in mental health treatment. *Journal of Consulting and Clinical Psychology,* 1973, **40,** 356–364.

Graziano, A. M., Hastrup, J., & Pearlson, H. Behavioral treatment of an adolescent school phobic. Unpublished manuscript, State University of New York at Buffalo, 1975.

Graziano, A. M., & Kean, J. E. Programmed relaxation and reciprocal inhibition with psychotic children. *Behaviour Research and Therapy,* 1968, **6,** 433–437.

Guerney, B. B. (Ed.) *Psychotherapeutic agents: New roles for non-professionals, parents, and teachers.* New York: Holt, 1969.

Hall, R. V., Axelrod, S., Tyler, L., Grief, E., Jones, F. C., & Robertson, R. Modification of behavior problems in the home with a parent as observer and experimenter. *Journal of Applied Behavior Analysis,* 1972, **5,** 53–64.

Hall, R. V., & Broden, M. Behavior changes in brain-injured children through social reinforcement. *Journal of Experimental Child Psychiatry,* 1967, **5,** 463–474.

Hall, R. V., Cristler, C., Cranston, S. S., & Tucker, B. Teachers and parents as researchers using multiple baseline designs. *Journal of Applied Behavior Analysis,* 1970, **3,** 247–255.

Hanf, C. Modifying problem behaviors in mother–child interaction: Standardize laboratory situations. Paper read at the Association of Behavior Therapies, Olympia, Washington, April 1968.

Hanf, C. A two-stage program for modifying maternal controlling during Mother–child (m-C) interaction. Paper read at the Western Psychological Association, Vancouver, April 1969.

Hanf, C., & Kling, J. Facilitating parent-child interaction: A two-stage training model. Unpublished manuscript, University of Oregon Medical School, 1973.

Hawkins, R. P., Peterson, R. F., Schweid, E. L., & Bijou, S. W. Behavior therapy in the home: Amelioration of problems parent-child relations with the parent in a therapeutic role. *Journal of Experimental Child Psychology,* 1966, **4,** 99–107.

Herbert, E., & Baer, D. Training parents as behavior modifiers Self-recording of contingent attention. *Journal of Applied Behavior Analysis,* 1972, **5,** 139–149.

Herbert, E. W., Pinkston, E. M., Hayden M. L., Sajwaj, T. E., Pinkston, S., Cordua, G., & Jackson, D. Adverse effects of differential parental attention. *Journal of Applied Behavior Analysis,* 1973, **6,** 15–30.

Hersch, C. The discontent explosion in mental health. *American Psychologist,* 1968, **23,** 497–506.

Hersen, M. Treatment of a compulsive and phobic disorder through a total behavior therapy program: A case study. *Psychotherapy: Theory, Research and Practice,* 1968, **5,** 220–225.

Hersen, M. Behavior modification approach to a school phobia case. *Journal of Clinical Psychology,* 1970, **26,** 128–132.

Hersen, M. The behavioral treatment of school phobia. *Journal of Nervous and Mental Disease,* 1971, **153,** 99–107.

Hewett, F. M. Teaching speech to autistic children through operant conditioning. *American Journal of Orthopsychiatry,* 1965, **35,** 927–936.

Hirsch, I., & Walder, L. Training mothers in groups as reinforcement therapists for their own children. *Proceedings, 77th Annual Convention, American Psychological Association,* 1969, **4,** 561–562.

Holland, C. J. Elimination by the parents of fire-setting behavior in a seven-year-old-boy. *Behaviour Research and Therapy,* 1969, **7,** 135–137.

Howlin, P., Marchant, R., Rutter, M., Berger, M., Hersov, L., & Yule, W. A home-based approach to the treatment of autistic children. *Journal of Autism and Childhood Schizophrenia,* 1973, **3,** 308–336.

Jackson, D. D., (Ed.) *Communication, family and marriage.* Palo Alto, Calif.: Science and Behavior Books, 1968.

Jersild, A. T. *Child psychology.* Englewood Cliffs, N. J.: Prentice-Hall, 1968.

Johnson, C. A., & Katz, C. Using parents as charge agengs for their children: A review. *Journal of Child Psychology and Psychiatry,* 1973, **14,** 181–200.

Johnson, S. M., Bolstad, O. D., & Lobitz, G. K. The generalization of children's behavior and behavior change across settings. Paper read at the Banff International Conference on Behavior Modification, Banff, Canada, May 1974.

Johnson, S. M., & Brown, R. A. Producing behavior change in parents of disturbed children. *Journal of Child Psychology and Psychiatry,* 1969, **10,** 107–121.

Joint Commission on Mental Health of Children. *Crisis in child mental health: Challenge for the 1970's.* New York: Harper, 1969.

Jones, H. G. The behavioral treatment of enuresis nocturna. In H. J. Eysenck (Ed.), *Behaviour therapy and the neuroses.* Oxford: Pergamon, 1960.

Kennedy, W. A. School phobia: Rapid treatment of fifty cases. *Journal of Abnormal and Social Psychology,* 1965, **70,** 285–289.

Knight, M., & McKenzie, H. S. Elimination of bedtime thumbsucking in home settings through contingent reading. *Journal of Applied Behavior Analysis,* 1974, **7,** 33–38.

Koegel, R. L., & Rincover, A. Treatment of psychotic children in a classroom environment: I. Learning in a large group. *Journal of Applied Behavior Analysis,* 1974, **7,** 45–59.

Kolansky, H. Treatment of a three-year-old girl's severe infantile neurosis: Stammering and insect phobia. *Psychoanalytic Study of the Child,* 1960, **15,** 261–285.

Kubie, L. Resolution of a traffic phobia in conversations between a father and son. *Psychoanalytic Quarterly,* 1937, **6,** 223–226.

Kushner, M. The operant control of intractable sneezing. In D. Spielberger, B. Fox, & B. Masterton (Eds.), *Contributions to General Psychology.* New York: Appleton, 1968.

Lal, H., & Lindsley, O. R. Therapy of chronic constipation in a young child by rearranging social contingencies. *Behaviour Research and Therapy,* 1968, **6,** 484–485.

Lasser, B. R. Teaching mothers of mongoloid children to use behavior modification procedures. *Dissertation Abstracts,* 1970, **30,** 5239A–5340A.

Lavigueur, H., Peterson, R. F., Sheese, J. G., & Peterson, L. W. Behavioral treatment in the home: Effects on an untreated sibling and long-term follow-up. *Behavior Therapy*, 1973, 4, 431–441.

Levine, M., & Levine, A. *A social history of helping services.* New York: Appleton, 1970.

Levine, R. A. Treatment in the home. *Social Work*, 1964, 9, 19–28.

Levitt, E. E. The results of psychotherapy with children: An evaluation. *Journal of Consulting Psychology*, 1957, 21, 189–196.

Lick, J. Statistical vs. clinical significance in research on the outcome of psychotherapy. *International Journal of Mental Health*, 1973, 2, 26–37.

Lick, J., & Unger, T. The external validity of laboratory fear assessment: Implications from two case studies. *Journal of Consulting and Clinical Psychology*, 1975, 43, 864–866.

Lindsley, O. R. An experiment with parents handling behavior at home. *Johnstone Bulletin*, 1966, 9, 26–36.

Lindsley, O. R. An experiment with parents handling behavior at home. In F. A. Gargo, C. Bahrns, & P. Nolen (Eds.), *Behavior modification in the classroom.* Belmont, Calif.: Wadsworth, 1970. Pp. 310–316.

Lovaas, O. I., Koegel, R., Simmons, J. Q., & Long, J. S. Some generalizations and follow-up measures on autistic children in behavior therapy. *Journal of Applied Behavior Analysis*, 1973, 6, 131–166.

Love, L. R. Information feedback as a method of clinical intervention. Paper read at the American Psychological Association, New York, September 1966.

Lovibond, S. H. *Conditioning and enuresis.* New York: Pergamon, 1964.

MacGregor, R., Ritchie, A., Serrano, A. C., Shuster, F. P., MacDonald, E. C., & Goolishian, H. A. *Multiple impact therapy with families.* New York: McGraw-Hill, 1964.

MacNamara, M. Helping children through their mothers. *Journal of Child Psychology and Psychiatry*, 1963, 4, 29–46.

Madsen, C. H. Positive reinforcement in toilet training of a normal child: A case report. In L. P. Ullmann & L. Krasner (Eds.), *Case studies in behavior modification.* New York: Holt, 1965. Pp. 305–306.

Marks, I. M., & Gelder, D. M. Different ages of onset in varieties of phobia. *American Journal of Psychiatry*, 1966, 123, 218–221.

Martin, B., & Kubly, D. Results of treatment of enuresis by a conditioned response method. *Journal of Consulting Psychology*, 1955, 19, 71–73.

Martin, S. The comparability of behavioral data in laboratory and natural settings. Paper read at the Banff International Conference on Behavior Modification, Banff, Canada, May 1974.

Mathis, M. I. Training of a "distrubed" boy using the mother as therapist: A case study. *Behavior Therapy*, 1971, 2, 233–239.

Miller, L. C., Barrett, C. L., Hampe, E., & Noble, H. Comparison of reciprocal inhibition, psychotherapy and waiting list control for phobic children. *Journal of Abnormal Psychology*, 1972, 79, 269–279.

Miller, N. E. Comments on strategy and tactics of research. In A. E. Bergin & H. H. Strupp (Eds.), *Changing frontiers in the science of psychotherapy.* Chicago: Aldine, Atherton, 1972. Pp. 348–350.

Minuchin, S. Conflict-resolution family therapy. *Psychiatry*, 1965, 28, 278–286.

Mira, M. Results of a behavior modification training program for parents and teachers. *Behaviour Research and Therapy*, 1970, 8, 309–311.

Moore, N. Behavior therapy in bronchial asthma: A controlled study *Journal of Psychosomatic Research*, 1965, 9, 257–276.

Morrey, J. G. Parent training in precise behavior management with mentally retarded children. *Dissertation Abstracts,* 1971, **31,** 3376A.

Moustakas, C. W. *Psychotherapy with children.* New York: Harper, 1959.

Mowrer, O. H. Apparatus for the study and treatment of enuresis. *American Journal of Psychology,* 1938, **51,** 163–166.

Munro, D. M. G. An experiment in the use of group methods with parents in a child guidance clinic. *British Journal of Psychiatric Social Work,* 1952, **6,** 16–20.

Murphy, C. M., & Bootzin, R. R. Active and passive participation in the contact desensitization of snake fear in children. *Behavior Therapy,* 1973, **4,** 203–211.

Neisworth, J. T., & Moore, F. Operant treatment of asthmatic responding with the parent as therapist. *Behavior Therapy,* 1972, **3,** 95–99.

Nolan, D. J., & Pence, C. Operant conditioning principles in the treatment of a selectively mute child. *Journal of Consulting and Clinical Psychology,* 1970, **35,** 265–268.

Nordquist, V. M., & Wahler, R. G. Naturalistic treatment of an autistic child. *Journal of Applied Behavior Analysis,* 1973, **6,** 79–87.

O'Dell, S. Training parents in behavior modification: A review. *Psychological Bulletin,* 1974, **81,** 418–433.

O'Leary, K. D., O'Leary, S., & Becker, W. C. Modification of a deviant sibling interaction pattern in the home. *Behaviour Research and Therapy,* 1967, **5,** 113–120.

Ollendick, T. H., & Gruen, G. E. Treatment of a bodily injury phobia with imposive therapy. *Journal of Consulting and Clinical Psychology,* 1972, **38,** 389–393.

Ora, J. *Instruction pamphlet for parents of oppositional children.* Regional intervention Project for Preschoolers and Parents. Nashville, Tenn.: George Peabody College, 1971.

Parsons, B. V., & Alexander, J. F. Short-term family intervention: A therapy outcome study. *Journal of Consulting and Clinical Psychology,* 1973, **41,** 195–201.

Paschalis, A. P., Kimmel, H. D., & Kimmel, E. Further study of diurnal instrumental conditioning in the treatment of enuresis nocturna. *Journal of Behavior Therapy and Experimental Psychiatry,* 1972, **3,** 253–256.

Patterson, G. R. Fathers as reinforcing agents. Paper read at the Western Psychological Association, San Diego, April 1959.

Patterson, G. R. A learning theory approach to the treatment of the school phobic child. In L. P. Ullmann & L. Krasner, (Eds.), *Case studies in behavior modification.* New York: Holt, 1965. Pp. 279–284.

Patterson, G. R., & Brodsky, G. A behaviour modification programme for a child with multiple problem behaviours. *Journal of Child Psychology and Psychiatry,* 1966, **7,** 277–295.

Patterson, G. R., Cobb, J. A., & Ray, R. S. A social engineering technology for retraining aggressive boys. In H. Adams & L. Unikel (Eds.), *Georgia symposium in experimental clinical psychology* Vol. 2. Oxford: Pergamon, 1972. Pp. 139–210.

Patterson, G. E., & Gullion, M. E. *Living with children: New methods for parents and teachers.* Champaign, Ill.: Research Press, 1968.

Patterson, G. R., McNeal, S., Hawkins, N., & Phelps, R. Programming the social environment. *Journal of Child Psychology and Psychiatry,* 1967, **8,** 181–195.

Patterson, G., Ray, R., & Shaw, D. Direct intervention in families of deviant children. *Oregon Research Institute Bulletin,* 1968.

Patterson, G. R., & Reid, J. B. Intervention for families of aggressive boys: A replication study. *Behaviour Research and Therapy,* 1973, **11,** 383–394.

Patterson, G. R., Shaw, D., & Ebner, M. Teachers, peers and parents as agents of change in the classroom. In F. A. M. Benson (Ed.), *Modifying deviant social behaviors in various classroom settings.* Monograph No. 1. Eugene: University of Oregon, 1969. Pp. 13–47.

Paul, G. L. Behavior modification research: Design and tactics. In C. M. Franks (Ed.), *Behavior therapy: Appraisal and status.* New York: McGraw-Hill, 1969. Pp. 29–62.

Pechey, B. M. The direct analysis of the mother-child relationship in the treatment of maladjusted children. *British Journal of Medicine and Psychology*, 1955, **28**, 101–112.

Peed, S., Roberts, M., & Forehand, R. Generalization to the home of behavior modified in a parent training program for non-compliant children. Unpublished manuscript, University of Georgia Psychological Clinic, 1975.

Peine, H. A. Programming the home. Paper read at the Rocky Mountain Psychological Association, Albuquerque, N. M., May 1969.

Peine, H. A. *Effects of training models on the modification of parent behavior.* (Doctoral dissertation, University of Utah) Ann Arbor, Mich. University Microfilms, 1971. No. 71-24641.

Peine, H. A., & Munro, B. Training parents using lecture demonstration procedures and a contingency management program. Unpublished manuscript, University of Utah, 1970.

Pinkston, E. M., & Herbert, E. W. Modification of irrelevant and bizarre verbal behavior using mother as therapist. Paper read at the American Psychological Association, Washington, D.C., September 1971.

Rangell, L. A treatment of nightmares in a seven-year-old-boy. *Psychoanalytic Study of the Child*, 1952, **5**, 358–390.

Redd, W. H. Effects of mixed reinforcement contingencies on adults control of children's behavior. *Journal of Applied Behavior Analysis*, 1969, **4**, 249–254.

Risley, T. R. The effects and side effects of punishing the autistic behaviors of a deviant child. *Journal of Applied Behavior Analysis*, 1968, **1**, 21–34.

Risley, T. R., & Wolf, M. M. Experimental manipulation of autistic behaviors and generalization in to the home. In R. Ulrich, T. Stachnick, & J. Mabry (Eds.), *Control of human behavior*. Glenview, Ill.: Scott, Foresman, 1966. Pp. 187–198.

Ritter, B. J. The group treatment of children's snake phobias using vicarious and contact desensitization procedures. *Behaviour Research and Therapy*, 1968, **6**, 1–6.

Rose, S. D. A behavioral approach to the group treatment of parents. *Social Work*, 1969, **14**, 12–29.

Rose, S. D., Sundel, M., DeLange, J., Corwin, L., & Palumbo, A. The Hartwig project: A behavioral approach to the treatment of juvenile offenders. In R. Ulrich, R. Stachnik, & J. Mabry (Eds.), *Control of human behavior.* Vol. 2. Glenview, Ill.: Scott, Foresman, 1970. Pp. 220–230.

Ruben, M., & Thomas, R. Home training of instincts and emotions. *Health Education Journal*, 1947, **5**, 119–124.

Russo, S. Adaptations in behavioral therapy with children. *Behaviour Research and Therapy*, 1964, **2**, 43–47.

Rutter, M., & Bartak, L. Special education treatment of autistic children: A comparative study-II. Follow-up findings and implications for service. *Journal of Child Psychology and Psychiatry*, 1973, **14**, 241–270.

Sacks, S., & DeLeon, G. Conditioning two types of enuretics. *Behaviour Research and Therapy*, 1973, **11**, 653–659.

Sajwaj, T., Twardosz, S., & Burke, M. Side effects of extinction procedures in a remedial pre-school. *Journal of Applied Behavior Analysis*, 1972, **5**, 163–175.

Salzinger, K., Feldman, R. S., & Portnoy, S. Training parents of brain-injured children in the use of operant conditioning procedures. *Behavior Therapy*, 1970, **1**, 14–32.

Sarason, S. B. *The creation of settings and the future societies.* San Francisco: Jossey-Bass, 1972.

Sarason, S. B., Levine, M., Goldenberg, I. I., Cherlin, D. L., & Bennett, E. M. *Psychology in community settings.* New York: John Wiley, 1966.

Schwarz, H. The mother in the consulting room: Notes on the psychoanalytic treatment of two young children. *Psychoanalytic Study of the Child,* 1950, **5**, 343–357.

Schwitzgebel, R. L. *Streetcorner research.* Cambridge, Mass.: Harvard University Press, 1964.

Schwitzgebel, R. L. Short-term operant conditioning of adolescent offenders on socially relevant variables. *Journal of Abnormal Psychology,* 1967, **72**, 134–142.

Schwitzgebel, R. L. Preliminary socialization for psychotherapy of behavior-disordered adolescents. *Journal of Consulting and Clinical Psychology,* 1969, **33**, 71–77.

Schwitzgebel, R., & Kolb, D. A. Inducing behavior change in adolescent delinquents. *Behaviour Research and Therapy,* 1964, **1**, 297–304.

Seitz, S., & Hoekenga, R. Modeling as a training tool for retarded children and their parents. *Mental Retardation,* 1974, April, 28–31.

Seitz, S., & Terdal, L. A modeling approach to changing parent-child interactions. *Mental Retardation,* 1972, June, 39–43.

Sergeant, H. G. S., & Yorkston, N. J. Verbal desensitization in the treatment of bronchial asthma. *Lancet,* December 20, 1969, 1321–1323.

Silver, A. A. Progress in therapy with children. In L. E. Alt & B. F. Riess (Eds.), *Progress in clinical psychology.* Vol. 5. New York: Grune & Stratton, 1963.

Sloane, H. N., Johnston, M. K., & Bijou, S. W. Successive modification of aggressive behavior and aggressive fantasy play by management of contingencies. *Journal of Child Psychology and Psychiatry,* 1967, **8**, 217–226.

Smith, M. B., & Hobbs, H. The community and the community health center. *American Psychologist,* 1966, **21**, 499–509.

Smith, R. E., & Sharpe, T. M. Treatment of a school phobia with implosive therapy. *Journal of Consulting and Clinical Psychology,* 1970, **35**, 239–243.

Straughan, J. H. Treatment with child and mother in the playroom. *Behaviour Research and Therapy,* 1969, **2**, 37–41.

Stuart, R. B. *Trick or treatment: How and when psychotherapy fails.* Champaign, Ill.: Research Press, 1970.

Stuart, R. B. Behavioral contracting within the families of delinquents. *Journal of Behavior Therapy and Experimental Psychiatry,* 1971, **2**, 1–11.

Sulzer, E. S. Reinforcement and the therapeutic contract. *Journal of Counseling Psychology,* 1962, **9**, 271–276.

Tahmisian, J., & McReynolds, W. Use of parents as behavioral engineers in the treatment of a school-phobic girl. *Journal of Consulting Psychology,* 1971, **18**, 225–228.

Tasto, D. L. Systematic desensitization, muscle relaxation and visual imagery in the counter conditioning of a four-year old phobic child. *Behaviour Research and Therapy,* 1969, **7**, 409–411.

Tavormina, J. B. Basic models of parent counseling: A review. *Psychological Bulletin,* 1974, **81**, 827–835.

Tavormina, J. B. Relative effectiveness of behavioral and reflective group counseling with parents of mentally retarded children. *Journal of Consulting and Clinical Psychology,* 1975, **43**, 22–31.

Terdal, L., & Buell, J. Parent education in managing retarded children with behavior deficits and inappropriate behaviors. *Mental Retardation,* 1969, **7**, 10–13.

Tharp, R. G., & Wetzel, R. J. *Behavior modification in the natural environment.* New York: Academic Press, 1969.

Toepfer, C., Reuter, J., & Maurer, C. Design and evaluation of an obedience training program for mothers of preschool children. *Journal of Consulting and Clinical Psychology*, 1972, 39, 194–198.

Tretakoff, M. Counseling the parents of handicapped children—A review. *Mental Retardation*, 1969, 7, 31–35.

Verville, E. *Behavior problems of children*. Philadelphia: Saunders, 1967.

Wagner, L., & Ora, J. Parental control of the very young severely oppositional child. Paper read at the Southeastern Psychological Association, Louisville, Ky., April 1970.

Wagner, M. K. Parent therapists: An operant conditioning method. *Mental Hygiene*, 1968, 52, 452–455.

Wahler, R. G. Behavior therapy with oppositional children: Attempts to increase their parents' reinforcement value. Paper read at the Southwestern Psychological Association, April 1967.

Wahler, R. G. Oppositional children: A quest for parental reinforcement control. *Journal of Applied Behavior Analysis*, 1969, 2, 159–170. (a)

Wahler, R. G. Setting generality: Some specific and general effects of child behavior therapy. *Journal of Applied Behavior Analysis*, 1969, 2, 239–246. (b)

Wahler, R. G., & Erickson, M. Child behavior therapy: A community program in Appalachia. *Behaviour Research and Therapy*, 1969, 7, 71–78.

Wahler, R. G., Winkel, G. H., Peterson, R. F., & Morrison, D. C. Mothers as behavior therapists for their own children. *Behaviour Research and Therapy*, 1965, 3, 113–124.

Walder, L. O., Cohen, S. I., Breiter, D. E., Daston, P. G., Hirsch, I. S., & Leibowitz, J. M. Teaching behavioral principles to parents of disturbed children. Paper read at the Eastern Psychological Association, Boston, 1967.

Walder, L. O., Cohen, S. E., Breiter, D. E., Daston, P. G., Hirsch, I. S., & Leibowitz, J. M. Teaching behavioral principles to parents of disturbed children. In B. G. Guerney (Ed.), *Psychotherapeutic agents: New roles for non-professionals, parents and teachers*. New York: Holt, 1969. Pp. 443–449.

Walter, H. I., & Gilmore, S. K. Placebo vs. social learning effects in parent training procedures designed to alter the behavior of aggressive boys. *Behavior Therapy*, 1973, 4, 361–377.

Walton, D. The application of learning theory to the treatment of a case of bronchial asthma. In H. Eysenck (Ed.), *Behaviour therapy and the neuroses*. Oxford: Pergamon, 1960.

Weber, H. An approach to the problem of fear in children. *Journal of Mental Science*, 1936, 82, 136–147.

Webster, C. D., McPherson, H., Sloman, L., Evans, M. A., & Kuchar, E. Communicating with an autistic boy by gestures. *Journal of Autism and Childhood Schizophrenia*, 1973, 4, 337–346.

Welsh, R. S. A highly efficient method of parental counseling. Paper read at the Rocky Mountain Psychological Association, Albuquerque, N. M., May 1966.

Welsh, R. S. The use of stimulus satiation in the elimination of juvenile fire-setting behavior. Paper read at the Eastern Psychological Association, Washington, D.C., April 1968.

Wetzel, R., Baker, J., Roney, M., & Martin, M. Outpatient treatment of autistic behavior. *Behaviour Research and Therapy*, 1966, 4, 169–177.

Williams, C. D. The elimination of tantrum behaviors by extinction Procedures. *Journal of Abnormal and Social Psychology*, 1959, 59, 269–270.

Wiltz, N. A. *Modification of behaviors through parent participation in a group technique*. (Doctoral dissertation, University of Oregon) Ann Arbor, Mich. University Microfilms, 1969, No. 70-9482.

Wiltz, N. A., & Patterson, G. R. An evaluation of parent training procedures designed to alter inappropriate aggressive behavior of boys. *Behavior Therapy*, 1974, 5, 215–221.

Wolf, M. M., Risley, T., Johnson, M., Harris, R., & Allen, E. Application of operant conditioning procedures to the behavior problems of an autistic child: A follow-up and extension. *Behaviour Research and Therapy*, 1967, 5, 103–111.

Wolf, M. M., Risley, T. R., & Mees, H. Application of operant conditioning procedures to the behavior problems of an autistic child. *Behaviour Research and Therapy*, 1964, 1, 305–312.

Wright, L., Nunnery, A., Eichel, B., & Scott, R. Application of conditioning principles to problems of tracheostomy addiction in children. *Journal of Consulting and Clinical Psychology*, 1968, 32, 603–606.

Wulbert, M., Nyman, B. A., Snow, D., & Owen, Y. The efficacy of stimulus fading and contingency management in the treatment of elective mutism: A case study. *Journal of Applied Behavior Analysis*, 1973, 6, 434–441.

Young, G. C. The problem of enuresis. *British Journal of Hospital Medicine*, 1969, 2, 628–632.

Young, G. C., & Morgan, R. T. T. Overlearning in the conditioning treatment of enuresis. *Behaviour Research and Therapy*, 1972, 10, 147–151.

Young, G. C., & Morgan, R. T. T. Overlearning in the conditioning treatment of enuresis: A long-term follow-up. *Behaviour Research and Therapy*, 1972, 10, 419–420. (b)

Zeilberger, J., Sampen, S. E., & Sloane, H. N. Modification of a child's problem behaviors in the home with the mother as therapist. *Journal of Applied Behavior Analysis*, 1968, 1, 47–53.

Zlutnick, S. The control of seizures by the modification of pre-seizure behavior: The punishment of behavioral chain components. Unpublished doctoral dissertation, University of Utah, 1972.

A REVIEW OF THE THEORETICAL RATIONALE AND EMPIRICAL SUPPORT FOR THE EXTINCTION APPROACH OF IMPLOSIVE (FLOODING) THERAPY

DONALD J. LEVIS AND NATHAN HARE

Department of Psychology

State University of New York at Binghamton

Binghamton, New York

The number of individuals seeking psychological aid has increased markedly in recent years, placing considerable pressure on the mental health field to develop effective short-term treatment techniques. Treatment approaches labeled behavioral represent one possible answer to our mental health problems. The available array of behavioral techniques is impressive and the movement as a whole offers certain distinct advantages (Levis, 1970a). Nevertheless, serious criticism has been raised (Bernstein & Paul, 1971; Breger & McGaugh, 1965). The main concern, which also applies to most nonbehavioral techniques, centers around the unsupported claims of therapeutic efficacy that not only accompany the introduction of each technique but frequently are perpetuated in the literature as accepted fact. A case in point is the premature claims of 90% effectiveness which were made in the infancy of the behavioral movement (Eysenck, 1960). Since that time, little has been done to correct the initial impression given. It is the authors' contention that not one of the existing behavioral techniques has been substantiated by sufficient well-controlled outcome research to make any strong claims for effectiveness. For example, the frequently recommended technique of systematic desensitization (Wolpe, 1958) is supported primarily by analogue, non-patient research using college students. After 20 years of research, only a few controlled studies using clinical populations are to be found in the literature. Methodological sophistication of researchers in the behavioral area is, in general, lacking (Bernstein & Paul, 1971), including serious problems associated with the use of the frequently employed ABA design (Stampfl, 1970, pp. 102–107). Furthermore, many techniques are founded on either underdeveloped or outmoded theoretical models which are still in need of empirical validation (Breger & McGaugh, 1965). Nevertheless, despite some unfulfilled objectives, the behavioral movement has made important theoretical and empirical contributions to clinical knowledge, with some of the techniques showing considerable potential. As the history of psychotherapy indicates, the evaluation process is by nature complex and long-term (Tourney, 1967).

I. THE APPROACH OF THOMAS G. STAMPFL

The purpose of this article is to review the contributions of one behavior technique described as promising (Krasner, 1971). The technique under discussion was developed by Thomas G. Stampfl and is referred to as implosive therapy (IT) or flooding. Stampfl developed a therapeutic procedure designed to emphasize one basic principle, that of experimental extinction. In general terms, this principle states that learned fears can be unlearned or extinguished by simply repeating the stimuli conditioned to elicit the fear in the absence of any inherent aversive stimulation (e.g., physical pain). The presentation of fear cues is expected to elicit a strong emotional response at first, but with repetition the emotional responding should subside. Although the importance of having clients respond emotionally during treatment has been recognized by many other theorists, Stampfl's technique represents a different strategy toward this objective. The attempt is made to re-present, reinstate, or symbolically reproduce those emotionally evoking cues believed motivating symptomatology of the client via instructions to imagine scenes directed by the therapist (Stampfl & Levis, 1967a).

At a clinical level, Stampfl found the technique useful for treatment of a wide variety of psychoneurotic problems including anxiety, phobic, obsessive-compulsive, and depressive reactions, and behavior labeled as psychotic, including affective, schizophrenic, and paranoid reactions. Marked reduction in symptomatology is reported to occur, usually within 15 therapy sessions. However, Stampfl has been careful not to use such clinical observations in the scientific defense of the position's efficacy. Perhaps better than most, he understands the dangers of case history material. This is the primary reason why 10 years elapsed before Stampfl published the first major paper describing his approach (Stampfl & Levis, 1967a). Those 10 years (1957–1967) were spent documenting the principle of experimental extinction upon which IT is based, treating numerous clinical cases to insure that at the "personal" level the technique was effective and nonharmful, and waiting for the completion of some outcome studies (Stampfl, personal communication).

A review of Stampfl's papers reveals that he has provided the field with more than a description of the clinical treatment technique. He has attempted to outline a comprehensive model of psychopathology, suggesting how fears are learned, how they are maintained over time, and how they can be unlearned. In developing his formulations, Stampfl has drawn extensively upon the learning as well as the clinical literature. This article will provide a detailed outline of Stampfl's theoretical model as well as a critical but constructive review of the existing literature on the effectiveness of the implosive and related extinction techniques. As will be shown later in this paper, a credible evaluation of the treatment literature cannot be made in the absence of a thorough understanding of the theoretical model underlying the technique. Previous reviews of the implosive literature (Ayres, 1972; Frankel, 1972; McNamara, 1972; Morganstern, 1973; Smith, Dickson, & Sheppard, 1973) frequently have failed to consider whether important points of the model were incorporated into a given research design. This lack of understanding of the conceptual model has led to a number of theoretical misconceptions and erroneous conclusions as well as to frequent misapplication of the IT procedure. It is hoped that the current review will correct such misinformation and point the way toward theoretical and empirical issues in need of study.

To achieve the above objective, this article is divided into three general sections. The first part deals with issues of theory concerning how psychopathology develops, how symptoms are maintained over extended periods of time, and how they can be extinguished. The second section deals with issues related to the implosive technique, including a review of methods used for classifying the cue content of scenes and for distinguishing the techniques of implosive therapy from flooding. The final section provides a review of the existing research literature evaluating the technique's efficacy. Human analogue studies and studies with client populations are reviewed separately. Inferences are drawn from existing data and research directions are suggested.

II. THE DEVELOPMENT OF PSYCHOPATHOLOGY

In the administration of an extinction approach like that of implosive therapy, it is important that the therapist be able to restructure a close approximation of the client's conditioning history. To achieve this objective, Stampfl realized that a theoretical working model was needed to provide a conceptual framework for the origin and development of psychopathology. The basic assumption made in the model offered (Stampfl & Levis, 1967a, 1969) is that maladaptive behavior, in most cases, is learned behavior. A common element of many contemporary behavior theories is the distinction made between independent variables that seem to have motivational effects upon behavior and those that direct or guide behavior. Intermediary constructs have been introduced by several theorists which correspond with these two groups of variables. Thus, drives, motivations, emotions, conations, and libidos are constructs considered to function as the activating agents; whereas cognitive maps, associative tendencies, and habit strength serve, in conjunction with external and internal stimuli, to determine the direction of behavior (Brown, 1961). The term "drive" will be used in this paper to refer to the motivational or activating aspects of behavior, and "habit strength" will be used to indicate directive functions.

The assumption is made that maladaptive behavior that is likely to be labeled symptomatic is motivated by a strong drive state. Traditionally, drives have been classified into primary and secondary sources of motivation (Brown, 1961). In general, primary or innate drive states like hunger, thirst, sex, and pain are those that produced their effects through the action of inherited bodily mechanisms and are not dependent upon learning. Secondary drives differ from primary drives in that their ability to serve as motivators is dependent upon learning. These drives play an important role in the development of human behavior; they include the strivings for prestige, social mobility, money, power, love, and status. In terms of developing maladaptive behavior, however, learned fear or "anxiety" appears to be one of the most important drives of all. Fear is important to symptom formation because it can be a very strong source of motivation, because it can be attached to new cues so easily through learning, and because it is the source of motivation that produces the inhibiting responses in most conflicts (Dollard & Miller, 1950, p. 190).

A. Two-Factor Learning Theory

The model of psychopathology adopted here essentially involves an extension by Stampfl to human behavior of Mowrer's two-factor theory of avoidance learning (Mowrer, 1947, 1960; Rescorla & Solomon, 1967). Mowrer departed from the monistic reinforcement theory of Hull (1943) mainly because of the latter theory's awkwardness in dealing with the infrahuman avoidance literature. According to this position, at least two response classes are believed inherent to the development of psychopathology. The first consists of the organism's learning to respond in a fearful manner to previously nonfearful stimuli. The sequence of events required for fear acquisition is well established in the experimental literature. Its development simply results from the pairing of initially nonfearful stimuli with an inherent aversive event producing pain. The primary drive or unconditioned response (UCR) of pain can be elicited by a variety of unconditioned stimuli (UCSs), such as those involved in physical punishment or generated by severe states of primary deprivation such as hunger. Following sufficient repetition of a neutral stimulus with a UCS, the nonfearful stimulus will acquire the capability of eliciting a fear response. At this point in time the nonfearful stimulus is appropriately labeled a conditioned stimulus (CS) and is capable of eliciting fear even when not followed by the inherent aversive event (UCS). The aversive emotional reaction elicited by the presentation of conditioned fearful stimuli is referred to as the conditioned fear response (CR). Although some theorists believe that the fear response solely reflected conditioning of the autonomic nervous system (Mowrer, 1947; Wolpe, 1958), recent data have questioned this assumption (Rescorla & Solomon, 1967). Nevertheless, in most cases of fear conditioning the autonomic nervous system is affected. It is also safe to say that the fear response does not involve a unitary, well-defined set of response topographies. Many theorists believe fear learning is governed by the laws of classical conditioning and is based solely on the principle of contiguity, the pairing of the CS and UCS (Hilgard & Bower, 1966).

The conditioned fear response is also viewed as a secondary source of drive, possessing motivational or energizing effects (Amsel & Maltzman, 1950; Brown, Kalish, & Farber, 1951; Meryman, 1952, 1953) as well as reinforcing effects (Brown & Jacobs, 1949; Kalish, 1954; Miller, 1948). The drive properties of the fear response set the stage for learning of the second class of responses, referred to as avoidance behavior. Avoidance behavior is governed by the laws of instrumental learning which are believed to include both a contiguity and drive reduction notion of reinforcement (Mowrer, 1947, 1960). Avoidance behavior is learned because of the effect of this response class to terminate or reduce the presence of the conditioned aversive state. The resulting reducing of fear (drive reduction) serves as the reinforcing mechanism for the learning of the avoidance behavior. Symptoms and defensive maneuvers developed by humans are viewed as being equivalent to avoidance behavior (Freud, 1936; Stampfl & Levis, 1967a; Wolpe, 1958). They are assumed to result from attempts on the individual's part to avoid previously conditioned aversive stimuli which function as "danger" signals. Symptoms, as was the case with the fear response, produce varied response topographies. Although two-factor theory has not been free of criticism (Herrnstein, 1969), the theory is still considered a viable explanatory model for infrahuman and human avoidance data. The experimental evidence previously mentioned lends support to the basic assumptions of the position.

It should be noted, however, that the learning of the above two response classes is not, in and of itself, a sign of psychopathology. On the contrary, human survival is in large part dependent upon emotional learning and subsequent avoidance responding which protects the individual from a potential source of physical pain and tissue damage. Psychopathology is assumed to occur when a very low or zero correlation exists between the occurrence of the above response classes and the potential presence of physical danger to the organism.

Thus, for some individuals, being on the tenth floor of a building leads to a strong emotional reaction and subsequent avoidance of the building. Yet, the nonoccurrence of such reactions would not physically endanger the individual. Or, in the case of compulsive behavior, the failure to wash one's hands over and over again after turning on a light switch or touching money would not significantly increase the probability of danger to the organism. Such behaviors are labeled maladaptive because their occurrence is not biologically protective, is usually not under the individual's control, and frequently interferes with the functioning of desired, socially adaptive responses.

B. The Nature of Symptom Formation

Rats and other infrahuman organisms have been trained to perform a variety of response topographies to avoid aversive conditioned stimuli including running, jumping, turning wheels, pressing bars, and remaining passive. However, the avoidance response topographies of humans, manifesting signs of psychopathology, are usually far more complex than reported in the typical laboratory experiment. Perhaps the closest analogy between the two situations is the response topography associated with the typical human phobic reaction. In the case of both the human and the rat, the organism simply avoids the aversive stimulus situation, whether the CS is an airplane, tall building, car, or black box with grid floors. The response is reinforced by its ability to remove or reduce the source of aversive stimulation.

As is the case with the infrahuman analysis, the avoidance response or symptom of the human is believed to be functional in that it reduces stress immediately upon its execution. The response topography of the human avoidance behavior also appears to make sense from a *utility* point of view. If one is afraid of a given stimulus situation, what better way is there to reduce the fear than to avoid directly the fear situation? *It is argued that all symptoms make sense in a functional way if the source of conditioned aversive stimulation is taken into consideration.*

From the viewpoint of an observer, however, it might seem puzzling that certain kinds of symptoms develop. Consider the unusual behavior of an individual who repeatedly upon touching a dollar bill has to wash his hands. If the CS pattern involved in the original conditioning trials of the compulsive handwasher were known and if these events led to a strong fear of dirt or disease, the avoidance response of washing one's hands to remove dirt clearly makes sense. Or if one is afraid of thinking sexual thoughts, counting one's heartbeats may well provide a nice distraction, preventing the occurrence of such thoughts. Usually, such avoidance behavior produces only a temporary relief. With exposure to a similar anxiety situation, the individual is again motivated to repeat the avoidance act.

The above point of symptom utility is perhaps more obvious in the case of hysterical conversion reactions. Consider the case of a soldier who following a minor injury in combat develops a paralyzed leg or the case of combat aviators who develop disturbances in depth perception or night vision. The presence of such a conversion reaction has the immediate effect of preventing the individual from re-entering the feared combat situation. Furthermore, the individual's inability to understand the relationship between the conversion reaction and the desired avoidance behavior, which usually accompanies such cases, results in the avoidance of an additional source of anxiety generated by feelings of guilt.

Similarly, in cases of depression it makes sense to become depressed and despondent if one is afraid of being exposed to rejection cues or fears of failure in work or interpersonal relationships. The depressive response allows the individual to withdraw from activities in which failure or rejection are viewed as likely. Additionally, considerable positive secondary reinforcement (gain) is frequently achieved by friends telling the individual how much they care or how much potential the depressed person really has. Defense mechanisms such as repression, rationalization, projection, and displacement serve a similar function. That is to say, they help the individual to avoid aversive internal cues such as thoughts, memories, or images, which, if not avoided through the execution of the defense mechanism, would cause considerable anxiety. Further consideration of other symptom nosologies should bring to mind many other examples of the utility function of symptoms. Symptoms are not an effect of anxiety but a stratagem to circumvent or avoid painful consequences.

To summarize the preceding analysis, fear learning and subsequent avoidance of aversive conditioned stimuli are viewed as essential ingredients in the development of human psychopathology. We also maintain that the diversity of unusual and puzzling behavior patterns evinced by persons who are labeled as neurotic or psychotic can more easily be understood following a thorough analysis of the array of conditioned stimuli driving the individual's symptomology. Although the CS complex conditioned frequently involves many fear-eliciting cues, a common pattern or theme usually develops, such as fear of bodily injury, fear of rejection, or fear of failure. The avoidance conditioning paradigm investigated in the laboratory provides a useful model in studying fear acquisition and subsequent avoidance behavior. However, the etiology of symptom formation at the human level can be motivated by more than a single drive, and involves learning paradigms more complex than that suggested by the simple avoidance model. To illustrate this point, an outline of five different learning situations believed embedded in the development of psychopathology will briefly be described.

1. SYMPTOM FORMATION MOTIVATED BY A SINGLE DRIVE SOURCE, THAT OF CONDITIONED FEAR

In this category, the straightforward model of avoidance conditioning previously described is operating. Most phobic reactions are believed to have developed from this learning process, which simply results from past specific experiences of punishment and pain conferring strong emotional reactions to initially nonpunishing (neutral) stimuli. The acquisition of fear to previous neutral stimuli in the human may have resulted from aversive events in the early socialization period of the child (spanking, slapping, etc.) for the transgressive (forbidden) behavior. Other significant conditioning factors may be events related to aversive peer group experiences (being bullied, teased, or beaten) or from aversive natural events (injuries resulting from falling, being burned, being cut, etc.). Current aversive events (trouble with one's in-laws, losing one's job, ill health, etc.) also may help to perpetuate the affective arousal. Defensive maneuvers and symptoms of the individual are believed to result from attempts on his or her part to avoid or terminate the conditioned stimuli which function as danger signals. A source of fear common to this category is the fear of bodily injury (Stampfl & Levis, 1973a).

2. SYMPTOM FORMATION ORIGINALLY MOTIVATED BY THE PRIMARY DRIVE OF HUNGER

The hunger drive and strong responses it excites may pave the way under certain circumstances for important learning, especially in reference to childhood developmental patterns. As Dollard and Miller (1950, p. 132) pointed out, if a child is repeatedly left to "cry itself out" when hungry, the child may learn that no matter what is tried there is nothing that can be done which will elevate the painful experience of hunger. Such training may lay the basis for the habit of apathy or helplessness, the behavior of not trying to avoid when in pain (Seligman, 1975). Furthermore, if an intensive hunger develops, the responses involved can attach fearfulness to situational cues like the bedroom, darkness, quietness, being alone, or to the absence of parental stimuli. An approach—avoidance conflict may develop between two primary drives (hunger and externally induced pain) if the child cries when hungry and is subsequently punished for crying or is directly punished for certain eating behaviors which meet the displeasure of the parents. Thus, by pitting two drives against each other, the desire to eat and the fear of being punished for eating, the resulting conflict can heighten fearfulness and the conditionability of situational cues associated with the stressful situation.

3. SYMPTOM FORMATION ORIGINALLY MOTIVATED BY THE PRIMARY DRIVE OF SEX

Probably no other primary drive is so severely inhibited in our society than sex. Research has indicated that the sex drive can produce positive reinforcement effects early in life. For example, Kinsey, Pomeroy, and Martin (1948) concluded that small boys acquire the capacity for orgasm long before they become able to ejaculate. Yet, many parents view such reinforcement as "nasty," "dirty," and "evil." Even in the present "enlightened" age, it is not uncommon for parents to inhibit their childrens' sexual play by directly punishing such behavior or threatening to administer punishment such as cutting off the penis if the undesired behavior reoccurs. It is also not uncommon for parents to create an approach—avoidance conflict by directly stimulating their children sexually and then punishing the child's response. It is little wonder that sexual inhibitions play such an important role in the development of many cases of psychopathology. Since sex is a relatively weak primary drive, a frequent response learned is to remove the conflict and guilt associated with the response by avoidance of (repressing) sexual feelings and thoughts. Such conflicts frequently reemerge in adult life when society partially removes its taboos and places strong pressure on the individual to be active in this area.

4. SYMPTOM FORMATION ORIGINALLY MOTIVATED BY THE WITHDRAWAL OF POSITIVE REINFORCING CUES LABELED "AFFECTION" OR "LOVE"

Stimuli made contingent with positive reinforcement can acquire the capacity to elicit a positive emotional response in the same manner as described for stimuli conditioned to elicit negative effect. To describe an individual as feeling good emotionally, or as having a feeling of well-being and of security, is to say in learning terms that environmental and internal cues previously conditioned to produce positive affect are currently being elicited. A decrease in the positive emotional state experienced is considered to be a direct function of eliminating or reducing the cues eliciting the positive affect. This is true whether they are labeled conditioned or unconditioned stimuli. If the loss of positive affect is of sufficient magnitude, the experience will generate a negative emotional state resulting in the aversive conditioning of those situational cues correlated with the reduction in stimulation of the positive affective cues. Depending upon the individual's previous conditioning history, such a sequence of events can elicit additional cues (thoughts, images, memories) representing similar conditioning sequences. The resulting compounding of negative affective stimuli can generate strong negative emotional states frequently described by clinicians as representing feelings of guilt, worthlessness, and depression (Stampfl & Levis, 1969).

Thus, goal-directed behavior designed to elicit a positive emotional state may become inhibited because of the presence of previously conditioned stimuli which were associated with a reduction in the positive emotional state (e.g., rejection). The presence of such aversive stimuli may result in an anticipatory response that such negative consequences may occur again if the positive goal-directed behavior is carried out. This in turn should result in an inhibition of such behavior in an attempt to avoid the possible negative outcome. Whether such behavior will be engaged in will depend on the conditioning and motivational strength of the two sets of approach–avoidance stimuli (Miller, 1951). For a fairly typical conditioning sequence depicting the above process and believed to reflect a common childhood occurrence, the reader is referred to an article by Stampfl and Levis (1969).

5. SYMPTOM FORMATION ORIGINALLY MOTIVATED
    BY THE CONDITIONED INHIBITION OF BEHAVIOR
    ELICITED BY THE EMOTION LABELED ANGER

As previous models have suggested, the excessive or severe use of punishment as a behavioral controller leads to the conditioning of fear to previous nonfearful stimuli. Punishment can also have the effect of inhibiting on-going, goal-directed behavior. The blocking of such responses frequently creates a state of frustration which has been shown experimentally to lead to an increase in drive (anger) and to behavior labeled as aggression (Amsel, 1958). The effects of the interaction of these two emotions (fear and anger) on the development of psychopathology are well documented in the clinical literature. It is not surprising that Dollard and Miller (1950) concluded: "Lift the veil of repression covering the childhood mental life of a neurotic person and you come upon the smoking responses of anger" (p. 148).

The conflict resulting from the interaction of fear and anger frequently can lead in theory to behavior best described in the context of a multiprocess approach–avoidance paradigm (see Stampfl & Levis, 1969). The first stage consists of conditioned anxiety being associated to cues correlated with a desired approach response. This is achieved by pairing the goal-directed response with punishment (pain). Because the goal-directed behavior is thwarted, frustration is elicited in addition to pain and may lead to aggressive behavior. Especially in the case of children, such aggressive tendencies are usually followed by more punishment, inhibiting the aggressive responses. With sufficient repetition of the above sequence, aggressive responses will, in turn, become inhibited by conditioned anxiety.

By channeling the aggressive behavior into internal cues involving thoughts, images, or ruminations toward the punishing agent, a partial discharge of the anger response can occur. However, if the punishing agent is a source of considerable positive primary and secondary reinforcement, such as the case of a mother who provides a protective, nurturant role, the stage is set for an additional conflict. By the child's harboring aggressive impulses toward such a figure, the strength and positive reinforcement obtained from viewing the mother as a supportive, loving figure will be decreased.

The above conflict can be resolved by avoiding (suppressing) the aggressive fantasies and responses associated with the aggressive behavior. Such behavior is engaged in so as to avoid diminishing the positive reinforcement associated with the child's conceptualization of the punishing agent and to reduce additional secondary anxiety (guilt) over expressing the internal aggressive cues. If the avoidance pattern is not completely successful in removing the conflict, defense mechanisms such as displacement, reaction formation, and projection may develop. A depressive reaction is also believed to be a frequent outgrowth of such conditioning sequences.

Depression can serve added functional roles in that the self-punitive effects of the reaction may help reduce secondary anxiety of guilt as well as setting the stage for the attainment of positive responses from the punisher or other individuals (secondary gain). Furthermore, such conditioning experience usually leads to a decrease in assertive behavior in order to avoid increasing the probability of additional conditioning trials.

The above five conditioning models are only suggestive of some possible interactions that can occur to produce symptoms. Clearly, the models are speculative in nature and in need of scientific evaluation at the human level of analysis. Yet, as Stampfl suggests, such speculation may prove to be useful in determining directions in which therapy might proceed. Direct observation of symptom formation in childhood is needed since it is impossible to be certain, using a retrospective analysis, of what actually were the historical conditioning sequences of a given client. Although it is probably safe to say that conditioned aversive sequences comprising human psychopathology may involve multiple stimulus and avoidance response patterns, these patterns can be viewed in some cases as being unrelated or in other cases as being highly interactive.

C. Conditioned Fear Transference

As the foregoing discussion suggests, cues can be conditioned directly by pairing them with an aversive UCS. However, it should be explicitly stated that it is not necessary that all fear-eliciting cues, whether internal or external, be conditioned directly by a primary drive. Actually, a great deal of human emotional learning occurs because fear learned to one set of cues can transfer to other nonfearful stimuli. Children fear ghosts and skeletons, yet they have not been directly hurt by them. Many adults fear riding in an airplane even though such an experience has never been followed by bodily injury or physical pain. To account for such fear transfer, learning theorists appeal to such concepts and processes as those involved in secondary conditioning, higher-order conditioning, primary stimulus generalization, response-mediated generalization, and/or the principle of memory redintegration of past aversive events. Such principles also provide an explanation for the development of symbolism and displacement (Miller & Kraeling, 1950). Thus, if the sight of a knife has been conditioned to elicit a strong fear reaction, the fear may generalize to all sharp objects or to objects that can potentially produce bodily injury, such as guns, cars, unprotected high places, airplanes, and so on. If the sight of feces has been conditioned as well as the fear of disease, the cue transference may include such items as dirt, money, water fountains, public toilets, etc. Thus, fear of the phallus may generalize to other objects like snakes, telephone poles, knives, etc., which are seen as similar to the actual fear object (Kimble, 1961; Stampfl & Levis, 1967a).

D. A Distinction between Conditioned and Unconditioned Aversive Events

From the point of view of the learning position adopted, it is important to make a careful distinction between aversive stimuli, which function as secondary reinforcers (CSs), and stimuli which function as inherent or primary reinforcers (Stampfl & Levis, 1969). The basic distinction resides in the functional analysis of the properties of a given stimulus in eliciting emotional responding prior to any exposure to conditioning sequences. The CS only acquires the ability to elicit an emotional reaction in the organism by being paired with another aversive stimulus. Furthermore, repeated exposure to the CS complex in the absence of further UCS presentation will result in the loss of fear to the CS (extinction). That is to say, with sufficient repetition, each CS, in principle, can be returned to its original nonfearful state. On the other hand, an aversive UCS is a primary drive stimulus which must involve, in principle, physical pain arising from harmful external stimuli or inherently painful states within the organism. Repetition of the UCS will either increase the strength of the aversive reaction or at least maintain the aversive-eliciting strength of stimulation correlated with it (excluding temporary effects of habituation or adaptation).

Learning theorists have little difficulty making the above distinction or classifying stimuli as CS or UCS when referring to infrahuman research. Therefore, it is somewhat surprising that so much confusion exists when such an analysis is applied to human situations. Morganstern (1973), for example, expressed concern over the implosive therapist's attempts to present to their clients aversive images which he labeled as "horrifying" and "cruel." Images are not inherently aversive (primary reinforcers), and if they possess aversive properties the effect has been imposed by a conditioning sequence. Dollard and Miller (1950, p. 294) also expressed a similar concern about conventional "insight" treatment techniques. They pointed out that an awkward, stupid interpretation by the therapist which elicits strong fear is equivalent to a cruel therapist attaching a grid to the patient's chair and giving him a strong electric shock. Like Morganstern, these authors also failed to distinguish between the primary and secondary reinforcers outlined above. Visual representations (e.g., the sight of blood), words, thoughts, memories, or images which elicit fearful responses are not, in and of themselves, capable of eliciting unconditioned responses (i.e., producing physical pain). They acquire their affective aversive arousal because of their pairing with another CS or CS sequence which was at some point in time paired with a UCS. The fear associated with such CS stimulation can be unlearned, which is not the case with UCSs. It should be noted, however, that such CSs, if not extinguished, can produce upon exposure strong conditioned emotional reactions and act as powerful secondary reinforcers for the learning of new behavior to remove such stimulation.

E. The Role of the CS Complex

It should be clear by now that both internal and external cues are viewed by Stampfl as being conditionable. In fact, any environmental change discerned by an organism may serve as a conditioned stimulus if it is followed by an aversive event. Laboratory demonstrations of conditioning have included visual stimuli such as lights, colors, papers, moving objects, and geometrical forms; auditory stimuli such as tones, buzzers, horns, bubbling water, metronomes; and various thermal, tactual, olfactory, and proprioceptive stimuli. The effectiveness of some stimuli may depend on their sudden onset or termination, on a change in stimulus intensity or appearance, and yet other stimuli may depend for their effectiveness on summation (Kimble, 1961, p. 52).

One should, however, when attempting to reconstruct or determine what cues have been conditioned, be careful not to assume that the CS in question involves a single discrete event. Many behavior therapists and some conditioning researchers appear to make this assumption when they describe the CS as a tone, a light, the sight of a tall building, or the sight of a snake or rat. Laboratory evidence again has demonstrated quite convincingly that conditioning occurs not simply to a discrete stimulus but to a stimulus complex potentially including all the cues which immediately precede the UCS (see McAllister & McAllister, 1971). This point is central to the model proposed by Stampfl.

Many of the cues responsible for motivating psychopathology are believed to be historical in origin. On the basis of available clinical and experimental data and on the basis of common sense, it is safe to assume that a child during the first 5 or 6 years of life is forced into many significant changes in behavior. Although considerable knowledge has been accumulated on the physical motivation of the child, little is known experimentally about the child's emotional development. It is clear, however, that at an emotional level children are frequently rendered helpless by harsh and confusing patterns of training. Clinicians repeatedly have warned parents about the emotional dangers associated with harsh and punitive training resulting from weaning, the feeding situation, cleanliness training, and early sexual experiences. The acquisition of fearful stimuli in the human not only involves early socialization periods of parent–child interactions but can include aversive events associated with sibling rivalry, peer group interaction, parental conflicts, illness, or the death of a loved one (Stampfl & Levis, 1967a).

As some of the previously described models of symptom formation emphasized, intense conditioned aversive situations are believed to be represented neurally, and the neural engram (thoughts, memories, images) can be considered to have the potential to function as a stimulus. Any stimulus object or event in the external environment (e.g., a phobic object) or response-produced stimulation such as the impulse to act sexually or aggressively (or even the impulse to act morally), if associated with a stimulus pattern originally paired with pain, will tend to reactivate or redintegrate the anxiety-arousing associations or memories. Thus, it is argued that a given environmental event which elicits fear and subsequent avoidance may also elicit a chain of memories of similar fear-eliciting situations as well as the neural representation of the unconditioned stimuli employed (Stampfl, 1970; Stampfl & Levis, 1967a, 1969).

In attempting to restructure an individual conditioning history, it is important, as Stampfl noted, not only to consider the neural representation of external events, but also internal events which were directly conditioned. For example, consider a child who is repeatedly punished by a parent. Any overt or verbal expressions of anger by the child are also directly inhibited. Under such circumstances, it would not be surprising if the child wished secretly that his parent would die. If this thought process becomes paired with the physical pain or another aversive stimulus, it will acquire aversive properties in the manner of an extroceptive cue. It is also conceivable that internal cues which exist prior to the full development of perceptual and discrimination skills of the child play an important role in the conditioning sequence. As dynamic theory suggests (Fenichel, 1945), such internal cues might seem strange and bizarre to an adult, especially if they involve fantasies and thought patterns comprising cannibalistic, or oral-incorporative behavior (Stampfl & Levis, 1967a). As the learning theorist, Kimble (1961), noted:

One advantage of the view that anxiety is a conditioned fear reaction is that it leads to the search, in the life history of the individual, for traumatic occasions which may provide the origin of anxiety. This has led to the emphasis on certain events in childhood which are often responsible for the development of anxiety. These events include some of the same episodes stressed by the psychoanalysts in their theory of psychosexual development, such as toilet training and the inhibition of infantile sexuality and aggression. One of the important points about such fears is that they are acquired before the child can talk. This appears to contribute to the difficulties encountered later on in trying to remember traumatic events which led to the development of anxiety (p. 474).

Such internal cues as thoughts, desires, images, or memories are believed to follow the same conditioning laws that apply to external cues. Although the above assumption is still an open experimental question, the evidence available appears to favor such a conclusion (Dollard & Miller, 1950, p. 99).

III. SYMPTOM MAINTENANCE

As previously suggested, human methods of dealing with fear-provoking situations essentially follow the same strategy as the conditioned rat (i.e., to escape as quickly as possible the feared CS). Such a position is consistent with a number of behaviorists (e.g., Wolpe, 1958) and nonbehaviorists (e.g., Freud, 1936, p. 85). Although important differences exist between laboratory and real-life conditioning situations in terms of the nature of the CS complex and the avoidance response topography, both situations are assumed to be governed by similar conditioning principles. Furthermore, the original Pavlovian principle that exposure to the CS in the absence of the UCS will lead to extinction has been documented by a vast amount of evidence at both the infrahuman and human level of analysis. This principle appears to be valid whether overt or emotional states have been learned. Unfortunately, the abundance of laboratory evidence falls far short in producing resistance to extinction results comparable to those obtained from the clinical literature. Reports of nearly total failures to obtain successful avoidance conditioning with infrahuman subjects and of short-lived conditioning are strikingly in evidence (Anderson & Nakamura, 1964; Feldman &

Bremmer, 1963; Fitzgerald & Brown, 1965; Meyer, Cho, & Wesemann, 1960). Only a handful of studies exist which demonstrate that
infrahuman avoidance learning is relatively efficient and persistent
(Brush, 1957; Solomon & Wynne, 1954).

The finding that symptoms of clients can markedly resist extinction presents a paradox for the two-factor theory of conceptualization. Clearly, increased CS exposure should produce a subsequent
extinction effect. Clinical evidence also suggests that any attempt by
an individual to increase CS exposure by "fighting" the symptomatic
behavior regularly results in an unbearable anxiety reaction that
frequently progresses to a panic-like intensity. In effect, rather than
obtaining a decrease in anxiety as theory would suggest, these individuals are punished by an increase in anxiety for trying to prevent
symptom onset. No wonder, a "why try?" reaction frequently develops. This state appears to be quite similar to Seligman's concept of
"learned helplessness" (Seligman, 1975; Stampfl & Levis, 1973b).

The Role of CSs Ordered Serially

Stampfl attempted to explain the seeming paradox of why infrahuman avoidance responding produced only occasional examples of
extreme resistance to extinction while conditioned avoidance
responses that take the form of neurotic and psychotic symptoms
apparently resist extinction for years. He observed that most of the
conditioning laws developed in the laboratory stemmed from a
paradigm in which only one external cue was manipulated. On the
other hand, he noted from his work with clients that the CS patterns
that appeared to be avoided involved rather complex and varied
stimulus elements which were frequently ordered in a serial CS
pattern. Surprisingly, the variable of CS complexity has remained a
relatively unexplored parameter in the American infrahuman avoidance conditioning literature (Baker, 1968; Razran, 1965).

After analyzing the infrahuman situation in great detail, Stampfl
noted that much of the conditioning apparatus used failed to make
the situation following the avoidance response highly distinctive
from the situation present during the CS. For example, the subject
frequently jumped from a black box or grid floor situation with tone
present to a black box or grid floor situation with tone absent. In
theory, the avoidance response of the subject does not result in the
removal of a large element of the total CS complex, which, in turn,
should retard both acquisition and resistance to extinction. He also
found that by presenting the animal with a series of different stimuli

(e.g., tone, followed by lights, followed by buzzer), resistance to extinction of the avoidance response could be greatly increased.

The above infrahuman work conducted by Stampfl led him to provide a theoretical extension of the Solomon and Wynne (1954) conservation of anxiety hypothesis, to encompass the presentation of complex stimuli, and to extend the model to human psychopathology. The theoretical objective was to provide a rationale of how fear can be maintained in the absence of further presentation of a primary aversive event.

Stampfl (see Levis, 1966a) suggested that by dividing the CS–UCS interval into distinctive components and ordering them sequentially, one could maximize the principle of anxiety conservation. He reasoned that after the attainment of short latency responses to the first stimulus component in the sequence, S_1, subsequent extinction effects to this component will result in less generalization of extinction to the second component in the sequence, S_2, if the S_2 segment is highly dissimilar to the S_1 segment. The greater the reduction in generalization of extinction effects from the early part of the CS–UCS interval to the later portions, the greater the amount of anxiety that will be conserved to the components closer to the UCS onset. As fear to the S_1 stimulus extinguishes, the response latencies will become longer, eventually resulting in the exposure of the S_2 stimulus. At this point, a stimulus change in the organism from a low-fear to a high-fear state will occur. The S_2 component, upon exposure, is viewed as being capable of functioning as a secondary conditioning stimulus, driving the avoidance latencies back to the S_1 stimulus. In theory, this process will continue to repeat itself until the S_2 stimulus is sufficiently exposed to produce a subsequent extinction effect. By adding further distinctive components (i.e., S_3) to the original conditioning sequence, the process of reacquiring shorter avoidance response latencies via the principles of anxiety conservation and secondary intermittent reinforcement can be maximized. Empirically, serial CS procedures when compared to nonserial CS procedures have been found to produce reliably more resistance to extinction (Kostanek & Sawrey, 1965; Levis, 1966a, 1966b; Levis, Bouska, Eron, & McIlhon, 1970).

The model offered by Stampfl concerning acquisition and fear maintenance of complex and serially ordered CSs has generated a number of predictions at the infrahuman level which have undergone analysis. Although support of these predictions is important to the defense of the model, a review of these results is beyond the scope of this article. The interested reader is referred to several articles (Boyd & Levis, 1976; Dubin & Levis, 1974; Levis, 1966a, 1970c; Levis *et al.*, 1970; Levis & Boyd, 1973; Levis & Dubin, 1973; Levis & Stampfl, 1972; Shipley, 1974).

IV. FEAR EXTINCTION

As noted in the introduction to this article, the procedures employed in the techniques of implosive therapy and flooding are designed to maximize the principle of direct experimental extinction. This principle states that the presentation of the CS in the absence of the UCS will lead to extinction of the conditioned response. Laboratory evidence suggests that the most efficient way this can be achieved is to present the total CS complex in the absence of primary reinforcement. For example, Miller (1951) advocated this strategy when he stated that: "Experimental extinction is more effective when the animal is in the original punished situation that evokes the most intense fear." It is interesting to observe that Solomon, Kamin, and Wynne (1953) adopted the same strategy:

. . . the best way to produce extinction of the emotional response would be to arrange the situation in such a way that an extremely intense emotional reaction takes place in the presence of the CS. This would be tantamount to a reinstatement of the original acquisition situation, and since the UCS is not presented a big decremental effect should occur (p. 299).

Many studies are available which have corroborated this interpretation (Baum, 1970; Black, 1958; Denny, Koons, & Mason, 1959; Hunt, Jernberg, & Brady, 1952; Knapp, 1965; Weinberger, 1965).

According to Mowrer's two-factor theory, the repeated presentation of the total CS complex will result in extinction of the emotional fear response. Once the drive value of the CS has been eliminated, CS presentation will cease to serve as a discriminatory cue to escape (avoid) the CS. One method used in the laboratory to achieve the objective of total CS exposure is to block escape from the CS by inserting a barrier between the shock and safe compartments of the apparatus during extinction. This procedure is commonly referred to as the response prevention technique of extinction. Overwhelming evidence at the infrahuman level indicates that a response prevention procedure does indeed facilitate extinction of the previously conditioned avoidance response. There is some controversy, however, over whether such a procedure leads to extinction of the fear response or to incompatible response tendencies such as freezing (Coulter, Riccio, & Page, 1969; Page, 1955). Recent work directed to resolving this issue suggests that although incompatible responses may develop initially, fear does extinguish through the use of a response prevention procedure (Shipley, Mock, & Levis, 1971). The total amount of CS exposure also appears to be a critical factor as fear reduction seems to be related directly to the amount of CS exposure (Shearman, 1970; Shipley, 1974; Shipley et al., 1971). A corollary to this principle applied at the human level is that the more clearly the subject perceives the anxiety-eliciting stimuli when followed by nonreinforcement, the more rapid will be the extinction of the emotional response (Lowenfeld, Rubenfeld, & Guthrie, 1956; Wall & Guthrie, 1959).

V. THERAPEUTIC APPLICATION OF THE EXTINCTION PROCEDURE

Analyzing the laboratory principle of experimental extinction via "forced" CS exposure to the treatment of human symptoms poses some obvious procedural questions. First, in the case of the human subject, unlike that of the laboratory rat, the contingencies of the conditioning history usually are unknown. The therapist is forced to rely mainly upon verbal reports of the client in the attempt to restructure the conditioning paradigms. Independent validation of the accuracy of such reconstructions is difficult if not impossible to obtain. Second, the issue of the method of CS presentation needs to be raised. The theoretical model suggests that the CS complex representing the past conditioned specific experience of punishment and pain is represented in the human being neurally via images, thoughts, and memories. Furthermore, the ideational representation (level of reported awareness) of the anxiety-eliciting associations need not be present to function as an elicitor of the anxiety state. A subliminal area of neural function is necessary to account for some of the phenomena associated with the defensive maneuvers of the individual (Stampfl & Levis, 1967a). Last, one must consider the issue of the subject's cooperation or willingness to be exposed to anxiety-eliciting material.

Stampfl (Stampfl & Levis, 1967a, 1969) acknowledges the apparent difficulty of accurately determining each client's conditioning history but stresses that most trained therapists, after only a few diagnostic interviews, usually find themselves in the position of being able to speculate about the significant personal, environmental, and dynamic interactions shaping the client's behavior. That is to say, by asking the question of what cues the subject is avoiding, hypotheses can be formulated as to the type of traumatic events which give rise to the problem areas. Complete accuracy of such hypothesized formulations is not viewed as essential, since some effect through the principle of generalization of extinction would be expected when an approximation is presented. Stampfl and Levis (1967a) suggest that the merits of a given hypothesis can be determined operationally by directly monitoring autonomic responding such as galvanic (GSR) or heart rate change. If the hypothesized cues elicit anxiety upon presentation, the assumption is made that the subject has been previously conditioned to them. The greater the degree of anxiety elicited by a given cue pattern the greater the support for continuing with the hypothesis. If the hypothesis is not confirmed by the subject's reactions, a new hypothesis is formulated.

Because, in theory, many of the cues originally conditioned are believed to involve not only auditory but also visual and tactual modalities, Stampfl suggests the mode of presentation should involve imagery rather than a simple verbal reproduction. In cases where the anxiety appears bound to only external cues, in vivo presentation may produce worthwhile effects (Stampfl & Levis, 1973a).

One may ask at this point: Why would a client cooperate in a procedure that is designed to elicit high degrees of anxiety? The term "cooperation" must be emphasized since experience indicates that no matter how potentially anxiety-eliciting the scene, whether the client be labeled neurotic or psychotic, the material can be avoided if complete cooperation is lacking (see Boudewyns & Levis, 1975). Experience also indicates that in most cases clients do cooperate and that it is a rarity if a case is terminated prematurely by the client. The rationale of the technique is easily understood and usually makes sense. Finally, and perhaps most importantly, once a considerable amount of emotion is discharged to a given hypothesized CS complex, considerable relief appears to occur, which in turn reinforces involvement in the technique (Levis, 1977; Stampfl & Levis, 1969).

VI. THE IMPLOSIVE THERAPY PROCEDURE

The procedure for administrating the implosive technique will be described only briefly since it has been described in detail in other sources (Levis, 1977; Stampfl, 1970, 1975; Stampfl & Levis, 1967a, 1967b, 1968, 1969, 1973a, 1973b). The first task of the therapist is to identify the aversive cues presumed to be mediating the subject's emotional responding and subsequent symptomatic behavior. Two or three diagnostic interviews usually provide sufficient information to begin the procedure. This phase is followed by a session of "neutral" imagery, to allow the therapist to establish a crude baseline for the ability of the client to imagine various stimuli. The client is then asked to imagine various scenes presented by the therapist. Belief or acceptance of the themes introduced in a cognitive sense is not requested. The therapist attempts to maximize emotional arousal (anxiety, anger, guilt, etc.) by describing the hypothesized aversive stimuli as vividly and realistically as possible. Repetition of the main components of the avoided CS complex introduced is followed by progressive expansion to other sets of cues thought to be related to the client's symptoms. Any attempt on the part of the client to avoid the imagined aversive stimuli is matched by the therapist's attempt to discourage such behavior. The essence of the procedure is to repeatedly expose in imagery the aversive stimuli assumed to be underlying the client's difficulties until an extinction effect is obtained. Following each session, the client is assigned "homework" scenes in order to maximize the extinction effect and to bring the process under personal control.

Stimulus Cue Categories

A critical step in the above outline description of the IT procedure involves the selection of cues to be incorporated into a given scene presentation. In the Stampfl and Levis (1967a) article two main categories of cues were outlined for consideration. These categories were labeled "symptom-contingent cues" and "hypothesized sequential cues." Symptom-contingent cues were defined as those situational or environmental cues which are highly correlated with the occurrence of the client's symptom. They can be identified by analyzing the contingencies surrounding the occurrence of the symptom. Selecting an example from the human analogue area, the sight of a white rat or snake may well fall within this category when the subject behaviorally avoids the object in question. The second general category of hypothesized cues was defined as those which are not directly correlated with symptom onset but which represent "guesses" as to the remaining components of the avoided CS complex. In the case of the fear of a harmless laboratory rat, one might ask if it is reasonable to assume that the sight or touch of the rat comprises the whole stimulus complex to be extinguished. Perhaps it is not solely the sight of the rat per se which is feared, but rather what the subject anticipates the rat might do if physical contact is made (e.g., bite the subject) and the resulting consequences (e.g., bleeding, tissue damage, infection, or even death). With analogue subjects and with simple clinical cases, empirically one might obtain sufficient generalization of extinction by just presenting the symptom-contingent cues. However, at the clinical level, Stampfl predicted that by incorporating hypothesized cues into scene presentation a greater success rate in reducing symptomalogy is expected. In the 1967 article ten general cue areas which were found useful at the clinical level of analysis were outlined. The categories mentioned were as follows: aggression, punishment, oral material, anal material, sexual material, rejection, bodily injury, loss of control, acceptance of conscience, and autonomic nervous system and central nervous system reactivity. As was pointed out in the article, some of these general cue areas have previously been suggested by psychoanalytic theorists (Fenichel, 1945).

In a later article, Stampfl (1970), in the interest of clarity, subdivided the hypothesized sequential cue category into three levels of analysis: *reportable internal elicited cues; unreportable cues hypothesized to relate to reportable internally elicited cues;* and *hypothesized dynamic cues.* Examples of each of these cue categories are given in the above-cited articles and should prove helpful in determining the functional role and importance of each cue set. Unfortunately, little systematic work has been conducted in isolating (for a given symptom) the importance of introducing these different sets of cues. Researchers have also been negligent in systematically outlining the type of cues they have presented.

To provide an intelligent review of the existing treatment literature, it is believed essential to take into consideration the general category of cues introduced. Terms like flooding and implosive therapy, as used by various authors, provide little aid to the reader in differentiating the type of cues presented. For purposes of the present review, a slightly different cue category distinction will be used in the hope of increasing operational specificity and stimulating further work (Levis, 1975).

1. INHERENTLY NONHARMFUL SITUATIONAL AND
   ENVIRONMENTAL CUES (CSs) PRECEDING
   SYMPTOM ONSET AND BELIEVED CORRELATED
   WITH IT

Category (1) cues comprise the presentation of those stimulus situations which lead up to the point of symptom onset but which occur prior to actual avoidance behavior (e.g., sight of snake, car, plane, tall building, stage, money, dirt, etc.). If one avoids being on top of a tall building, the visualization of tall buildings would be classified as being in this cue category as long as one is not doing it from a high point. The sight of a feared snake would fit this category as long as one is not touching it. For inclusion in this category, the general operating rule is that only stimulation preceding the actual engagement with the phobic situation be depicted. This category of cues can also be subdivided into presentation of scenes via instructions to imagine (1a) or in vivo presentations (1b).

2. INHERENTLY NONHARMFUL SITUATIONAL ENVIRONMENTAL CUES (CSs) DIRECTLY AVOIDED BY SYMPTOM ONSET

Cues in category (2) represent those contextual cues which are partially or completely avoided by symptom onset. Cues presented in this category are those situational or environmental stimuli which would have a high probability of occurring in real life situations if the phobic reaction were not activated (e.g., driving a car, taking a plane, touching a harmless snake, riding an elevator, looking out a window of a tall building, speaking in public, meeting people, being assertive, not repeatedly washing hands, etc.). The general operating rule for inclusion in this category is the presentation of all those cues which one would normally be exposed to if symptom onset did not occur. This category can also be subdivided into presentation of scenes via instructions to imagine (2a) or in vivo presentations (2b). Categories (1) and (2) are similar to the symptom-contingent cue classification previously discussed.

3. PHYSICALLY HARMFUL CUES (USs) HYPOTHESIZED TO BE ANTICIPATED WITH THE FAILURE OF SYMPTOM ONSET

Category (3) cues represent the presentation via instructions to imagine those internal and external contextual cues hypothesized to represent aversive unconditioned consequences (e.g., bodily injury, severe states of deprivation) protected by symptom onset. This category is given great importance by implosive therapists and in most cases is totally ignored by other behavioral approaches. Implosive therapists take the position that it is incorrect to assume that the only cues avoided by a client are those situational cues involved in direct engagement with the phobic stimulus. For example, is one only afraid of the situational cues associated with being in an airplane in flight or is it possible that the low probability of danger associated with the situation is what is really feared? In the case of the airplane phobic, the stimulus situation binding most of the affect may be the fear that the plane will crash and the client will die, not the cues associated with flying per se. These hypothesized internal cues can be logically deduced from an analysis of the nature of the symptom itself. With externalized phobic reactions, the hypothesized cues may involve fear of bodily injury cues and death (e.g., car crashing, snake biting, falling off a high building, etc.). In cases involving an obsessive fear of dirt, scenes might be presented in which the client, as a result of having contact with dirt, becomes infected or acquires a disease that causes pain and possibly death. Obsessional cases might involve a scene in which the obsessions are acted out in imagery (e.g., killing a loved one) and followed by a punishment sequence for having engaged in such taboo behavior. For individuals afraid of social interaction or public speaking, scenes might be presented which include rejection and loss of love or status cues. If the situation is one of avoiding the opposite sex, scenes involving rape or scenes depicting pain with sexual encounter might be presented as well as cues associated with any related guilt feelings. Loss of control scenes (e.g., becoming insane with accompanying acting out of bizarre behavior) would fall under this category. The general operating rule is to develop scenes in imagery which depict the worst possible event (UCS or threat of UCS) that could possibly occur following the client's engaging in the feared situation (e.g., scenes involving bodily injury, punishment, severe rejection, loss of love, loss of control, bizarre acting out, etc.).

4. HYPOTHESIZED EXTERNAL ENVIRONMENTAL
    CUES DEDUCED TO BE ASSOCIATED WITH THE
    ORIGINAL (HISTORICAL) CONDITIONING
    SEQUENCES

Category (4) includes the presentation of imagined scenes designed to reactivate in memory those earlier life events which may have contributed to the formation of symptoms. These hypotheses are usually generated from interview material conducted prior to the start of therapy or recalled during the process of treatment. Scenes in this category usually consist of possible (either reported or suspected) historical events associated with stimulus complexes involving rejection, punishment, guilt, bodily injury, religious experiences, and potentially traumatic sexual experiences. Such scenes usually include significant individuals (e.g., parents, teachers, siblings, peer group members, or police). The general operating rule for this category is to include anxiety scenes which have a reasonable probability of actually having occurred in the past.

5. HYPOTHESIZED INTERNAL THOUGHT PROCESSES
   DEDUCED TO BE ASSOCIATED WITH THE ORIGINAL
   (HISTORICAL) CONDITIONING SEQUENCES

Category (5) covers those hypothesized internal avoided conditioned cues which are assumed to have originated historically as a result of the external conditioning sequences. For example, if the male client had been severely beaten by his father at the age of 4 for touching his genitals, part of the original conditioning sequence might well include internal thought processes such as the desire to kill his father, fear of bodily injury via castration, fantasies associated with incestuous desires, or other "primary process" thought patterns. If these thought processes are activated immediately prior to the administration of physical punishment, they should acquire aversive loading in the same manner that exteroceptive stimuli are conditioned. The general operating rule for this category is the inclusion of hypothesized thought processes involving the eliciting of strong emotions which usually are considered taboo by society and are believed to be part of the original conditioning sequence.

6. HYPOTHESIZED STIMULUS GENERALIZATION
   EQUIVALENT OF THE PRESENTING PHOBIC
   STIMULUS

Cue category (6) incorporates the hypothesized assumption that in certain cases the phobic stimulus reported may involve predicated thinking on the client's part, a process involved in symbol development similar to the process of stimulus generalization. For example, the phobic stimulus of a knife may represent the male organ because both are long and pointed, both can be viewed as a symbol of aggression, and both may produce harm (see Dollard & Miller, 1950; Kimble, 1961). The use of this category can be viewed mainly from a research standpoint of testing certain hypotheses related to symptom development.

7. HYPOTHESIZED AVOIDED CUES ELICITING
    EMOTIONAL REACTIONS OTHER THAN THOSE
    REPRESENTED BY THE LABEL OF FEAR OR
    ANXIETY

Category (7) represents an attempt to present and subsequently extinguish directly avoidance patterns inhibiting other emotions such as anger, love, hope, and happiness. Scenes are depicted in which clients are asked to imagine themselves engaging in assertive behavior, expressing behaviors associated with love, happiness, or success. In many cases, such scenes elicit considerable anxiety upon initial presentation. The general operating rule for labeling a scene in this category is that the major emphasis of this scene is on eliciting emotions other than fear.

In practice, many of the above cue categories may be used during the treatment process. It is hoped, however, that by separating cues into the above general classification scheme, some indication of the kind of material introduced into therapy can be obtained. Further descriptive subdivision of the above categories may also be worthwhile.

VII. REVIEW OF THE LITERATURE

We have so far described the theory, rationale, and technique of implosive therapy. Such a review is believed essential before an evaluation of the experimental literature concerned with the use of the technique can be made. As noted earlier, about a decade has passed since the first publication on the IT procedure appeared in a major psychological journal (Stampfl & Levis, 1967a). Over 60 articles evaluating the technique can currently be found. For purposes of organization, these can be divided into case reports, analogue studies using nonpsychiatric populations, and studies using psychiatric populations. This review will concentrate on the latter two subdivisions. Although the case studies confirm that the IT technique has been applied to a wide variety of treatment problems, they will not be considered here because they provide little direct information concerning the technique's effectiveness or ineffectiveness.

Although the overall quality of the published studies to be reviewed varies, many were considered methodologically weak and poorly executed. Furthermore, most studies failed to take into account important procedural and theoretical issues central to the exccution of the technique. Nevertheless, it is our hope that the following review will lead to some tentative conclusions in addition to pointing the way to important unanswered research issues.

A. Studies Using Analogue, Nonpsychiatric Populations

Our literature search uncovered 23 studies that can be classified as analogue studies with nonpsychiatric populations. Although analogue studies can serve as a useful vehicle by which methodological and theoretical issues can be investigated in a well-controlled laboratory situation, such work should not be used to validate the efficacy of a therapy technique designed for patient populations (Levis, 1970b). Therefore, the purpose of this section is to summarize the methodological and theoretical issues which have been raised and point out those in need of further study. To achieve this objective we have divided our review into the following issues: (a) the analysis of the stimulus cue-category employed; (b) the length of scene duration and total scene exposure; (c) the mode of treatment presentation; (d) comparative studies; and (e) the issue of determining whether boundary conditions of the technique have been met.

Table I provides a brief summary of each of the analogue studies reviewed. At the head of each column are descriptions of the experimental factors on which each of the existing studies has been rated. In Column (1), the type of group used is labeled. The term implosive therapy (IT) will be used to describe the experimental extinction group even if the author labeled the group as "flooding." As noted earlier, the techniques differ procedurally only in the type of cue category selected for presentation. In Column (2) the number and sex of subjects in each group are presented. In Column (3), the target behavior selected is listed. Column (4) lists the type of cue category selected for the IT condition. These numbers refer directly to the classification schemes outlined earlier in this article, which included seven categories. In Columns (5), (6), and (7), the number of IT sessions given, the scene exposure per session, and the total scene exposure (exposure per session times the number of sessions) are listed, respectively. In some cases, ratings on Columns (4) through (7) represent only estimates. Column (8) lists the mode of therapy presentation. The letter T stands for taped sessions and the letters LT

TABLE I[a]

Study	Groups	No. of subjects per group and sex	Target stimulus	Cue category	No. of IT sessions	Scene Exposure per sessions (min)	Scene Exposure per study (min)	Mode of scene presentation	Boundary conditions met	% Touch/pick-up P-T	% Touch/pick-up F-U	BAT P-T	BAT F-U	Ss Report P-T	Ss Report F-U	Follow-up duration
Kirchner & Hogan (1966)	Implosive therapy	16 F	Rat	1,2,3	1	45	45	T	No	62(+)						
	Positive imagery control	19 F														
Rachman (1966)	Implosive therapy	3 F	Spider	1,2	10	20	200	LT	No	26(−)		(−)	(−)	(−)	(−)	3 months
	Systematic desensitization	3 F										(+)	(+)	(+)	(+)	
	No treatment control	3 F										(0)	(0)	(0)	(0)	
Hogan & Kirchner (1967)	Implosive therapy	21 F	Rat	1,2,3	1	39	39	LT	No	66(+)						
	Neutral imagery control	22 F								9(−)						
Hogan & Kirchner (1968)	Implosive therapy	10 F	Snake	1,2,3	1	45	45	LT	No	70(+)						
Barrett (1969)	Electric verbal therapy	10 F	Snake	1,2,3	2	NR		LT	No	40(0)						6 months
	Bibliotherapy	10 F								10(−)						
	Implosive therapy	12 F-M								83(+)	75(+)	(+)	(+)	(+)	(+)	
	Systematic desensitization	12 F-M								92(0)	100(0)	(0)	(0)	(0)	(0)	
	No treatment control	12 F-M								8(−)	25(−)	(−)	(−)	(−)	(−)	
Willis & Edwards (1969)	Implosive therapy	16 F	Mouse	1,2	2–5			LT	No	(−)		(−)		(−)	(0)	7–8 weeks
	Systematic desensitization	16 F								(+)		(+)		(+)	(0)	
	Contact time control	16 F								(0)		(0)		(0)	(0)	

Study	Treatment	N	Phobia															Follow-up
DeMoor (1970)	Implosive therapy	9 F	Snake	1,2	4	20	80	LT	No	77	44	(+)	(0)	(+)	(0)	(0)	(0)	6 months
	Systematic desensitization	9 F								77	77	(0)	(0)		(0)	(0)	(0)	
	No treatment control	9 F								33	33	(−)	(0)		(0)	(0)	(0)	
Calef & MacLean (1970)	Reactive inhibition (IT)	10	Speech anxiety	1,2	5	60	300	LT	No					(+)				
	Reciprocal inhibition (SD)	10						G						(0)				
	No treatment control	10												(−)				
Fazio (1970, Exp. I)	IT-relevant imagery	6 F	Cockroach	1,2,3,7	3	29	87	T	No	33(−)	40			(0)				
	Irrelevant imagery and discussion and IT	6 F		1,2,3,7						50(0)	50			(0)				8 weeks
	Irrelevant imagery and discussion	6 F		3						100(+)	80			(0)				
Fazio (1970, Exp. II)	Implosive therapy (3) and discussion (2)	6 F	Cockroach	1,2,3,7	3	29	87	LT	No	33	(−)			(0)				
	Discussion (3) and IT (2)	4 F		1,2,3,7	2	29	58	T		71	(+)			(0)				
	Irrelevant image (3) and discussion (2)	7 F		3						25				(0)				
Hodgson & Rachman (1970)	Implosive therapy	10 F	Snake	1,2,3	1	40	40	T	No	10(0)				(−)				
	Aversive imagery (30) and Implosive therapy (10)	10 F		1,2,3	1	10	10	G		0(0)				(0)				
	Aversive image (30) and implosive (10)	10 F		1,2,3	1	10	10			0(0)				(0)				
	Aversive imagery	10 F								39(0)				(0)				
	Pleasant imagery	10 F								0(0)				(+)				

Continued

TABLE I—Continued

Study	Groups	No. of subjects per group and sex	Target stimulus	Cue category	No. of IT sessions	Scene exposure per study (min)	Scene exposure per study (min)	Mode of scene presentation	Boundary conditions met	% Touch/pick-up		BAT		Ss Report		Follow-up duration
										P-T	F-U	P-T	F-U	P-T	F-U	
Prochaska (1971)	IT (symptom cont. cues)	13 M	Test anxiety	1,2	3	46	138	T	No			IQ Scores (+)		(+)		
	IT (dynamic cues)	13 M		5,7								(0)		(+)	(0)	
	Anxiety scenes	12 M										(−)		(0)		
	Placebo-neutral scenes	12 M										(−)	(−)	(−)	(−)	
	No treatment	11 M														
Mealica & Nawas (1971)	Implosive therapy	10 F	Snake	1,2,3	5	30	150	T	No	20(−)	10(−)	(−)	(−)	(0)	(0)	
	Implosive desensitization	10 F								20(0)	30(0)	(0)		(0)	(0)	
	Systematic desensitization	10 F								80(+)	80(+)	(+)	(+)	(0)	(0)	1 month
	Pseudotherapy	10 F								10(0)	30(0)	(0)	(0)	(0)	(0)	
	No treatment	10 F								10(0)	10(0)	(0)	(0)	(0)	(0)	
Fazio (1972)	Implosive therapy	7 F	Insect	1,2,3,7	4	NR		LT	No	57(0)				(0)	(+)	
	Supportive and directive	7 F								85(0)				(0)	(−)	
Mylar & Clement (1972)	Implosive therapy	13 M	Speech anxiety	1,2	5	60	300	T	Yes			Speech (+)	(+)	(0)	(0)	
	Systematic desensitization	13 M										(0)	(0)	(0)	(+)	
	No treatment control	13 M										(−)	(−)	(0)	(−)	
Borkovec (1972)	IT (neutral expectancy)	6 F	Snake	1,2	3	50	150	LT	Yes			(−)	(+)	(0)		
	IT (positive expectancy)	6 F										(+)	(+)	(0)		
	Systematic desensitization (N.E.)	6 F												(0)		
	Systematic desensitization (P.E.)	6 F												(0)		1 month
	Avoidance response placebo (N.E.)	6 F												(0)		

Study	Condition	N/Sex	Target					Type	AR	Outcome	Symbols
Dee (1972)	Avoidance response placebo (P.E.)	6 F									
	No therapy (N.E.)	7 F									
	No therapy (P.E.)	7 F									
	IT-no explanation	12 F	Snake	1,2,3	4	30	120	T	No	0(−)	(↓) (0)
	IT-positive expectancy	11 F								36(+)	(0) (0)
	IT-rational	12 F								33(+)	(↓) (↑) (0) (0)
	IT-positive expectancy and rational	12 F								25(0)	(+) (0)
	Neutral imagery	11 F								18(0)	(0) Test Anx. (+)
Smith & Nye (1973)	Implosive therapy	11 F–M	Test anxiety	1,3,7	5	45	225	LT	No		A-state (0); (↓) (+)
	Systematic desensitization	11 F–M									(+) (↑) (0) (↓)
	No treatment	12 F–M									(+) (↓)
Cornish & Dilley (1973)	Implosive therapy	10 F–M	Test anxiety		4	40	160	T	No	(0)	(+) (+)
	Systematic desensitization	10 F–M								(0)	(+) (0)
	Study counseling	10 F–M								(0)	(0) (↓)
	No treatment	9 F–M								(0)	
Mathews & Shaw (1973, Exp. I)	IT-massed (high arousal)	10 F	Spider	1,2,3	1	48	48	T	No		(0) (0) (0)
	IT-spaced (high arousal)	10 F		1,2,3							(0) (0) (0) 1 month
	IT-massed (low arousal)	10 F		1,2							(0) (0) (0)
	IT-spaced (low arousal)	10 F		1,2							(0) (0) (0)
Mathews & Shaw (1973, Exp. II)	IT low arousal–high arousal	10 F		1,2,3	1	48	48	T	Yes		(0) (0)
	IT high arousal–low arousal	10 F		1,2,3							(0) (0)

Continued

TABLE I—Continued

(1) Study	(1) Groups	(2) No. of subjects per group and sex	(3) Target stimulus	(4) Cue category	(5) No. of IT sessions	(6) Scene Exposure per sessions (min)	(7) Scene Exposure per study (min)	(8) Mode of scene presentation	(9) Boundary conditions met	(10) % Touch/pick-up P-T	(10) F-U	(11) BAT P-T	(11) F-U	(12) Ss Report P-T	(12) F-U	(13) Follow-up duration
Hekmat (1973)	Implosive therapy	10 F–M	Rat	1,2,3	1	40	40	LT	No			(−)		(−)		
	Systematic desensitization	10 F–M										(+)		(+)		
	Semantic desensitization	10 F–M										(+)		(+)		
	Pseudo desensitization	10 F–M										(+)		(0)		
Dawley & Wenrich (1973)	Implosive therapy	12	Test anxiety	1,2	5	30	150	LT	No					(+)	(+)	1 month
	Placebo	12						G						(0)	(0)	
	No treatment control	12												(−)	(−)	
McCutcheon & Adams (1975) Exp. I	IT-relevant imagery	4 F	Surgery	1,2	1	20	20	T	No			(0)		(0)		
	IT-irrelevant imagery	4 F										(0)				
	Control imagery	4 F										(0)				
McCutcheon & Adams (1975, Exp. II)	IT-relevant imagery	6 F	Surgery	1,2	1	60	60	T	Yes			(+)		(0)		
	IT-irrelevant imagery	6 F										(−)				
	Control-no imagery	6 F										(−)				
Orenstein & Carr (1975)	Implosive therapy	8 F	Rat	1,2,3	1	39	39	T	Yes				(0)	(−)		1 week
	Information placebo	8 F										(0)	(0)	(+)		
	No treatment	8 F										(0)	(0)	(0)		

aThis table is designed to provide only a cursory overview of the analogue studies received. Dimensions selected for inclusion are not all-inclusive. For complete statements of procedure and data analyses, the reader is referred directly to the primary source. A detailed description of how to interpret this table can be found on pp. 327 and 333.

stand for presentation by a "live" therapist. The letter G means the therapy was presented in a group session. Column (9) rates each study as to whether the data suggest that the boundary conditions of the technique were met. That is to say, was a diminution of anxiety (self-report, therapist's observation, physiological recordings) for the IT group shown either during the individual therapy session or with repeated sessions? These data are considered critical since repeated presentation of scenes is required until diminution of the anxiety response is observed.

    Columns (10) through (12) provide a summary of the obtained results. Column (10) lists the percentage of subjects in each group that touched or made contact with a given phobic target stimulus. We believe that this measure provides the most stringent test of treatment effectiveness. Column (11) includes an analysis of the frequently used Behavioral Avoidance Test (BAT). This test combines an approach (distance) and contact measure into one rating scale. The measure usually involves a difference score between pre- and post-test avoidance of a given phobic test stimulus. Column (12) reports differences obtained on subjective indices such as paper-pencil rating scales. Columns (10) through (12) are divided into two parts. The first includes a report of results during the post-test period (PT) whereas the second considers the follow-up period (FU), if administered.

    Significant differences ($p < .05$) between groups on each of the measures in Columns (10) through (12) are reported by either a (+) or a (−) sign. Nonsignificant differences are indicated by (0). The (+) sign indicates the group which showed the greater improvement. The implosive therapy group serves as the reference group for all comparisons. Thus, if in a given study a (+) appears after the IT group, one need only look down the column until the group with a (−) is found. It is these two groups which were found to differ reliably from each other, with the (+) group showing the greater improvement. If the IT group is followed by a (0), this indicates the IT group was not found to be significantly different from any other group. If the IT group receives either a (+) or (−) designation and is compared with a group receiving a (0), no reliable difference was found between these groups. For a reliable difference to have occurred, a (+) and a (−) condition must be compared.

    Column (13) indicates the duration of the follow-up (FU) period. If data are not available the appropriate space is left blank. Remember that Columns (4) through (7) sometimes involve estimates, since many studies failed to be specific about these factors.

1. STIMULUS CUE CATEGORY LEVEL

Although the principle of experimental extinction appears straightforward in theory, implementation can be extremely complex, requiring a good deal of clinical sensitivity. The cues introduced should be tailor-made to each subject's history. Although it was suggested earlier in the theory section that certain stimulus situations may be correlated with certain target behaviors, one must always take into consideration the individual difference variable. For example, we have found that although many rat phobic subjects are afraid that they might be bitten, some seem more afraid of, or repulsed by, other aspects of the rat (e.g., the tail). The point is that as there is no "universal" hierarchy for administration of systematic desensitization, there is no universal implosive scene. Yet, in many of the studies reviewed, one received the impression that this was the case. Most experiments failed to provide any systematic description of the type of cues introduced. Furthermore, it was not uncommon to find experimenters presenting material from stimulus cue categories (3) through (7) to subjects receiving implosion, while subjects receiving systematic desensitization were presented material from levels (1) and (2).

It was surprising to find that most investigators failed to justify or document the relevance of the cue category introduced. Many of the cues selected by experimenters seemed irrelevant and often were associated with negative results. For example, Fazio (1970) presented implosive scenes which included material involved with loss of control, aggression, and "other psychodynamic themes" to subjects fearful of cockroaches. We fail to see the importance of such material, and Fazio failed to document the rationale for their inclusion. Nor did he objectively establish that the introduction of such cues led to an increase in anxiety. If we are correct that such cues had little to do with the fear of cockroaches, then the results of such a tactic would be to provide too little exposure to more appropriate cues, decreasing the possibility of extinguishing the fear response to the target behavior.

Many of the analogue investigations reviewed, especially those using standardized taped procedures, appeared to make assumptions regarding the appropriate cue content which were not only undocumented but from experience seemed incorrect. Most failed to produce any positive results for the IT subjects. One is still left with the problem of determining whether the procedure was inappropriately applied or whether an extinction technique failed to work at this level of analysis. In the analogue therapy situation, this problem might be conceived of as a problem in generalization. A study by Mealiea and Nawas (1971) serves to illustrate this point. Fifty female snake phobics selected on the basis of a BAT were randomly assigned to groups receiving either no treatment, systematic desensitization, pseudotherapy, implosive desensitizations (implosive scenes presented in a systematic desensitization context), or implosive therapy. Subjects in the systematic desensitization group received a hierarchy based on the 20-step BAT (cue levels 1 and 2). Subjects in the implosive therapy group received scenes of giant snakes choking them and killing them (cue level 3). Not only does this confound the treatment manipulation, but since this material is so far removed from the actual situation on which the subject is tested, it is possible that a generalization of extinction decrement occurred.

A study by Mylar and Clement (1972) suggests that the above conclusion is indeed likely. In this experiment, theology students displaying speech anxiety were either imploded or systematically desensitized (SD). The investigators held scene content constant across groups. Although not as rigorously as possible, an attempt was made to equalize scene exposure, in that the number of visualization periods per session was controlled. The results of the experiment showed no significant differences on several dependent measures between the IT and SD groups. Such an outcome would be predicted from the hypothesis that extinction is a function of total nonreinforced CS exposure (Shipley *et al.*, 1971). Thus, the findings of this study indicate that when the same material is presented in both SD and IT scenes for approximately the same duration, identical results occur in terms of anxiety reduction. However, this material should be effective. Otherwise, little behavioral change is expected to take place. Again, the data of Mealiea and Nawas (1971) support this hypothesis in that the implosive group showed no change on behavioral avoidance measures whereas significant changes were observed on attitudinal measures. Considering the situational specificity of human behavior (Mischel, 1968), these results might have been expected.

Summarizing the above point, many of the negative results found using implosive therapy (Fazio, 1970; Mathews & Shaw, 1973; Mealiea & Nawas, 1971) may have resulted from experimenters presenting material inappropriately related to the subjects' fears. It would appear that presentation of material above stimulus cue levels (1) and (2) may not be appropriate for isolated fears studied in the analogue situation. If such material (level 3 and above) is to be effective, it is likely that substantial amounts of exposure to cue levels (1) and (2) may have to be given first. Such a tactic is often used in IT when it is applied to clinical cases. That is to say, it is often necessary to extinguish material believed located at a point further removed from the original UCS before proceeding to higher levels of anxiety-eliciting material believed to be more closely associated with the original UCS (Stampfl & Levis, 1967a).

One notable exception to the above observation involves a study by Prochaska (1971). He compared test-anxious groups imploded on symptom-contingent cues (levels 1, 2) and "dynamic cues" (levels 5, 7). The target behavior selected deviated from the usual approach of using small animals. His results indicated that both were equally effective in producing positive increases on test scores. It is important, however, to note that work has been done that suggests that test anxiety consists of both of these components. Thus, either set of material should be effective (see Prochaska, 1971, p. 133).

Clearly, more parametric work is needed in this area, not only in the comparison of IT's effectiveness in using different levels of cue categories, but also in the investigation of individual differences in affinity to particular cue levels and content.

2. SCENE DURATION AND TOTAL EXPOSURE

Surprisingly little work has been done in the analogue area on the importance of duration of scene presentation and total scene exposure. In fact, only two studies (Mathews & Shaw, 1973; McCutcheon & Adams, 1975) were found which directly relate to these variables. From the standpoint of the IT technique, it is critical that scene material be presented until diminution of the anxiety response is obtained (Stampfl & Levis, 1967a, 1969, 1973b; Staub, 1968). Related also to this issue is the possibility raised by Wolpe (1958) and Eysenck (1968) that termination of treatment before anxiety reduction has taken place may actually serve to sensitize the subject. The McCutcheon and Adams' experiment is especially relevant in light of this warning. These authors report a study in which female subjects were selected on the basis of being able to view a film depicting surgery for less than a 3-minute period. Following this pretest, subjects were assigned to one of three groups: a group receiving relevant imagery (witnessing an operation), one receiving irrelevant imagery (anxiety-provoking scenes involving snakes), or a no-treatment control group. The treatment period lasted 20 minutes.

Nonspecific GSR fluctuations were recorded during the entire procedure as a measure of arousal. The results showed that there were no significant differences among the groups in film-viewing time during the post-test. However, GSR fluctuations during the post-test increased for the relevant imagery group. Thus, these data suggest that sensitization (at least at the physiological level) may have taken place. However, this interpretation must be considered in light of the second experiment carried out by these investigators. The procedures of the second experiment were similar to those of the first, except that the groups (relevant, irrelevant, and control) received 60 minutes of treatment rather than 20 minutes. The post-test data showed that the relevant-imagery group significantly increased their viewing time of the film and showed fewer GSR fluctuations (less arousal) than either of the other groups. These data strongly suggest that scene duration is a critical factor in the subsequent reduction of avoidance behavior, and that sensitization may take place if scene duration is not sufficient to bring about a reduction in anxiety to the material being presented.

Similar results are presented by Mathews and Shaw (1973), who had spider phobic subjects undergo either massed or spaced flooding trials. In addition, the arousal value (high arousal vs. low arousal) of the material was manipulated, yielding a 2 X 2 factorial design. Unfortunately, the high arousal material used by these experimenters was found to have little effect, perhaps because it was introduced too early in the treatment process (Stampfl & Levis, 1967a). However, the low arousal material did produce an extinction effect. Returning to the main point of the discussion, massed (48 minute) presentation of the low arousal material was more effective in reducing avoidance behavior on the post-test BAT than spaced six (8 minute) presentations of the same material separated by 4 minute neutral stories. These data appear to support the notion that a single massed exposure is more effective than several shorter exposures of the same *total* duration. Such results contradict recent infrahuman research (Shipley, 1974), demonstrating that *total* duration is the important variable in fear extinction. Clearly, more work is needed on this important topic.

Inspection of Table I gives credence to the suggestion that the duration variable is important. With the exception of two studies reviewed (Mealiea & Nawas, 1971; Rachman, 1966), positive results were obtained with the implosive procedure when total durations of 100 minutes or more were used at the analogue level. An exception to this finding is the study by Hogan and Kirchner (1968), in which only a 45 minute scene was given and a positive effect was obtained. The studies showing negative results (Mealiea & Nawas, 1971; Rachman, 1966) with long exposure durations suffer from design problems which may have contributed to the negative findings.

In summary, scene duration and total scene exposure appear to be important variables in need of systematic parametric manipulation both at the patient and analogue level.

3. MODE OF SCENE PRESENTATION

As previously suggested by Levis (1974), the use of tape recordings in presenting IT material potentially violates the IT procedure in two important ways. First, the cues presented are not tailor-made to a given subject or altered by a subject's feedback or lack of it. Second, avoidance responses on the part of the subject during the session cannot be blocked or extinguished. Both of these problems relate to issues discussed in the preceding section concerning negative results that often appear correlated with inappropriate use of the cue content levels, as well as inappropriate selection of scene material. Although it is legitimate to hypothesize that certain material is often correlated with a particular problem (i.e., bodily injury with phobias), the validity of such notions must be demonstrated experimentally. It is critical that the hypothesized material introduced be shown to activate motivational properties correlated with the subject's pathology. This point appears to be neglected frequently by analogue investigators.

Referring again to Table I, interesting trends can be found. Looking down Column (8), one finds that in a number of cases in which taped therapy was used, negative results were shown (Dee, 1972; Fazio, 1970; Hodgson & Rachman, 1970; Mealiea & Nawas, 1971; Orenstein & Carr, 1975). However, because so many other factors varied among these studies (e.g., scene duration and target behavior) it would be difficult to attribute the lack of results only to the taped versus live-therapist distinction. On the other hand, some studies apparently found taped therapy presentations to be effective in changing some or all of the dependent measures manipulated (Cornish & Dilley, 1973; Kirchner & Hogan, 1966; Mathews & Shaw, 1973; McCutcheon & Adams, 1975, Experiment 2; Mylar & Clements, 1972; Prochaska, 1971).

Similarly, studies using live therapists have shown mixed results.

Borkovec (1972), Calef and MacLean (1970), Dawley and Wenrich (1973), DeMoor (1970), Hogan and Kirchner (1967), and Smith and Nye (1973) all found decreases in avoidance behavior or anxiety ratings with implosive techniques. Fazio (1972) found that supportive therapy was superior to implosive therapy in the reduction of avoidance of cockroaches. Hekmat (1973) provides data that suggest systematic desensitization is better at reducing rat avoidance than implosive therapy, although his systematic desensitization group received more therapy sessions than the IT group. Both of the other two remaining studies showing a lack of effects with implosive therapy suffer from methodological difficulties (Rachman, 1966; Willis & Edwards, 1969). The Willis and Edwards study presented little data in regard to the inclusion of subjects. Subjects were assigned to the groups on the basis of Fear Survey scores (FSS), in spite of the fact that a behavioral avoidance test was conducted. The possibility exists that some of the subjects may have been able to touch or pick up the mouse prior to therapy. The Rachman study allows even fewer conclusions to be drawn since the groups contained only three subjects, and the flooding group was completed at a different time than the systematic desensitization and control group.

Considering the above data, it would seem that the more appropriate question to ask might be: Under what conditions are taped therapy procedures effective or ineffective? Differences may result from an uninvestigated third factor (e.g., subject expectation, demand characteristics, subject's ability to imagine with affect). What is being stated here is that the relevant literature does not currently answer these questions. To our knowledge, no experiment has been done in which taped versus live presentation of the same material has been administered to comparable groups of subjects. The closest any experiment has come to looking at these effects was a study by Kirchner and Hogan (1966), which essentially replicated the results of another experiment by these same authors in which a live therapist was used (Hogan & Kirchner, 1967). However, such a demonstration is not an appropriate test of the differences in live versus taped presentations since the experiments were separated in time and differed on a variety of dimensions (e.g., the tape study used group administration of material). In addition, these experiments can be criticized for a variety of methodological problems that occurred during the administration of the procedure and during testing. Thus, questions as to whether the effects of implosive therapy are specific to the IT procedure, to some nonspecific effects produced by the therapist, or perhaps to the interaction of the two are still open.

4. STUDIES CONTRASTING IMPLOSIVE THERAPY WITH OTHER TREATMENT TECHNIQUES

A number of experiments have compared IT with other treatment techniques. Generally, the choice for the comparison treatment has been systematic desensitization (SD), since differences in the theoretical rationale between the two treatments make it possible to generate contrasting predictions. Before we review these studies, it is important to discuss an important procedural issue relating to the contrasting predictions mentioned above.

It should be noted that embedded within the countercondi- tioning procedure used during SD is an extinction procedure. A review of the relevant infrahuman literature by Wilson and Davison (1971) concluded that it was this extinction procedure that results in the anxiety decrement observed, not the counterconditioning manip- ulation. Considering the above data as well as infrahuman data indicating that extinction is a function of time in the presence of the nonreinforced CS (Shipley, 1974; Shipley et al., 1971), it becomes imperative that studies contrasting these techniques equate not only the material to which the subject is exposed, but also the length of time the subject is exposed to this material. It is not sufficient to equate therapy time, since it is generally true that only a portion of each session is spent visualizing material from the hypothesized avoidance hierarchy. Only one study was found which attempted to control stimulus exposure time. This experiment, carried out by Mylar and Clement (1972), found no differences between SD and IT procedures. Unfortunately, in order to control the above-mentioned variable, it was necessary for the authors to run a nonstandard SD procedure. Such changes reduce generalization to the typical SD technique employed in the clinical setting (Bernstein & Paul, 1971). However, Mylar and Clement's study does serve as a starting point for future comparisons of the procedures.

Returning to the review of the literature relevant to this section, we find very little adequate work contrasting SD and IT procedures. The emphasis will be placed upon studies in which a live therapist was used and in which appropriate clinical representations of the procedure (either SD or IT) were used.

One of the first studies to meet these criteria was a design carried out by Barrett (1969). In this study, IT was contrasted with SD and a waiting list control. Subjects who were unable to hold or touch a harmless snake were used. The IT group received two 50-minute clinical interviews followed by two sessions of implosive therapy of unspecified duration. According to Barrett's report, scenes included two standard themes which involved confrontation with snakes or death resulting from interactions with a snake. Implosive sessions were carried out until a significant diminution in anxiety was observed. Systematic desensitization was continued for up to 11 sessions to a criterion such that the entire hierarchy could be presented twice without signs of anxiety by the subject. Hierarchy material was individually designed for each subject. The nontreated control group received the pretest, the post-test, and the follow-up testing at the same intervals as the experimental groups.

Barrett's results showed that nearly all of the subjects who received IT or SD picked up the snake on the post-test. Statistical analysis indicated that these two groups differed significantly from the control group, but not from each other. Changes in other dependent measures, FSS-III snake fear rating, total FSS-III score, also followed this pattern. Although no reliable differences were found between SD and IT groups during the 6-month follow-up period, Barrett analyzed the variance in the avoidance test change scores. He reported that the variance decreased for both the IT and SD groups from the pretest to the post-test. However, from the post-test to the follow-up, the variance scores continued to decrease for the SD group while the variance scores for the IT group increased. Barrett, as well as others (e.g., Morganstern, 1973), cite these findings as evidence for a deterioration effect with IT. Levis (1974) has recently reviewed these arguments, citing unpublished portions of the dissertation on which Barrett's paper was based. He reports that the difference in variance occurred only on one of the measures (the avoidance test change scores). Further, these differences are attributed to only three subjects, two of whom changed in the negative directions. Clearly, the variance analysis is inappropriate since the implosive groups received only two sessions of therapy, while the SD groups received up to 11 sessions. The use of an F test to anaylze differences in variance is also questionable. Since the two groups were not equated on either therapy or visualization time or on content of stimulus materials, it would seem that no strong statements can be made from this study regarding deterioration effects. Conversely, it would seem that the IT treatment was remarkably effective considering the limited time spent in therapy by the IT subjects.

Willis and Edwards (1969) also compared SD and IT procedures. In addition, a therapy contact placebo group was used as a control. It is extremely difficult to critically evaluate the Willis and Edwards study since these authors present almost none of the procedural specifics. For example, it is impossible to conclude from their published report how long the therapy sessions were, how many therapy sessions were given, and what cue content was used. Further, as discussed earlier, it would appear that subjects were assigned to groups such that the distribution of FSS scores (total and mouse rating) were similar within each of the groups rather than on the basis of pretest BAT scores. Considering the generally low correlation that is found between BAT scores and self-report measures (Lang, 1969), it is possible that a bias could have developed such that the behaviorally less fearful subjects ended up in the SD group. However, Willis and Edwards present no means nor did they test this possibility. In addition, no significant differences were shown between therapy groups on the most stringent measure of fear reduction, the pick-up and hold measure.

Hekmat (1973) compared SD, semantic desensitization, and IT procedures with a neutral scene semantic control group. Rat phobic college students served as subjects. The results showed that the two desensitization procedures produced a greater reduction in avoidance when compared to the neutral scene control group. The implosive group did not differ from the controls. However, it would seem, if the 100-minute exposure hypothesis presented earlier is considered, that Hekmat did not present enough exposure to the material (see Table I) to produce sufficient anxiety reduction. Hekmat (1973) himself acknowledges this point (pp. 207–208), stating that exposure to the scenes was not as long as with previous successful studies.

Another study in the literature which used a live therapist and closely approximated clinical procedures was conducted by Borkovec (1972). Borkovec's study consisted of four groups: SD, IT, an avoidance response group in which subjects received anxiety scenes and were instructed to visualize an avoidance response when they experienced anxiety, and a no-treatment group. Half the subjects in each group were exposed to a positive-expectancy manipulation and half to a neutral-expectancy condition. Actual therapists were used, and each treatment subject was seen for 4 contact hours, 3 of which actually involved formal treatments. All subjects were defined as snake phobics. Borkovec concluded that, regardless of expectancy condition, both the SD and IT groups resulted in lowered pulse rate and tended to produce decreases in self-reported fear. The avoidance response group (which can also be viewed as an extinction group) demonstrated nearly equal improvement. Interestingly, a strong expectancy effect was obtained on the overt behavioral avoidance test measure. The positive expectancy condition produced the biggest effect on the IT group and also affected the avoidance response group. The SD group was not reliably affected by the expectancy manipulation and did not improve either at the post-test or follow-up period on the avoidance measure when compared to the no-treatment control. On the other hand, the IT group differed reliably from the no-treatment group at the post-test period. The IT group also produced a reliable reduction in avoidance behavior at the follow-up period in a similar comparison, which was also the case for the avoidance response group. None of the neutral-expectancy therapy groups differed reliably in avoidance behavior from the no-treatment control group.

Borkovec's findings suggest an interesting hypothesis. It is quite possible that a positive expectancy statement is needed in conjunction with an extinction therapy like IT to facilitate behavioral change on the avoidance measurement. This hypothesis appears especially reasonable when normal subjects are being tested, where the motivation for treatment is perhaps not as strong as that at the patient level. To many "phobic" individuals, an extinction or forced CS exposure procedure may well be viewed as a counterintuitive procedure which, when used on a given subject, may well elicit the implicit self-instruction that experiencing an increase in anxiety might "make me worse." A trained IT therapist would implode this defense, but it is unlikely that defenses of this nature were dealt with in the Borkovec study. A positive expectancy statement or well-worked rationale presented prior to therapy could serve to eliminate the defense which could partially block therapy gains. It is also possible that expectancy rather than the IT procedure produced most of the change but physiological and rating scale changes were reported in the neutral IT expectancy group. Unfortunately, few investigators have provided sufficient information in their articles to determine what instructional sets or rationales were administered. More work is definitely needed in this area.

Smith and Nye (1973) selected test-anxious college students as subjects. The dependent measures consisted of two questionnaires: the Test Anxiety scale and the A-State Anxiety scale. In addition, subjects' pre- and post-therapy grade point averages (GPA) were analyzed. Treatment consisted of seven 45-minute sessions. Subjects assigned to the SD group underwent desensitization to a 16-item hierarchy dealing with academic test situations. Implosive therapy subjects were imploded on material previously disclosed by the subject to be anxiety provoking. Although these procedures are very much analogous to those used in clinical practice, scene content was allowed to vary and thus the specific treatments are difficult to compare. The results showed that the IT group decreased on test anxiety questionnaire scores as did the SD group. In addition, the SD group also decreased on the A-State questionnaire. On the GPA dependent measure, the SD group showed a significant increase from pre- to post-therapy while the implosive group remained the same. However, as Smith and Nye noted, the groups were not equivalent at the start of therapy, as the IT group had a higher GPA. Because of the nonequality of the experimental groups prior to treatment, conclusions from the data presented in this study are difficult.

Rachman (1966) treated three spider phobics using an IT technique. Each subject received 10 sessions in which 10 scenes were presented for 2 minutes. Fear assessment was made with a behavioral avoidance test prior to treatment, after treatment, and 3 months later. These data were compared to data from subjects tested in an earlier experiment who underwent a desensitization or relaxation control procedure. The results of this comparison indicated that both at the time of testing and at the 3-month follow-up the desensitization and relaxation group estimated that they were less fearful and showed closer approach on the BAT. However, because of the time confound outlined above, these data might also be explained by a number of alternate factors and thus provide no information in regard to differences in effectiveness of the two techniques. Further, since no information is provided as to the procedures used in the desensitization–relaxation procedure, it is not known how these groups compare on several important variables (e.g., stimulus cue level, exposure duration).

DeMoor (1970) did a study in which SD was contrasted with IT with snake phobic college students. Five sessions of each treatment were provided. According to DeMoor's analysis, there were no significant differences between the treatment groups on any of the dependent measures, including the behavioral avoidance test scores. DeMoor did note, however, that deterioration effects were present during the follow-up test (6 months) in that some of the IT subjects who had picked up the snake on the post-test later failed to do so on follow-up. Fortunately, DeMoor presented the individual subject data in his report. If one inspects these data, it becomes apparent that several of the subjects in the treatment and control groups touched the snake on the pretest. If these subjects are dropped from the analysis (since in most studies such subjects would not be considered to be phobic), the results of the treatments are nearly identical. The only deterioration that is shown on the follow-up test by the IT group results from one subject who rapidly touched the snake on the post-test and later only opened the window used to gain access to the animal. Thus, the effectiveness and stability of the treatment seem comparable.

The final study on this subject to be reviewed was carried out by Calef and MacLean (1970). Although these investigators attribute the IT-like procedure used to a reactive inhibition process, explaining its effectiveness on a cognitive basis, the procedure essentially reflects the IT procedures followed in the previous studies. College students were separated into high and low speech-anxiety groups on the basis of a rating scale (PRCS). The subjects were then randomly assigned to groups receiving either reciprocal inhibition (SD), reactive inhibition (IT), or no treatment. The Taylor Manifest Anxiety Scale (TMAS) was used as an additional dependent measure. Following treatment, the results indicated that both the reciprocal inhibition and reactive inhibition groups showed reduced anxiety scores on the PRCS. No differences were shown on the TMAS. From these data, Calef and MacLean concluded that the reactive inhibition procedure was more efficient because it was simpler. Although these results suggest that the reactive inhibition procedure produces reports of reduced anxiety on a questionnaire, it is unknown what relationship these questionnaire scores have to actual public speaking ability or performance. Certainly, this study should have included an actual behavioral speech test as a dependent measure rather than only questionnaire data.

In summary, it would seem that no strong statements can be made in regard to an analogue comparison between IT and SD procedures. Most of the relevant studies contained procedural or methodological flaws. Clearly, more parametric research is needed in this area.

5. EVIDENCE FOR OBTAINMENT OF BOUNDARY CONDITIONS

The final research issue to be discussed in this section involves the importance of presenting evidence that the boundary conditions of the implosive procedure have been met for each subject treated.

This issue is central to the evaluation of any treatment process. By adopting such a strategy for each subject, the process of therapy evaluation can be shortened, as well as reducing arguments about a given therapist's effectiveness, about the relevance of a given scene or issue related to duration of scene presentation. In establishing the boundary conditions for effective IT presentation, it is important to obtain individual measurements on each subject to determine objectively the following points: (1) Do the cues introduced lead to an increase in anxiety? (2) Does their continual repetition produce an extinction effect? (3) Does the extinction effect correlate positively with a reduction in symptomology? If points (1) and (2) are established and point (3) does not occur, then the procedure used is clearly ineffective. If points (1) and (2) are not met and point (3) materializes, then the effect is unrelated to the theoretical structure outlined for the implosive therapy technique.

It will be clear from the above that the appropriate point at which the subject should be tested is when points (1) and (2) are met, not at some time arbitrarily set by the investigator. Although such a procedure does not control for total contact time, a more accurate analogue of the technique is treated since clinical patients are not terminated based on time schedules, but rather when anxiety is reduced. It is believed that this design could be used with any technique or in the comparison of any technique.

In light of this proposal we will now consider those studies in which data were provided that suggest that the boundary conditions of implosive therapy were met. However, some clarification may be necessary here in that there are two processes by which anxiety reduction can appear to have taken place. In the first process, the subject actually experiences a reduction in anxiety to the material. This is the boundary condition which was referred to above and thus should be correlated with symptom reduction. In the second process, the subject learns an avoidance or blocking response to the material being presented, which inhibits rather than extinguishes the occurrence of anxiety. Such an effect will not lead to symptom reduction. It is because of this latter possibility that taped implosive sessions may provide an inappropriate test of the effectiveness of implosive therapy. Avoidance behavior on the part of the subject cannot be monitored easily or dealt with directly. Unfortunately, none of the existing studies on this topic presents individual subject data on either of these points. Therefore, we must be content, at present, with group analysis.

The first experiment to take account of these issues was carried out by Hogan and Kirchner (1967). During this experiment, female college students who refused to pick up a rat during a pretest were randomly assigned to two groups, one receiving implosion and one receiving neutral imagery. During the therapy session, subjects were connected to a polygraph which monitored their heartbeat and GSR. Therapy time was allowed to vary since the scientists felt it was appropriate to let the therapy session proceed at a pace set by the subject's progress. Physiological data were recorded in order to demonstrate that the subject who received implosion became more anxious during the sessions, as would be predicted from the implosion model. An analysis of the polygraph records by blind raters confirmed this hypothesis. Following the therapy session, two-thirds of the group that had received implosive therapy picked up the rat, while only 9% of the control group were able to perform this task. From these data, Hogan and Kirchner concluded that IT is an effective method of fear reduction. However, Hogan and Kirchner's post-test procedure was marred by the fact that the individual administering the post-test was aware of group membership. Unfortunately, Hogan and Kirchner do not present enough details of the post-test procedure to evaluate how large an effect this may have been. Nonetheless, the study was the first attempt to use an objective measure of anxiety (heart rate, GSR) to show that at least part of the boundary conditions of implosive therapy were met. Data were not presented to show whether a diminution in these measures occurred as the therapy session progressed.

The next study to appear on this topic was done by Mealiea and Nawas (1971), with snake phobic coeds. These experimenters monitored anxiety during taped IT sessions using a paper-pencil measure (Paul, 1966). Although no formal analysis of the data was carried out, Mealiea and Nawas reported that the mean number of anxiety-related behaviors decreased over sessions. Although the direction of positive change for the IT subjects on the behavioral avoidance measure was greater than the non-treated control, the difference was not found to be reliable by the conservative test used (Tukey HSD). It should be recalled from our earlier description of this study that the material presented to the implosive group may have been inappropriate to their fears and too far removed from the situation in which the subjects were tested, thus leading to a generalization decrement. Also, as outlined earlier, this material differed in content from the material given the comparative treatment groups.

Borkovec (1972, 1974) presents data relevant to the hypothesis that a decrease in symptoms is correlated with reduction of anxiety responding during therapy sessions. As discussed earlier, Borkovec's study compared the effectiveness of SD and IT to an avoidance response placebo group using snake phobic college students. In addition, half the subjects underwent an expectancy manipulation designed to establish a positive set while the other half received a neutral expectancy instructional set. Therapy sessions were carefully equated for time and content. During each of the sessions, physiological variables (heart rate and skin conductance) were recorded during visualization of the cue items. The results showed that the basal skin conductance level decreased over ordinal hierarchy items, which suggests an extinction-like function. The heart-rate data indicated that subjects receiving IT showed greater reduction in heart rate over hierarchy items than the SD group. Both the SD and IT groups showed reduction in heart rate when compared with the avoidance response placebo. To a certain extent, the heart-rate differences between SD and IT groups might be artifactual, since the SD group, by virtue of its relaxation training, was at a lower level of arousal to begin with. Considering these physiological data, it would appear that the boundary conditions of the implosion model were met. The behavioral avoidance post-test revealed that the IT group showed significant improvement when compared to controls but only under conditions of positive expectancy.

Mylar and Clement (1972) employed a self-report measure of anxiety to evaluate the treatment process. Three groups were tested: SD, IT, and a no-treatment control. These experimenters used speech-anxious theology students as subjects. As with the Borkovec study, therapy duration and content were controlled. The process variable used by Mylar and Clement was the subject's report of the subjective unit of distress level (SUD) which he experienced to the scene just presented to him via a tape recorder. Five sessions were given. These data showed reductions in the reported SUD levels for both treatment groups (IT and SD) across sessions, providing evidence that the boundary conditions had been met. As would be predicted from the implosion model, the IT group reports were higher, probably because they were not relaxed during the procedure. Unfortunately, Mylar and Clement did not analyze these data statistically. A rating of each subject's performance during a 6-minute speech showed that the treatment groups differed significantly from the no-treatment control group at the post-test in terms of overt anxiety displayed. As in the studies previously discussed, these data support the notion that once the boundary conditions of IT are met symptom reduction occurs.

Despite the positive findings of the above studies, results that do not support the boundary condition hypothesis have also been reported. Orenstein and Carr (1975) conducted an experiment in which heart rate was monitored during tape-recorded implosive sessions. Two control groups were used, an information placebo group and a no-treatment group. The subjects were rat phobic coeds. In spite of the fact that heart rates of the implosive group first increased and then decreased to the level of the subjects in the information placebo group, no significant change was observed on the behavioral avoidance test. However, there appear to be several problems with the procedure used in this experiment. First, therapy was administered by tape recording, which, as discussed earlier, does not prevent the subject from engaging in defensive tactics. Thus the observed diminution might have resulted from defensive tactics on the part of the subject rather than actual extinction to the material. Second, the therapy session was only 39 minutes long. According to the observation made earlier with regard to Table I, few positive affects from implosive therapy occur when less than 100 minutes of scene exposure are given. Third, the cue content of the implosive scenes was not separated by the investigators. As discussed above, it is possible that a generalization decrement might have occurred from therapy session to the post-test situation if this material were at an inappropriate cue level. Nevertheless, the available evidence is against predictions made from the implosive model.

The final study to be discussed here is by McCutcheon and Adams (1975). It should be recalled that portions of this experiment were reviewed during the discussion of scene duration. Once again, the subjects of this study were college women who terminated viewing a film depicting surgery in less than 3 minutes. Similarly, the post-test measure was the amount of time the subject was able to view the film before terminating its showing. Two experiments were run. In experiment 1, the therapy session was 20 minutes long. Groups received either surgery-related imagery, irrelevant but arousing imagery consisting of scenes involving snakes, and a control group receiving no treatment. Nonspecific GSR fluctuations were recorded throughout the procedure. Analysis of these data revealed that both the "relevant" and "irrelevant" imagery groups showed significant increases in nonspecific fluctuations in comparison to the control group. These increases did not decrease during the therapy session. Post-test viewing time did not differ among the groups nor did viewing time change from pretest levels. Experiment 2 followed the same procedure except that 60-minute therapy sessions were used. The GSR data recorded during these sessions replicated the results for the "relevant" and "irrelevant" image groups for the first 20 minutes. However, as the therapy session progressed past this point, the arousal level decreased and finally reached the low level displayed by the no-treatment group. The post-test data revealed that only the relevant-imagery group showed significant increases in viewing time. Overall, the results of these two studies indicate that when therapy fails to meet the boundary conditions outlined earlier (Experiment 1), no behavioral change is shown. However, when the boundary conditions are met, significant reduction in avoidance behavior results. A further implication of this study is that meeting the boundary condition is closely related to total duration of scene exposure, although it is probable that other variables play a significant role (e.g., scene content).

In summary, the boundary conditions of implosive therapy must be met before symptom reduction can take place. Specifically, these boundary conditions are an initial increase in anxiety, followed by a decrease. It seems apparent that two further stipulations must be placed on the obtainment of these boundary conditions. First, diminution in anxiety must result from habituation or extinction effects and not from the operation of defensive or blocking mechanisms of the subject. Indirect support for this stipulation comes from the general ineffectiveness of taped therapy procedures, which do not control these defensive tactics. However, more direct evidence of this hypothesis is needed through studies that objectively measure defensive tactics of the subject. A step in this direction is a recent study by Boudewyns and Levis (1975), which investigated a personality variable (ego strength) hypothesized to be a measure of the patient's defensiveness. The second stipulation that must be considered in relation to the boundary condition hypothesis is that the material presented must be relevant to the target behavior analyzed. As demonstrated by the McCutcheon and Adams (1975) study, an identical arousal function (increase followed by decrease) was generated by the "irrelevant" imagery group. However, no change in the target behavior (film viewing) was observed. Both of these issues need further investigation so that the parameters for the effective utilization of implosive therapy can be known. Greater operational specificity is clearly needed.

It should be apparent that none of the issues discussed above has been sufficiently investigated, utilizing parametric designs. Such a conclusion seems at variance with the rationale generally given for the analogue therapy experiment (Levis, 1970b). Considering this observation, it seems clear what direction future research should take. Before gross comparisons between two techniques are made, parametric research should be undertaken in which the possible effective components of a single technique are investigated.

Although no strong conclusions can be reached, some evidence exists at the analogue level that the implosive procedure is effective in reducing objectively defined avoidance behavior. The obtainment of positive results appears to be related to whether the technique is procedurally administered in the manner suggested by Stampfl. In this respect, Morganstern (1973) appears to be correct in his generalization that many of the investigators who are able to obtain positive effects are those who are proponents of the technique. One possible reason for this is that these investigators are probably cognizant of the important variables in the use of the procedure (e.g., scene duration, assessment of subject avoidance tactics, cue content level, etc.). In light of this possibility, a statement might be made in closing that before an investigator begins work with any therapy technique, he should be thoroughly familiar with the procedure clinically in order that the laboratory analogue to be used accurately represents the technique. Bernstein and Paul (1971) expressed a similar view. If this were uniformly done by all investigators, many of the procedural problems found in the studies reviewed would not hamper meaningful interpretation of the data.

B. Studies Using Psychiatric Populations

The ultimate validation of a therapeutic technique's effectiveness can only come about through systematic study of the technique using clients as the subject of study. The critics of analogue study are quite correct in pointing out that one cannot overgeneralize from the data collected on nonpatient populations. However, therapy outcome research with client populations is extremely difficult to execute (Levis, 1970b; Stampfl, 1970). Paramount are problems in the operational definition of independent and dependent measures, selection and implementation of appropriate control conditions, control of medication type and dose level, client selection, equation of therapist skills, and ethical considerations.

Given the current state of affairs, criticism of outcome work should center mainly on what questions were raised by the researchers, did they reasonably answer these questions, and was the reader cautioned as to design problems and the validity of the conclusions drawn? Finally, it should be realized that validation of a therapeutic technique cannot be based on just a few studies, but requires the completion of numerous outcome investigations. It would seem that the best that can be done at this time is to look for trends across studies rather than drawing definitive conclusions from a given investigation.

Fifteen studies using an extinction approach were found in the literature. Unlike the situation noted with analogue studies, a reasonable correlation with patient studies exists between the use of the terms implosive therapy and flooding and the category of cues employed. As far as we can determine, studies labeled "IT" drew upon all seven cue categories if the therapist believed the use of such cues was warranted. Studies labeled "flooding" generally restricted cue usage to categories (1) through (3), with the emphasis on the first two categories.

1. TREATMENT OF INPATIENT AND OUTPATIENT POPULATIONS

Hogan (1966) was the first to conduct a study using the IT procedure with patients. Fifty patients on the intensive treatment ward of a state hospital were assigned to either implosive or conventional therapists on the basis of the time available in their schedules. Assignment was made by a ward physician who did not know a study was in progress. Twenty-six patients were treated with implosive therapy, while 24 received conventional treatment. The two groups of patients were not statistically different from each other on the following variables: sex, age, education, intellectual ability, and length of previous treatment. The pretherapy MMPI scores were used to establish similarity between groups with regard to the character and degree of initial disturbance. The pretreatment MMPI was administered at the time of the patient's arrival on the ward, while the posttreatment MMPI was given at the time the patient was released or transferred from the ward. Release or transfer was determined by the ward physician after consultation with the members of the ward staff. Treatment time differed between the groups, with the implosive group averaging 4.9 months in treatment while the conventional group averaged 8.2 months. Psychologists of similar academic and therapy experience served as the therapists. In addition to the individual treatment techniques used, each patient received group therapy, occupational therapy, recreational work, and educational programs. These treatments were outlined for all patients in this hospital setting.

Comparison of the pre- and post-MMPI's of the implosive and nonimplosive groups revealed that the implosive group showed a significant shift away from pathology on 5 MMPI scales. The conventional group showed no significant shift. When T-scores of 70 or above were considered (those traditionally indicative of pathology), an average drop of −11.47 T-scores was shown by the implosive group. The conventional group displayed a mean shift of −.59 T-scores. For scores above 80, the implosive group changed an average of −8.12 T-scores, as opposed to the control group's shift of +.88 T-scores. Since there were differential drops between the groups, explanation in terms of regression towards the mean is implausible. Hogan also tabulated data in regard to post-therapy hospitalization status one year after treatment. Patients were considered successful if they had been released or discharged from the hospital; patients were considered unsuccessful if they had been transferred or rehospitalized. Statistically reliable differences were shown between the groups on these measures, with 18 out of 26 implosive patients classified as being successful as opposed to 8 out of 24 control patients falling in this classification.

Hogan's study can be criticized for its failure to control the treatment time and for the fact that post-therapy testing was carried out at different times. However, as noted earlier, the attempt to hold treatment time constant may well reduce the ability of the therapists to meet the boundary conditions of the technique for each patient treated. However, Hogan should have used a process variable (such as anxiety responding to the scene presentation, ward behavior, etc.) in order to pinpoint each therapy's progress so that comparison could be made at specific points in time and not just at termination of therapeutic contact.

The use of the MMPI as a dependent measure can be questioned. The major problem here is the lack of knowledge of the behavioral correlates of the scores on this instrument. However, as discussed by Stampfl and Levis (1973a), there is little agreement as to the appropriate measure of change in a therapy outcome study. The MMPI does provide certain advantages in that it is well constructed, empirically derived, and extensively validated (Dahlstrom & Walsh, 1960). In addition, it has been previously used as a measure of treatment evaluation (Barron & Leary, 1955; Gallagher, 1953; Kaufman, 1950; Mogar & Savage, 1964; Schofield, 1950, 1953). In spite of these advantages, the addition of behaviorally oriented measures such as ward behavior rating, ability to become and remain gainfully employed, or ratings of family function would be welcome.

Levis and Carrera (1967) carried out a similar study with outpatients, also using the MMPI as a dependent measure. Forty clients were placed in one experimental group which received 10 hours of IT and three control groups (two active treatment and one waiting list control). The first control group (CT1) received a combination of supportive and insight therapy for 10 hours and served as a control for the number of therapy sessions and duration of treatment received by Group IT. Four therapists treated the patients assigned to Group CT1. The second control group (CT2) received the same kind of treatment as Group CT1, but no restrictions were placed on treatment time (average time: 37 hours). This group was treated by one of the IT therapists before he had a knowledge of IT. Group CT2 was a control for possible skills and personality characteristics of this therapist. The final control group was a waiting list control group. MMPI evaluation of this latter group was made at approximately the same times as those of Group CT1. In all groups, pre- and post-MMPI assessment was made within a week prior to and a week after therapy. The MMPI profiles of the clients included in the study were evaluated as to validity such that to meet the requirements for inclusion, the question raw score was below 30, the L scale T-score was below 60, and the F-K raw score difference was below 9. In addition, three or more T-scores above 70 on any of the 10 clinical scales was required. No subclassification of type of disorder was made because of the difficulty in objectively determining diagnosis. All clients were judged as capable of functioning in society without hospitalization.

The results of this study showed that Group IT had a greater drop on each of the 10 standard scales except Ma. The overall mean drop of −53.10 was significantly different from the control groups' drop of −7.96. There is some justification for such a comparison since Johnson and McNeal (1965) found, using follow-up data, that patients showing drops of 20 T-scores or more can be considered improved. When T-scores above 70 were considered, it was shown that for Group IT, 17 of the 48 pretest scores dropped into the normal range. This can be contrasted to 5 of 42 in Group CT1; 4 of 46 in Group CT2; and 3 of 41 in group WT. Similar changes were shown for T-scores above 80 as 15 of 26 of these scores dropped below 80 for the IT group, while no change in the total number of scores dropping below 80 was shown for the control groups combined. The mean T-score decrease for scores above 70 was −8.3; −1.0;

−.3; and −1.9 for Groups IT, CT1, CT2, and WT, respectively. The differences in the rank of the mean drop for scores above 70 for group IT versus all of the control groups was significant according to Fisher's test of exact probability. Comparison was also made between the groups (Group IT and Group CT2) treated by the newly trained IT therapist before and after training in the technique. The mean difference between these groups was −50.9. For scores above 70 the difference was −8.7. Levis and Carrera (1967) report that these changes correlated with clinical observation and verbal report of the clients, although no systematic data were reported.

Again, the main criticism of this study is the failure to collect behavioral data in addition to the MMPI data and the failure to include a process variable. Furthermore, not all groups were treated at the same point in time, and subjects were not assigned randomly to conditions. However, the investigators appear to have been cognizant of a variety of empirical issues which bear further investigation. These include treatment time, the effect of commitment and expectation of professional treatment, and therapist personality and skill. It is also important to note that these authors consider their effort a pilot study, indicating that they feel further refinements are necessary.

A well-executed study by Boudewyns and Wilson (1972) compared implosive therapy with a desensitization procedure using free association (DT) developed by Wilson and Smith (1968). Thirty-six V.A. hospital patients were assigned to three groups that received either IT, DT, or the standard milieu therapy available to all hospital patients (MT). This consisted of occupational therapy, industrial therapy, physical therapy, and individual counseling by a variety of hospital staff. During therapy, the patients were not allowed to take antipsychotic medication. The active treatments were provided by four therapists (two clinical psychologists and two trainees). Each therapist treated three patients with each technique. The criterion measures used were the depression (D) and psychasthenia (Pt) scales on the MMPI, as well as the Mooney Problem Checklist. In addition, prior to therapy the subjects were asked to rate their psychological distance from a goal that they wished to obtain from therapy. Significant others (e.g., wife, mother, father) of the patients were also asked to specify and rate goals that they thought the patients should obtain. The final dependent measure that was used was the patient's employment and hospitalization status for one year following treatment. Evaluations were conducted three times during the course of the study: prior to therapy, immediately following therapy, and following a 6 month or 1 year post-therapy period. Process variables were also monitored during the study in that a rating scale of perceived physiological arousal (PPA) during therapy was used. The authors hypothesized that the amount of anxiety shown during therapy would correlate with outcome.

The results of the study revealed that for the MMPI criterion score (the T-score on the D or Pt scale), the changes were ordered in terms of magnitude IT > DT > MT. Statistical comparisons showed the only difference that was significant ($p < .06$) was the contrast between the IT and MT groups. At the 6-month follow-up, this comparison reached the .05 level of significance. For the remaining MMPI scales, the mean T-score for scales (Hy, Pt, and Sc) fell within normal limits for the IT group. In the DT group only one scale (Hy) fell to within the normal range. There were no changes recorded in Group MT. At the 6-month assessment, two of the three scales showing decreases with IT treatment remained in the normal range. Considering changes in overall MMPI performance, the sum of 10 individual MMPI clinical scales showed interesting trends. Citing data of Johnson and McNeal (1965), Boudewyns and Wilson (1972) argued that a drop of 20 T-scores or more is often predictive of hospital release. Considering this, six subjects in Group IT, nine in DT, and four in MT met this post-therapy criterion. At the time of follow-up, seven, three, and one subject in the IT, DT, and MT groups, respectively, met this criterion. The difference between the IT and MT groups was significant. When the total number of elevated MMPI scales was analyzed, 45.3% of those in Group IT fell into the normal range after therapy. This is contrasted to 34.5 and 14.6% for groups DT and MT, respectively. Of these gains, 83% in Group IT, 36% in Group DT, and 25% in Group MT retained these gains at the 6-month follow-up. For the goal rating variable, a gains score was created (pre-post therapy). Gains were significantly greater for Groups IT and DT than for Group MT. When the gains in goals as rated by significant others were calculated, only the gains shown by Group IT were significant when compared to the gains for the patients in DT. At the 1-year follow-up, one subject from Group IT, two subjects in DT, and four subjects in Group MT were readmitted to the hospital for psychiatric reasons. These results did not differ statistically. The number of months spent in gainful employment also did not differ. For the process measure, Group IT showed significantly greater PPA scores (indicative of greater anxiety during therapy) than Group DT. However, these scores were not predictive of therapeutic outcome as hypothesized. There were no therapist or therapist–therapy interactions.

From these results, Boudewyns and Wilson concluded that Group IT was more effective than MT alone. The effectiveness of DT was considered equivocal since the gains made by this group post-therapy did not continue at follow-up. Further, since the patients had not volunteered for therapy, it was felt that their motivational levels were not as high as would have been liked. Thus, the study may represent a rather conservative test of the techniques used.

Boudewyns (1975) recently published a 5-year follow-up of these data. Most of the subjects (N = 11 and N = 10 for the IT and MT groups, respectively) were contacted, although a high attrition rate reduced the DT group to half its original size. The 5-year data revealed that the IT group showed fewer psychiatric rehospitalizations than the MT group. Comparisons of the DT and MT, and the IT and DT groups on the number of months spent in gainful employment failed to reveal any significant differences. It is unfortunate that Boudewyns did not include the MMPI and Mooney Problem Checklist in the follow-up so that the gains recorded on these measures following therapy could be assessed. Work such as this is desperately needed, if the long-term effectiveness of therapy techniques is to be evaluated.

The above three studies were not restricted to the types of cue category used. The populations tested also showed signs of severe pathology. The studies still to be reviewed selected for investigation more homogeneous populations in terms of client-target behaviors. Furthermore, the content of scene material presented in these studies appeared to be restricted mainly to cue categories (1) and (2), although category (3) was sometimes used.

2. TREATMENT OF CLINICAL PHOBIC CASES

Boulougouris and Marks (1969) reported the outcome of four phobic cases treated with flooding. They reported that three out of the four cases treated showed significant improvement, both according to their own ratings and in clinical assessment of impairment of functioning. The mean number of sessions used was 14, and therapeutic gains were found maintained over a 6-month follow-up period. It is interesting to note that these investigators emphasized the need for in vivo exposure of the patient to the feared situation, in addition to exposure in imagery. In almost all studies reported by the English group, both imagery and in vivo exposure to feared objects or situations were provided by the therapist. The extent to which this improves treatment efficacy is unknown as no systematic trials have been undertaken. Relating to this, at least one theorist (Mathews, 1971) has proposed a two-stage model of fear reduction. Mathews suggests that exposure in imagery to feared situations reduces anxiety to such an extent that in vivo exposure can be tolerated to the point where actual anxiety decrement occurs.

A study with patients by Watson, Gaind, and Marks (1972) provides some support for these hypotheses. Utilizing 10 patients suffering from various specific phobias, these investigators monitored the patient's physiological responses (heart rate) to repeated exposures in imagery and later to in vivo presentations of the patient's feared stimulus. Several general findings were noted. First, repeated exposure to phobic stimuli resulted in diminished physiological response. Second, imaginal sessions evoked less tachycardia than in vivo exposure. Third, in vivo stimulation evoked considerable tachycardia even after such responses had decreased to imaginal presentation; however, with repeated in vivo exposure the response diminished. Finally, it was reported that reduced physiological arousal was accompanied by cognitive and behavioral changes. However, it was noted that changes in these response systems took place at different rates such that cognitive changes generally followed rather than preceded physiological changes. These data not only provide evidence for Mathew's proposal but also would be predicted by the implosive model. The data also suggest that in vivo exposure to the feared situation given during the course of therapy may expedite the fear reduction process. A number of studies (Crowe, Marks, Agras, & Leitenberg, 1972; Emmelkamp, 1974; Emmelkamp & Wessels, 1975; Watson, Mullett, & Pillay, 1973) have used such a technique and will be reviewed later.

Returning to work which extended the Boulougouris and Marks study, Boulougouris, Marks, and Marset (1971) contrasted flooding and systematic desensitization in a crossover design. Sixteen psychiatric patients suffering from phobias were treated. Nine of the patients were diagnosed as agoraphobics; the other seven suffered from specific phobias. The mean age of these patients was 33 years. Six sessions of IT and six sessions of systematic desensitization were given to two groups of patients in counterbalanced order. The majority of the patients did not receive drugs during the therapy. Five of the patients were inpatients; the other 11 were outpatients. Each patient saw the same therapist for both treatments. All 10 therapists participating in the study were novices to both techniques. Implosive scene content was kept at levels 1 and 2. The dependent measures used included ratings by the patient, the therapist, and an independent medical assessor of each patient's main phobia and minor phobias. For the purpose of analysis, the therapist's and independent assessor's ratings were combined, since the measures were shown to correlate highly. In addition, physiological assessments were made of the patient's heart rate, spontaneous skin conductance fluctuations, and maximum skin conductance deflection during periods when the patient imagined standard scenes relating to the main and minor phobias. This assessment was also made while the therapist described standard test scenes to the patient.

The results showed that, although both treatments produced improvements on the doctor's ratings (combined rating of the therapist and independent assessor) of the main and total phobias, implosion produced significantly greater improvement. The physiological assessment reflected these findings in that implosion produced greater decrease in heart rate during periods when the patient imagined phobic material. For periods when the therapist was presenting the standard scenes, a greater reduction in the number of spontaneous fluctuations and maximum deflection was found for the group receiving implosive treatment. Other data provided by these investigators show that when treatment type was correlated with the type of phobia treated (specific vs. agoraphobia), desensitization produced greater improvement with specific phobias. Implosion, on the other hand, produced greater improvement in agoraphobics. Follow-up data available at the time of publication (6–12 months) indicated that gains made during therapy had not disappeared. However, these results cannot be interpreted clearly since some of the patients received continued treatment during this period. Further caution must be exercised since all patients received both treatments.

The use of the crossover design in the Boulougouris, Marks, and Marset experiment enabled the experimenters to use fewer subjects. However, its use seems inappropriate for studies in which follow-up data are required since at the time of follow-up both groups have received both treatments. The use of the crossover design also leaves open the possibility of carry-over effects of the previous treatment, thus preventing clear assessment of the effects of the individual treatments. Data presented by Boulougouris et al. suggest this was the case in their study since they noted that some differences in physiological data were exaggerated due to flooding having a greater effect when used as the first treatment. In light of this information, it would seem that the crossover design is inappropriate when one wishes to analyze the uncontaminated effects of individual treatment techniques.

Drug-assisted flooding was attempted by Hussain (1971). Two groups of 40 phobic patients were formed, one receiving desensitization, while the other received flooding. Each of these groups received its treatment under both barbiturate and saline control conditions. Half the group received a barbiturate—saline order, while the other group received a saline—barbiturate order. Six sessions were given under each condition. The dependent measure used was a rating by the therapist and the patient of his phobia and anxiety. The flooding procedure differed slightly from standard in that in addition to instructions to imagine material, pictorial representation was presented to the patient. It should be noted that use of differential material between the treatment types confounds this manipulation.

The results indicated that the average amount of change in rating shown under the drug-assisted flooding was 50% greater than under either drug-assisted desensitization or saline control flooding. In his interpretation of his results, Hussain (1971) indicated that the effect of the drug in the flooding situation is to allow clearer visualization of the scenes and thus experience the appropriate emotions to them. He states:

In this state the patient accepts suggestions more readily, can visualize the versions of the situations suggested more realistically, and experiences the appropriate emotional response; thus the patient's excitement and fear can be stimulated to a climactic phase, which usually passes into a state of temporary general inhibition (p. 1512).

Thus, it would appear that the drug state tends to reduce defenses, increasing the subject's motivation to experience the avoided CS complex. The extent to which one needs to resort to this kind of a manipulation is still unknown. A trained implosive therapist attempts to provide such motivation by carefully presenting the treatment rationale and instructional sets. Certainly, analogue work with expectancy (Borkovec, 1972) and instructional sets (Dee, 1972) should be extended to client populations.

Crowe et al. (1972) report a study in which 14 phobic patients received four 50-minute sessions of each of three therapeutic techniques. The three techniques were systematic desensitization, flooding, and shaping. The sequence of the three treatments for each patient was determined on a random basis. There were 4 to 10 days between treatments, during which assessment took place. One therapist applied all three treatments for each of the patients. The dependent measures used in assessment were phobic rating scales in which the rater (patient, therapist, and an independent rater) judged the patient's feelings about and avoidance tendency toward the most intense phobic situations. In addition, a behavioral avoidance test was used in which the patient was instructed to approach the feared object or situation until he experienced anxiety. For example, an agoraphobic might be asked to walk on a certain route, reporting landmarks. Most of the patients were assessed both on the treated and untreated phobia. The techniques were applied in the usual clinical manner except that the treatment time of each was limited to four sessions. Each desensitization session consisted of 10 minutes of relaxation followed by 40 minutes of scene presentations. Flooding sessions were also 40 minutes long as were the shaping sessions. Shaping was basically a graduated in vivo treatment approach, although some modeling was used. Stimulus exposure time was equated for the three therapies.

The results showed that on the phobic rating scales, there were no significant differences between the therapies. However, on the behavioral avoidance test, the change scores indicated that shaping was superior to desensitization. Flooding resulted in changes intermediate between shaping and desensitization, but not statistically different from either. For the untreated phobias, only shaping produced a specific effect on the avoidance measure such that the change score for the treated phobia was significantly greater than for the untreated phobia. When the patients were divided as to the specific type of phobia, agoraphobic versus specific, differences in the order of effectiveness were shown. Agoraphobics showed the greatest response to shaping, the next greatest to flooding, and the least response to desensitization. For the specific phobics, no differential effectiveness was shown. From these data, the authors conclude that shaping and flooding show promise in the treatment of phobias. However, as the authors note, desensitization was limited in sessions and thus the boundary conditions may not have been met. This could also be true of the flooding group since session number was fixed. It should be noted that only the shaping group received direct CS exposure to the phobic situation.

Watson, et al. (1973) present data from a study in which 19 female agoraphobic patients were given both imaginal and in vivo exposure to their feared situations. Patients were treated in groups, each group receiving 9 hours of treatment. Three sessions of 3 hours each were given. The first 2 hours of each session were arranged in a crossover design, with imaginal and in vivo treatments being presented. During the third hour the patient was allowed to choose which of the two treatments she would like to experience. Imaginary exposure was presented via tape recording and thus it varied from standard clinical treatment procedure. The tape presented several phobic "stories," each depicting a situation typically feared by this group (shopping in a busy supermarket, traveling by bus, etc.). The in vivo exposure consisted of a combination of shaping and modeling with groups of patients accompanied by a therapist traveling increasing distances from the hospital gates. Clinical assessment consisted of rating scales filled out by the patient. They were given at the beginning and end of each session, as well as within each session between treatment hours. A behavioral test consisting of walking a prescribed course away from the hospital gates was given before and after each session but not between treatments. The results showed that for overall treatment (imagery plus in vivo), improvement was found on both phobic ratings and avoidance behavior between the beginning and end of all three treatment sessions and between the beginning of treatment, end of treatment, and follow-up. For the phobic ratings, there was a significant increase between sessions 1 and 2 and between the end of treatment and the follow-up. The increase between the first and second sessions seems predictable since the patients were being exposed to fearful situations which had been avoided in the past. The increase at follow-up most likely represents incomplete treatment effects.

When each treatment was considered separately, both produced improvement although the in vivo condition produced more improvement than the imaginal condition. The imaginal condition had little effect past the first session. Overall, the results of the Watson et al. (1973) study suggest that a gradual introduction of the patient into the in vivo phobic situation has anxiety-reducing effects. The effect of the imaginal exposure is questionable in this study since it was presented via tape, as well as the fact that after the first session the two treatments were mixed and thus the individual effects could not be separated. Further, since the in vivo exposure situation included elements of other techniques (i.e., modeling), the contribution of each of these is unclear. Nevertheless, since an exposure procedure is embedded in each of the treatment procedures, it is possible that this variable is the change agent. Again, research is needed to separate the specific contribution of the in vivo and imaginary presentation. Such questions can best be answered by a between-group design.

A between-group design was used by Emmelkamp (1974). Emmelkamp compared the effects of 12 sessions of flooding treatment, three sessions of flooding followed by nine sessions of self-observation, or 12 sessions of self-observation. Agoraphobic clients served as subjects. In addition to the active treatment groups, a waiting list control group was used. Treatment sessions were 90 minutes long. The flooding sessions consisted of 45 minutes of flooding in imagination followed by 45 minutes of flooding in vivo. The cue content levels used during flooding came from levels (1) and (2). Flooding in vivo required the client to walk a predetermined path alone. Self-observation treatment required the client to go outside and remain outside until he or she felt anxious. When this occurred, the clients were asked to return to their home and record the duration that they had been outdoors. After two sessions the clients carried out the self-observation treatment by themselves. Twenty-nine clients began the study; however, nine dropped out during the course of treatment. Four were from the flooding group, four were from the self-observation group, and one was from the combination group. The authors report that two of the dropouts did so following their going out into the street and experiencing panic. The remainder were due to illness or the client's inability to meet the methodological demands of the experiment. The dependent measures consisted of an in vivo test in which the client remained outside until anxiety was felt. The time outside was measured, as well as paper-pencil anxiety and avoidance scales filled out by the client, therapist, and an independent observer. Assessments were made after the first three sessions, after the nine additional sessions, and after 3 months following the termination of treatment.

Assessments after three treatment sessions showed no significant differences between groups. The results of the experiment at the end of treatment indicated that all three treatment groups displayed significant improvement on both the rating scale and time-outside data after 12 treatments. The waiting list control group showed no change. When the individual groups were contrasted, the flooding plus self-observation treatment condition showed significantly greater improvement than either of the other treatment groups. The flooding alone and self-observation alone groups did not differ from one another. Follow-up data were confounded by other treatments, but the flooding self-observation group showed continued improvement. The author interpreted these data as suggesting that the combination treatment was the most effective, although he noted that all treatments were effective.

From a critical standpoint, Emmelkamp's study is one in which the effects of treatment can be meaningfully separated. However, it must be kept in mind that the flooding treatment used in this study consisted of both imaginal and in vivo exposure and thus differs from the self-observation group in the amount of in vivo exposure provided. It is unfortunate that data were not provided concerning duration of exposure for the self-observation subjects. It is also unfortunate that an attempt was not made to control in vivo and self-observation exposure times and to make them equal. Had this been done, it is conceivable that no differences between the groups would have been shown. Nonetheless, the study is important as a preliminary step in demonstrating that exposure to a feared situation [either at the client's pace (self-observation) or at a pace set by the therapist] is effective in the reduction of anxiety.

In a later study, Emmelkamp and Wessels (1975) attempted to separate the effects of flooding in imagination from those of flooding in vivo. Four 90-minute sessions were given in which clients received either prolonged flooding in vivo, flooding in imagination, or 45 minutes of flooding in imagination followed by 45 minutes of flooding in vivo. Following an intermediate test, eight 90-minute sessions of self-observation similar to the treatment used in the previous study were given. A post-test was administered following this treatment. Twenty-six clients took part in the experiment, although following the first phase of treatment three dropped out. Clients were matched on the amount of time they were able to remain outdoors. As in the previous study, the dependent measures were a series of phobic anxiety and rating scales as well as a behavioral test. Phobic rating scales were also administered for phobias other than the main street phobia. Because of differences between the groups on ratings of other phobias at the time of the pretest, the authors used an analysis of covariance on all of the results. This is unfortunate since such an analysis is inappropriate for use on measures that did not differ, such as the street phobia in vivo test and ratings.

The results showed that at the time of the intermediate measure (prior to the self-observation treatment), flooding in vivo was more effective on the in vivo dependent measure than flooding in imagination. These two groups also differed on several of the phobic rating scales. The combined group was more effective than flooding in imagination alone for the phobic rating scales. The prolonged exposure and combined group did not differ on any of the measures of the main (street) phobia. On the post-test which followed self-observation, additional improvements were shown on the rating scales by the prolonged exposure and combined treatment groups. The flooding in imagination group showed improvement on the in vivo measure as well as on the rating scales. No treatment was given between post-testing and follow-up. There were no significant differences between the groups at the time of follow-up. These results are interpreted to indicate the superiority of flooding in vivo. To support this interpretation, the authors cite not only their data but also reports that clients undergoing the flooding in imagination treatment, who felt this treatment was of little value and actually made them more anxious. On the other hand, the authors also cite reports of clients who were unable to endure the prolonged exposure condition. Such data suggest the possibility that insufficient therapeutic rationale was given prior to treatment. If this were the case, it would underscore the need for systematic research on the effects of rationale presentations to client populations.

As with previous studies, the differences between the groups at the time of the intermediate test may be important. More specifically, the distance of the test situation from the therapy situation may be critical in terms of differential generalizations of extinction effects. Stated another way, improvement in the actual behavioral situation is probably a function of two variables, one being stimulus exposure, and the other and equally important, being possible differences in terms of decrements of generalization of extinction between the therapy and test situations. Data presented by Emmelkamp and Wessels (1975, p. 13, Figure 2) clearly support this observation. Although the prolonged exposure and combination treatment groups (both of which received exposure to the actual test situation prior to self-observation treatment) differ from the flooding in imagination group at the time of the intermediate test (before the imagination group received in vivo exposure), rapid gains are shown by the flooding in imagination group following self-observation treatment. These data are suggestive of the possible key role played by generalization of extinction effects in these procedures. Since the situations in which prolonged exposure, self-observation, and in vivo tests are applied are quite similar, little generalization of extinction decrement results. However, since the imaginary flooding treatment differs in many ways, it is possible that a decrement develops and is reflected on the behavioral tests. Such a formulation suggests a two-stage treatment strategy. First, the patient would be imploded in imagination. Once anxiety to these situations had been extinguished, in vivo exposure would be given. This is similar to the formulation given by Mathews (1971) and is supported not only by Emmelkamp's (Emmelkamp, 1974; Emmelkamp & Wessels, 1975) data, but also by data provided by Watson et al. (1972). The problem with such a formulation develops when there is no clearly defined behavioral situation or phobic object. However, such cases may require exposure to a variety of situations, thus increasing the probability that emotional response to the entire CS complex will be extinguished.

3. TREATMENT OF OBSESSIVE-COMPULSIVES
AND ALCOHOLICS

Hodgson, Rachman, and Marks (1972) and Rachman, Marks, and Hodgson (1973) used flooding in vivo and modeling in the treatment of obsessive-compulsive behavior. The results of treatment of the Hodgson et al. (1972) experiment, in which a combination of modeling and flooding in vivo was given to five obsessive-compulsive patients, were compared with previous work (Rachman, Hodgson, & Marks, 1971) in which each of these two treatments was individually compared to a relaxation control procedure. These comparisons on a variety of dependent measures (clinical rating, interference with life activities, fear thermometer, etc.) indicated that the combination of modeling and flooding in vivo was superior to either treatment alone. Each individual treatment was shown to be effective when compared to the relaxation control group. Two criticisms can be applied to these studies. First, since the treatments occurred at different times, the treatment manipulation was confounded by the time of treatment and lack of randomization of subjects to treatment conditions. Second, as recognized by the authors, the modeling manipulation has an extinction component embedded in it, and thus modeling may serve only to facilitate exposure to the anxiety-arousing situation that triggers the obsessive-compulsive behavior. Thus, it is possible that the superiority of the modeling plus flooding is simply that the procedural combination provides for more CS exposure. The obvious manipulation necessary to test this hypothesis would be to equalize exposure time for all treatment conditions before testing. Treatment of an additional five patients by these methods (Rachman et al., 1973) replicated the findings discussed above. In addition, a 2-year follow-up of the previously reported patients indicated that no deterioration had occurred. However, these follow-up data must be interpreted with caution since in some cases additional treatment was provided in the period following the study.

Newton and Stein (1974) turned their attention to the treatment of alcoholism. Sixty-one alcoholic men were treated with either implosive therapy, brief traditional therapy, or ward milieu. Fifteen therapy sessions were used. The dependent measures were Gaugh's

Adjective Checklist, the Standard Situations Test, and rating by the ward physician. The results showed that neither treatment was significantly more effective than milieu therapy on any of the measures. Unfortunately, active drinking behavior was not assessed. Furthermore, the rationale for inclusion of implosive therapy as a treatment can be raised. According to the authors' statements, IT was used because of the belief that excess anxiety plays a key role in the maintenance of alcoholism. The question now becomes: Is this assumption correct? Clearly, it would seem that alcoholism is a polygenic disorder, and thus treatment by implosive therapy should only be effective in cases in which excess anxiety provides the main motivational base for drinking. More work with the population is needed before any definite conclusions can be reached.

4. STUDIES ADDRESSING THEORETICAL ISSUES

At least two studies at the patient level have attempted to investigate theoretical research hypotheses outlined under the discussion of analogue work. The first study to be reviewed was executed by Watson and Marks (1971), who investigated the effects of relevant and irrelevant cue content. Sixteen phobic patients were divided into two groups, each of which received eight sessions of flooding on relevant cues (cues at levels 1 and 2 that dealt with their phobias) and eight sessions of flooding in which the cue content consisted of material that would ordinarily be frightening to anyone (i.e., a tiger escaping from the zoo and mauling the patient) in counterbalanced order. However, as was pointed out by Stampfl and Levis (1969), bodily injury cues are often the central CS complex for most phobic cases. Thus, rather than being irrelevant, bodily injury cues theoretically represent cue content level (3) for this sort of patient. Dependent measures used were ratings of the patient's phobic anxiety and avoidance made by the patient, therapist, and an independent assessor, as well as physiological response to phobic material test scenes imagined by the patient. The results showed that when both treatments were combined, significant reductions took place in ratings of the phobia by all raters. In addition, the patient's heart rate increases to phobic imagery also decreased significantly.

When the two treatments (flooding and "irrelevant" fear) were considered separately, both treatments produced improvements on clinical ratings. However, only the irrelevant material treatment produced significant improvement of physiological arousal to the phobic test scenes. There were no interactions of the treatment material with order of presentation. There were order effects, however, during the treatment sessions as flooding sessions produced more report of anxiety when given during the second treatment block, while irrelevant fear scenes were more anxiety provoking during the first treatment block. It was also noted that anxiety peaked approximately midway through the session, regardless of the treatment, and then diminished. At the end of a 6-month follow-up period, most patients continued to improve. However, since many of the patients received additional treatment, the continued improvement cannot be entirely tied to the original treatment. The data from this study indicate that, considering predictions based on the stimulus complex notion, material that can be tied to the patient's behavior and also produces anxiety in the patient must be considered relevant. As noted before, this area is clearly in need of further study.

A second study which concerned itself with a theoretically related research issue was recently conducted by Boudewyns and Levis (1975). The study was an attempt to determine whether scenes designed to elicit anxiety produced an autonomic extinction effect with repetition and whether the degree of arousal elicited was differential for subjects labeled moderate or low in ego strength as defined by the Barron (1960) scale. Forty-eight male psychiatric inpatients volunteered for the study. None of the subjects was receiving a major antipsychotic drug during the course of the study. Half the subjects were assigned to an experimental group and half to a nontreated control. The experimental subjects were presented anxiety scenes, neutral scenes, and a balloon-stressor test. The anxiety material selected was geared to responses on an FSS and not to the patient's presenting problem. Cue content of scenes was limited to categories (1), (2), and (3). The high ego-strength experimental subjects initially responded to anxiety scenes with reliably more affect than to the neutral scenes as indexed by their skin conductance level, heart rate measures, and by responses to a Fear Thermometer and Affect Adjective Checklist. With repeated presentations of the anxiety scenes (15 minutes in duration) across four sessions (60 minutes total scene duration), a rapid extinction for the autonomic measures was obtained. Identical comparisons over these indices for the low ego-strength subjects failed to produce any reliable differences. This was found despite the fact the low ego-strength subjects reported reliably more psychopathology on the pretest MMPI and FSS. Differences in baseline autonomic reactivity and responding to a standard stressor test were not obtained between ego-strength conditions. Data obtained from the nontreated subjects suggested that the anxiety scenes produced no ill effects for either ego-strength population. The finding that implosive-type material failed to elicit anxiety in subjects labeled low in ego-strength is in need of further study.

5. OVERVIEW OF PSYCHIATRIC POPULATION STUDIES

It would appear from the above review that, except for one study (Newton & Stein, 1974), improvement was found on a variety of dependent measures following the use of an extinction technique. Procedural variations such as self-observation and modeling may only affect motivational variables which encourage the client to expose himself or herself to the anxiety-provoking stimuli. The extent to which these methods are effective or can be duplicated by other means (demand, expectancy, etc.) has not been systematically investigated. Summarizing further, extinction techniques appear to be effective on a wide variety of patients, as positive results have been obtained with psychotics (Boudewyns, 1975; Boudewyns & Wilson, 1972; Hogan, 1966), outpatients (Levis & Carrera, 1967), phobics (Boulougouris & Marks, 1969; Boulougouris et al., 1971; Crowe et al., 1972; Emmelkamp, 1974; Emmelkamp & Wessels, 1975; Hussain, 1971; Watson & Marks, 1971; Watson et al., 1973), and obsessive-compulsives (Hodgson et al., 1972; Rachman et al., 1973).

The greatest problem with the studies using psychotic and outpatient samples was one of the dependent measures. Clearly, effects were shown on the MMPI. However, work is needed in which more behaviorally based outcome measures are used. For example, ward behavior might be monitored, or perhaps performance at tasks previously interfered with by psychiatric symptomology. The work using behavioral dependent measures is also not without fault. None of the studies reviewed attempted to systematically separate treatment effects through the use of a matched group design. Follow-up data were generally confounded since other treatments were provided following completion of the study. Further, investigators have failed to recognize that in many of the treatment procedures used, stimulus exposure is considered to be the major component. Unfortunately, this factor is rarely controlled. Considering this observation, many of the treatment effects found might also be explained in terms of differential stimulus exposure times.

It would appear that, at the patient level, the general principle of stimulus exposure is effective in the treatment of anxiety and fear. However, the conditions under which it operates most effectively are not well understood since little systematic parametric work has been

done in this area. Strong statements regarding any of the above
conclusions must await the gathering of additional data.

REFERENCES

Amsel, A. The role of frustrative nonreward in noncontinuous reward situations. *Psychological Bulletin*, 1958, 55, 102–119.

Amsel, A., & Maltzman, I. The effect upon generalized drive strength of emotionality as inferred from the level of consummatory response. *Journal of Experimental Psychology*, 1950, 40, 563–569.

Anderson, N. H., & Nakamura, C. Y. Avoidance decrement in avoidance conditioning. *Journal of Comparative and Physiological Psychology*, 1964, 57, 196–204.

Ayres, W. A. Implosive therapy: A review. *Psychotherapy: Theory, Research and Practice*, 1972, 9, 242–250.

Baker, T. W. Properties of compound conditioned stimuli and their components. *Psychological Bulletin*, 1968, 70, 611–625.

Barrett, C. L. Systematic Desensitization *vs* Implosive Therapy. *Journal of Abnormal Psychology*, 1969, 74, 587–592.

Barron, F. An ego-strength scale which predicts response to psychotherapy. In G. S. Welch & W. G. Dahlstrom (Eds.), *Basic readings on the MMPI in psychology and medicine*. Minneapolis: University of Minnesota Press, 1960.

Barron, F., & Leary, T. Changes in psychoneurotic patients with and without psychotherapy. *Journal of Consulting Psychology*, 1955, 19, 239–245.

Baum, M. Extinction of avoidance responding through response prevention (flooding). *Psychological Bulletin*, 1970, 74, 276–284.

Bernstein, D. A., & Paul, G. L. Some comments on therapy analogue research with small animal "phobias." *Journal of Behavior Therapy and Experimental Psychiatry*, 1971, 2, 225–237.

Black, A. H. The extinction of avoidance responses under curare. *Journal of Comparative and Physiological Psychology*, 1958, 51, 519–525.

Borkovec, T. D. Effects of expectancy on the outcome of systematic desensitization and implosive treatments for analogue anxiety. *Behavior Therapy*, 1972, 3, 29–40.

Borkovec, T. D. Heart-rate process during systematic desensitization and implosive therapy for analog anxiety. *Behavior Therapy*, 1974, 5, 636–641.

Boudewyns, P. A. Implosive therapy and desensitization therapy with inpatients: A five-year follow-up. *Journal of Abnormal Psychology*, 1975, 84, 159–160.

Boudewyns, P. A., & Levis, D. J. Autonomic reactivity of high and low ego-strength subjects to repeated anxiety eliciting scenes. *Journal of Abnormal Psychology*, 1975, 84, 682–692.

Boudewyns, P. A., & Wilson, A. E. Implosive therapy and desensitization therapy using free association in the treatment of inpatients. *Journal of Abnormal Psychology*, 1972, 79, 259–268.

Boulougouris, J. C., & Marks, I. M. Implosion (Flooding)—A new treatment for phobias. *British Medical Journal*, 1969, ii, 721–723.

Boulougouris, J. C., Marks, I. M., & Marset, P. Superiority of flooding (implosion) to desensitization for reducing pathological fear. *Behaviour Research and Therapy*, 1971, 9, 7–16.

Boyd, T. L., & Levis, D. J. The effects of single-component extinction to a three-component serial CS on resistance to extinction of the conditioned avoidance response. *Learning and Motivation,* 1976, in press.

Breger, L., & McGaugh, J. L. Critique and reformulation of "Learning-Theory" approaches to psychotherapy and neurosis. *Psychological Bulletin,* 1965, 63, 338–358.

Brown, J. S. *The motivation of behavior.* New York: McGraw-Hill, 1961.

Brown, J. S., & Jacobs, A. The role of fear in the motivation and acquisition of responses. *Journal of Experimental Psychology,* 1949, 39, 747–759.

Brown, J. S., Kalish, H. I., & Farber, I. E. Conditioned fear as revealed by magnitude of startle response to an auditory stimulus. *Journal of Experimental Psychology,* 1951, 41, 317–328.

Brush, F. R. The effects of shock intensity on the acquisition and extinction of an avoidance response in dogs. *Journal of Comparative and Physiological Psychology,* 1957, 50, 547–552.

Calef, R. A., & MacLean, G. D. A comparison of reciprocal inhibition and reactive inhibition therapies in the treatment of speech anxiety. *Behavior Therapy,* 1970, 1, 51–58.

Cornish, R. D., & Dilley, J. S. Comparison of three methods of reducing test anxiety: Systematic desensitization, implosive therapy, and study counseling. *Journal of Consulting Psychology,* 1973, 20, 499–503.

Coulter, X., Riccio, D. C., & Page, H. A. Effects of blocking an instrumental avoidance response: Facilitated extinction but persistence of "fear". *Journal of Comparative and Physiological Psychology,* 1969, 68, 377–381.

Crowe, M. M., Marks, I. M., Agras, S. W., & Leitenberg, H. Time-limited desensitization, implosion and shaping for phobic patients: A crossover study. *Behaviour Research and Therapy,* 1972, 10, 319–328.

Dahlstrom, W. G., & Welsh, G. S. *An MMPI handbook.* Minneapolis: University of Minnesota Press, 1960.

Dawley, H. H., Jr., & Wenrich, W. W. Treatment of test anxiety by group implosive therapy. *Psychological Reports,* 1973, 33, 383–388.

Dee, C. Instructions and the extinction of a learned fear in the context of taped implosive therapy. *Journal of Consulting and Clinical Psychology,* 1972, 39, 123–132.

DeMoor, W. Systematic desensitization *vs* prolonged high intensity stimulation (flooding). *Journal of Behavior Therapy and Experimental Psychiatry,* 1970, 1, 45–52.

Denny, M. R., Koons, P. B., & Mason, J. E. Extinction of avoidance as a function of the escape situation. *Journal of Comparative and Physiological Psychology,* 1959, 52, 212–214.

Dollard, J., & Miller, N. E. *Personality and psychotherapy.* New York: McGraw-Hill, 1950.

Dubin, W. J., & Levis, D. J. Influence of similarity of components of a serial CS on conditioned fear in the rat. *Journal of Comparative and Physiological Psychology,* 1974, 85, 304–312.

Emmelkamp, P. M. G. Self-observation *vs* flooding in the treatment of agoraphobia. *Behaviour Research and Therapy,* 1974, 12, 229–238.

Emmelkamp, P. M. G., & Wessels, H. Flooding in imagination *vs* flooding *in vivo:* A comparison with agoraphobics. *Behaviour Research and Therapy,* 1975, 13, 7–16.

Eysenck, H. J. (Ed.) *Behaviour therapy and the neuroses.* New York: Pergamon, 1960.

Eysenck, H. J. A theory of the incubation of anxiety/fear responses. *Behaviour Research and Therapy,* 1968, 6, 309–322.

Fazio, A. F. Treatment components in implosive therapy. *Journal of Abnormal Psychology,* 1970, 76, 211–219.

Fazio, A. F. Implosive therapy with semiclinical phobias. *Journal of Abnormal Psychology,* 1972, 80, 183–188.

Feldman, R. S., & Bremmer, F. J. A method for rapid conditioning of stable avoidance bar pressing behavior. *Journal of the Experimental Analysis of Behavior,* 1963, 6, 393–394.

Fenichel, O. *The psychoanalytic theory of neurosis.* New York: Norton, 1945.

Fitzgerald, R. D., & Brown, J. S. Variables affecting avoidance conditioning in free-responding and discrete-trial situations. *Psychological Reports,* 1965, 17, 835–843.

Frankel, A. S. Implosive therapy: A critical review. *Psychotherapy: Theory, Research and Practice,* 1972, 9, 251–255.

Freud, S. *The problem of anxiety.* H. A. Bunker, trans. New York: Psychoanalytic Quarterly Press & Norton, 1936. Pp. 85–92.

Gallagher, J. J. MMPI changes concommitant with client-centered therapy. *Journal of Consulting Psychology,* 1953, 17, 443–446.

Hekmat, H. Systematic vs. semantic desensitization and implosive therapy: A comparative study. *Journal of Consulting and Clinical Psychology,* 1973, 40, 202–209.

Herrnstein, R. Method and theory in the study of avoidance. *Psychological Review,* 1969, 76, 49–69.

Hilgard, E. R., & Bower, G. H. *Theories of learning.* New York: Appleton, 1966.

Hodgson, R. J., & Rachman, S. An experimental investigation of the implosion technique. *Behaviour Research and Therapy,* 1970, 8, 21–27.

Hodgson, R., Rachman, S., & Marks, I. M. The treatment of chronic obsessive-compulsive neurosis: Follow-up and further findings. *Behaviour Research and Therapy,* 1972, 10, 181–189.

Hogan, R. A. Implosive therapy in the short-term treatment of psychotics. *Psychotherapy: Theory, Research and Practice,* 1966, 3, 25–31.

Hogan, R. A., & Kirchner, J. H. Preliminary report of the extinction of learned fears via short-term implosive therapy. *Journal of Abnormal Psychology,* 1967, 72, 106–109.

Hogan, R. A., & Kirchner, J. H. Implosive, eclectic verbal and bibliotherapy in the treatment of fears of snakes. *Behaviour Research and Therapy,* 1968, 6, 167–171.

Hull, C. L. *Principles of behavior.* New York: Appleton, 1943.

Hunt, H. F., Jernberg, P., & Brady, J. V. The effects of electroconvulsive shock (E.C.S.) on a conditioned emotional response: the effects of post-E.C.S. extinction on the reappearance of the response. *Journal of Comparative and Physiological Psychology,* 1952, 45, 589–599.

Hussain, M. S. Desensitization and flooding (implosion) in treatment of phobias. *American Journal of Psychiatry,* 1971, 127, 1509–1514.

Johnson, R., & McNeal, B. F. Residual psychopathology in released psychiatric patients and its relation to readmission. *Journal of Abnormal Psychology,* 1965, 70, 337–342.

Kalish, H. I. Strength of fear as a funciton of the number of acquisition and extinction trials. *Journal of Experimental Psychology,* 1954, 47, 1–9.

Kaufman, P. Changes in the MMPI as a function of psychiatric therapy. *Journal of Consulting Psychology,* 1950, 14, 458–464.

Kimble, G. A. *Hilgard and Marquis' Conditioning and Learning.* New York: Appleton, 1961.

Kinsey, A. C., Pomeroy, W. B., & Martin, C. E. *Sexual behavior in the human male.* Philadelphia: Saunders, 1948.

Kirchner, J. H., & Hogan, R. A. The therapist variable in the implosion of phobias. *Psychotherapy: Theory, Research and Practice,* 1966, 3, 102–104.

Knapp, R. K. Acquisition and extinction of avoidance with similar and different shock and escape situations. *Journal of Comparative and Physiological Psychology,* 1965, 60, 272–273.

Kostanek, D. J., & Sawrey, J. M. Acquisition and extinction of shuttlebox avoidance with complex stimuli. *Psychonomic Science,* 1965, 3, 369–370.

Krasner, L. Behavior therapy. *Annual Review of Psychology*, 1971, **22**, 483–532.

Lang, P. J. The mechanics of desensitization and the laboratory study of human fear. In C. M. Franks (Ed.), *Behavior therapy appraisal and status*. New York: McGraw-Hill, 1969. Pp. 160–191.

Levis, D. J. Effects of serial CS presentation and other characteristics of the CS on the conditioned avoidance response. *Psychological Reports*, 1966, **18**, 755–766. (a)

Levis, D. J. Implosive therapy, Part II: The subhuman analogue, the strategy, and the technique. In S. G. Armitage (Ed.), *Behavioral modification techniques in the treatment of emotional disorders*. Battle Creek, Mich.: V. A. Publication, 1966. Pp. 22–37 (b)

Levis, D. J. Behavioral therapy: The fourth therapeutic revolution? In D. J. Levis (Ed.), *Learning approaches to therapeutic behavior change*. Chicago: Aldine, 1970. Pp. 1–35. (a)

Levis, D. J. The case for performing research on nonpatient populations with fears of small animals: A reply to Cooper, Furst, and Bridger. *Journal of Abnormal Psychology*, 1970, 76, 36–38 (b)

Levis, D. J. Serial CS presentation and shuttlebox avoidance conditioning: A further look at the tendency to delay responding. *Psychonomic Science*, 1970, **20**, 145–147 (c)

Levis, D. J. Implosive therapy: A critical analysis of Morganstern's review. *Psychological Bulletin*, 1974, **81**, 155–158.

Levis, D. J. IT stimulus cue categories. Paper read at Wayne State University, Detroit, February 1975.

Levis, D. J. Implementing the technique of implosive therapy. In E. B. Foa & A. Goldstein (Eds.), *Handbook of behavioral interventions*. New York: Wiley, 1977, in press.

Levis, D. J., Bouska, S., Eron, J., & McIlhon, M. Serial CS presentations and one-way avoidance conditioning: A noticeable lack of delayed responding. *Psychonomic Science*, 1970, **20**, 147–149.

Levis, D. J., & Boyd, T. L. Effects of shock intensity on avoidance responding in a shuttlebox to serial CS procedures. *Psychonomic Bulletin*, 1973, **1**, 304–306.

Levis, D. J., & Carrera, R. Effects of ten hours of implosive therapy in the treatment of outpatients. *Journal of Abnormal Psychology*, 1967, **72**, 504–508.

Levis, D. J., & Dubin, W. J. Some parameters affecting shuttle-box avoidance responding with rats receiving serially presented conditioned stimuli. *Journal of Comparative and Physiological Psychology*, 1973, **82**, 328–344.

Levis, D. J., & Stampfl, T. G. Effects of serial CS presentation on shuttlebox avoidance responding. *Learning and Motivation*, 1972, 3, 73–90.

Lowenfeld, J., Rubenfeld, S., & Guthrie, G. M. Verbal inhibition in subception. *Journal of General Psychology*, 1956, **54**, 171–176.

Mathews, A. M. Psychophysiological approaches to the investigation of desensitization and related procedures. *Psychological Bulletin*, 1971, 76, 73–91.

Mathews, A. M., & Shaw, P. Emotional arousal and persuasion effects in flooding. *Behaviour Research and Therapy*, 1973, **11**, 587–598.

McAllister, W. R., & McAllister, D. E. Behavioral measurement of conditioned fear. In F. Robert Brush (Ed.), *Aversive conditioning and learning*. New York: Academic Press, 1971. Pp. 105–182.

McCutcheon, B. A., & Adams, H. E. The physiological basis of implosive therapy. *Behaviour Research and Therapy*, 1975, **13**, 93–100.

McNamara, J. R. Systematic desensitization vs. implosive therapy: Issues in outcomes. *Psychotherapy: Theory, Research and Practice*, 1972, 9, 13–17.

Mealiea, W. L., & Nawas, N. M. The comparative effectiveness of systematic desensitization and implosive therapy in the treatment of snake phobia. *Journal of Behavior Therapy and Experimental Psychiatry*, 1971, 2, 85–94.

Meryman, J. J. Magnitude of startle response as a function of hunger and fear. Unpublished master's thesis, State University of Iowa, 1952.

Meryman, J. J. The magnitude of an unconditioned GSR as a function of fear conditioned at a long CS-UCS interval. Unpublished doctoral dissertation, State University of Iowa, 1953.

Meyer, D. R., Cho, C., & Wesemann, A. F. On problems of conditioning discriminated lever-press avoidance responses. *Psychological Review*, 1960, 67, 224–228.

Miller, N. E. Studies of fear as an acquirable drive: I. Fear as motivation and fear-reduction as reinforcement in the learning of a new response. *Journal of Experimental Psychology*, 1948, 38, 89–101.

Miller, N. E. Learnable drives and rewards. In S. S. Stevens (Ed.), *Handbook of experimental psychology*. New York: Wiley, 1951. Pp. 435–472.

Miller, N. E., & Kraeling, D. Displacement: Evidence for more generalization of approach than avoidance in an approach-avoidance conflict generalized to a new stimulus situation. *Journal of Experimental Psychology*, 1950, 43, 217–221.

Mischel, W. *Personality and assessment*. New York: Wiley, 1968.

Mogar, R. E., & Savage, C. Personality change associated with psychedelic (LSD) therapy: A preliminary report. *Psychotherapy: Theory, Research and Practice*, 1964, 1, 154–162.

Morganstern, K. P. Implosive therapy and flooding procedures: A critical review. *Psychological Bulletin*, 1973, 79, 318–334.

Mowrer, O. H. On the dual nature of learning—a re-interpretation of "conditioning" and "problem-solving". *Harvard Educational Review*, 1947, 17, 102–148.

Mowrer, O. H. *Learning theory and behavior*. New York: Wiley, 1960.

Mylar, J. L., & Clement, P. W. Prediction and comparison of outcome in systematic desensitization and implosion. *Behaviour Research and Therapy*, 1972, 10, 235–246.

Newton, J. R., & Stein, L. I. Implosive therapy in alcoholism: Comparison with brief psychotherapy. *Quarterly Journal of Studies on Alcohol*, 1974, 35, 1256–1265.

Orenstein, H., & Carr, J. Implosion therapy by tape-recording. *Behaviour Research and Therapy*, 1975, 13, 177–182.

Page, H. A. The facilitation of experimental extinction by response prevention as a function of the acquisition of a new response. *Journal of Comparative and Physiological Psychology*, 1955, 48, 14–16.

Paul, G. L. *Insight vs. desensitization in psychotherapy*. Stanford: Stanford University Press, 1966.

Prochaska, J. O. Symptom and dynamic cues in the implosive treatment of test anxiety. *Journal of Abnormal Psychology*, 1971, 77, 133–142.

Rachman, S. Studies in desensitization II: Flooding. *Behaviour Research and Therapy*, 1966, 4, 1–6.

Rachman, S., Hodgson, R., & Marks, I. M. Treatment of chronic obsessive-compulsive neurosis. *Behaviour Research and Therapy*, 1971, 9, 237–247.

Rachman, S., Marks, I. M., & Hodgson, R. The treatment of obsessive-compulsive neurotics by modelling and flooding *in vivo*. *Behaviour Research and Therapy*, 1973, 11, 463–471.

Razran, G. Empirical codification and specific theoretical implications of compound stimulus conditioning. Perception. In W. F. Prokasy (Ed.), *Classical conditioning: A symposium*. New York: Appleton, 1965. Pp. 226–248.

Rescorla, R. A., & Solomon, R. L. Two-process learning theory: Relationships between Pavlovian conditioning and instrumental learning. *Psychological Review*, 1967, 74, 151–182.

Schofield, W. Changes in response to the MMPI following certain therapies. *Psychological Monographs*, 1950, 64(5, Whole No. 311).

Schofield, W. A further study of the effects of therapies of MMPI responses. *Journal of Abnormal and Social Psychology*, 1953, 48, 67–77.

Seligman, M. E. P. *Helplessness. On depression, development, and death.* San Francisco: Freeman, 1975.

Shearman, R. W. Response-contingent CS termination in the extinction of avoidance learning. *Behaviour Research and Therapy*, 1970, 8, 227–239.

Shipley, R. H. Extinction of conditioned fear in rats as a function of several parameters of CS exposure. *Journal of Comparative and Physiological Psychology*, 1974, 87, 600–707.

Shipley, R. H., Mock, L. A., & Levis, D. J. Effects of several response prevention procedures on activity, avoidance responding, and conditioned fear in rats. *Journal of Comparative and Physiological Psychology*, 1971, 77, 256–270.

Smith, R. D., Dickson, A. L., & Sheppard, L. Review of flooding procedures in animals and man. *Perceptual and Motor Skills*, 1973 (Monogr. Suppl. 2-U37).

Smith, R. E., & Nye, S. L. A comparison of Implosive Therapy and Systematic Desensitization in the treatment of test anxiety. *Journal of Consulting and Clinical Psychology*, 1973, 41, 37–47.

Solomon, R. L., Kamin, L. J., & Wynne, L. C. Traumatic avoidance learning: The outcomes of several extinction procedures with dogs. *Journal of Abnormal and Social Psychology*, 1953, 48, 291–302.

Solomon, R. L., & Wynne, L. C. Traumatic avoidance learning: The principle of anxiety conservation and partial irreversibility. *Psychological Review*, 1954, 61, 353–385.

Stampfl, T. G. Implosive Therapy: An emphasis on covert stimulation. In D. J. Levis (Ed.), *Learning approaches to therapeutic behavior change.* Chicago: Aldine, 1970. Pp. 182–204.

Stampfl, T. G. Implosive therapy. In P. T. Olson (Ed.), *Emotional flooding.* New York, 1975. Pp. 62–79.

Stampfl, T. G., & Levis, D. J. Essentials of Implosive Therapy: A learning-theory-based psychodynamic behavioral therapy. *Journal of Abnormal Psychology*, 1967, 72, 496–503. (a)

Stampfl, T. G., & Levis, D. J. Phobic patients: Treatment with the learning theory approach of Implosive Therapy. *Voices, psychotherapy*, 1967, 3, 23–27 (b)

Stampfl, T. G., & Levis, D. J. Implosive Therapy—A behavioral therapy? *Behaviour Research and Therapy*, 1968, 6, 31–36.

Stampfl, T. G., & Levis, D. J. Learning theory: An aid to dynamic therapeutic practice. In L. D. Eron & R. Callahan (Eds.), *Relationship of theory to practice in psychotherapy.* Chicago: Aldine, 1969. Pp. 85–114.

Stampfl, T. H., & Levis, D. J. Implosive therapy. In R. M. Jurjevich (Ed.), *Direct Psychotherapy.* Vol. 1. Chapel Hill: University of North Carolina Press, 1973. Pp. 83–105. (a)

Stampfl, T. G., & Levis, D. J. *Implosive therapy: Theory and technique.* N. J.: General Learning Press, 1973. (b)

Staub, E. Duration of stimulus-exposure as determinant of the efficiency of flooding procedures in the elimination of fear. *Behaviour Research and Therapy*, 1968, 6, 131–132.

Tourney, G. A history of therapeutic fashions in psychiatry, 1800–1966. *American Journal of Psychiatry*, 1967, 124, 784–796.

Wall, H. W., & Guthrie, G. M. Extinction of responses to subceived stimuli. *Journal of General Psychology*, 1959, 60, 205–210.

Watson, J. P., Gaind, R., & Marks, I. M. Physiological habituation to continuous phobic stimulation. *Behaviour Research and Therapy*, 1972, 10, 269–278.

Watson, J. P., & Marks, I. M. Relevant and irrelevant fear in flooding—a crossover study of phobic patients. *Behavior Therapy*, 1971, 2, 275–293.

Watson, J. P., Mullett, G. E., & Pillay, H. The effects of prolonged exposure to phobic situations upon agoraphobic patients treated in groups. *Behaviour Research and Therapy*, 1973, 11, 531–545.

Weinberger, N. M. Effects of detainment on extinction of avoidance responses. *Journal of Comparative and Physiological Psychology*, 1965, 60, 135–138.

Willis, R. W., & Edwards, J. A. A study of the comparative effectiveness of systematic desensitization and implosive therapy. *Behaviour Research and Therapy*, 1969, 7, 387–395.

Wilson, A., & Smith, F. J. Counterconditioning therapy using free association: A pilot study. *Journal of Abnormal Psychology*, 1968, 73, 474–478.

Wilson, G. T., & Davison, G. C. Process of fear reduction in systematic desensitization: Animal studies. *Psychological Bulletin*, 1971, 76, 1–14.

Wolpe, J. *Psychotherapy by reciprocal inhibition*. Stanford: Stanford University Press, 1958.

SUBJECT INDEX

A

Aftercare programs, 72–75
Aggressive behavior, parents as therapists
  for, 265–268
Alcoholics, implosive therapy for, 366–367
Anger, symptom formation and, 309–311
Assessment, demand characteristics and,
  146–148

B

Behavior maintenance, with reinforcement
  techniques, 58–59
Behavioral norms, 98–100
Biofeedback, 163–241
  discrimination and, 167–168
  future directions for, 238–241
  research and evaluation in, 169–171
  self-control and, 166–167
  self-management and, 165–166, 169
  self-reinforcement and, 168–169
  utility of
    cardiovascular responses, 171–199
    electroencephalogram, 209–219
    electromyographic responses, 199–209
    electrooculargram, 237
    galvanic skin response, 235–237
    gastrointestinal responses, 227–232
    penile erection, 232–235
    skin temperature, 219–227
    vaginal contractions, 237–238
Blood pressure, in biofeedback, 185–199

C

Cardiac arrhythmias, in biofeedback,
  173–176
Cardiac neurosis, heart rate control and,
  181–182
Cardiovascular responses, in biofeedback,
  171–172
  blood pressure, 185–199
  heart rate, 172–184
Community problems, 91–94
Contingencies, unresponsiveness to, 59–60
Corrections, 75–81
  nonresidential programs, 78–80
  residential programs, 76–78
Covert conditioning, obesity and, 22–23
Crime, ecology of, 106–107

D

Demand characteristics, 119–152
  as artifact, 128–129
    controlling for demand and, 143–146
    exploring demand sources and,
      140–143
    future research in, 138–140
    "one-shot" BAT performance and,
      129–132
    repeated BAT performance and,
      132–135
    subject variables and, 135–138
  as clinical tools, 146
    in assessment, 146–148

377

A
B
C
D
E
F
G
H
I
J